LIBERALISM, CONSERVATISM, AND CATHOLICISM:

An Evaluation of

Contemporary American

Political Ideologies

in Light of Catholic

Social Teaching

(Revised Edition)

BY STEPHEN M. KRASON, J.D., Ph.D

CENTRAL BUREAU
Catholic Central Verein of America
3835 Westminster Place
St. Louis MO 63108

Dedication

This book is dedicated to
our Holy Father,
Pope John Paul II,
and
to my beloved wife,
Therese Catherine Krason

Acknowledgements

I want to thank the following persons for assistance that made the completion of this book possible and insured the final product would turn out to be better than otherwise would have been the case: Rev. Robert J. Levis, for his guidance and advice when a part of this book was written to satisfy my M.A. thesis requirements in the Pontifical Center for Catechetical Studies at Gannon University; Dr. Rupert J. Ederer, one of the premier Catholic economists in America today, for kindly reading and commenting on two separate drafts of this manuscript; the national offices of the Democratic Party, the Republican Party, the Americans for Democratic Action, and the American Conservative Union in Washington, D.C., for sending me helpful materials and giving me needed information; the Department of History, Humanities and Political Science of Franciscan University of Steubenville and the University itself for financial assistance; Dan Gallio for help with proofreading and for compiling the index; Dr. James W. Salter for computer help; and Mrs. Elizabeth Atkins, Mrs. Theresa Araya, Nicholas C. Scarpone, Mrs. Lynn Cadman, Miss Stephanie Lester, and Miss Tammy Weiss who typed or corrected different drafts of the manuscript. I want to especially thank Catholics United for the Faith and its President, James Likoudis, for their interest in securing the original publication of this book, and Rev. John H. Miller, C.S.C., S.T.D., and the Catholic Central Verein of America for publishing this revised edition. I also thank the St. Martin de Porres Lay Dominican Community for their help and cooperation as well as the fine job they did in printing both editions of this book. Finally, as always, I am grateful to my wife, Therese C. Krason, for her loving support. I, of course, am the person exclusively responsible for the contents of the pages which follow.

Stephen M. Krason

Franciscan University of Steubenville

Steubenville, Ohio

January 1994

Table of Contents

Foreword

This is a time when the Church in the United States through various organs is intervening in public affairs to an unprecedented degree. It is also, however, a time when an unwarranted clericalism has manifested itself, and a time when Catholic politicians are manifesting less and less of a willingness to allow their thinking on basic moral questions (such as contraception and abortion and euthanasia) to be shaped by the infallible teaching of the Church. An accompanying erosion in the teaching of doctrine in Catholic universities and colleges, seminaries, and parochial schools has resulted in increased confusion among the laity, generally, and resistance to the role of the Church in shaping their political and socio-economic attitudes.

Too often, American Catholics fail to consult the clear teachings of the Church in making decisions affecting the political and social order. The political philosophy of too many American Catholics ignores the truth that God and politics are connected with each other. Thus do they appear to be "liberals" or "conservatives" first, and Catholics second. To the contrary, every serious and informed Catholic knows that "All things must be reestablished in Christ" (Eph. 1:10)—and that includes the political order. He realizes that political life, like all human activities, has a role in helping man move toward his rightful end, namely *Salvation*. As Pope John Paul II has emphasized:

> The temptation of the world today is to reduce the Gospel message to a form of humanitarianism...The Church's mission is not restricted to the framework of temporal existence nor completely identified with temporal desires, hopes, affairs and struggles. Rather, it is at the service of a transcendent and eschatological salvation, which has its beginnings in this life but which is fulfilled in eternity.
>
> (Address to Indonesian Bishops 10/13/89)

The Church is aware that politics plays a particularly significant role in fulfilling its purpose to secure that *common good* which is an indispensable precondition for the flourishing of religion.

The serious Catholic also knows that while the social doctrine and moral teachings of the Church (grounded in the Natural and Revealed Law of

God) must shape the contribution of Catholics to public discussion and dialogue, prudence also plays an important role and much is left to the individual judgment of Catholics where the Church acknowledges their freedom to act as informed citizens of the community. This has not always been recognized by Catholic "social activists" for whom the pronouncements of individual Bishops and national episcopal conferences have preempted the exercise of legitimate lay options. The truth is that Catholic teaching has always sought to insure that a proper balance be maintained between those moral decisions which the Church affirms to reflect the mind and will of God (and which are binding on the consciences of the faithful) and those moral positions which are rooted in legitimate political differences. The Church is always mindful of the fact that her role is not that of the ordinary political decision-maker or policy-maker. Her role is to guide and illuminate consciences regarding the Law of God, the care of fundamental human rights, the spread of the Kingdom of God and the salvation of souls. Nowhere is the splendid balance of Catholic social doctrine demonstrated more clearly than in the Papal social encyclicals which constitute the major teaching documents of the Magisterium of the Church on social matters.

It is regrettable that these social encyclicals are not better known by American Catholics. It is important to bring greater attention to them and to promote serious study of them. Dr. Stephen M. Krason's book accomplishes the task of clarifying Catholic social teaching for the American Catholic public and, in doing so, provides a valuable Catholic assessment of the actual direction of American politics at the very time when many Catholics appear to be in a veritable flight from their Catholicism.

A genuinely Catholic critique of America's reigning political ideologies, *liberalism* and *conservatism*, has been needed, and Dr. Krason is to be commended for undertaking this effort. Too many scholars have tilted their findings in the direction of their own predetermined liberal or conservative leanings. In this impressive study, Dr. Krason informs readers about the nature of American *liberalism* and *conservatism*, gives the background for Catholics' affiliating with each, details the major tenets of these ideologies as well as the major policy positions they have taken, and analyzes the reasons why each ideology deviates in various ways from Catholic social teaching. He also gives an excellent summary of the key tenets of Catholic social doctrine as contained in the Papal social encyclicals and the documents of the Second Vatican Council (1962-1965).

Today, we witness the capitulation of many American Catholics in public life and Church bureaucracies to *liberalism*. We also see prominent American Catholics remain fixated to *conservative* ideology. Dr. Krason points out the fatal consequence of such positions: namely, *the marginalization of*

Catholics in American public life. The danger of surrender to either ideological ethos is the forfeiting of the very possibility of effectively influencing and leavening society with Catholic truth. Dr. Krason realizes, as liberal and conservative Catholics do not, that the Church is *neither Left nor Right.* The Catholic Church does not—and cannot—endorse automatically the political, socio-economic or cultural perspectives identified with either *liberalism* or *conservatism,* if such positions are not compatible with the Gospel of Christ. Here Dr. Krason follows Pope John Paul II's proclamation in *Sollicitudo Rei Socialis*:

> The Church's social doctrine is not a "third way"...nor is it an ideology, but rather the accurate formulation of the results of a careful reflection on the complex realities of human existence, in society and in the international order, in the light of faith and of the Church's tradition...It therefore belongs to the field, not of ideology, but of theology and particularly of moral theology. (No. 41)

It is my hope that this excellent study will help strengthen American Catholics and others of good will with respect to their political, socio-economic and cultural obligations in the crucial years ahead.

James Likoudis
President
Catholics United for the Faith
January 1991

Prefatory Note

This revised edition is different from the original only in some brief, additional discussion which appears in the final section of Chapter Seven, the expanded treatment of *Centesimus Annus* in the Addendum, and in other slight updating and the correction of various errata throughout the book. The only significant area which includes statements which are dated since the original edition is communism. The original edition was written after the momentous events of 1989, but before the brief, failed Soviet coup of 1991, the dissolution of the Soviet Union, and the inconclusive events since that time. Thus, the discussion about the Cold War and other conditions and events will no longer be pertinent. This scarcely affects our analysis of the American ideologies' views of communism in comparison to the Church's teaching, however, because that comparison concerns not essentially events or current international conditions or foreign policy questions, but views about the very nature of the Communist ideology and radical totalitarian ideologies of the left generally. Moreover, it is far from clear that communism is dead—in practice, and certainly not in theory. As this new edition goes to the press in 1994, such nations as China, the most populous nation in the world, Cuba, and Vietnam remain under Communist control; the old Communists in other eastern European countries have reasserted themselves politically under different names; the Sandinistas are regaining strength in Nicaragua; and the political future of Russia is very much in doubt with the Communists again flexing their muscles. It is by no means certain that communism is no longer a major force in world politics or that the conflict between communism and the West is over.

ONE

INTRODUCTION:
LIBERALISM, CONSERVATISM, THE CHURCH,
AND AMERICAN CATHOLICS

Liberalism and conservatism, in at least some sense of the terms, are the prevailing political perspectives or "ideologies" in the United States today. Catholics, like all Americans, have to make political decisions—decisions about which of the two major parties to support, which candidates to vote for, whether they should support the policy proposals of the "liberals" or the "conservatives." For a long period of time, going back to the nineteenth century, American Catholics mostly supported the political party—the Democratic— and the politicians which were considered "liberal." They did this for reasons discussed in this Chapter. Catholics have also been known to support conservative ideas and politicians in our history, however. Catholics and all serious religious believers know that political ideologies must not be the basis for their world view; rather, the validity and worth of political ideas must be determined by the religious teachings they adhere to. They must be evaluated against those teachings and not the other way around. This is only because the theological and philosophical are indeed at the root of the political. As such eminent thinkers as Cardinal Manning and Irving Babbitt said, when we study matters of human society seriously we find that economic ideas are rooted in political ones and political ones in turn in philosophical ones and, finally, philosophical ones in religious or theological ones. In recent years, we have witnessed the emergence of typical positions being taken by American liberals and conservatives which have seemed to contradict Catholic teaching, or at least have been—or are frequently alleged to be—very questionable in light of that teaching. For example, the support for legalized abortion generally identified with liberalism—although some conservatives espouse it, too (and this may be happening more frequently as the 1990s unfold)—is with little doubt in opposition to the Church, especially when one considers that the legalization of abortion has made many people think that something utterly immoral and abominable is really morally licit and has led to its widespread availability and has drastically increased the number of abortions.[1] Liberalism has also been attacked as supporting other initiatives that damage the family. Conservatism has been alleged to be in favor of such uninhibited economic freedom that it has sanctioned excessive material accumulation and greed and fostered an obliviousness to the needs of the poor and the working man. It has also been accused of inhibiting the cause of world peace by not working sufficiently for arms control and by supporting military and paramilitary operations against certain governments in the underdeveloped world. Exactly how correct some of these characterizations of our leading American ideologies are will be taken up in this book. The important point here is that, if they *are* accurate, Catholic support for them is a problematical matter. Considering how each of these ideologies measures up to Catholic teaching is especially important nowadays when American politics is probably more ideologically polarized than it used to be, with liberalism and conservatism farther apart than previously, each standing, it has been argued, for more sharply different positions in various important issue areas than used to be the case.[2] It is less troublesome for Catholics to stand with ideologies that fudge exactly what they stand for and seem quite accommodationist-oriented than it is to do so with ideologies which are quite precise and militant in their positions. The important thing, in any event, is that Catholics need to know exactly how these ideologies can be judged against the tenets of their faith, especially the social ones, since it is this area that politics touches most directly.

The purpose of this book is to investigate the latter question, in sufficient detail and with the appropriate objectivity so that reasonably good conclusions can be made. It seeks to examine, in scholarly fashion, liberalism and conservatism since World War II—what we might call the "contemporary period" or "present-day"—exclusively in light of the teaching of the Church—of her Magisterium—without being bogged down by the baggage and biases of "left" and "right." It compares the thinking and important issue positions of each with Catholic social teaching. Its findings and conclusions, hopefully, will be a guide for serious American Catholics to consider and ponder in thinking about politics. The book then, may serve a practical purpose for Catholics, as well an interesting study for others, both scholars and laymen, who have wondered about the relationship of American politics to Catholicism. It seems to take on a special pertinence at a time when the Church in America has been involving itself in an array of controversial political issues, from abortion to nuclear arms.

This book proceeds in the following manner. In the present chapter it defines the key terms of "ideology," "liberalism," and "conservatism" and gives some essential background about the relationship of Catholicism and both liberalism and conservatism in American history. It also discusses the apparent change that occurred in American liberalism about fifteen or so years after World War II and explains the differences between the "old liberalism" (from 1945 or possibly the beginning of the New Deal in 1933 to 1960) and the "new liberalism" (from, roughly, 1960 to the present). Some have argued that this change makes it more difficult for Catholics, if they are committed to the teachings of the Church, to identfy with liberalism.

In Chapter Two, it summarizes and highlights the important "social teachings" of the Church (i.e., her teachings on social, economic, and political matters). Our primary sources are the papal social encyclicals from *Rerum Novarum* (1891) to *Sollicitudo Rei Socialis* (1987). (*Centesimus Annus* appeared as our first edition went to press.) These encyclicals are the main immediate source of Church social teaching, applying divine Revelation and the natural law—of which the Church is the authoritative interpreter—to important social questions of the times. This is why, when refering to the teachings put forth in Chapter Two, we freely interchange the terms "papal" and "Church" teaching. The evaluation of liberalism and conservatism will be made largely with reference to these encyclicals. Important Church moral teachings which relate to questions confronting the political order, such as abortion, will also be considered even though they are not generally discussed in the social encyclicals. In certain places, other papal statements on social questions and instructions promulgated by the Congregation for the Doctrine of the Faith, with papal permission, are cited. While such statements have a lesser degree of teaching authority than encyclicals, Catholics must still respond to them with an attitude of religious submission.[3]

In Chapter Three, the general philosophy of politics and of the purpose of the political order that is held by liberalism and its thinking on such fundamental matters as freedom, equality, and communism will be evaluated according to what the Church has said. In order to determine what these general perspectives of liberalism are, we examine leading works of prominent liberal thinkers and commentators from the two periods mentioned above—from the "old liberalism" and the "new liberalism." The two versions of liberalism will be compared to each other and then each will be compared to the Church's teachings and a conclusion drawn as to which is closest to them. As noted, 1933 has been chosen as the starting point of present-day liberalism because it marks the beginning of Franklin Delano Roosevelt's New Deal, which is generally acknowledged to have been the start of the contemporary liberal ascendancy and of the distinct brand of liberalism characteristic of twentieth century America. This type of liberalism was unlike that of the nineteenth century in that it has favored government intervention in the economy, substantial government social welfare programs, a strong and active national government and a deemphasis on "states' rights," and a "broad" interpretation of the Constitution to permit this greater role for the national government and the achievement of various social policy objectives.[4] Nineteenth century liberalism, on the contrary, was known for its belief that government should take a "hands-off," or *laissez-faire*, position with respect to the economy and social welfare. We will basically confine our discussion to liberalism after 1945 because it was then that its perspective became certain and clearly settled as we state in Chapter Three, even if it really came into existence in 1933.

Chapter Four will determine how closely specific "liberal" public policy proposals and positions on various domestic and foreign policy questions—again, examining both the "old" and "new liberalism"—accord with Catholic teaching. The policy areas focused on in this chapter are the following: economic, labor, and social welfare policy; agriculture and environmental policy; civil rights and civil liberties; education; foreign policy; and defense and disarmament policy. This chapter will use as its sources platforms of the Democratic Party—America's "liberal" political party—for two different representative presidential election years, one in each of the periods in which the different versions of twentieth-century liberalism—what we are calling the "old liberalism" and the "new liberalism"—held sway. The validity of the platforms as indicators of liberal public policy positions is affirmed by briefly examining the stands taken by probably the best known national liberal lobbying and political advocacy group, the Americans for Democratic Action. The final sections of both Chapters Three and Four will state conclusions about how each version of liberalism compares with Church teaching on the subject in question.

Chapter Five does with conservatism what Chapter Three does with liberalism: it compares the general philosophy of conservatism about politics and the purpose of the political order and its thinking about freedom, equality, and communism with that of the Church. Unlike liberalism, there does not seem to be a basis for a division of post-1932 conservatism—twentieth century conservatism, more generally—into "old" and "new" periods in which the perspective shifts. There are, however, various distinct identifiable schools of thought or perspectives in conservatism—which are not present in mainstream American liberalism in the post-1932 era—which are examined and compared against each other. Then, a set of what we might call "consensus" positions of conservatism is derived from this comparison and contrasted with Church teaching.

In Chapter Six, the same type of issue comparison between conservatism and Church teaching is made as is done in Chapter Four with liberalism. The most distinctly conservative of the post-World War II platforms of America's "conservative" party, the Republican, are selected for comparison with the Church. These give us a good idea of the public policy positions of American conservatives in general. To confirm the conservatism of the platforms, we examine the issue positions of one of America's leading conservative lobbying and political advocacy organizations, the American Conservative Union.

Chapter Seven brings the findings of the previous chapters together and makes the book's conclusions about which contemporary American ideology—liberalism (in its "old" and "new" versions) or conservatism—is closer to Church teaching. It also considers the question of *why* liberalism and conservatism stand as they do in relation to the Church and ponders whether Catholics have any alternatives in American politics to lining up with the liberals or conservatives and the two dominant political parties which represent their perspectives, respectively.

Definition of "Ideology"

We use the term "ideology" to describe liberalism and conservatism in this book. This term can have several different definitions, certain of which are appropriate for usage here and certain of which are not. It is thus essential that we define the term.

In his very good *Principles of Politics: An Introduction*, John J. Schrems of Villanova University provides two brief definitions of the term ideology. The first is simply "an attempt to understand or describe the political world."[5] The second, which he takes from political scientist Leon Baradat, says an ideology is "action-oriented, materialistic, popular, and simplistic."[6] It is "action-oriented" and "popular" because it seeks "to persuade large groups for specific purposes." It is "simplistic" because it intends, to at least some degree, to have mass appeal. Thus it must be made *understandable* to the mass of people, It is "materialistic" because it generally deals with and seeks to accommodate itself to social and economic conditions.[7] This same definition is expressed only slightly differently by University of Missouri political scientist Max J. Skidmore: "Political ideology is a form of thought that presents a pattern of complex ideas simply and in a manner that inspires action to achieve certain goals."[8]

Liberalism and conservatism, as we are using the terms, are clearly ideologies in the first sense that Schrems speaks of. Each of the various thinkers that are discussed in Chapters Three and Five possess a certain understanding or interpretation of political life, which is seen in their thought about the particular areas examined. Schrems' second definition (from Baradat) and Skidmore's also seem to apply to our investigation because, first, these thinkers each have a "goal" or set of goals for politics that corresponds to a general vision of the good political society, and, more basically, the good life for men that they hope by their writings to persuade or urge men toward. Even though the thinkers surveyed in the respective chapters do not have *identical* views, they are close enough in their thought that we can say that one group espouses a common perspective or ideology and the other, a different one (i.e., liberalism and conservatism). Liberalism and conservatism can be said to be "action-oriented" partly because these thinkers would, for the most part, like to see their ideas influence, or be practiced in, actual political life. Mostly, however, we can say they are action-oriented because major political parties and lobbying groups, such as those discussed, seek to promote specific public policies based upon general, foundational thought (such as that discussed in Chapters Three and Five). They do this by working to gain popular support and political power or influence. Most of these policy aims concern the social and economic conditions of the political order in some way. Indeed, political parties, lobbying groups, and all political actors operate within the context of a political order or society (embodying a particular set of fundamental social and economic characteristics) and are shaped by it and have the furthering of *its* interests—as opposed to those of *all* political societies or political life per se — as their ojective. "Simplistic," or perhaps we should say simplifying, elements come into play with the fact that popular support is gained in contemporary democracies by garnering enough votes and support from the masses, so perspectives and policy ideas must be made understandable to the masses.

The above definitions of ideology would fit almost any political perspective, even one that is relatively vague and unfocused. Virtually any activity of seeking to effect practical political life in a democratic republic would seem to fall into them. The definitions do not suggest that an ideology necessarily has to have a rigid or even extremely cohesive set of doctrines or principles that it seeks to promote, nor does it have to have a clear scheme—winning elections—for gaining political power and putting its ideas into effect. In fact, an important aspect of the nature of both liberalism and conservatism is their adaptability to new circumstances and their eschewing of dogmatic solutions. It is ideology in this other sense—what one major dictionary calls "a body of doctrine, myth, symbol, etc. of a social movement..., class, or large group...with reference to some political and cultural plan for putting it into operation"[9] — which is what we do *not* mean in our use of the term. This is a definition of ideology we would attach to such twentieth century totalitarian ideologies as Nazism and Communism, which have very well developed, highly structured, and rigid sets of doctrines—the validity of which their adherents are oblivious to—and a usually comprehensive plan to propagandize and seize political control—forcibly if necessary—through the efforts of a highly organized and supremely well disciplined cadre. This kind of ideology has never characterized the main political perspectives in America, including the post-World War II liberalism and conservatism we are examining.

For example, we note that the eminent conservative scholar Russell Kirk (who will frequently be mentioned in this book), while strongly emphasizing the "permanent things" which are part of the nature of man and social life,[10] criticizes self-proclaimed "conservatives" who dogmatically adhere to certain ideas and prescriptions when the evidence is clearly against them.[11] While it is argued herein that American liberalism has become more dogmatic in recent years, by no means can we say that the liberal ideology fits this particular definition of the term.

Finally, liberalism and conservatism also do not satisfy one other definition of the term "ideology": "theorizing of a visionary or impractical nature."[12] While it can be argued that some of the liberal social engineering schemes of the past three decades in America might represent precisely this, our politics throughout our history—with both good and bad results—has been distinguished for its pragmatism. It has addressed real-life concerns in a piecemeal way with approaches "that work."

Definitions of "Liberalism" and "Conservatism"

Clear definitions of "liberalism" and "conservatism" will emerge implicitly from Chapters Three through Six, so the definitions given here will be brief and general, which will simply serve to make clear what is under discussion. This is necessary because terms such as "liberal," "conservative," "moderate," "socialist," etc. have taken on so many different meanings and shades of meaning that in order to have an intelligent discussion of them the definition must be put forth at the outset.

Let us consider liberalism first. It should be emphasized that what is *not* meant by liberalism is the nineteenth century type of liberalism (i.e., "classical" or *laissez-faire* liberalism). This was basically an economic ideology and, as indicated, held that economic actors—employers and entrepreneurs, workers, purchasers, etc.—should be permitted to carry out their efforts completely unencumbered by government. It contended that government should not even make laws to insure certain basic protections for workers on the job (which it viewed as constituting interference with the worker's right to enter into an employment contract). It believed that there are certain "laws" at work in the natural course of human economic activity that would insure that society and all of its members would benefit most if everyone simply could carry out, unimpeded, their individual efforts and preferences. It also, for the most part, held that social welfare functions should be handled by private organizations, such as churches, not government. This brand of liberalism has been condemned by the popes from Leo XIII on and is primarily what is meant by the term in the social encyclicals when they discuss the morality of economic activity. (We shall see that in its essence, however, the popes' understanding of the term goes far beyond this and their criticism of liberalism applies most fundamentally to the general philosophical and moral perspective it embodies. It should also be pointed out that the liberalism of twentieth century America is primarily a reaction to the nineteenth century version.)

A beginning definition of twentieth century—that is, post-1932 or "contemporary"—American liberalism can perhaps be gleaned from what was said above.[13] A precautionary note is first in order, however. As Professor Harry K. Girvetz writes in his book *The Evolution of Liberalism,* "Contemporary [i.e., twentieth century] liberalism...is not a fixed or systematically elaborated body of doctrine...[it] is essentially a fluid and frequently elusive doctrine. It is eclectic in point of view." Writing in 1962, he contrasts it on these points with "the doctrinaire Left."[14] As we have noted, however, and as we shall go on to explain in this book, liberalism has probably become more doctrinaire in the last two and a half decades than it previously was and has assumed more of a militantly left-wing stance—perhaps because its ranks have been populated more and more by people schooled in the leftism of the Vietnam War era.

To speak first in general terms about liberalism, per se, whether of the contemporary or the older ("classical") variety, we must say that it is irreverent about the status quo, very willing to entertain new ideas, and, because of its confidence in modern science, "hopeful of the possibilities of exploration, experiment, and discovery."[15] Political scientist Francis Canavan, S.J., tells us that liberty and equality are the primary principles of liberalism, although liberty seems to be *the* most basic one. As Canavan puts it, "The right to pursue one's own happiness is freedom, equality is the guarantee of the same right to everyone."[16] This emphasis on liberty—an idea of liberty much broader and applicable to many more areas of life than the early modern notions of the idea which applied essentially to politics—has inclined contemporary liberalism to assume a morally neutral stance. Political scientist Walter Berns makes this unflattering comment about it: "The one inexpiable sin [according to liberalism] is for government to get into the business of distinguishing good from evil."[17] David Spitz, another political scientist and an avowed liberal, explains this:

> Skepticism about ultimate values...is often associated with the liberal creed; but while it is appropriate to that creed it is not necessary to it...liberalism repudiates the conservative claim to absolute and infallible truth...The basic value of the liberal is...the value of free inquiry; his basic attitude, the skeptical, or at least the inquiring, mind....Liberalism need not, however, be identified only with this skeptical approach to knowledge. It is altogether possible for one to believe that the truth is known and still hold to a liberal defense of toleration....in a society constituted of diverse men and groups many may claim to know the truth...the political problem is to deal with a situation in which all believe they are right.[18]

We must comment that, while what Spitz says does not necessarily indicate that liberalism espouses relativism, it is certainly easy to see how it has led to essentially this on many public issues, such as abortion. Political scientist Joseph Cropsey of the University of Chicago tells us that "for the sake of avoiding a reliance upon notions of the common good [i.e., endorsing some notion of the truth, which Spitz fears], liberalism recurs to the theory of interest groups."[19] (Whether and to what extent he is correct in saying that liberalism dispenses with the notion of the common good is taken up in Chapter Three).

Cropsey also tells us about two other basic tenets of contemporary liberalism: its suspicion of propertied interests—which it sees as promoting selfishness and creating division in society—and an internationalist orientation, motivated by its concern that the division of men into nations is an obstacle to peace.[20] Thus, contrary to conservatism, it deemphasizes patriotism in deference to "the love of mankind." Its suspicion of property is, more generally, a suspicion of wealth. It has strongly favored the reduction of great inequalities of wealth, the elimination of hereditary privilege, and the dissolution of racial, religious, and sex discrimination.[21] It traditionally sought equality of opportunity as a key goal, but there is substantial evidence that in recent years it has gone beyond this to "equality of outcome." This is discussed in Chapter Three.

As stated above, contemporary liberalism has favored a strong and active national government. Noted political scientist Samuel N. Beer, another self-proclaimed liberal, says that the major reason for this, especially since the New Deal, has been to give greater economic power and security to groups that did not previously have them.[22] Although the reasons for promoting government action, in the minds of liberals, today go beyond just economic concerns, they probably still relate, in large part, to the more basic aims above of eliminating inequality and discrimination (even if some of the groups liberalism chooses to support today are dubiously classified as "victims"). Beer says that one of the key ways in which American liberalism has worked as a "nationalizing" force has been in trying to integrate "into the national community groups which had previously been marginal or excluded."[23] He also tells us about another objective which contemporary liberalism has sought to use governmental power to promote (which we believe is both subsumed in the aim of ending inequality and discrimination and makes it comprehensible): "'the increase of American individuality.'"[24]

The above, then, gives us a good initial understanding and introductory definition of contemporary liberalism. As stated, the discussion in Chapters Three and Four will fill out the picture.

Now let us turn to a definition of conservatism. Historian Clinton Rossiter says the following about conservatism:

> *Conservatism* is committed to a discriminating defense of the social order against change and reform. The conservative knows that change is the rule of life among men and societies, but he insists that it be sure-footed and respectful of the past....[H]is natural preferences are for stability over change, continuity over experiment, the past over the future.[25]

Conservatism, Rossiter contends, is not "standpattism." "The conservative conserves discriminately, the standpatter indiscriminately, for he fears movement in any direction." Nor is the conservative a reactionary, who "sighs for the past and feels that a retreat back into it, piecemeal or large-scale, is worth trying."[26] The conservative knows better. It is sometimes thought that conservatives favor order, simply, as against liberty. Rossiter insists this is not true: "his [the conservative's] concern is *ordered* liberty rather than order pure, simple, and at any cost."[27]

Along these lines, further dispelling a misconception—usually held by those left of center—about conservatism, Rossiter says that it "is as much an enemy" of fascism as of communism, even though it "may appear on the surface to share some of the former's notions about authority, obedience, and inequality." It is true that the conservative is suspicious of democracy, but is "[d]eeply if not joyfully aware that democracy is the only real alternative to totalitarianism." Conservatism seeks to "domesticate" democratic government "with the aid of constitutionalism and tradition."[28] It "accepts and defends most of the institutions and values of the contemporary West...it...hold[s] in trust the great Western heritage from Israel, Greece, Rome, and all Christianity."[29]

Conservatism, like liberalism, is undogmatic and adaptable, to a certain degree. As Russell Kirk says, "[c]onservatism is not a fixed and immutable body of dogmata, and conservatives inherit from [Edmund] Burke a talent for re-expressing their convictions to fit the time."[30] Nevertheless, he tells us, conservatism has definite beliefs. There are "six canons of conservative thought": 1) the belief in "a transcendent order or body of natural law, which rules society as well as conscience" signifying that political problems, in the final analysis, are religious and moral problems (as Manning, Babbitt and other of his conservative predecessors thought); 2) a rejection of uniformity, egalitarianism, and a utilitarian orientation, and an "[a]ffection for the proliferating variety and mystery of traditional life"; 3) the belief that "civilized society requires orders and classes as against the notion of a 'classless society'...[and i]f natural distinctions are effaced among men, oligarchs fill the vacuum" (levelling of all sorts, including economic levelling, is rejected); 4) the conviction that private property is essential to maintain freedom; 5) a faith in "[c]ustom, convention, and old prescription" to restrain men's "lust for power" and anarchic tendencies and a rejection of schemes to "reconstruct society upon abstract designs" (i.e., social engineering); and 6) a suspicion of hasty change and innovation—fearing that it can be "a devouring conflagration"—and espousal of the idea that change, while essential, must be prudent.[31]

While the above characteristics are the essence of conservatism and especially are seen with those who are philosophical and intellectual conservatives—such as the thinkers we shall be surveying in Chapter Five—there are a number of other positions that are popularly associated with conservatism (and which, in fact, are observed in the thought of most conservatives). These are: an emphasis on private initiative as opposed to state control or regulation of the economy (even to the point where the stress on individual action in this area stands in marked contrast to that on the community and social wholes in other areas. This is the area in which the roots of conservatism are actually in the classical liberalism spoken of above); an opposition to centralization, especially in government, and a preference for matters to be dealt with by lower levels of government if they must be addressed by government at all (hence, in the American context, the conservative has been an exponent of "states' rights"); a general suspicion of the increase in governmental power per se; a strong military and defense establishment, especially in the face of the threat of communism that arose after World War II; an emphasis on public morality and restraint on excesses of individual freedom in areas involving sexual conduct, literature, the media, and the visual arts; concern about protecting private institutions, such as churches, from government encroachment; a general belief that social welfare functions ought to be handled, whenever possible, by private organizations instead of government; and opposition to forced equality, especially an equalization of conditions or outcomes.

This, then, is an initial characterization of conservatism. As noted, a fuller picture of it shall be drawn in the chapters examining conservative thought and public policy positions in detail.

A Note About What the Church Has Taught About Liberalism

We have distinguished between the liberalism of the nineteenth and twentieth (since 1932) centuries, indicating that it has represented two substantially different perspectives, even if they share certain basic assumptions. (We have noted that there have been two different versions of liberalism since World War II, the period of our examination, but these have not been as substantially and fundamentally different as the liberalism of the twentieth and nineteenth centuries). In 1888, Pope Leo XIII issued what was essentially a condemnation of liberalism and a number of its tenets in the encyclical *Libertas Praestantissimum* (*On Human Liberty*). The liberalism he was speaking about, essentially, was classical liberalism, since that was the type that was predominant and was what people meant at that time when they used the term. In the encyclical, he equated liberalism in the political and moral realm with rationalism in the philosophic. Like rationalism, it denies "the existence of any divine authority to which obedience is due" and saw man trying to style his own morality which turned true liberty into "boundless license."[32] He acknowledged the existence of a more moderate version of liberalism which rejected this extreme notion of individual freedom and accepted the reality of a divine law. He rejected this version, too, however, because it saw no obligation to follow the divine law.[33] He pointed to one of the logical consequences of liberalism: the tyranny of the state, since the law of God was no longer acknowledged as a buffer against it (i.e., since there was no transcendent restraint on the will of the individual, there was none on the state which simply is made up of the multitude of individual wills).[34] He singled out for particular criticism some of the specific expressions of liberalism's more extreme notions of freedom. One is the absolute liberty of speech and of the press. This right, he said, must be used in moderation; there is no right to propagate untruth or undermine sacred things.[35] Another is the liberty of teaching. There can be no right to teach error, but rather a solemn duty of those giving instruction to teach truth.[36] Yet another is a confused notion of liberty of conscience, which holds—apart from the Church's teaching that every person be free to follow God's will without hindrance—that one is free to worship God or not.[37] He also rejected the idea of liberalism—which stands behind his rebuke of the "Americanists," discussed below—that there should be a radical separation of church and state, meaning either that "the State...[should] be separated from the Church wholly and entirely, so that with regard to every right of human society, in institutions, customs, and laws, the offices of State, and the education of youth, they would pay no more regard to the Church than if she did not exist" or that the Church should not be acknowledged as having "the nature and rights of a perfect society" with the power "to legislate, to judge, or to punish" or to do anything more than "exhort...[and] to advise."[38]

This same description of liberalism was taken up by a Spanish priest, Father Felix Sarda y Salvany, in an obscure book published in 1886 entitled *El Liberalismo es Pecado* ("Liberalism Is a Sin"—later translated into English under the title *What Is Liberalism?*). He concluded that "[l]iberalism, whether in the doctrinal or practical order, is a sin."[39] We need not discuss liberalism in the doctrinal order here; that is outside the scope of this book. In the practical order, Sarda contended that liberalism is a sin because it rejects a transcendent standard for morality. Only God's law can "be the principle or rule of morality." Liberalism's espousal of the notion of "the absolute sovereignty of human reason" is its reason for rejecting this principle. Thus, "in the order of action...[it] is license." It thereby commits the "very grievous and deadly sin of...rebellion against God."[40] In 1887, the Sacred Congregation of the Index declared that Sarda "merits great praise for his exposition and defense of the sound doctrine" in his book.[41]

With the above said, one is prompted to ask, what is the point of a study to see if American liberalism is in conformity with the Church? Hasn't the Church already rejected it, since it has rejected liberalism per se? The answer is not so simple. First, it must be recalled that Pope Leo separated different versions of liberalism and saw the need to address the question of whether a more moderate version did not conflict with the Church. Thus, we have the suggestion that he did not condemn it—or everything that goes under the label of "liberalism"—per se; *perhaps* some version of "liberalism" could be acceptable to the Church. Since the version of liberalism which has characterized post-World War II America has been so different from that of the nineteenth century—it has particularly been noted for restricting freedom of a questionable sort in some ways and in fact, developed as a reaction to the liberalism of the last century—it is *possible* that it could be acceptable to the Church. At least, it is necessary to undertake a renewed analysis. If twentieth century liberalism is to be criticized for the same reason as the nineteenth century version was, it has to be shown that in spite of differences its basic nature is the same. Also, because of the pragmatism characteristic of American politics, it is *possible* that what goes by the name of liberalism in this country is actually something entirely different—that it is a misnomer. This is another matter to explore. Finally, if we are to automatically call contemporary liberalism into doubt because of the Church's past pronouncements, without any further analysis in light of the complete corpus of major (and more recent) encyclicals and consideration being given to the changes which have occurred in liberalism, then we should even more automatically be ready to do the same with contemporary conservatism, some of whose schools of thought are really, or are close to, the classical liberalism which Leo XIII condemned.

In summary, this study will investigate if contemporary liberalism—and contemporary conservatism for that matter—embodies the beliefs and perspectives attacked in Leo's encyclical.

American Catholics, Liberalism, and Conservatism: The Historical Background

It was noted above that Catholics have "lined up" with liberalism (that is, liberal political efforts) in the twentieth century. It is necessary to elaborate on this phenomenon and provide substantiation and examples. First, Catholics, who made up a good chunk of the immigrant groups that came to the United States in the nineteenth and early twentieth centuries, tended disproportionately to attach themselves to the political party that was pro-immigrant. This was the Democratic Party, which also happened to be the more liberal one, (especially as it moved into the twentieth century). It was probably not entirely accidental, however, that the party that the immigrant Catholics were attracted to was the liberal one. They were also perhaps favorably disposed to the Democratic Party *because* of its very liberalism, which—demonstrated by its openness to the immigrants—had as one of its components support for the underdog. American political historian Thomas A. Bailey states the following:

> The Democrats were more likely to be immigrants or second-generation Americans; they were also more likely to be Jews or

Catholics....The Republicans [the more conservative party] were more generally of "native" American stock...and hence more nativist, more Nordic, more Anglo-Saxon, more anti-Semitic, more anti-Catholic, more pro-Protestant. The heirs of Hamilton [the Republicans] were WWASPS; well-born, white, Anglo-Saxon Protestants.[42]

We see early on in American Catholic history the political and social reform efforts that express a sympathy with the twentieth century New Deal liberalism that would later emerge under Franklin D. Roosevelt. The social reform activities of German-American Catholics, largely in the Midwest, were a case in point. Their efforts centered around their group called the Central-Verein, which started out as a fraternal and benevolent organization to help German-Catholic immigrants participate in American life.[43] In the late nineteenth century, the Central-Verein was a major opponent of the liberal Americanizers in the Catholic Church in the U.S. (the Americanist question is discussed below).[44] Professor Philip Gleason, historian of the German Catholic reformers in the U.S., writes that, "[i]n 1901 it solemnly pledged itself to work for the reform of society according to the principles laid down in Pope Leo XIII's *Rerum Novarum*, and from that time forward it consistently made the study of social questions, social criticism, and social reform its leading concerns."[45] Before World War I, the social reform program of the Central-Verein had a number of accomplishments to its credit, including the setting up of a national office to coordinate its work, the organizing of lecture tours and "social study" courses, and the starting of a news service for religious and reform items for the Catholic press. It also sought to gain support for many legislative efforts of the Progressive Movement, aided by the labor movement, and promoted the creation of Catholic workingmen's societies. After the War, the Central-Verein's leaders helped found such Catholic social action organizations as the National Catholic Rural Life Conference and the Catholic Conference on Industrial Problems.[46] Some of these leaders, such as Frederick P. Kenkel and Father Peter E. Dietz, became prominent figures in the Catholic social reform movement. It also established the bilingual (German and English) *Central-Blatt and Social Justice,* the predecessor of *Social Justice Review,* which, in Gleason's words, was "devoted specifically to examination of the social question in the light of Christian principles."[47] Interestingly, the national Catholic newspaper *The Wanderer,* which is known today for its staunchly conservative political positions, supported and worked with the Central-Verein in its social reform work.[48]

Another early example of the Catholic Church in America associating with political liberalism was the "Bishops' Program of Social Reconstruction" which was promulgated in 1919. Written by the noted Catholic social reformer Monsignor John A. Ryan, it foreshadowed many elements of the New Deal program. It supported federal work projects for returning servicemen, keeping intact the War Labor Board, the expansion of the U.S. Employment Service, using the federal taxing power to end child labor, state minimum-wage laws, comprehensive social insurance, widespread vocational education, and even government competition with monopolies that could not be checked by anti-trust laws.[49]

Monsignor John A. Ryan was perhaps the preeminent example of an American Catholic figure earlier in this century who was involved actively with liberal efforts. Ryan was probably the foremost Catholic spokesman for social reform in the U.S. He authored two very important and influential books on social justice and the economy. The first one, *A Living Wage,* was published in 1906 and both gave a moral basis for the effort to establish minimum wage laws and set forth the notion of the "family wage" (i.e., the idea that a living wage had to be sufficient to insure maintenance of the worker's family), which was later endorsed by Pope Pius XI in the encyclical *Quadragesimo Anno.* It made Ryan a major progressive figure. The second, *Distributive Justice,* spelled out a program for reconstructing the entire American economy on the basis of principles that would help social justice to be realized.

Ryan spearheaded the social justice efforts of the U.S. bishops for many years as head of the Social Action Department of the National Catholic Welfare Conference, the predecessor of the United States Catholic Conference. Widely respected in the American liberal community despite battling it on artificial birth control and support for leftist anti-Church regimes abroad, Ryan was active in such liberal organizations as the Consumers League, the Public Ownership League, the National Conference of Charities and Correction, and the American Civil Liberties Union (ACLU). Besides writing about the necessity of minimum wage legislation, he worked actively for its passage in several states.[50] He was a vigorous supporter of the New Deal and served both as an advisor to President Roosevelt and in a number of other official capacities, most notably as a member of the Industrial Appeals Board of the National Recovery Administration.[51] He also strongly promoted the Congress of Industrial Organizations (C.I.O.), the more liberal of the two labor federations (the American Federation of Labor [A.F. of L.] was the other), and its principle of industry-wide unionism.[52] He often seemed like an unabashed political partisan in his strong attacks on Hoover Republicanism and critics of the New Deal. He developed a general program of industrial democracy which called for increased wage levels, profit-sharing, cooperative employee-management decisionmaking on the plant level, and worker ownership of stock.[53] Many think that Ryan had a definite impact on his fellow American Catholics, making them less politically conservative, more socially concerned, and more aware of economic and social injustices in their country.

Other examples of American Catholic political liberalism during and after the New Deal period include the continuous efforts of the Church to be involved in pro-labor efforts, the short-lived plan of a number of bishops to push for closed shop laws in the 1950s, the work of the Association of Catholic Trade Unionists, the activism of the Dorothy Day-led Catholic Worker Movement, and the outspoken endorsement of liberal positions and politicians by *Commonweal* magazine.

The association of American Catholics with liberalism is seen not only in the examples of prominent Catholic leaders and groups promoting liberal objectives, but also in the political affiliation, voting behavior, and political views of the Catholic population as a whole over the years. We have already spoken about the reason for the attraction of the Catholic immigrants to liberalism and the Democratic party. Catholic affiliation with the Democratic party has continued, by and large, over the years.[54] Catholics were particularly responsive to the liberal New Deal, which not only featured appealing economic policies but also a *social* equalitarianism which sought to elevate underdog groups in American society, like themselves.[55] Survey research indicates that this New Deal liberalism continued among Catholics through the 1950s,[56] in spite of the willingness of many of them, perhaps for emotional reasons, to cast their ballots for Eisenhower.

By the 1970s, the Catholic population at large had become more conservative both on domestic and foreign policy issues. The survey research tells us that this shift was not pronounced, however.[57] It *may* have reflected the alleged transformation of liberalism referred to above. It is not possible to prove this point; that would involve a substantial survey research study well beyond the focus of this book. Nevertheless, the fact that one of the major studies of voting behavior and public opinion tells us that this greater conservatism has manifested itself in such issues as welfare, race questions, and the Cold War, suggests that some insight may be gotten about this point from the comparative examination of Chapters Three and Four. Could there be reasons, based ultimately in Catholic teaching, for the divergence of many Catholics from liberalism on these subjects? This same study makes the point that while more Catholics have moved to the "conservative" side of the political spectrum, a substantial percentage—albeit smaller than the "conservative" one—remains *very* "liberal." The Catholic population has thus become more politically polarized.[58]

This conservatism continued to manifest itself in the 1980s on such issues as abortion—which Catholics overall were more inclined to be against than Protestants—and cutting government social and economic programs—which Catholics were a bit more in favor of than other religious groups in the U.S. This was the case even while Catholics were more likely to identify themselves as liberals than Protestants were.[59]

The greater political polarization within the American Catholic polulation may have been reflected in the conflicts between certain Catholic politicians and the Church hierarchy and orthodox spokesmen that we have seen in the 1980s and are continuing to see at present (e.g., Cardinal John J. O'Connor and Governor Mario Cuomo and Representative Geraldine Ferraro Zaccaro in 1984 and Bishop Leo Maher and California State Senator Lucy Killea in 1989). In the 1980s, as further evidence of the Catholic abandonment of liberalism, we have witnessed a sharp decline of Catholic support for liberal Democratic presidential candidates. There was a fairly consistent pro-Democratic bias among Catholics in presidential elections from the New Deal until 1980 (i.e., a plurality of Catholics went for the Republican candidate in only three elections from 1932 to 1976). In 1980 and 1984, however, they gave a clear plurality of their votes to avowed conservative Ronald Reagan (in 1984 it was a strong majority of 56%). In 1988, Catholics returned to the Democratic fold, but in much smaller numbers. They gave liberal Michael S. Dukakis 52% of their vote to 48% for George H. Bush.[59] The trend of Catholic support away from the Democrats continued in 1992, when Bill Clinton received only 44% of the Catholic vote and the more conservative George Bush (36%) and H. Ross Perot (20%) divided 56% of it.[60]

In spite of the Catholic connection with liberalism, Catholic association with what has been called "conservatism" has not been unknown in American history. Russell Kirk notes that Alexis de Tocqueville, the famous French writer on American democracy and perhaps the first sociologist, "described...[Catholicism's] conservative tendency in American life."[61] He perhaps was referring to Tocqueville's following remarks in his mammoth *Democracy in America*, written in the 1830s:

> People in democracies are...very prone to shake off all religious authority, but if they do consent to submit to any such authority, they want it to be at least single and uniform...Our contemporaries are naturally little disposed to belief, but once they accept religion at all, there is a hidden instinct within them which unconsciously urges them toward Catholicism. Many of the doctrines of the Roman Church astonish them, but they feel a secret admiration for its discipline, and its extraordinary unity attracts them.[62]

Catholicism's conservatism for Tocqueville, then, was based on its unity, the cohesiveness and integrity of its doctrine, and the emphasis it places on discipline and authority. Tocqueville's telling us how a democratic ethos tempts men to an ever more irresponsible use of freedom and pursuit of material pleasure enables us to readily see how Catholicism is in tension with principles such as these.[63] The fact that he sees American democracy as continuing and flourishing, and of all religions "the Roman Catholic religion...making the most progress" and gaining the most adherents in 1830s,[64] gives one the sense of the influence he saw Catholicism, with its "conservative tendency," as having on America.

Besides John Courtney Murray, S.J., spoken of elsewhere in this book, probably the only Catholic political thinker of any renown that America has produced is Orestes Augustus Brownson. (It is interesting that the two most eminent American Catholic political thinkers have both been conservative.) Brownson was a restless spirit whose intellectual and spiritual odyssey involved commitments to Congregationalism, Presbyterianism, Universalism, socialism, atheism, and Unitarianism before he entered the Catholic Church in 1844. Kirk says that Brownson "is the most interesting example of the progress of Catholicism as a conservative spirit in America."[65] In the pages of *Brownson's Quarterly Review*, which he edited for a generation, and in his main work, *The American Republic*, Brownson developed his theory of politics in general and of American government specifically. He wrote that religious sanctions are essential to the safeguarding of freedom and justice; it is only through them that men's passions, which lead to the threatening of freedom and justice when they are unleashed, can be held in check. Contrary to what the ascendant lberalism of the nineteenth century believed, Brownson held that "[t]he sovereignty of God, far from repressing liberty, establishes and guarantees freedom;" authority is not to be seen as threatening to freedom, "but is its vindicator." He advocated the "sacredness and supremacy of law," and emphasized the Thomistic notion of the hierarchy of law. Like the great English conservative Edmund Burke, he viewed constitutions as "the product of slow growth, the expression of a nation's historical experience," having their basis in Providence not human will, and requiring amendment and change from time to time. He feared the tendency in the American people to "ceas[e]...regard[ing] anything as sacred or venerable, spurning what is old, injuring what is fixed, setting adrift all religious, domestic, and social institutions" and to repudiate experience and the past.[66]

During the Civil War, many Catholic leaders aligned themselves on the "conservative" side in the sense of wanting to conserve and not abolish the slavery status quo in the South. As David O'Brien writes in *Public Catholicism*, a volume in the historical series of the Church in the U.S. authorized by the U.S. Catholic Bishops to commemorate the bicentennial of American Catholicism, "Church leaders north and south believed that antislavery, nativism, and anti-Catholicism were parts of a reform package at once utopian and hypocritical, threatening the church but also offering it an opportunity to contrast such unstable radicalism with its own sound conservatism."[67] As Archbishop John Hughes said of the reformers who spearheaded movements such as abolitionism, the Church "'had little confidence in theoretical systems which assume that great or enduring benefit is to result from the sudden or unexpected excitements.'"[68] In the 1850s, the U.S. bishops were conspicuous for their refusal when they met as a body to denounce slavery. When the Civil War actually broke out, Hughes and other northern bishops rallied to the support of the Union—as those in the South did to the Confederacy, with varying degrees of enthusiasm—but not so much for the antislavery cause, but to preserve the United States. If Catholics became more liberal, in part, because of their attachment to the Democratic party, their views about slavery and the Civil War were somewhat shaped by the party as well (but on these questions it was the more conservative of the two parties).

Catholic conservatism was also manifested—ironically, in light of what has been said in the discussion of liberalism—in the labor ferment that gripped America in the late nineteenth and early twentieth centuries. At least this was the case until the end of World War I. Many of the workers experiencing unfair treatment in this period of burgeoning industrialization were Catholic and members of recent immigrant groups. O'Brien writes that the Church leadership in America during this period saw itself, in general, as "exert[ing] a conservative influence in a too individualistic and undisciplined society," and "therefore felt compelled to demonstrate their capacity to persuade Catholic workers to be patient and orderly in the pursuit of their legitimate rights."[69] At this point in time, the labor movement was associated—to some degree fairly, to some degree unfairly—with radicalism and socialism. As O'Brien puts it, "[m]ost Catholic commentators...were suspicious of labor organizations, some from fear of socialism, others out of dislike for secret societies, which had undercut clerical authority in Ireland."[70] Probably other factors influenced this early American Catholic attitude toward labor unions, as well. O'Brien mentions that there was a strong "conservative impulse" among the pre-Civil War urban Irish immigrants. This was because of their having "ties...to Old World ways." He also speaks of the growth, in the late nineteenth century, of "a substantial Catholic middle class drawing the Church more deeply toward conservative social attitudes."[71]

The American hierarchy and prominent Catholic lay spokesmen became distinguished for their opposition to socialism. The hierarchy, concerned about the assault on private property, opposed the Henry George single-tax movement, the Eugene Debs-led Socialist party, and (by and large) the Knights of Labor, whose secret society aspects it found especially objectionable.[72] William Onahan, a prominent Catholic political figure in Chicago, switched from the Democrats to the Republicans to help defeat the United Labor Party, whose members he characterized as "'socialists, anarchists and other undesirable elements.'"[73] Martha Moore Avery and David Goldstein became two prominent Catholic lay opponents of socialism in the first decades of the twentieth century after previously having been socialists before their conversions. The two authored *Socialism: The Nation of Fatherless Children*, which attacked the anti-family ethos of socialism, and Avery became a leading opponent of women's suffrage.[74] O'Brien contends that the threat of socialism did have the effect of stimulating the hierarchy to a more active effort for social reform of a sort that conformed to the Church's teachings.[75]

Even the reputedly most "liberal" members of the American Church hierarchy in the late nineteenth and early twentieth centuries, James Cardinal Gibbons and Archbishop John Ireland, were fairly conservative politically. As O'Brien says, Gibbons "was far more conservative than most Protestant spokesmen."[76] Although Gibbons had defended the rights of workers to organize and the Knights of Labor,[77] and had condemned child labor and advocated a living wage,[78] he also opposed strikes and boycotts and gained the sympathy of certain anti-union partisans.[79] He was a fierce opponent of socialism. His fervent commitment to the American republican idea led him to strongly advocate limited government and states' rights. He feared a strong national government, partly because of the threat it could pose to the Church. This fear led him to oppose such Progressive Era demands as direct popular election of U.S. senators and referendum and recall. He also was a leader among Catholic spokesmen in opposing woman's suffrage, seeing it as a threat to the family and no help to politics. As O'Brien puts it, Gibbons was not an apostle of change: "[n]ot every change, whether in politics or religion, was a reformation" for Gibbons, so it was better to bear difficulties than face the uncertainties that came with it.[80] Ireland supported the cause of labor but was also suspicious that some labor activists were waging an attack on private property. He believed the Church should act as a force to uphold "'social order and law.'"[81] He was an active Republican and gave advice to Republican presidents, including the conservative Taft. He opposed Woodrow Wilson in 1912, believing him to be anti-Catholic.[82]

In the years between World Wars I and II, American Catholic leaders distinguished themselves for their opposition to communism, the threat of which heightened with the Bolshevik Revolution of 1917. When Franklin Roosevelt recognized the Soviet government in 1933, he was vigorously attacked by Catholic journals and groups. Most Catholic leaders in the U.S. supported Franco's side in the Spanish Civil War.[83] Catholic Mayor Frank Hague of Jersey City vigorously opposed Communist influence in labor unions.[84] Catholic labor leader George Meany was an unrelenting opponent of Communist efforts to control unions. Generally, the Church in the U.S. was known for its outspoken anti-communism. After World War II, Bishop Fulton J. Sheen became a leading spokesman for this cause[85] and rank-and-file Catholics were among the biggest supporters of Catholic Senator Joseph R. McCarthy's anti-Communist investigations of the 1950s.[86]

The New Deal, as noted, attracted much Catholic support, but it also had its Catholic opponents. Important German-American Catholic writers, who as noted had been distinguished for their support of social reform, lashed out at the New Deal and the continuation of economic liberalism that it represented. A leading critic of this group was Frederick P. Kenkel, mentioned above.[87] A number of the members of the Church hierarchy were also critical, including William H. Cardinal O'Connell—who was especially known for his political and social conservatism—and Archbishop John R. McNicholas. McNicholas became particularly known for his opposition to legalizing divorce and his insistence that the First Amendment did not give the press such absolute freedom that it could print materials that morally degrade the public. Also, many bishops were incensed by Roosevelt's "court packing" plan, which they saw as an overreach of federal power and opening the door to more centralized government control.[88] Perhaps the best known Catholic critics of the New Deal, however, were Al Smith, the 1928 Democratic presidential candidate, and Father Charles E. Coughlin. Smith was initially a Roosevelt supporter, but later broke with him to embrace the conservative Liberty League.[89] Coughlin promoted a program of social reform, including constitutional change to permit representation of vocational groups in the U.S. Congress and government ownership of natural monopolies.[90] He was a populist of sorts, but refused to embrace the new notion of liberalism that was being defined by the New Deal. The main targets of Coughlin were Communists, big business interests, and Jewish international bankers.[91] He saw both communism and capitalism, the latter of which the New Deal was upholding, as causes for the woeful economic situation of the 1930s. Other Catholic spokesmen and editorialists attacked the New Deal as eroding personal liberties, expanding executive authority, and being unconcerned about the suppression of the Church abroad in its foreign policy.[92]

One other expression of Catholic conservatism in the 1930s—although it was shared also by some Catholics on the left of the political spectrum—was isolationism (i.e., the withdrawal of America from world affairs and a general retreat into our own concerns). Isolationism was generally associated at that time with conservatism in American politics.

What we can see from the above, then, is that Catholics in a significant way have been involved with conservative efforts and objectives, or at least with those that in the minds of the public or typical political commentators have been considered "conservative."

The "Old Liberalism" and the "New Liberalism"

The noted Catholic scholar, Professor James Hitchcock of St. Louis University, has put forth the notions of an "old liberalism" and a "new liberalism" in the United States in the years since World War II or perhaps the New Deal. He distinguishes these two liberalisms primarily on the basis of their avowed moral positions and the tolerance of each for traditional religion, especially Catholicism. He wrote about the old and new liberalisms in an article entitled, "Catholics and Liberals: Decline of Detente," in *America*, March 16, 1974.[93]

According to Hitchcock, the background of the detente between Catholics and the liberal community in twentieth century America began ninety years ago with the efforts of Americanizers like Cardinal Gibbons and Archbishop Ireland. The essence of the Americanist position, as it applied to politics, was that the American scheme of church-state separation, in which the state had no concern with the affairs of the Catholic Church and did nothing to promote it, was the ideal for all political societies. In his 1895 encyclical letter, *Longinque Oceani (Catholicity in the United States)*, Pope Leo XIII said that even though Catholics were treated equally with other Americans because of good laws and customs and the Church was protected by law and "free to live and act without hindrance," this contention of the Americanists was not valid because the Church "would bring forth more abundant fruits if, in addition to liberty, she enjoyed the favor of the laws and the patronage of the public authority."[94]

Hitchcock tells us that in spite of this "rebuff from Rome," those who wanted American Catholicism to take its place in the mainstream of American culture, seeing it as fully compatible with it, "largely won the day" in their struggle with those who believed that the Church had to remain an essentially separatist entity in the U.S. What resulted later from this struggle was the alliance between Catholics and secular liberals in the New Deal coalition. The characteristic pragmatism of liberalism enabled it to join Catholics in a common front on economic and political issues, while avoiding other issues, such as those involving sexual morality, birth control, abortion, Church-state questions, etc., about which there was likely to be much disagreement. At some point—Hitchcock does not say when, but we believe it occurred with certainty at the dawn of the 1960s—the old liberalism, which enabled the consensus to occur, gave way to the new liberalism, in which "moral relativism has moved to the forefront and has become militant." This version of liberalism was no longer willing to sublimate such issues as the above. In fact, it became a forcefully insistent advocate for positions in these and other areas that are at variance with the Church's teaching. This led Hitchcock, writing in 1974, to state that "the relationship between the Church and American liberalism may have to be laboriously and painfully rethought."[95] What we have said about Catholic voting indicates that in certain quarters in the Catholic community this separation indeed seems to have happened.

Let us consider Hitchcock's further description of the new liberalism and his explanation of how it differs from the old. Many of the old liberals, Hitchcock tells us, "were privately skeptical about religion," but, "for the most part they kept their skepticism to themselves." The new liberalism, by contrast, is openly hostile to traditional religion and, in fact, is of the nature of a secular religion itself. He says that it seems willing to relegate religion to strictly a private affair and does not make religious liberty an important part of its agenda. In spite of this anti-religious stance, the new liberalism is a kind of substitute religion: it is fervently absolutistic and moralistic, it is "quick to discover and exclude heretics...[and c]onverts are eagerly welcomed," it passionately pushes a "new morality" at odds with traditional morality, and, with religion pushed aside, lets the civil law be the prime determiner of moral beliefs. Hitchcock contends that it is actually "the religion of many intellectuals."[96]

Hitchcock states that an important—perhaps the most important—aspect of the new liberalism's anti-religious attitude is its anti-Catholicism. The Church, with its millions of official members, is seen—maybe correctly—as the major obstacle to its prime objective of "ushering in a period of general permissiveness." Thus it has adopted, as "a semiofficial tenet," that the Church is repressive and tyrannical. Its adherents in the media—who are abundant in number—readily give center stage to former Catholics eager to claim that their experience confirms this attitude. The Catholic Church and other groups that challenge certain practices, such as abortion, to which the civil law has given its imprimatur, "run the risk of being read out of the American consensus."[97]

Where the old liberalism submerged its heterodox moral views for the sake of consensus, the new liberalism, as stated, aggressively and intolerantly promotes them. This approach is clearest on matters involving sex and the family, where not only its approach but many of its views differ from the old liberalism. It has already been mentioned that new liberalism favors a "general permissiveness" (thus its enthusiasm for the "sexual revolution" and abortion). Its views that are perhaps the most wrought with threatening implications for Christians, however, are those concerning the family. Hitchcock tells us that in this area, the new liberalism "frankly invokes the prospect of legal coercion to achieve its goals." These goals include, among other things, sharp limitation of family size (some new liberals have talked of compulsory contraception, abortion, and sterilization), changing the nature of marriage (since 1974, it has achieved considerable success in doing this through changes in the law and social attitudes), and radically restructuring the parental-child relationship (since the new liberalism views the traditional exercise of parental authority as "'uncreative,'" "'rigid,'" and "'authoritarian'"[98]). One other aspect of the new liberalism sharply distinguishes it from the old, according to Hitchcock. This is its un- or anti-democratic ethos and lack of civility. This attitude is demonstrated in the new liberalism's extremism and willingness to turn to coercion, its "willingness to polarize and fragment in the name of ideological purity," and its "deep...distrust...of popular wisdom" and readiness to circumvent the democratic process to promote its agenda in areas where it can win without popular support, such as the schools, courts, and media. (Hitchcock speaks of the new

liberals' "disdain for the old liberals' preoccupation with democratic procedures.")[99]

Hitchcock does not say for sure when the old liberalism gave way to
the new. He seems to suggest that it was in the late 1960s when that the former
"splintered...as many of the new liberals gave their support to...the New Left."[100]
As stated above, I am inclined to think it was earlier—by 1960. These are a few
of the events that signalled the detente was over, and that symbolized the
precedence that liberalism was openly giving to the secular over the religious
(indeed, even signalled that the era of its militant secularism had arrived): John
F. Kennedy's famous 1960 campaign announcement in Houston that his commitment to the Constitution would have to take precedence over his commitment to the Catholic Faith[101] and the succession of Supreme Court decisions
during the course of his Administration which held that nontheistic movements
such as Secular Humanism and Ethical Culture were religions, and that vocal
prayer and devotional Bible-reading in public schools are unconstitutional.[102]

It is correct, we believe, that the New Left had a substantial influence
on American liberalism. After the late 1960s, some old liberals continued to
hold sway over the Democratic party, more or less, until the rise of the George
McGovern wing in 1972. After that, however, the views of the "McGovernite"
left-wing of the party, which espoused moral postions at sharp odds with
traditional religion, became its mainstream views. It seems that there was not
just a break-off of the new liberals from liberalism, but that the old liberals were
co-opted by the new. This is seen by the fact that virtually all the figures of the
old liberalism who are still prominent liberals today support the ideas that
emerged from the "new politics" agenda of the 1960s, such as legalized abortion, rigid separation of Church and state, secularization of American public
life, and support for a revamping of the family along the lines suggested by the
contemporary feminist movement. Indeed, the old liberals that Hitchcock mentions as being the likely stimulus for the restoration of the old liberalism, such
as Michael Novak, Norman Podhoretz, and Nathan Glazer (they have sometimes
been called "neo-conservatives"; the work of one of their members, Irving
Kristol, is examined in this book), have since either sought to distance themselves from liberalism and moved toward the Republican party, or have finally
succumbed to the new liberalism (e.g., Daniel Patrick Moynihan). Thus, the old
liberalism seems hardly to exist anymore.

Hitchcock's thesis about there being an old and new liberalism, with
the latter hostile to Catholicism, was the inspiration for the comparative examination, in Chapters Three and Four, of the thinking of liberalism in the two time
periods mentioned. In a sense, those chapters are something of a test of the
Hitchcock thesis. Although he may be the only writer who has considered
where the change in post-World War II liberalism stands in relation to Catholic
teaching, he is not the only one to point to the fact that such a change has

occurred (although, in fact, even this has not been studied very extensively or in much detail). Podhoretz, mentioned above, has written about the changed perspective of the new liberalism from the old on foreign policy and communism. While it is *possible* that this issue may no longer be a crucial or viable one, we are of the opinion that it is premature to conclude that communism and the threat represented to the U.S. and Western Europe by the major Communist powers is simply dead. In any event, we certainly cannot say that communism as an ideology is dead; the Church's teaching about it or whatever has characteristics like it will always remain in force. Podhoretz mentions how the old liberalism had been more aggressive in action, although not in rhetoric, than even conservatives in using American political, economic, and military power to promote an anti-Communist foreign policy. The new liberalism has not seen the Communist threat so strongly, has stressed cooperation instead of competition with the Communist powers (at a time before there was any sense at all that ideological changes had occurred in Communist countries or that they had abandoned it as an ideology), and has more isolationistic.[103] David L. Schaefer has written that the egalitarianism of the new liberalism distinguishes it from the old.[104] Joseph Sobran has discussed various aspects of the difference between the old and new liberalisms periodically in his weekly columns in *The Wanderer*. We shall examine particular points such as these in Chapters Three and Four.

TWO

PAPAL TEACHINGS ON THE FAMILY,
THE STATE, AND THE "SOCIAL QUESTION":
A SUMMARY

This chapter summarizes Church teachings, as discerned primarily from papal documents, in the areas that will be the most pertinent to this inquiry into liberalism and conservatism. These are the teachings that relate to the public questions and issues that liberalism and conservatism have addressed. They fall basically into five categories: the family, the obligations owed to human life, the role of the state, the "social question" (involving the moral issues concerning economic activity and the relationship between capital and labor and the taking care of the needy), and the "international question" (relations among nations, war and peace, and human rights). Most of the summarization of these teachings in this chapter comes from the papal social encyclicals. The limits of this book do not permit a detailed examination of all the social encyclicals. Instead, the major ones of the nineteenth and twentieth centuries—from the time of the earliest social encyclicals in the latter half of the nineteenth century—are focused on. The summarization of the social teachings, then, will come mostly from the following encyclicals: *Rerum Novarum* (*The Condition of Labor* [1891]), *Quadragesimo Anno* (*Reconstructing the Social Order* [1931]), *Divini Redemptoris* (*Atheistic Communism* [1937]), *Mater et Magistra* (*Christianity and Social Progress* [1961]), *Pacem in Terris* (*Peace on Earth* [1963]), *Populorum Progressio* (*On the Development of Peoples* [1967]), *Laborem Exercens* (*On Human Work* [1981]), and *Sollicitudo Rei Socialis* (*The Social Concern of the Church* [1987]). Other Church documents, encyclicals, and secondary source materials will also be referred to at different points in the summary.

We are taking all these major encyclicals together as comprising the corpus of the Church's social teachings. There is no change of the teaching from encyclical to encyclical, only a further development and application of it to new questions. The moral principles involved remain the same over time.

Thus, it is correct to look at all the major encyclicals, not just the most recent ones.

These points were made well by Pope John XXIII in *Mater et Magistra*. Tracing the development of the Church's social teaching from Pope Leo XIII's *Rerum Novarum* through Pope Pius XI's *Quadragesimo Anno* to Pope Pius XII's statements, he pointed out that *Rerum Novarum* "is known even to the present day as the *Magna Carta* for the reconstruction of the economic and social order," and "the solidly grounded principles, the norms of action, and the potential admonitions" in it "retain their original worth," and that *Quadragesimo Anno* "reaffirmed those [*Rerum Novarum's*] principles and directives...clarif[ied] certain points of doctrine...but...also showed how the principles and directives themselves regarding social affairs should be adapted to the changing times."[1] The reason Pope John says he is writing *Mater et Magistra* is "to keep alive the torch lighted by our great predecessors...to confirm and explain more fully what...[they] taught, and to set forth the Church's teaching regarding the new and serious problems of our day."[2] We can thus see why one Catholic scholar of the social teachings instructs us to take the social encyclicals "*in toto*" — their cumulative teaching — in determining what the Church's "social doctrine" is comprised of.[3]

The Family

The first area to be considered is the family. As the previous chapter indicated, this area has become one of increasing contention in the public realm. According to Hitchcock, it is one of the key areas on which acrimony has developed between Catholics and liberals and on which Catholicism cannot accommodate itself to the contemporary liberal agenda.

The central role of the family in the Church's teaching is clear and does not need much elaboration here. It is appropriate that it is discussed first in this chapter because the Church has viewed the family as "'the first and vital cell of society'" and thus must be a necessary initial focus of attention before undertaking any consideration of the social question.[4] Its importance to the larger society is seen clearly in Pope John Paul II's apostolic exhortation *Familiaris Consortio*: "It is from the family that citizens come to birth and it is within the family that they find the first school of the social virtues that are the animating principle of the existence and development of society itself."[5]

Catholic teaching, based in all cases on the natural moral law of which God is the Author, makes it clear that the family exists independently of the state and that parents do not depend upon the state for their authority. As Pope Leo XIII said in *Rerum Novarum*: "Parental authority can be either abolished nor absorbed by the State; for it has the same source as human life itself." He says this in conjunction with a condemnation of socialists for "setting aside the parent and setting up a State supervision."[6]

One area in which parental authority over their children has been increasingly challenged has been in education. The Church, however, has constantly insisted that parents are the primary educators of their children. As *Familiaris Consortio* puts it: "The right and duty of parents to give education is essential, since it is connected with the transmission of human life. . .it is irreplaceable and inalienable and therefore incapable of being entirely delegated to others or usurped by others."[7]

Sex education is singled out for particular attention in *Familiaris Consortio.* It calls it "a basic right and duty of parents" and says sex education "must always be carried out under their attentive guidance whether at home or in educational centers chosen and controlled by them."[8]

Despite its emphasis on the rights and prerogatives of the family, the Church, in her concern about the rights and dignity of the individual person, has made clear that there are limits to family authority. In *Rerum Novarum*, Leo XIII set down the conditions for what today we might call state "intervention" in the family. It is "a great and pernicious error" to believe that the state "should at its option intrude into and exercise intimate control over the family." The conditions for "intervention" are strict and limited: the state may aid the family if it is in "exceeding distress, utterly deprived of the counsel of friends, and without any prospect of extricating itself," and it may intervene "if within the precincts of the household there occur grave disturbances of mutual rights."[9]

In *Populorum Progressio*, Pope Paul VI said that "[t]he family's influence may have been excessive at some periods of history and in some places when it was exercised to the detriment of the fundamental rights of the individual."[10] *Familiaris Consortio* specifies the respect for the rights and dignity that must be present within the family context for its various members, especially those who are the weakest: women, children, and the elderly.[11] The Church has *not* taught that individual rights have primacy over family rights, but simply that individuals also have rights that must be respected in the family context.

Familiaris Consortio is particularly noteworthy for its attention to the situation of women in an era when this subject is discussed so much. John Paul II enunciates a reasonable and moderate position on this matter when he says:

> There is no doubt that the equal dignity and responsibility of men and women fully justifies women's access to public functions. On the other hand the true advancement of women requires that clear recognition be given to the value of their maternal and family role, by comparison with all other public roles and all other professions.[12]

In accordance with this position, the Holy Father speaks of ending "discrimination" in education and work, and also of structuring society "in such a way that wives and mothers are not in practice compelled to work outside the home." He continues that "the mentality which honors women more for their work outside the home than for their work within the family must be overcome."[13] These points are repeated in his encyclical *Laborem Exercens*.[14]

Further, John Paul speaks strongly against "offenses against women's dignity," that include not only the above kinds of discrimination, but pornography, prostitution, and unfair treatment of childless wives, widows, separated or divorced women, and unmarried mothers.[15]

While calling for respect for these latter groups of women, papal teaching on moral matters involving marriage and sexuality has been clear and distinct. The modern encyclicals, for example, have strongly emphasized the Church's constant teaching about the immorality of divorce and contraception. Pope John XXIII stated in *Mater et Magistra*: "We strongly affirm that human life is transmitted and propagated through the instrumentality of the family, which rests on marriage, *one and indissoluble*."[16] In this century, of course, two major encyclicals have specifically upheld the teaching on contraception: *Casti Connubi* (1930) and *Humanae Vitae* (1968). The subject of abortion is treated in the next section. The only thing that needs to be said now about it is that the Church emphasizes that the rights of women do not justify abortion. As was stated in the Sacred Congregation for the Doctrine of the Faith's *Declaration on Procured Abortion*: "The movement for the emancipation of women, insofar as it seeks essentially to free them from all unjust discrimination, is on perfectly sound ground. . . .But one cannot. . .exempt women, any more than men, from what nature demands of them."[17]

The attempts in the contemporary world to eliminate the moral stigma of homosexual behavior and to view it as "normal"—which would be a terrible blow to the family if widely accepted—led to the Church's firmly restating its traditional teaching on homosexuality, also. The Sacred Congregation for the Doctrine of the Faith stated this in its *Declaration on Certain Questions Concerning Sexual Ethics*: "[A]ccording to the objective moral order, homosexual relations are acts which lack an essential and indispensable finality. . . .homosexual acts are intrinsically disordered and can in no case be approved of."[18]

Quite pertinent to a consideration of how a major political ideology fares against Catholic teaching is a consideration of the views the ideology has about the various rights of the family as stated by the Church. The 1980 Synod of Bishops, which focused on the family, gave a long list of these rights in the contemporary world, which was repeated by Pope John Paul II in *Familiaris Consortio*.[19] They will be consulted when later drawing the comparisons between liberalism, conservatism, and the Church.

Abortion and the Respect for Human Life

The Church, both from Rome and in the United States, has distinguished itself by speaking up against the legalization of abortion. It is a clearcut example of a basic point of Christian morality that has become an important issue in the public forum.

In standing four-square against abortion, the Church is defending her age-old teaching. In his *Catholic Catechism*, Father John A. Hardon, S.J., a leading Catholic theologian, emphasizes this fact, telling us that the Church's teaching was first set out clearly in the Apostolic Era when the *Didache* instructed, "'You shall not procure abortion. You shall not destroy a newborn child.'"[20] The latter sentence, of course, meant that infanticide was also rejected. The most recent formal document of the Church that was specifically devoted to reaffirming the Church's teaching on abortion was the *Declaration on Procured Abortion* noted above, which was issued in 1974. The Congregation followed this document in 1980 by issuing the *Declaration on Euthanasia*, which restated the Church's traditional teaching against so-called "mercy-killing."

In the *Declaration on Procured Abortion*, the Congregation also addressed the question of what the civil law should do about abortion and what the response of the individual to the civil law should be. The *Declaration* clearly suggests that the civil law should prohibit and punish abortion when it says the following:

> One must. . .be attentive to what a change in legislation can represent. Many will take as authorization what is perhaps only the abstention from punishment. Even more, in the present case, this very renunciation seems at the very least to admit that the legislator no longer considers abortion a crime against human life, since murder is always severely punished. It is true that it is not the task of the law to choose between points of view or to impose one rather than another. But the life of the child takes precedence over all opinions. One cannot invoke freedom of thought to destroy this life.[21]

The *Declaration* goes on to say that not only can medical personnel and others not take part in abortion procedures or the procurement of abortion, but an individual—this would seem to be especially pertinent to the individual carrying out his duties as citizen and legislator—"can never obey a law which is itself immoral, and such is the case of a law which would admit in principle the liceity of abortion," nor "can he take part in a propaganda campaign in favor of such a law, or vote for it."[22] This clearly disallows Catholic politicians from taking positions on the public policy about abortion (mentioned in Chapter One) which are contrary to the teaching of their Church.[23]

Another moral question involving respect for human life, war, is taken up in the section on "'The International Question.'"

The Role of the State

The discussion in this chapter of the role of the state in the political thought set forth by the popes will admittedly be limited. Any more detailed examination of this role would go well beyond the purposes of this book. Nevertheless, by considering what the popes wrote in the aforementioned encyclicals we can get an adequate general understanding of the Church's thinking on this matter, which will help us in comparing the thought of liberalism and conservatism in the following chapters.

The first, most basic point to take note of is that the popes hold firmly that God must be acknowledged to be at the foundation of every political order, and that the state must act positively to protect and favor religion.[24]

Rerum Novarum presents us with the following defintion of "the State" and statement of its basic purpose:

> [T]he State. . .[is] not the particular form of government prevailing in this or that nation, but the State rightly apprehended, that is to say, any government conformable in its institutions to right reason and natural law. . .The foremost duty. . .of the rulers of the State should be to make sure that the laws and institutions, the general character and administration of the commonwealth, shall be such as of themselves to realize public well-being and private prosperity. . . .a State chiefly prospers and thrives through moral rule, well-regulated family life, respect for religion and justice, the moderation and fair imposing of public taxes, the progress of the arts and of trade, the abundant yield of the land—through everything, in fact, which makes the citizens better and happier.[25]

Elsewhere, this encyclical tells us that "the safety of the commonwealth is not only the first law, but it is government's whole reason for existence." It further sets out the basis for the respect of human rights by government: "[t]he State must not absorb the individual or the family; both should be allowed free and untrammeled action so far as is consistent with the common good and the interests of others."[26] This was put another way by Pope John XXIII in *Pacem in Terris*: "[o]ne of the fundamental duties of civil authorities. . .is to coordinate social relations in such a fashion that the exercise of one man's rights does not threaten others in the exercise of their own rights nor hinder them in the fulfillment of their duties."[27]

The purpose of government in promoting the dignity and ends of the individual and human rights is a theme frequently sounded by the popes. *Rerum Novarum* says simply that "the end of society is to make men better."[28] *Pacem in Terris* contends that the civil authorities must understand that "the common good touches the whole man, the needs both of his body and of his soul" and "should promote simultaneously both the material and spiritual welfare of the citizens."[29]

The state's responsibility, then, is the maintenance of the common good, which, as the above makes clear, relates not only to the good of the community as a whole but to that of the individuals in it as well. According to *Pacem in Terris*, "the very nature of the common good requires that all members of the political community be entitled to share in it, although in different ways according to each one's tasks, merits and circumstances."[30] The popes do not say that all persons in the community must be treated exactly alike, but instead there must be no undue preference shown on the basis of such criteria as race, ethnic group, religion, economic or occupational status, etc.[31] This dual responsibility of respecting both the whole community and the parts of it that is dictated by a true respect for the common good places on the state the special duty mentioned in *Populorum Progressio*: "[i]f there should arise a conflict 'between acquired private rights and primary community exigencies,' it is the responsibility of public authorities 'to look for a solution with the active participation of individuals and social groups.'"[32]

Let us consider the rights of men further at this point. The basis for human rights, the popes state, is simply that man is a rational creature "endowed with intelligence and free will." His rights and duties flow "directly and simultaneously from his very nature, which are therefore universal, inviolable and inalienable."[33] This emphasis on human rights is consistently coupled with an emphasis on duties. One of the themes of Part I of *Pacem in Terris* seems to be that men must be equally conscious of both their rights and duties, both of which are mandated by the natural moral law and are oftentimes flip-sides of the same matter, since whenever there are rights there must be a corresponding duty to respect them.[34]

This encyclical lists the various natural rights and duties of man which the public authority must respect and protect. The rights mentioned, by category, are the following: the right to life and a worthy manner of living (rights to life, bodily integrity, and to means necessary for the development of life, including food, shelter, rest, medical care, "necessary" social services, and the right to security when deprived of the means of subsistence through no fault of his own); rights "pertaining to moral and cultural values" (rights to respect for his person, his good reputation, freedom in searching for truth and in expressing and communicating his opinions, and in the pursuit of art, and related to these, "the right to be informed truthfully about public events"; the right to a basic education and to technical and professional training "in keeping with the stage of educational development in the country to which he belongs"); the "right to honor God according to the dictates of an upright consicence, and therefore the right to worship God privately and publicly"; the right to choose freely the state of life preferred (the right to establish a family or to follow a vocation to the priesthood or religious life); rights pertaining to economic life (rights to free initiative in the economic field, to work, to working conditions in which health, morals, and the special needs of women and the young are protected, to a proper wage, and to private property, including productive goods) (these economic rights will be discussed further in the next section); rights of meeting and association (e.g. the right to form and act in societies to achieve goals); the right to move freely about one's own country and to emigrate to other countries; and rights in the political order (the right to take an active part in public affairs, to contribute one's part to the common good of citizens, and to juridical protection of one's rights).[35]

In connection with the rights of communication mentioned above, it must be noted that Vatican II's *Inter Mirifica* (*Decree on the Means of Social Communication* [1963]) states that "[i]t is for the civil authority. . .to defend and safeguard—especially in relation to the press—a true and just freedom of information, for the progress of modern society demands it. . . .It should guarantee to those who use the media the free exercise of their lawful rights."[36]

In mentioning duties in *Pacem in Terris,* Pope John singles out only a few specific ones, but says that all human rights have corresponding duties that are, in effect, the other side of the respective rights. As Pope John explains:

> [T]he right of every man to life is correlative with the duty to preserve it; his right to a decent manner of living with the duty of living it becomingly; and his right to investigate truth freely, with the duty of seeking it and of possessing it ever more completely and profoundly.... to one man's right there corresponds a duty in all other persons: the duty, namely, of acknowledging and respecting the right in question. For every fundamental human right draws its indestructible moral force from the natural law, which in granting it imposes a corresponding obligation....A well-ordered human society requires that men recognize and observe their mutual rights and duties. It also demands that each contribute. . .to the establishment of a civic order in which rights and duties are. . .acknowledged and fulfilled.[37]

In *Sollicitudo Rei Socialis,* Pope John Paul II reiterates the various categories of rights above, but without being so specific.[38] He also discusses the rights of entire nations and peoples, which are mentioned in the section on "The International Question" below.

Church teaching does not specify any one particular form of government that states must adopt to carry on the basic purposes above, so long as the common good (i.e., "public well-being and private prosperity") is being promoted. This is so in spite of *Pacem in Terris'* speaking about the right to take an active part in public affairs and *Sollicitudo Rei Socialis'* insisting that "nations need to reform. . .their political institutions, in order to replace corrupt, dictatorial, and authoritarian forms of government by *democratic* and *participatory* ones."[39] In saying this, the popes are simply insisting that governing authorities acknowledge that consent plays a vital part in any state. If popes have shown a recent preference for democracy, it is because of the contemporary forms it has best upheld popular consent and the common good.

As Father Thomas J. Higgins, S.J., states in his solidly Catholic ethics textbook, *Man as Man: The Science and Art of Ethics*, consent (at least tacit) is the juridic cause of any actually existing state and that a particular ruler's authority to rule must rest ultimately upon the permanent consent of the people. These are both requirements of the natural law. In the modern world, particularly, "the development of the republican ideal and the increasing power of the masses. . .are gradually rendering the consent of the governed more and more indispensable, at least as a condition of rightful rule."[40] As *Pacem in Terris* stipulates, "[i]n determining the structure and operation of government which a State is to have, great weight has to be given to the historical background and circumstances of the individual peoples." The encyclical goes on to mention just one likely requirement of any type of government: "[I]n keeping with the innate demands of human nature. . .the State should take a form which embodies the threefold division of powers corresponding to the three principal functions of public authority" (i.e., legislative, judicial, and executive).[41]

It makes clear that, contrary to what some, at different times, have accused the Church of, she is not opposed to democratic regimes. Even though she asserts that all political authority comes from God—and all human law, to be valid, must be derived from the eternal law and correspond to right reason—this does not preclude a regime in which the governed choose their rulers.[42]

The "Social Question"

The papal social and economic teachings touch a substantial number of questions, so, again, it will be possible to go into them only to the extent necessary for the inquiry in this book. We discuss just the major points from the encyclicals under consideration. There are a number of areas that will be surveyed: the teachings about private property, the rights and duties of workers and employers, the role of the state in economic life, the structuring of industry, and the treatment of the agricultural sector.

Private Property and Private Enterprise

As already mentioned, the Church has stressed that men have a natural right to private property, including productive goods. This right includes the right of inheritance.[43] The Church has defended private property as a way of insuring human liberty generally.[44] She has also endorsed private economic activity for the same reason. In *Mater et Magistra*, Pope John states the following:

> Experience. . .shows that where private initiative of individuals is lacking, political tyranny prevails. Moreover, much stagnation occurs in various sectors of the economy, and hence all sorts of consumer goods and services, closely connected with needs of the body and more especially of the spirit, are in short supply. Beyond doubt, the attainment of such goods and services provides remarkable opportunity and stimulus for individuals to exercise initiative and industry.[45]

The Church has also made clear, however, that the right of private property and the prerogatives attached to it are not absolute. Ownership has a "social or public aspect" as well as a private one that cannot be denied. This means that God has given men the right to own private property "not only that individuals may be able to provide for their own needs and those of their families, but also that by means of it, the goods which. . .[He] has destined for the human race may truly serve this purpose."[46] This means that private property must not be used only for self-interested ends and to help oneself, but also to further the common good. As *Populorum Progressio* puts it, "each man has ...the right to find in the world what is necessary for himself. . . .'Thus, as all men follow justice and unite in charity, created goods should abound for them on a reasonable basis.' All other rights whatsoever, including those of property and of free commerce, are to be subordinated to this principle."[47] It is no doubt in the spirit of such a teaching that *Rerum Novarum* urges that "[t]he law... should favor ownership, and its policy should be to induce *as many as possible of the people to become owners*."[48]

Obligations of Employers and Workers

The obligations of the possessors of private property, especially productive property, are spelled out in the encyclicals in the form of the duties of employers toward their workers and the rights of workers. The Church has clearly allied herself with the cause of workers who have been disadvantaged and oppressed by production arrangements and employment practices. As we shall see, however, she has also emphasized that workers likewise have obligations to their employers.

In *Mater et Magistra*, we are told that there is a two-fold dimension to justice in the economic order which affects the dignity of workers: one aspect relates to the distribution of wealth, the other to the conditions under which men engage in productive activity. Both must be operational for an economic order to be just, as the encyclical states:

> There is. . .an innate need of human nature requiring that men engaged in productive activity have an opportunity to assume responsibility and to perfect themselves by their efforts.

> Consequently if the organization and structure of economic life be such that the human dignity of workers is compromised, or their sense of responsibility is weakened, or their freedom of action is removed, then we judge such an economic order to be unjust, even though...[its] distribution conforms to the norms of justice and equity.[49]

In *Laborem Exercens*, Pope John Paul II emphasizes that man's dignity requires that he not be treated as "an instrument of production"—as has so often happened in modern times—but rather as "the effective subject of work and its true maker and creator."[50] He attacked "the error of economism"—which is part of the more broadly encompassing "error of materialism"—that "consider[s] human labor solely according to its economic purpose."[51]

Probably the major duty of employers to their employees—which has been stressed over and over again and elaborated on in the social encyclicals—is the payment of a just wage. In *Quadragesimo Anno*, Pope Pius XI states that this is to consist of a wage which would be "sufficient for the support of. . .[the workingman] and his family." It should be "adequate to meet ordinary domestic needs," so that mothers do not have to neglect their children by working outside of the home and young children do not have to work.[52] *Rerum Novarum* says that a workman's wages must "be sufficient to enable him to comfortably support himself, his wife, and his children," and to permit him, if he "practice[s] thrift. . .to put by some little savings and thus secure a modest source of income."[53] *Quadragesimo Anno* holds that "[i]f in the present state of society this [a just wage] is not always feasible, social justice demands that reforms be introduced without delay which will guarantee every adult workingman just such a wage."[54] In *Mater et Magistra*, Pope John spells out further what a just wage requires and how it is to be derived:

> [W]orkers [must] receive a wage sufficient to lead a life worthy of man and to fulfill family responsibilities properly. But in determining what constitutes an appropriate wage, the following must necessarily be taken into account: first of all, the contributions of individuals to the economic effort; the economic state of the enterprises within which they work; the requirements of each community, especially as regards over-all employment; finally, what concerns the common good of all peoples, namely of the various States associated among themselves, but differing in character and extent.[55]

He emphasizes that "just as renumeration for work cannot be left entirely to unregulated competition, neither may it be decided arbitrarily at the will of the more powerful."[56] *Laborem Exercens* proposes two ways in which this just wage can be given: the "family wage," wherein "a single salary [is] given to the head of the family for his work, sufficient for the needs of the family without the other spouse having to take up gainful employment outside the home," or through "other social measures," "such as family allowances or grants to mothers devoting themselves exclusively to their families." This encyclical also mentions the obligation to provide "*'social benefits'*. . .to ensure the life and health of workers and their families," including inexpensive or free health insurance, especially in the case of work-related accidents, and pension rights and old-age insurance.[57]

Another point involving obligations of employers to workers that the popes have consistently raised concerns unemployment. *Quadragesimo Anno* speaks of it being "necessary. . .that employment opportunities be provided those able and willing to work." Issued at the time of the worldwide Great Depression, it says that "unemployment, particularly if widespread and of long duration. . .is a dreadful scourge." It views the problem of unemployment as connected to the general level of wages, saying that wages either too high or too low cause it. It states that "[t]o raise or lower wages unduly, with a view to private profit, and with no consideration for the common good, is contrary to social justice."[58] By the time of *Laborem Exercens*, Pope John Paul II refers to unemployment as "in all cases an evil."[59] We shall return to this subject shortly to discuss the obligations of the state to the unemployed.

There are other obligations of employer to employee that the popes have put forth. A listing of these obligations appears in *Rerum Novarum*: the worker must be given time for his religious duties (in *Laborem Exercens*, faced with a tendency in Western countries to treat Sundays like any other business day, John Paul II asserted the existence of a "right to rest," comprising Sunday and some vacation time).[60] The worker also has the right to be shielded from "corrupting influences and dangerous occasions," not to be put in a position that leads him to neglect his home and family or squander his earnings, not to be taxed beyond his strength, and not to be assigned work unsuited to his sex or age.[61] Further, workers have a right to form or join unions.[62] These unions may employ "*the strike* or work stoppage" as "*[o]ne method*. . .in pursuing the just rights of their members."[63]

In *Laborem Exercens*, Pope John Paul II addresses the matter of the application of workers' rights to new areas gaining attention in the contemporary world. He states that "disabled persons. . .should be helped to participate in the life of society in all its aspects and at all levels accessible to their capacities." To do otherwise "would be to practice a *serious form of discrimi-*

nation, that of the strong and healthy against the weak and sick."[64] They should be offered work according to their capabilities. John Paul also states that discrimination on the basis of nationality, religion, or race in determining renumeration for work has no place, and that those who emigrate to a new country in search of work "should not be *placed at a disadvantage* in comparison with the other workers in that [new] society in the matter of working rights."[65]

While concerned about protecting the woman's unique, "irreplaceable" role as mother, John Paul also makes clear that women should not be discriminated against in consideration for or excluded from jobs they are capable of undertaking to the extent their nature will permit. They must be allowed to join men in their efforts to contribute "to the good of society." He also says, however, that a society's notion of work should take account of women's "family aspirations" and, in fact, that work "should be structured in such a way" that they can still hope to advance in it even if they devote themselves to a family calling.[66]

As mentioned, the popes have not only insisted on the obligations of employers to workers, but also of workers to their employers. The popes have stated both specific obligations to individual employers and obligations to respect the rights and system of private ownership. Leo XIII lists the following specific duties:

> [To] fully and faithfully perform the work which has been freely and equitably agreed upon; never to injure the property, nor to outrage the person, of an employer; never to resort to violence in defending their own cause, nor to engage in riot or disorder; and to have nothing to do with men of evil principles, who work upon the people with artful promises of great results, and excite foolish hopes which usually end in useless regrets and grievous loss.[67]

As far as respect for the system of private ownership is concerned (the legitimacy of profit is also implicitly shown), Pius XI says this:

> By. . .[the] principles of social justice one class is forbidden to exclude the other from a share in the profits. This law is violated by an irresponsible wealthy class who. . .deem. . .that they should receive everything and the laborer nothing. It is violated also by the propertyless class, when, strongly aroused because justice is ignored and too prone to vindicate improperly the one right well known to them, they demand for themselves all the fruits of production. They are wrong in thus attacking and seeking the abolition of ownership and all profits deriving from sources other than labor. . .[68]

Pope Pius XI is quick to make clear that respect for the rights of workers does not mean that idleness should be tolerated. He says that St. Paul's teaching that "[i]f any man will not work, neither let him eat" means that we must "use deligently our time and our powers of body and mind, and not...become burdensome to others as long as we are able to provide for ourselves." Additionally, this teaching is not to be taken as an endorsement of a "labor theory of value" as some contended.[69]

Workers' associations—i.e., unions—are similarly restricted in what they can do. As *Laborem Exercens* says, they must be viewed as "*a mouthpiece for the struggle for social justice,* for the just rights of working people," but not a "reflection of the 'class' structure of society" or "a mouthpiece for a class struggle." It goes on to say that "[u]nion demands cannot be turned into a kind of *group or class 'egoism,'*" although they can aim at correcting defects in the economic system. Unions "do not have the character of political parties struggling for power. . .[and] they should not. . .have too close links with them [parties]." The strike "*must not be abused. . .*especially for 'political' purposes. . . .[E]ssential community services. . .must in every case be ensured. . ."[70] (The reference to union demands and the affirmation of the right to strike, of course, indicate *a fortiori* that workers and unions also have a right to collective bargaining and other peaceful collective action.)

Agricultural Labor

While the earlier social encyclicals specifically addressed the plight of industrial workers, the more recent ones have expanded upon this theme to address the needs of farmers and agricultural workers also. *Mater et Magistra,* concerned so much with the moral imperative of economic development, tells us that this development is best accomplished if it "proceed[s] in an orderly fashion. . .preserving appropriate balance between the various sectors of the economy," including agriculture.[71] This involves "public authorities giv[ing] heed and tak[ing] action in the following matters: taxes and duties, credit, insurance, prices, the fostering of requisite skills, and. . .improved equipment for rural enterprises."[72] Attention to the economic situation of those in the agricultural sector is morally required and the language of the encyclical on the foregoing particular points indicates that they are, in some sense, also morally required or at least come close to being moral mandates in order to help a depressed sector of the economy.

On the other hand, the encyclical endorses the family farm concept as something desirable, not morally mandated. This means of organization is not mandated—the encyclical says "no person can lay down a universal rule" about this—although it suggests that it may be the most conducive to "hold[ing] man and the family in proper esteem."[73] It is clear that it is a moral requirement that farmers be able to acquire "money income sufficient for decent and human family living."[74] It also states, by way of "opinion" (i.e., it is not morally mandated), "that in rural affairs, the principal agents and protagonists of economic improvement, of cultural betterment, or of social advance, should be the men personally involved, namely, the farmers themselves."[75] He also speaks of the need for farmers to join together in associations in order to "achieve an importance and influence in public affairs proportionate to their own role."[76] He thus urges that they be involved in the decisions that affect their endeavors and way of life.

Laborem Exercens speaks of specific injustices and needs of persons in agriculture that must be addressed: the fact that in developing countries peasants are exploited by powerful landowners and can never gain land of their own, the lack of legal and social insurance protection, long hours and poor pay, poor training and equipment, the exclusion of these workers from decisions involving their services, and the denial to them of the right of free association.[77] Moreover, *Mater et Magistra* holds that rural dwellers must be provided with "the principal services needed by all," including highway construction, transport services, marketing facilities, pure drinking water, housing, medical services, schools, things needed for religion and recreation, and furnishings and equipment needed in the modern farm home.[78]

Communism, Socialism, and Equality

Let us now turn to what the social encyclicals have said about the role of the state in economic matters, or, more broadly, its role in securing social justice. Again, this will be a brief survey of major points, since there is much more in the various encyclicals than space permits us to go into here.

First, communism has been consistently condemned. This was first done in 1846 by Pope Pius IX and was the subject of Pope Pius XI's entire encyclical *Divini Redemptoris* (*Atheistic Communism*) in 1937. In this encyclical, communism is attacked for the following: its atheism; its gross materialism and rejection of anything spiritual; its exploitation of the antagonisms existing among classes in society and "consequent violent hate and destruction"; its "strip[ping of] man of his liberty, rob[bing of] the human personality of all its dignity, and remov[ing of]. . .all moral restraints"; its unwillingness to recognize "any right of the individual in his relations to the collectivity"; its denunciation of private property; and its repudiation of the spiritual and natural origins of marriage and the family.[79] Regarding the latter, communism rejects "any link that binds the woman to the family and the home." and denies the inherent right of parents to educate their children.[80]

In the document *Instruction on Certain Aspects of the "Theology of Liberation,"*[81] the Congregation for the Doctrine of the Faith took a strongly critical view of the Marxist-inspired "liberation theology" that has in recent years made gains in the underdeveloped world, especially Latin America. In the document written by the Congregation as a follow-up to this one, entitled

Instruction on Christian Freedom and Liberation[82]—the Congregation issued this in order to put forth the chief aspects of a genuine Christian perspective on freedom and liberation[83]—there is an implicit criticism of the view of liberation theology adherents and Marxists generally that "sin" is found basically in unjust social and political structures. The latter document does not specifically call this a Marxist perspective, though it is clear enough that the Congregation had Marxism, particularly, in mind. Nevertheless, the document suggests that there may be some validity to the argument that there are "sinful structures"; it sees these merely as reflections of "sinful man." It puts it this way: "Having become his own center, sinful man tends to assert himself and to satisfy his desire for the infinite by the use of things: wealth, power and pleasure, despising other people and robbing them unjustly and treating them as objects or instruments. Thus he makes his own contribution to the creation of those very structures of explitation and slavery which he claims to condemn."[84]

Thus, while making it clear that Christian tradition understands that sin is something that issues forth from the hearts of men, the document it acknowledges that there can indeed be sinful structures due to the actions of sinful man.[85] Pope John Paul II takes up this point in *Sollicitudo Rei Socialis*:

> [I]t is not out of place to speak of "structures of sin," which. . .are rooted in personal sin, and thus always linked to the *concrete acts* of individuals who introduce these structures, consolidate them, and make them difficult to remove. Thus they grow stronger, spread, and become the source of other sins, and so influence people's behavior.[86]

Next, socialism also has been condemned repeatedly, in both its more extreme and moderate forms, because of its basic materialistic premises, its essential opposition to private property, its support for antagonism among classes in society, its basic atheism, its view of the individual as just a part of a socialized mass, and its belief in compulsion to secure its objectives.[87] One recalls the well known line from *Quadragesimo Anno*: "No one can be at the same time a sincere Catholic and a true socialist."[88]

In connection with this, we have already indicated that the Church says that all people in society must have their basic rights respected, all have an equal human dignity, and all must be guaranteed equal opportunity in society. She does not support the view that all must be treated exactly alike, or be entitled to the same station or the same amount of wealth or property, or be assured equal results in whatever they undertake. Pope Leo XIII's encyclical *Quod Apostolici Muneris* (*On Socialism* [1878]) says the following:

> [T]he socialists...always...maintain that nature has made all men equal, and...therefore, neither honor nor respect is due to magesty...

> But, on the contrary, in accordance with the teachings of the Gospel, the equality of men consists in this: that all, having inherited the same nature, are called to the same most high dignity of the sons of God, and that, as one and the same end is set before all, each one is to be judged by the same law and will receive punishment or reward according to his desserts. The inequality of rights and of power proceeds from the very Author of nature...For, He who created and governs all things has, in His wise providence, appointed that the things which are lowest should attain their ends by those which are intermediate, and these again by the highest. . . .He [has] appointed that there should be various orders in civil society, differing in dignity, rights, and power, whereby the State, like the Church, should be one body, consisting of many members, some nobler than others, but all necessary to each other and solicitous for the common good.[89]

and

> For, while the socialists would destroy the "right" of property, alleging it to be a human invention altogether opposed to the inborn equality of man, and claiming a community of goods, argue that poverty should not be peaceably endured, and that the property and privileges of the rich may be rightly invaded, the Church, with much greater wisdom and good sense, recognizes the inequality among men, who are born with different powers of body and mind, inequality in actual possession, also, and holds that the right of property and of ownership, which springs from nature itself, must not be touched and stands inviolate. For she knows that stealing and robbery were forbidden in so special a manner by God. . .that He would not allow man even to desire what belonged to another. . .[90]

It should be mentioned that, in spite of the above, the Church does not necessarily condemn redistribution of wealth by public authorities. As the Vatican II document *Gaudium et Spes* (the *Pastoral Constitution on the Church in the Modern World*) says, "God destined the earth and all it contains for all men and all peoples so that all created things must be shared fairly by all mankind" and "men are bound to come to the aid of the poor and to do so not merely out of their superfluous goods." The meaning of this age-old teaching of Christianity is that "[w]hen a person is in extreme necessity, he has the right to supply himself with what he needs out of the riches of others."[91] It specifies that "[i]n this case the old principle holds good: 'In extreme necessity all goods are common, that is, they are to be shared.'" Certain "moral conditions...must be fulfilled" in the doing of this, however, and Church teaching would be violated if it were done in the wrong manner or done beyond a certain extent.[92] On this latter point, the document refers readers to St. Thomas Aquinas' *Summa Theologica.*[93]

Ordering Principles in Economic Affairs
and the Role of the State

While condemning communism and socialism, however, the social encyclicals have made it clear that individualistic, laissez faire capitalism—a central aspect of classical or nineteenth century liberalism—is also to be rejected. Pius XI instructs us as follows:

> [T]he proper ordering of economic affairs cannot be left to the free play of rugged competition. . . .Free competition. . .though justified and quite useful within certain limits, cannot be an adequate controlling principle in economic affairs. . . .Still less can this function be exercised by the economic supremacy which. . .has taken the place of free competition.[94] [Elsewhere, he refers to the latter as a "concentration of power" which has led to "domination." In other words, he is condemning monopoly.[95]]

In spite of her rejection of the various modern economic ideologies, the Church's teaching must not be understood as just another approach or perspective. As *Sollicitudo Rei Socialis* says:

> The Church's social doctrine *is not* a "third way" between *liberal capitalism* and *Marxist collectivism*, nor even a possible alternative to other solutions less radically opposed to one another. . .Nor is it an ideology, but rather the accurate formulation of the results of a careful reflection on the complex realities of human existence, in society and in the international order, in the light of faith and of the Church's tradition. . . .It therefore belongs to the field, not of *ideology*, but of theology and particularly of *moral theology*.[96]

Pius XI tells us what should be looked to as the true controlling principles in economic matters and what the state must do:

> More lofty and noble principles must. . .be sought. . .to wit, social justice and social charity. . . .[A]ll institutions of public and social life must be imbued with the spirit of justice. . .It is the duty of the State to safeguard effectively and to vindicate promptly this [juridical and social] order.[97]

While the state, then, clearly has an important role to play, its role is limited. The basic principle limiting the state is subsidiarity. This principle is stated well in *Quadragesimo Anno*:

> [I]t is a fundamental principle of social philosophy, fixed and unchangeable, that one should not withdraw from individuals and commit to the community what they can accomplish by their own enterprise and industry. So, too, it is an injustice and. . .a grave evil and a

disturbance of right order, to transfer to the larger and higher collectivity functions which can be performed and provided for by lesser and subordinate bodies. Inasmuch as every social activity should...prove a help to members of the body social, it should never absorb them.

The State authorities should leave to other bodies the care and expediting of business and activities of lesser moment. . .[98]

Taking this principle of subsidiarity as a starting point, the popes have addressed the general prerogatives and functions the state may assume in the economy as well as the specific duties it has to its citizens to insure their economic well-being. So, on the one hand, "complete collectivisation" and "arbitrary planning," such as has characterized Communist countries, are condemned.[99] On the other hand, the state has a duty, as "'indirect employer,'" to "make provision for *overall planning*" in order "to meet the danger of unemployment and to ensure employment for all."[100] *Mater et Magistra* tells us that "it is lawful for States and public corporations to expand their domain of ownership," but only if the principle of subsidiarity is closely observed, the common good clearly requires it, and safeguards are taken to insure that the right of private property continues to be respected.[101] *Quadragesimo Anno* also makes clear that the public authority may decide "what is licit and what is illicit for property owners in the use of their possessions," so long as the divine and natural law are followed.[102]

This right of the state is indicated by the principle that "*the right to private property is subordinated to the right to common use,* to the fact that goods are meant for everyone."[103] This principle also legitimizes "*socialization,* in suitable conditions, of certain means of production."[104] By "socialization" is meant taking ownership of the means of production out of private hands and making them the property of organized society. *Laborem Exercens* makes it clear that this is not satisfied simply by the state taking possession, but when "on the basis of his work each person is fully entitled to consider himself a part-owner of the great workbench at which he is working with everyone else," and when basic human rights are protected.[105] How this can be done is seen in our discussion of the popes' recommendations for restructuring industry.

The State also may not levy excessive taxation on its citizens. It acts unjustly if it deprives a person of "more than is fair" by taxation, and it certainly cannot use taxation as an indirect means of violating the right of private property.[106] *Mater et Magistra* enunciates the general principle to be followed to insure a just taxing policy: "As regards taxation, assessment according to ability to pay is fundamental to a just and equitable system."[107] This is based simply on the principles of distributive justice.

The popes have said that the law should give special protection to workers and to the poor because, as Leo XIII pointed out, the rich have their own resources to protect themselves, but the poor do not "and must chiefly depend upon the assistance of the State."[108]

The state, Leo XIII also said, should act to eliminate the causes of labor-management problems before they develop by legislating proper standards for wages and working conditions, etc. (i.e., by making sure that the duties owed to workers mentioned above are carried out). It must also, of course, safeguard private property, to protect it from being seized by others even "under the futile and shallow pretext of equality." Indeed, the state has a duty to restrain those "firebrands" among the working class who seek violent, revolutionary change.[109] It also has the right to prevent the forming of associations "which are evidently bad, unlawful, or dangerous" to it.[110]

The popes mention a number of things that persons must have access to if their economic well-being is to be insured. They have said that the public authorities have a particular obligation to see that these are provided. The state may provide relief (i.e., welfare) for the poor, but its use of its laws to help alleviate the situation of the poor by other means should not make this so necessary. Also, its system of relief should not take precedence over the Church's charitable works, and it should view the relief effort as a cooperative one with other human agencies.[111] *Laborem Exercens* tells us that there is a "duty to make suitable grants. . .for the subsistence" of the unemployed and their families. Besides unemployment benefits, this ostensibly also includes relief. The state, as "indirect employer," is "responsible" for seeing that this is done in some way.[112] *Mater et Magistra* states that social insurance and social security (including old-age insurance) are necessary,[113] and what was stated above suggests that it views public authorities as especially responsible for this.

The Church has reemphasized recently her particular love of the poor and has said that this must be shared by others and particular attention given to the plight of the poor. She has called this "the *option* or *love of preference* for the poor,"[114] and it is based directly on Jesus' teaching.[115]

Cooperation: The Basis for Reconstructing the Social Order

The social encyclicals have had running through them the theme of reconstructing the social order. The first point the popes have made clear is that there can be no reconstruction, nor any real solution to the social problem, without religion and the Church.[116] It "must be preceded by a profound renewal of the Christian spirit."[117]

This reconstruction of the social order called for by the popes involves, most basically, a substitution of a cooperative spirit between labor and employers for the prevalent antagonistic and even hostile attitude. This cooperative spirit is based on the belief, as enunciated by Leo XIII, that "it is ordained by nature that these two classes should dwell in harmony and agreement. . .to maintain the balance of the body politic. Each needs the other: capital cannot do without labor, nor labor without capital."[118]

This need for a partnership between capital and labor has led the popes to call for employees to "have an active part in the affairs of the enterprise wherein they work, whether. . .private or public," especially in medium-size and large enterprises.[119] A more fundamental restructuring of the economic order called for by the popes has involved the call for the establishment of functional or vocational groups. These would not be unions, but would involve the coming together into associations of all those involved in the same trade or profession, both from the side of labor and of ownership and management. These common associations would enable all those involved in a profession to work for its common benefit and for the common good of society. Joining such associations must be a free choice of individuals and, in doing so, they retain their right to join other associations.[120] (The popes make it clear that both workers *and* employers have a right to organize their own groups to promote their objectives.)[121] *Rerum Novarum* states that these associations can be the means of correcting unjust or unsatisfactory conditions in industries and protecting workers' rights "in order to supersede undue interference on the part of the State," although, if circumstances dictate, the state can be appealed to "for its sanction and protection."[122]

The "International Question"

Finally, let us consider what the social encyclicals have said about the moral rules governing the relations between nations, war and peace, and international human rights questions.

Building a Just International Order

The first point of the popes that should be noted in building a just international order is the same as for building a just domestic social order: God and "a moral law rooted in religion" must be the basis of it.[123] Although, as we shall see, the popes point to many international problems—economic injustice, warfare, suppression of human rights—the most basic problem, as Pope Paul VI tells us, in a "world [which] is sick" is "the lack of brotherhood among individuals and peoples."[124] Individual countries can no longer just be concerned about indigenous social problems and divorce themselves from these problems as they afflict other nations. Both Paul VI and John Paul II declare that the "social question" has become worldwide in scope. John Paul states that economic conditions and problems in particular nations and regions of the world "are not to be considered as isolated cases with no connection" since "they depend more and more on the influence of factors beyond regional boundaries and national frontiers."[125] First, Second, Third, and even Fourth World...*interdependence* remains close...development either becomes shared in common by every part of the world or it undergoes a *process of regression* even in zones marked by constant progress."[126]

International Economic Matters and International Cooperation

We now consider the popes' teachings on the international economic question, most of which has been put forth from the time of John XXIII. (John's *Pacem in Terris,* Paul VI's *Populorum Progressio,* and John Paul II's *Sollicitudo Rei Socialis* all deal primarily with questions concerning the international community.) Much of this teaching deals with the treatment of poor countries by rich ones and the matter of the economic development of the poor countries.

John Paul II says that all peoples have the "right...to share in the process of full development,"[127] and insists that there be "an ever greater degree of rigorous respect for justice and consequently a fair distribution of the results of true development."[128] Paul VI admonishes us to understand that development does not have "increased possession" or wealth as the "ultimate goal of nations"; it must permit "man to develop as a man," to make "the transition from less human conditions to those which are more human." Less human conditions include insufficient material necessities, moral deficiencies, oppressive social structures, and exploitation of workers. Conditions which are more human include the opposite of these, along with greater respect for others' dignity, cooperation for the common good, the desire for peace, and, most of all, "the acknowledgement...of supreme values, and of God as their source...[and] faith...and unity in the charity of Christ."[129] True development "respect[s] and promote[s] *human rights...including the rights of nations and of peoples.*"[130] Along with the latter in the shaping of "a *real international system*" must go an acknowledgement of "the *equality* of all peoples" and a "respect for their legitimate differences,"[131] which include "the identity of each people, with its own historical and cultural characteristics."[132] (By "identity," John Paul II seems to mean a national and ethnic or racial uniqueness, with particular traditions developing as part of it.)

The popes instruct that the developed and economically better-off nations have an obligation to assist the poorer nations in their development efforts. "Every nation must...contribute to the common development of the human race....[T]he superfluous wealth of rich countries should be placed at the service of poor nations." They should devote some of their production to them and should train persons to be available to them to assist in their needs.[133]

Private enterprises and organizations should assist them also.[134] The popes have said that not only must nations work together to bring about development—both rich and poor nations and poor nations in concert—but there must be a truly cooperative effort by public authorities, private persons and organizations, and international bodies.[135] As Paul VI says, the situation demands "concerted planning"; he even calls for the creation of a *"World Fund"* established from part of the money spent on arms to help the most destitute of the world.[136] He insists that the aid given to developing nations, either by nations or other institutions, be truly disinterested: "[R]eceiving countries could demand that there be no interference in their political life or subversion of their social structures." They could be held accountable, however, for the legitimate use of the aid: "Guarantees could be given to those who provide. . .capital that it will be put to use according to an agreed plan and with a reasonable measure of efficiency."[137]

As far as international organizations are concerned, it must be noted that the popes have frequently spoken well of them. In fact, in *Pacem in Terris*, John XXIII talks of the need for an international public authority to further the universal common good which is not being sufficiently promoted in the present international order. He says this authority would have to be entered into freely by governments, and he does not specify if it should have the same power as a national government. He does make it clear that it is not to be a substitute for individual political communities—i.e., not a world government—and its actions would be governed by the principle of subsidiarity, so that it would be concerned only with world-wide problems.[138]

By the time of *Sollicitudo Rei Socialis*, twenty-five years later, Pope John Paul II is saying that "[i]n the opinion of many, the *International Organizations* seem to be at a stage of their existence when their operating methods, operating costs and effectiveness need careful review and possible correction." He demonstrates a regretful awareness that these organizations have been manipulated for national and political reasons. He nevertheless endorses such organizations, as John XIII did, and says that the world actually needs "a *greater degree of international ordering*, at the service of the societies, economies, and cultures of the whole world."[139] In other words, international organizations are an obvious way of bringing about necessary unity amidst a desirable diversity.

John Paul also elaborates on a particular form of international cooperation that Paul VI briefly mentioned in *Populorum Progressio*: regional cooperation. Both urge especially underdeveloped nations in the same geographical areas to join together to promote the economic and material advancement of each. This sharing can aid them in achieving economic independence, promoting trade with each other, and distributing productive capital among themselves. While Paul VI seems to speak mostly about bilateral and multilateral agreements among countries to accomplish this, John Paul goes beyond just this to suggest their setting up *"new regional organizations.*[140]

The popes address specific èconomic rights and prerogatives in the international sphere. They tell us that the same standards that apply in the domestic realm —regarding considerations of justice taking precedence over free contractual agreement, "the law of free competition," and prices set by the market—apply also in economic relations among nations. The rule of free trade cannot be a dogma. Trade must be "subject to the demands of social justice," and "[w]ithout abolishing the competitive market, it should be kept within limits which make it just and moral, and therefore human."[141] Areas singled out for particular concern in *Sollicitudo Rei Socialis* are the world monetary and financial system which hurts the debt situation of the poor countries, the discrimination of the international trade system against those of the latter countries that would be capable of being raw materials producers, and problems with technology transfer that often result in these countries not receiving the kind of technology they desperately need.[142] Expropriation of property is permissible in the following circumstances:

> If certain landed estates impede the general prosperity because they are extensive, unused or poorly used, or because they bring hardship to peoples or are detrimental to the interests of the country, the common good sometimes demands their expropriation.[143]

Also, available revenue cannot be used by persons in whimsical or speculative ways. Furthermore, if people have abundant incomes, they should not transfer substantial amounts of their money out of their country when it needs their investment.[144] A further indigenous problem in some of the underdeveloped countries which stands in the way of true progress for their people is the existence of "unjust structures" seen, as noted above, in corrupt and authoritarian political institutions.[145]

Colonialism and International Human Rights

Populorum Progressio presents a balanced view of colonialism, stating that "a certain type" of it caused damage, but acknowledging benefits resulting from it to many of the former colonies.[146] It states that "racism" and "nationalism" in the former colonies stand in the way of international cooperation (although nationalism can be a positive force if it is a moderate, not extreme, expression of pride in a certain cultural patrimony).[147] Previous papal teachings give us the basis for the rejection of these attitudes and the specter of employment discrimination discussed by Pope John Paul II (noted above). They say that all human beings "are equal by reason of their natural dignity,"[148] even though "there will ever be differences and inequalities of condition in the State" since "it should not be supposed that all can contribute in a like way and to the same extent"[149] (the previous points made about inequality when discussing socialism are also pertinent here). There is also a condemnation of revolution (except in an extreme case) which the popes see as causing new injustices.[150]

The various human rights the popes have enunciated and defended have already been mentioned. When examining the encyclicals, we see two additional points that need to be mentioned on the subject of human rights on the international plane. One, closely related to the above, is that the rights of ethnic minorities must be respected. This is stated along with an exhortation to these minorities to not exalt themselves and their culture or to view what is advantageous to them as advantageous to everyone.[151] The other point concerns political refugees. Refugees retain their human rights even though they have left their states. They should be accepted and these rights acknowledged by the states they seek to enter.[152] (We have already mentioned that the employment rights of emigres must be fully respected.)

In *Mater et Magistra*, John XXIII addresses the purported problem of an imbalance between population growth and the means of subsistence in the whole world or at least in some countries (i.e., the growth in population is outstripping the growth in food and resources necessary for maintaining it). He contends that the facts to back up this theory are inconclusive. He says, however, that if it is the case, the population policies developed to address it would have to follow "the moral law laid down by God," "regard the life of man as sacred," and avoid the use of "methods and procedures which may indeed be permissible to check the life of plants and animals" but not man.[153] This means that such methods as contraception, abortion, and infanticide would be morally unacceptable. In *Sollicitudo Rei Socialis*, John Paul II singles out for "the most forceful condemnation" the launching of "*systematic campaigns against birth*" that are against both the "cultural and religious identity of the countries" they are directed at—usually, he notes, poor countries—and "true development." He says further that "this sometimes leads to a tendency towards a form of racism."[154]

The Environment

Pursuant to, or in conjunction with, his discussion of underdevelopment, Pope John Paul II has recently addressed the question of the physical environment. In *Sollicitudo Rei Socialis*, he says that natural resources cannot be treated as if man has absolute dominion over them, as if they are inexhaustible, and that we must be concerned about the pollution of the environment and the health dangers of it. "[T]he way in which resources are used must include respect for moral demands. . . .The dominion granted to man by the Creator is not an absolute power. . .[W]hen it comes to the natural world, we are subject not only to biological laws but to moral ones, which cannot be violated with impunity."[155]

Pope John Paul II devoted one of his last statements of the 1980s to environmental concerns. This December 8, 1989 statement, called *Peace With God the Creator, Peace With All of Creation*,[156] speaks about the "ecological crisis" as a "moral problem."[157] He states that it is a consequence, most fundamentally, of man "turn[ing] his back on the Creator's plan."[158] It has been caused by such factors as: "the indiscriminant application of advances in science and technology"; a concern for "the interests of production" over human dignity (the same theme as is sounded in the social encyclicals when discussing labor) resulting in an ensuing disregard for physical nature; the "uncontrolled destruction of animal and plant life" and "a reckless exploitation of natural resources" often "in the name of progress"; and subsistence farming in underdeveloped countries—caused by deep-seated conditions of rural poverty and unjust land distribution—which leads to exhaustion of the soil and "accelerating uncontrolled deforestation."[159]

Also, the not-so-distant future holds the grave threats of "biological disturbance...from indiscriminant genetic manipulation" and warfare—either conventional, thermonuclear, or chemical-biological—on a worldwide or even more localized scale that can massively harm the environment.[160] John Paul II calls upon men to realize that the earth is their common heritage, the fruits of which all should partake of—not just the weathly—and all should be reponsible for.[161] He insists that, while not seeking to escape the modern world, men must seek a more restrained "lifestyle" which is characterized by "[s]implicity, moderation...discipline...[and] a spirit of sacrifice."[162] He charges governments with particular responsibility to do the following:

> [M]ake or facilitate necessary socio-economic adjustment within...[their] own borders, giving special attention to the most vulnerable sectors of society....[A]ctively endeavor within...[their] own territory to prevent destruction of the atmosphere and biosphere, by carefully monitoring, among other things, the impact of new technological or scientific advances....[And] ensuring that...[their] citizens are not exposed to dangerous pollutants or toxic wastes.[163]

This language, of course, does not say that governments must actually do all these things themselves, but must insure that they be effectively done. They also have the responsibility of joining with other states in cooperative efforts to work for a better environmental situation. There is especially the need for cooperation between developed and underdeveloped states. The latter "are not morally free to repeat the errors made in the past" by the former as they industrialize, but the former must not expect the latter to follow "restrictive environmental standards" if the former do not adopt them first.[164] A truly "internationally coordinated approach" is needed for "the management of the earth's goods" (just as we have seen the popes call for in other areas). John Paul even suggests that "[t]he right to a safe environment...be included in an updated Charter of Human Rights."[165]

War and Peace

We now briefly consider war and peace. It is first necessary to consider the general moral teaching of the Church about warfare. The Church has never had a pacifist tradition, in spite of what some have said in recent years. She has always taught that the Christian may bear arms and may participate in a *just* war.[166] In order for a war to be just, the Church in modern times has set out these four conditions: it must be on the sovereign's authority, the cause must be just, the belligerents should have a rightful intention, and the war must be waged by "proper means." The second of these conditions has been further elaborated: for the cause to be just the nation's rights, independence, or possession of vital national resources must have been unjustly violated or imminently threatened, other means of preventing the aggression against it have been tried and failed, and there has to be a proportion between the foreseen evils of the conflict and the hoped-for benefits from it.[167]

The Second Vatican Council addressed the matter of means in warfare in the contemporary world: "Every act of war directed to the indiscriminate destruction of whole cities or vast areas with their inhabitants is a crime against God and man, which merits firm and unequivocal condemnation."[168] Higgins writes that "[c]ivilians, who only remotely and indirectly promote military effort, are not to be classified as combatants and their persons and homes may not be the objects of direct attack."[169]

Pacem in Terris tells us that nations possess various rights that other nations may not violate, including their freedom, integrity, and security. Smaller states, as much as larger ones, have a right to economic development and to neutrality in the case of conflicts between other states. No state may unjustly involve itself in another's affairs.[170] Pope Paul reiterates this position in speaking particularly of developing countries: "[S]overeign states. . .have the right to conduct their own affairs, to decide on their policies, and to move freely towards the kind of society they choose."[171] Pope John maintains also that nations have an obligation to try to settle their differences amicably, through negotiation and agreement instead of warfare.[172] Pope John Paul II has emphasized that in the absence of the kind of supranational authority spoken of by Pope John, "the only realistic response to the threat of war is. . .negotiation."[173]

Pope Pius XII's encyclical *The Function of the State in the Modern World* held that nations have a moral obligation to live up to treaties they have entered into, even when they become "unjust, impracticable, or too burdensome for one of the parties." If such a situation of inconvenience occurs—perhaps after not being foreseeable when the treaty was made—"recourse should be had in good time to a frank discussion with a view to modifying the treaty or making another in its stead." For nations "tacitly to assume the authority of rescinding them unilaterally when they are no longer to one's advantage, would be to abolish all mutual trust among States."[174]

Pacem in Terris also calls for an end to the arms race, saying that "the stockpiles which exist in various countries should be reduced *equally and simultaneously by the parties concerned.*"[175] Echoing this, the Fathers of the Second Vatican Council say that "[r]ather than eliminat[ing] the causes of war, the arms race serves only to aggravate that position."[176] *Pacem in Terris* also advocates the banning of nuclear weapons and says that "a general agreement should eventually be reached about progressive disarmament and an effective method of control."[177] Pope John Paul II later speaks of the need for a "general verifiable disarmament."[178] Pope John was realistic about these possibilities, however, as can be seen from his words in *Pacem in Terris*:

> All must realize that there is no hope of putting an end to the building up of armaments, nor of reducing the present stocks, nor still less, of abolishing them altogether, unless the process is complete and thorough and unless it proceeds from inner conviction: unless, that is, everyone sincerely co-operates to banish the fear and anxious expectation of war. . .[T]he true and valid peace of nations consists not in equality of arms but in mutual trust alone.[179]

Pope John Paul II, writing almost twenty years later (but not in an encyclical), echoes what Pope John said above. He states that "[n]o negotiations about armaments would be complete if they were to ignore the fact that 80 percent of the expenditures for weapons are devoted to conventional arms" and calls for "[e]very step to limit. . .[their] production and traffic."[180] Calling also for "progressive disarmament," he says that "[i]n current conditions 'deterrence' based on balance [of forces on each side], certainly not as an end in itself but as a step toward [this] may still be judged morally acceptable." To insure peace, however, nations cannot "be satisfied with this minimum which is always susceptible to the real danger of explosion."[181]

Father Hardon has noted that there is today substantial agreement among Catholic moralists that although nuclear war is defensible in theory, it is almost impossible to justify in practice.[182] The above statements of the popes raise the question if it is even justified in theory.

Sollicitudo Rei Socialis decries the division of the world since World War II into two blocs "each suspicious and fearful of the other's domination." There is a military opposition based on an ideological opposition between a system in the West "historically inspired " by liberal capitalism and one in the East "inspired by. . .Marxist collectivism."[183] The result is both a kind of imperialism on the part of both sides toward the underdeveloped countries—referring basically to the latter being put in a position of being subjected to the objectives of the former—and "an unacceptably exaggerated concern *for security*" that both "deadens" the cooperation of men toward achieving the common good and impedes the development of the other, weaker countries.[184*]

Terrorism, which had become increasingly frequent in the twenty years between *Populorum Progressio* and *Sollicitudo Rei Socialis*, is singled out, not surprisingly, for specific condemnation in the latter.[185]

Finally, the popes have had no illusion about what peace consists of. As Paul VI says in *Populorum Progressio*:

> Peace cannot be limited to a mere absence of war. . .[It] is something...built up day after day, in the pursuit of an order intended by God, which implies a more perfect form of justice among men.[186]

Now that we have completed our survey of the Church's teachings on pertinent questions concerning the political and social orders (a few more specific points will be brought up in the course of discussion), let us turn our attention to evaluating contemporary liberalism and conservatism in light of these teachings.

---

* Obviously, some of the conditions of the world pointed to in *Sollicitudo Rei Socialis* have changed since the fading of the Cold War.

THREE

COMPARING AMERICAN LIBERALISM
AND CHURCH TEACHING, PART I:
THE GENERAL PHILOSOPHY OF
POLITICS AND GOVERNMENT

This chapter examines the broad political philosophy of American liberalism—its view of the general role of government, the basis for political authority, and the rights and duties of the individual in the political order—and compares it with the papal teaching discussed in Chapter Two. The focus here is on the general philosophy of liberalism. In Chapter Four, specific liberal policies and program ideas will be evaluated in the same way.

On the basis of the presentation of the papal teaching in Chapter Two, primarily in the section on "The Role of the State" and to some extent also in the sections on "The 'Social Question'" and "The 'International Question,'" we can identify five areas that should be considered to enable an intelligent comparison to be drawn between the Church's and liberalism's positions. These areas are: the views about the purposes of government; the understanding of the role of God, religion, and the natural law as the basis for the political order; and the views on freedom, equality, and communism.

These are the general areas that we can identify as being the most important ones in the encyclicals, at least for a comparison with political ideologies. The economic and, for the most part, international areas are best compared with reference to the various public policy positions in Chapter Four.

It should be noted that most of this book was composed before the dramatic developments which occurred in world communism in 1989. We have tried to note positions, where appropriate, that seem to have been proved or disproved by these developments. It is clear that the basic conclusions regarding communism are not much affected by these events, however, since the comparisons between the two ideologies and Church teaching are mostly on the level of principles (i.e., the beliefs associated with what we have called "communism" in the nineteenth and twentieth centuries). There is no evidence at all that *these* have changed, even though the praxis of most Communist states may have changed. Actually, it is not even clear that the latter has changed. If a number of nations that have been Communist for decades no longer are, there are others that remain so, such as China.

Perhaps the changes that have occurred are really due to the fact that many of the formerly Communist states no longer believe in communism and have implicitly abandoned it. Where the points made involve views about American policy toward the Soviet Union, it is not entirely clear that the situation has changed. In 1990, as this is being written, relations between the U.S. and the U.S.S.R. are in a state of flux. There is promise of a better, less hostile relationship in the future, but no clear evidence of substantial dismantling of the Soviet military apparatus or a conclusive change in its foreign policy.

Morever, the analyses of the Church and the two ideologes about communism was made during the lengthy era when what we clearly understood to be *communism* was in place in many nations throughout the world. Therefore, the assessments made are of this pre-1990 communism, and not of its most current, yet still not totally defined form which now exists in some of the former Soviet bloc countries.*

Morever, the analysis of how liberalism and conservatism have viewed and dealt with communism retains its pertinence, in our judgment, because it tells us something about how they would deal with any totalitarian ideology of the radical left and regimes based upon it. It is not impossible that some other such ideology that is not really Communist could rise up in the future. Indeed, there are many "Third World" regimes existing today which are not really Communist but would somewhat fit into a totalitarian category.

This chapter will be structured as follows: the first section will consider the view of the old liberalism about each of the five areas above, comparing them to the Church teachings; the same will be done with the new liberalism in the second section; and the final section will come to some conclusions about which version of liberalism comes closest to the Church's teachings.

Only a limited number of sources could be used to draw a picture of both the old and new liberalism, in order to produce a work of manageable length. The works dealt with here—and this is also the case in Chapter Five on conservatism—are being used as sources for the *general* thinking— the broad political philosophy—of liberalism in the five areas mentioned. It was for this purpose these works were selected. Most of them also present

---

* That communism in the U.S.S.R. has changed at all is unclear in early 1991.

specific policy proposals but, for the most part, have ignored these and are focusing primarily on the party platforms in Chapters Four and Six for this. We believe the latter to be a better and more integrated statement of the overall liberal and conservative programs.

The Old Liberalism

Four writers will be examined as a means of determining the thinking of the old liberalism. All were major spokesmen for, and shapers of, liberal thinking during that period, and so are good sources for determining what old liberalism's thinking was. These writers are: historian, political activist, and former White House staff member Arthur M. Schlesinger, Jr.; social science professor, editorialist, and radio commentator Max Lerner; historian, educator, and political commentator Henry Steele Commager; and Adlai E. Stevenson, Jr., Governor of Illinois and twice Democratic presidential candidate.

The source for Schlesinger's views is his well-known book *The Vital Center*,[1] which appeared in 1948. Lerner's *Actions and Passions* (1949), a compilation of his newspaper editorials and columns from late 1944 to mid-1948, that will be examined.[2] Two of Commager's books are considered: *Majority Rule and Minority Rights* (1943)[3] and *Freedom, Loyalty, Dissent* (1954).[4] Stevenson's thinking was derived from two books that are collections of speeches he gave in the 1950s, entitled *What I Think* (1956)[5] and *Putting First Things First* (1960).[6]

We draw from these various works as needed to give a good overall statement of the position of the old liberalism in the different areas. Some are relied on more than others. No attempt is made to discuss the overall thought of each particular writer or the points of difference among them since my purpose is to compare the views of the political ideology they represent and see if they agree with Catholic teaching. In a few isolated instances, another work of one of these writers is referred to.[7]

I. The General Purposes Of Government

As mentioned in Chapter Two, *Rerum Novarum* tells us that securing the safety of the state "is government's whole reason for existence."[8] While this position is not addressed directly in the works of the old liberalism, it is implicit in their discussion of containing communism and the military role of America in the world. Perhaps securing safety was so basic a governmental responsibility for them that it did not even have to be stated.

Considering the limited amount of attention devoted to this role of security in the old liberal literature, however, one wonders if another duty of government is not seen as paramount: protecting individual liberties.[9] Personal liberty is a preoccupation for Commager, in both of his works. Lerner, speaking specifically about black civil rights before the "civil rights revolution," seems to agree that protecting liberty is a duty of the state when he says "[w]hat we need is to make our Bill of Rights come alive."[10]

From what was said about the popes stressing the need for government to protect human rights, we can say that they would agree that this is one of government's key purposes (although, as *Rerum Novarum* states above, not its *most* important or most central one). The popes, of course, mention duties in association with rights. The old liberalism seems to acknowledge duties too, although generally they are specifically the duties of the individual to society (and involve limits to liberty). For example, Schlesinger speaks about "personal responsibility" as involving "[e]veryone of us ha[ving] a direct, piercing and inescapable responsibility in our own lives on questions of racial discrimination, of political and intellectual freedom. . ."[11] He also speaks of the capitalist system having, in effect, a duty to act in the interest of "the general welfare" and to "meet human needs."[12]

These are, of course, standard liberal social concerns. They are shared, as we saw, by the popes, but the latter's statement of personal duties goes well beyond them to include many things not in the realm of social morality. We do not see the old liberals, for example, speaking of a duty to live "becomingly" or of a duty to seek the truth.

Another basic purpose of government as put forth by Schlesinger is social control.[13] The same point is essentially observed in *Pacem in Terris* when it speaks of government having "to coordinate social relations"[14] so that persons will be able to exercise their rights and carry out their duties without others interfering. The old liberalism would concur with this, but, again, would press for a more restricted conception of duties.

A further difference arises with Schlesinger's positioning governmental social control as the only alternative to "the growing ineffectiveness of the private conscience."[15] Clearly, such a position is rejected by the Church. She would view moral restraint, based upon an informed conscience, as the *most* effective means of social control. The social encyclicals would suggest that Schlesinger's view contains the danger of the state becoming too powerful and, therefore, is plainly not the most basic solution. If social problems are to be overcome, man must conform his actions to the demands of God and the natural moral law.

In spite of the Church's position, the old liberalism did *not* take the view frequently attributed to liberalism that the correction of human problems is essentially a matter of correcting faulty institutions, not man himself. To be sure, the old liberalism saw the reform of institutions as important, but not the exclusive or most fundamental approach. As Schlesinger writes:

[T]he reform of institutions becomes an indispensable part of the enterprise of democracy. But the reform of institutions can never be a substitute for the reform of man.[16]

Schlesinger's view here is no doubt is due to his understanding of human nature, and, proceeding from it, of man in society, which he states as follows:

The people as a whole are not perfect; but no special group of the people is more perfect. . .Consistent pessimism about man, far from promoting authoritarianism, alone can inoculate the democratic faith against it. . . .[M]an is a creature capable of reason and purpose, of great loyalty and of great virtue, yet also he is vulnerable to material power and to spiritual pride.[17]

Lerner echoes Schlesinger as he ponders the evil that man is capable of as shown by the Nazi Holocaust of the Jews and other groups:

This is evil itself, positive, brutal, aggressive, organized. . .It is not simply evil, but powerful evil.

We must face its meaning. Don't fall back on your catchwords, O cultural progressive, brought up in the tradition of liberalism. Don't say it is due to the social environment or to faulty education, or to unemployment, or to the lack of religion. . . .

The fact is that evil and good are both basic thrusts in human nature. We had almost forgotten about evil and how powerful it is in all of us.[18]

We can conclude that the old liberalism had a view of human nature, and of the need to change man instead of just institutions, that was akin to the Church's, even if it did not entirely concur with the Church.

The above relates to another point the popes make about the role of government: it must promote the dignity and ends of the human person. This appears nowhere in the old liberal literature. Liberalism, old and new, *does* talk about man's "dignity,"[19] but almost never says that man has natural ends and that government should help him to achieve them, except for freedom (the comparative views of the old and new liberalism about freedom will be discussed later.) To say that man should be helped to achieve certain ends or purposes requires that government accept certain purposes as better or more worthy for man. Liberalism traditionally has been reluctant to make such judgments or permit government to make them, at least in principle.[20]

In addition, the popes also state, as noted, that government should help make men better and happier. Liberalism, to some extent, can make men happier. Greater political freedom, greater respect for individual rights, and a better material lot will help to do this. It will not help men to be happy in the more complete and profound sense that results from being morally virtuous and spiritually at peace with God, however. It cannot do this because it will not agree to trying to make men *better*, which is what genuine happiness would involve. Making men better, of course, involves a judgment about ends.

Stevenson states that "it is the duty of government to keep open to all people the avenues of opportunity."[21] Thus, another thing government must do is secure equal opportunity for its citizens. This is a traditional goal of American government. The popes do not mention this term *specifically*, but it is certainly indicated by their teaching against discrimination and other points they make about equality and rights.

Another aspect of the role of government, for Schlesinger, which seems to be part of this duty to secure equal opportunity, is combating economic privilege on behalf of the common man.[22] Certainly, the popes have been advocates for the poor and the working man and call for governments to end illegitimate inequalities and social injustice; so to this extent Schlesinger's view is compatible with the Church. His thinking on this point is likely based on the view that there is perpetual economic class conflict in society, however (which he contends is not specifically a Marxist notion). He sees class conflict as "essential if freedom is to be preserved" because it checks "class domination"— the task of the political order must be to contain it, in effect, by institutionalizing it. This may or may not be contrary to Church teaching. If he is simply endorsing something like the moderate restraint of class or other interests sought in Federalist Papers 10 and 51 for the sake of the common interest, there is no problem; but if he refers to a more militant confrontation of classes where basic suspicion and disdain is allowed to prevail there would be. He is in accord with the Church in believing in the value of cooperation between the classes (he says they "tend to forget their family relationship" of all being part of the same nation), but is in disagreement in thinking cooperation is not the natural state of things.[23]

Lerner seems to endorse government's role as being the promoter of equal opportunity also. This is implicitly observed in his support for federal aid for public (pre-college) educational institutions and federal college scholarship aid (this was before both came into existence). He says that the latter is needed to insure that no high school graduate "who wants to go to college, and...has the ability. . .shall be denied the chance because of belonging to the wrong income-group."[24] His position is also noticed in his insistence that government protect labor, the inherently weaker group in economic life,[25] and blacks (who at that time were only beginning their "civil rights revolution").[26]

Another part of government's role for the old liberalism, is to secure the "general welfare," which generally involves "a balancing of the rights of the one with the needs of many."[27] This is similar to what the popes say, although they use the term "common good." As one goes through the literature, he is led to believe that old liberals identified the common good as having both a material and moral dimension. Stevenson, for instance, speaks of the "danger" in America of "a spirit of materialism," in which we seek only "a never-ending increase of material comfort" with the "result [being] a moral and religious vacuum". He speaks about Americans being "inspired and motivated again by...the humanistic tradition of Western culture."[28] The old liberalism, then, clearly saw the "general welfare" as involving the presence of conditions that included not only material well-being, but also, in some sense, spiritual. Whether the latter consisted of the elements the popes mean when they say the common good involves the needs of both body and soul is unclear. Schlesinger's emphasis on alleviating material disadvantage whenever he refers to human well-being and his considerable discussion of government's economic and social welfare role and Commager's excessive emphasis on freedom and his endorsing of freedom of moral "experimentation"[29]—along with his other views stated in the next section—lead me to believe it does not. Possibly, the old liberalism, in the final analysis, actually did put most of its emphasis on the material—viewing the better quality of life that resulted from greater material security as a "spiritual" betterment of man—and, when it spoke of spiritual principles or values, referred mostly to secular notions of freedom. Nevertheless, it expressed a concern for the "higher" things in life—what Stevenson called the "things that are the essence of civilization" or, what we might call, the various elements of our Western tradition[30]—, even if these are not what Christianity would define, most basically, as the "spiritual things."

The old liberalism, in any event, placed a heavy emphasis on government's satisfying the material needs of people. This is clearly seen in its two other purposes put forth by Schlesinger: to create a favorable economic environment to assist business ("and then let the free market carry the ball as far as it can") and to help avert economic crises. He also rejects "total" planning.[31] All this accords with papal teaching, except the point about leaving things to the market. We shall look at the specific ideas and programs of the old liberalism in the next chapter to determine how far it was willing to rely on the market and competition. We can decide then how completely it squares with the popes on this.

Lerner also asserts that economics is part of the rightful and desirable role of government, but he wants to go beyond Schlesinger. He advocates moving in the direction of democratic socialism. Speaking of the rebuilding of Europe after World War II, he believes that for those countries "capitalism is no longer a viable choice" and they must turn to "socialism under democratic political controls."[32] He also refers to this as a "socialist mixed economy."[33] For the U.S., he favors the following: "The largest portion of American industry must be left under private ownership and operation, but under public regulation. Large sections of it, however, should be organized as co-operatives." Areas that are in the private domain but which function as monopolies, such as utilities and railroads, would be shifted to government control, run as public corporations with decentralized administration. Any industry that cannot operate according to the "competitive principle" should become public. Every industry, public and private, "must fit into a national economic plan," which would "not mean a rigid blueprint" but would insure that "we shall have our economic goals constantly in mind." The "larger policies" in the private industries would be shaped by a joint effort of "industry, labor, and the Government."[34] When evaluating Lerner against papal teaching, we come to ambiguous conclusions. On the one hand, he is with the popes in recognizing the need for cooperation and concerted planning in the economy. On the other hand, however, he sees nothing wrong with socialism, nor, where socialism is inappropriate, with competition essentially being the ruling principle of an economy. He seems impervious to the concern of the popes that the expansion of the state's role of owning economic enterprises be dictated only by considerations of the common good and that this expansion, simply, cannot be viewed as the guarantor of a true "socialization" of production. Lerner also gives no indication that he believes that the cooperation called for must be voluntary and not forced by the government or that it is necessary that the principle of subsidiary be respected. The last aspect of what the old liberalism seemed to view as part of the role of government involves assisting other countries. Stevenson expresses this as follows: "to help others help themselves…to share the burdens of the less fortunate, to raise the tide a little all around the world…"[35] This is clearly in the spirit of *Mater et Magistra, Populorum Progressio,* and *Sollicitudo Rei Socialis.* Of the writers and works surveyed, however, only one—Lerner—promotes world-wide political organization. He says he is for "world government," although most precisely it is "world federalism," which advocates the federal principle of organization insuring both "the necessary power at the center and the necessary autonomy for each member unit."[36] In general, the old liberals strongly favored the idea of the U.N., but here Lerner goes much further. While the popes would find his support for international cooperation laudable, Lerner seems to go beyond what they call for by way of international organization, perhaps, again thwarting the principle of subsidiarity.

(We shall see frequently in this book that subsidiarity is a problem both for the old and the new liberalism. It is pointed out, both when speaking about the works of the thinkers in this chapter and the platforms in Chapter Four, that subsidiarity is ignored or undercut. Some might argue that this is not really so, that it just is not explicitly mentioned by them. We find such an excuse to be lame: one can judge whether or not subsidiarity is being undercut regardless of whether the notion is mentioned or even if it is explicitly endorsed. The idea or lack of it are present, regardless of what the words say and the trend or effect of proposals or programs with regard to subsidiarity can be discerned. Morever, if liberalism is truly as supportive of subsidiarity as conservatism, as we'll see, why indeed doesn't it openly stress this fact as conservatism does? If liberalism truly upholds such a basic principle, why doesn't it say so?)

II. God, Religion, and the Natural Law as the Basis of the Political Order

None of the old liberal writers being surveyed asserts that religion—at least traditional (i.e., God-centered and doctrinal) religion, which the popes speak of—is actually necessary for man or for society to work justly. The farthest they seem willing to go is to say that religion can make valuable contributions to helping us deal with political problems. This is seen in Schlesinger's saying that Christianity helps us be aware of the dark side of human nature—Schlesinger's realism about human nature has already been noted—so we can recognize the malevolence of a Hitler or Stalin.[37] It is also seen in Stevenson's embracing of religious norms as a way of holding materialism in check.[38] Stevenson indicates that he believes in God, but seems to think that the laudatory norms we have gained from Christianity are not uniquely its own. He refers, for example, to "our devotion to the ideas of religious and secular humanism."[39]

Lerner's view is similar to Stevenson's, but he seems more prepared to simply replace religion—traditional religion—with some other "body of belief" that will better achieve what he sees as the pressing need of modern man: brotherhood and the "sense of society." While Christianity—he speaks specifically of Christianity, but doubtlessly is referring to all traditional religion—provided the great "gifts" of "Christian social teaching and the Christian conscience," he is skeptical it can accomplish this. "[S]omething has been lost out of the early dynamism of Christianity" which made possible the benefits it has given the world. What is needed now, he contends, is a new "belief" or "doctrine" whose stress is on "the linking of all men in the bond of the human plight and the human opportunity." "Democracy and socialism" are two modern secular substitutes that try to do this but cannot adequately command "men's imaginations."[40] (Schlesinger says the same sort of thing about only democracy.) The "tragic humanism" Lerner also speaks of (see below) seems to be another attempt at this.[41] The new belief must be religious in nature—it must bring "a new conception of the nature and destiny of man"—unlike "political religions" (e.g., communism). Perhaps yet, however, "the Christian idea may find new sources of vigor" to satisfy the "great. . .religious feeling among men. . .for whom none of the existing religious creeds serve as a stirring and fulfilling answer."[42] (Actually, though, the fact that he extols the Enlightenment makes one doubt that he has confidence Christianity could truly be the best doctrine possible, or even superior to many secular ones.[43])

The old liberalism seemed distinctly reluctant to acknowledge any set understanding of God, as seen by Commager's extolling the "spiritual diversity. . . characteristic of America" and pragmatism, "the philosophy of experimentation and pluralism."[44] Certainly, we can infer the same from the quotes from Lerner above. Although they do not say this, we are left to wonder if they believe God to be knowable at all. This would seem consistent with the skepticism characterizing all twentieth century liberalism, as mentioned in Chapter One. Clearly, what is said next about the old liberalism's view of natural law betrays its "skepticism about ultimate values."[45]

Commager, in defending pragmatism, strongly ridicules the claim that truth is "not relative but absolute," "universal and *a priori*," and not made by man but "rooted in the very nature of things."[46] He states that he believes truth exists—without saying anything about its content—but it is placed strictly in the context of a justification for freedom of inquiry and experimentation, similar to the argument of John Stuart Mill.[47]

What Commager says about truth is directly transferrable to the natural law since it is the embodiment of truth. His rejection of truth as being "rooted in the very nature of things" indicates also that he rejects the Christian conception of natural law. He does not like "set" conceptions of things, but prefers diversity.[48] As was mentioned before, this seems to apply even to morality. In different places, he identifies the natural law not with moral injunctions existing apart from the individual, but with the "dictates of conscience" (he does not say what they should be formed with reference to),[49] scientific principles,[50] and the individual's inalienable rights (there is no mention of duties).[51]

Lerner is something of a contrast to Commager, but he does not demonstrate a belief in natural moral norms that have the character of law (as the Church does). It has already been noted that he speaks about evil, which presumes a belief in there being some kind of set moral norms. This conclusion about him is reinforced by his speaking about "good" and also saying that, at least, one of the considerations that goes into determining whether an act is good or evil is "its nature."[52] Other things he says also make one conclude that he accepts the existence of moral norms which are not of man's making. For example, he speaks of the race question in moral terms,[53] and refers to "public morality"[54] and "business morality."[55] He also says that just as "the *laissez-faire* idea in economics" is being abandoned, "[w]e shall have to move away from the *laissez-faire* idea also in social and religious belief." He is especially insistent that there can be no "*laissez-faire* in social justice."[56] In other words, he is saying that men cannot themselves decide what is or is not moral, by reference only to their own opinions.

Thus, the view of old liberalism seems to range from being hostile to papal teaching on the natural law and society to being akin to it in at least an imprecise and general way.

III. The Thinking About Freedom

It has been mentioned that freedom was strongly emphasized by the old liberalism. Just how important it was to it can be seen in Commager's litany of the benefits of freedom:

> Only those societies that actively encourage freedom—...for example, scientific and scholarly research—...can hope to solve the problems that assail them...[57]

and

> A society that encourages state intervention in the intellectual area will find itself an easy prey to state intervention in other realms as well.
>
> That government which most scrupulously protects and encourages complete freedom of thought, expression, communication, investigation, criticism is the one which has the best chance of achieving security and progress. . .every society needs a continuous re-examination of old ideas and a continuous flow of new ideas.[58]

Another important aspect of freedom that Commager says must be preserved, as already mentioned, is freedom of conscience. This overall view of the need for freedom can best be summarized by Commager's saying that "[w]e protect freedom in order to discover truth."[59]

The following observations may be made about the comparison of the above with the Church's teaching. The Church has spoken of the need for freedom if one is truly to be led to the truth. The Second Vatican Council's document *Dignitatis Humanae* (*Declaration On Religious Liberty*), for example, states that while the Catholic Church is the true religion and "men are bound to seek the truth, especially in what concerns God and his Church...[t]ruth can impose itself on the mind of man only in virtue of its own truth, which wins over the mind with both gentleness and power."[60] So, the Church would be *somewhat* in agreement with the old liberalism here. She, however, would not endorse its smug confidence that freedom will insure that truth is acquired. Indeed, the very point of the social encyclicals is that no such certainty exists, in the economic realm as in others. *Laissez-faire* economics will not insure that social justice—which is part of the truth the Church teaches (because it is an aspect of morality)—will prevail. Rather, men must consciously shape their economic behavior and institutions in accordance with the Church's social teaching.

Lerner's comments about *laissez-faire* suggest that he would agree with the Church that truth will not necessarily prevail from the activity of freely expressing ideas. The positions he takes on certain particular applications of freedom seem to contradict this, however, as does the sweeping notion of press freedom he favors,[61] his glowing confidence in the "competition of ideas,"[62] and in his insistence that Communists be allowed to exist as a political party and compete in civil and union elections.[63] Like all the old liberals, however, he would not consider having men turn to the Church as the authoritative source of teaching about what the moral truth is.

The Church, also, would agree with the old liberalism about the primacy of the individual's conscience. She would say, however, unlike the old liberalism, that the individual has an obligation to make sure his conscience is rightly formed. Her flock must look to Church teachings to do this.[64] Lerner not only would not acknowledge such an obligation, but suggests—while fully supporting freedom of worship and not perhaps realizing the implication of his position—that the state can properly make it difficult for the Church to motivate men to do this. This is seen in his calling the Supreme Court's decision that parents be permitted to send their children to religiously-affiliated schools a "dangerous inroad. . .on the principle of the separation of Church and state" and damaging to "the nation's stake in having a common democratic education for its children."[65] The Church would certainly argue that if she is truly to be able to make Catholic children acknowledge their obligation to shape their consciences according to what she teaches and to learn what the teachings are, she must be free to educate them—in conjunction with their parents—in a full-fledged manner. Otherwise, there is a suppression of religious freedom.

From some of the broad applications of the notion of freedom that Lerner makes, we see conflict between the old liberalism and the Church. One such conflict is seen in the implicit rejection of parental rights in education (at least in terms of choosing the type of school they want their children to attend). Another is in his intense opposition to any state financial aid for sectarian schools, which the Church has been able to arrange in many countries and the Church in the U.S. has also favored.[66] The Church has often argued that this is discriminatory against her and makes it more difficult for her to effectively carry out an educational role in the face of the overwhelming near-monopoly of the public schools. Third, Lerner rejects the notion that restricting or suppressing economic liberty will also result in the restriction of political liberties. This is a position implicit in the thinking of all these old liberal writers, but Lerner seems to go beyond the others in insisting that political liberty won't be harmed even by Western European-type socialism.[67] While Lerner, then, endorses a seemingly broad notion of liberty, he is hostile to certain other, traditional liberties.

Even though Commager speaks of "complete" freedom, the old liberalism did not view the individual as totally free of restraints. This is seen in Lerner's comments above and in his general stress on the social obligations of men. Also, as Schlesinger emphatically points out (and the upshot of Lerner's comments is the same), man needs community and must be viewed as part of the community around him. Bemoaning a loss of this sense of commitment to the community, Schlesinger says, "Freedom has lost its foundation in community and become a torment; 'individualism' strips the individual of layer after layer of protective tissue."[68] Schlesinger speaks of individual responsibility, as mentioned. One of his comments about the relationship between the individual and the community sounds like the popes' conception of the common good as respecting both the individual and the community: "We require individualism which does not wall man off from community; we require community which sustains but does not suffocate the individual."[69] When Schlesinger says that "[t]he individual requires a social context, not one imposed by coercion, but one freely emerging in response to his own needs and initiatives,"[70] he speaks in the same spirit as the popes in saying that a reconstruction of the social order must be voluntarily, not forcibly, accepted by men. Lerner, similarly, echoes the popes in realizing that in order for freedom to flourish, there must be a strong framework of order (political order) in place.[71]

In stressing this need of the individual for community, Schlesinger echoes the popes on a further point: the importance of independent, intermediate groups for the individual. He contends that "the disappearance of effective group activity. . .leads toward emptiness in the individual. . .[and] compels the enlargement of the powers of the state."[72]

Schlesinger also raises fears about the future for democracy and freedom. He fears that democracy does not generate enough of a philosophical, moral, and religious-type of commitment, making men willing to "believe in it deeply enough to die for it." He says that to be an advocate of democracy means to be "for...certain *means*" and "other people...charge the means with content." Democracy has "no defense-in-depth against the neuroses of industrialism" and has a "thin optimism" which believes "the gnawing problems of doubt and anxiety could be banished by the advance of science or...a rise in the standard of living." Nevertheless, Schlesinger speaks against what he believes would be needed to cure democracy and give it the strength it needs: "[I]t seems doubtful whether democracy could...be transformed into a political religion... without losing its characteristic belief in individual dignity and freedom."[73] He sees the same problems with democracy that many others have pointed to: It lacks a spiritual element, something more for people to believe in than mere procedural mechanisms—"means"—and the opportunity for greater affluence and progress. Like any typical twentieth-century liberal, however, he is too entranced by prevailing notions of individualism and freedom to admit that what modern man needs is what democracy and any other type of political order cannot, by themselves, give him: revealed religion. The popes, of course, make clear that the opposite is true.

IV. The Thinking About Equality

The interesting thing about the old liberalism in regards to equality—the second section of this chapter and Chapter Four show how substantially it differs from the new liberalism on this point—is that it does not say much about it. The main references to equality in the books being considered were to racial equality[74] (the civil rights movement was then emerging), to the traditional notions of political and legal equality (i.e., equal political and legal rights), and to the notion of equal opportunity (Lerner even makes clear that he opposes racial, ethnic, and religious quotas[75]). These are all ideas which have been in force for most of American history.[76] What has already been said, plus Lerner's advocacy of a "thoroughly progressive" tax system,[77] makes apparent that the old liberals favored reducing the disparity of wealth between rich and poor—both within the U.S. and throughout the world. By no means did they favor economic levelling, however. By and large, they were against socialism,[78] although we have noted Lerner's favorable disposition to it (at least he favored government control of some parts of the economy). There is even a hint—as seen in Stevenson's saying that "education for all [i.e., mass education] may come to mean real education for none"[79] and Lerner's speaking about federal scholarships for *able*, needy students (noted above)—that they believed that inequalities based on excellence and competence are desirable. The old liberals, then, were not egalitarians; they favored guaranteeing equal rights and equal opportunity, not equal results. Their thinking on equality is basically in conformity with papal teaching.

V. The View of Communism

The popes have been unremitting in their condemnation of communism. The old liberalism, in general, also opposed and had a very tough-minded attitude about it and the Soviet Union, although there was something of a mix of views about this within its ranks. These differences can be observed in the thinking of Schlesinger and Stevenson on the one hand, and Lerner on the other.

Stevenson spoke about "expansive Communist imperialism" and "Communist ambition" that "[w]e and our allies must be strong to check."[80] Schlesinger's *The Vital Center* devotes much discussion to the Communist threat. This includes a pointing out of the evil of totalitarianism; an insistence that the ideological difference between the American and Soviet regimes is a significant factor in their rivalry; that this difference, especially from the Soviet perspective, renders any accommodation impossible; and a recognition that "Soviet power will surely spread everywhere that it meets no firm resistance." He also contends that this resistance cannot be carried out with economic and political aid alone without military strength.[81] He also says that internal subversion is clearly a threat, especially from the American Communist party and Communist front organizations. Like Lerner, he was not willing to outlaw the party just because it is Communist, and was as concerned as Commager and Lerner about civil liberties being harmed because of anti-Communist fervor (Commager even made the latter his major preoccupation when discussing communism.).[82]

Schlesinger has a rather hard-nosed approach for dealing with the problem of subversion and loyalty. For example, he favors keeping persons who *could* be security risks, even if this is not certain, out of government employment[83] (as we have seen, Lerner would never agree to this, nor probably would Commager). He also dismisses the claims of what later came to be called "revisionist history" that the U.S. and not the Soviet Union had been responsible for the Cold War.[84]

Schlesinger also says that in order to respond effectively to communism the U.S. should have a bipartisan foreign policy[85] and the non-fascist right and the non-Communist left should work together for "the expansion of free society," including the enactment of necessary social reforms.[86] This bipartisan approach demonstrates a characteristic of the old liberalism which James Hitchcock pointed to: its willingness to seek consensus. This characteristic is further emphasized by Schlesinger's saying that "compromise is the strategy of democracy."[87] Hitchcock says bipartisanship was a major point on which the new liberalism diverged from the old. We shall see how correct he is in the next section.

Lerner's thinking, while certainly anti-Communist, differs. He calls for "'a trade union and progressive movement which is clearly non-Communist'" and says that "to defend the civil rights of Communists does not mean to refrain from opposing them for their philosophy and attacking them for their tactics."[88] He acknowledges the police state repression and ruthlessness of totalitarian Communist regimes.[89] He is one of those American liberals who "differ. . .sharply with the Communists and refus[e]. . .to work with them."[90]

As we have seen, Lerner does indeed defend the civil rights of Communists to compete for federal jobs, to exist as a legal political party, and to compete in civil and union elections. He also does not seem to believe there ever was a Communist conspiracy to subvert the U.S. government from within,[91] nor that communism really poses a serious threat of taking hold in the U.S. ("our history and institutions and national character" have been drastically different than the Soviet Union's).[92] He says that pursuing a course of action that would suppress the civil liberties of Communists would be the thing that would most likely "play into the[ir] hands" by "weaken[ing] our own democracy by abandoning our democratic convictions."[93] Lerner seems to see the temptation to repress civil rights as presenting the greater threat to America: "the great enemy of American democracy is boom-and-bust reaction and its potential fascist sequel."[94]

Lerner demonstrates an almost astonishing optimism and belief in the benevolence of what communism as a doctrine is capable of achieving and in its accomplishments in Russia. (We now see just how untrue this is; the Communist party in the U.S.S.R. recently essentially admitted it.) He seems to see Communism as akin to what he believes to be the great humanist tradition of the West (he, of course, draws no distinction, as the popes would, between a God-centered humanism and the secular variety). He claims that "the Russian Revolution was the great historical event of our time and that the Soviet regime added a new dimension to the human effort—that of economic planning and new social forms" and that it sought "the dream of a socialist humanism" which was stifled by the rise of "the one-party totalitarian state, which Lenin and his comrades. . .never willed."[95]

He claims further that the Revolution—"violence and a moral overturn"—was necessary to wipe out the "rottenness and tyranny" and "deeply rooted" injustice of "the Czarist system"[96] and that the economic policies of the Soviets in his time have advanced those most in need of help, the workers and peasants.[97] Again, we now see how very doubtful Lerner's understanding of communism was; that, however, is not the significant question here. What is especially significant here is that his assessment of the nature of communism is in sharp contrast to Pope Pius XI's encyclical *Divini Redemptoris*. Lerner says nothing at all about the evil of the atheism of Communism, possibly because it does not bother a secular-minded thinker like himself.

As far as the Soviet Union's role in the world is concerned, Lerner sounds more like Schlesinger. Lerner believes world communism essentially to be monolithic and, despite his unwillingness to explicitly concede this, a conspiracy. He says, for example, that the American Communist party likely takes its cues, if not direct instructions, from Moscow and that the Soviet "Politburo....make[s] all the basic decisions for world Communism."[98] He acknowledges the Soviet Communist drive for world power, although only half-heartedly, and, like Schlesinger, sees it as rooted in the Communist ideology itself.

While in *Actions and Passions*, Lerner sees the conflict between the U.S. and the U.S.S.R. as being only partly, but genuinely, an ideological one,[99] in one of his other works of the same time period he talks about "Russia's ideological offensive" and "the revolutionary dynamism of 1917" which is "limited only by its capacity to absorb and to organize what it absorbs." Lerner realizes that a major "factor in Russian policy is the now habitual Russian sense of encirclement" which is based on the "Marxist doctrine" that capitalist governments must fight "imperialist wars" to survive and that they will try to crush socialism."[100] Lerner's belief in the existence of this imperialism is only half-hearted, however: Elsewhere, he refers to the "neurotic fear of the Western powers that Russia will dominate the world,"[101] contends that "[u]nlike the Nazis, the Russians do not make a cult of militarism and world rule,"[102] and suggests that the Truman administration spurned the Soviets' offers to negotiate after the Second World War.[103]

In bringing together these two perspectives about communism that existed within the old liberal ranks, we come to some overall conclusions. First, the old liberals saw Communist ideology as an evil—although how *intrinsically* evil is unclear—because it seeks to crush freedom and pluralism. It is silent about its assault on spiritual principles and the spiritual nature of man (which, of course, the popes stress). Second, the old liberals saw the Soviet Union essentially as an aggressive and imperialistic nation, at least in part because of its Communist ideology, although not all held the U.S. blameless for the U.S.-Soviet conflict. They thus took the ideological factor seriously. And, third, the U.S. and the West could have an accommodation with the Soviet Union in a geo-strategic sense, but not an ideological one. We conclude this even though at least some of the old liberals favored socialism to some extent and did not see it, or the desirable social orientation that they claimed was present in communism, as incompatible with the principles of the West. On this latter point, it would seem as if the old liberals would disagree among themselves about whether communism was akin to the humane traditions of the West.

In comparison to the popes, we can say that the old liberalism, for the most part, had the same general outlook about communism, except that it did not see communism as a phenomenon as bad as it really is, or for the full range of reasons. This is perhaps why some old liberals were willing to espouse a moderate variant of it—socialism—which the Church cannot. It seems that, in light of twentieth century history, as well as the recent admissions of its true character by the formerly Communist nations themselves, the Church has had a more realistic view of communism's nature and what it has done in practice. As we shall see, however, the old liberalism was closer to the Church than the new liberalism has been in its assessment of communism.

The New Liberalism

It is more difficult to find sources that give a representative view of the new liberalism than it is of the old. There do not seem to be many works—

especially full-length books—comparable to Schlesinger's *The Vital Center*
that clearly present the new liberalism's general principles and arguments.
While the adherents of the old liberalism clearly were distinguished from their
more leftist and radical cousins, this is not always the case with the new
liberals. Many people and many positions that are left of center in American
politics now are grouped under the general panoply of "liberalism," whereas
previously liberals—when one examined the matter with any degree of thor-
oughness and objectivity—were clearly seen as different from "radicals."

This change was due to the influence of the "New Left" and the
upheavals of the late 1960s, which caused many previously radical positions to
be adopted by "mainline" liberals (including a different view of communism
brought about by a liberal reassessment of the Cold War). This ideological
absorption was also due to the increasing—and increasingly open—secularism
of the liberals. The rethinking of positions by many old liberals led to a greater
willingness to work with persons farther on the left. Also, changes in the rules
for participation in the Democratic Party brought more "farther-out" leftists
into the mainstream of liberalism and was another factor in the blending of
radical with liberal positions. Moreover, new faces of this changed liberalism
have appeared, most notably the "neoliberal" movement. Consequently, it is
somewhat difficult to say for sure what the new liberalism precisely is and
stands for. Nevertheless, since the adherents of present-day liberalism—especially on the national level—do take common stances on political issues, it *is*
possible to identify new liberalism's characteristics and discuss it as a distinct
phenomenon. It must also be possible to find representative sources that embody it.

The sources chosen are, we believe, all representative of the new
liberalism and all share common perspectives, even though they occupy somewhat different places in the new liberal spectrum. The first source is a transitional figure who was a prominent old liberal but, as was the case with most of
them, shifted along with liberalism (even if he did so, in some respects, more
slowly than other liberals). This is the late Hubert H. Humphrey, former Vice
President of the United States. Two books of his are referred to: *The Education
of a Public Man*, his autobiography, published in 1976,[104] and *Beyond Civil
Rights: A New Day of Equality*, published in 1968.[105] In considering the autobiography, Humphrey's career and views espoused after 1960 are highlighted.

The second figure is George S. McGovern, who, in the minds of many
Americans, was the embodiment of the new liberalism when he ran for President in 1972. This was the first presidential year in which the new liberalism
strongly asserted its political muscle and made itself manifest to the public as a
new political ideology. McGovern's books that are used are his 1977 autobiography *Grassroots*[106] and *An American Journey*, the compilation of his key 1972
campaign speeches edited by him and published in 1974.[107]

The third source is the late U.S. Supreme Court Justice William O. Douglas. He was also once an old liberal, but was probably one of the more obviously secularized ones. Later in his career, his views on many issues seemed closer to those of the New Left. His works used here are his 1966 book *The Bible and the Schools*,[108] his 1971 book *International Dissent*,[109] and a number of his judicial opinions.

Finally, some attention is due, at least by way of comparison with the rest of the new liberalism, to that version of it called "neoliberalism." This is because neoliberalism has presented itself as being a somewhat different thing from mainstream liberalism—i.e., the "new liberalism" as we have defined it— even while its adherents call themselves liberals. To some degree, neoliberalism has made its presence felt in national politics—most notably in the presidential campaigns of Gary Hart, although there are indications it has influenced policy debate within the Democratic party more broadly[110]—and promises to be heard from much more in the future. Neoliberalism is being considered here as something different from most of the new liberalism, so a small amount of attention is given to its views in each of the following subsections after a discussion of the "normal" new liberal thinking. The work chosen for analysis is *A New Road for America: The Neoliberal Movement*, a compilation of the proceedings of the first major conference on neoliberalism (held in 1983). It was published in 1985 and edited by Charles Peters and Phillip Keisling.[111] The book is comprised largely of comments by panelists at the conference.

We now proceed to examine the new liberalism's views in each of the five areas under consideration.

I. The General Purposes of Government

The first purpose of government discussed when we speak about the old liberalism—although possibly not the most basic purpose, in its view—was to protect the state from aggression. The new liberalism agrees—as is seen in numerous places in McGovern's 1972 speeches—[112], but it places less emphasis on it. The lessened emphasis is suggested by McGovern's insistence that "[i]f we do not transfer funds from war to peace priorities, there will be no new peace priorities at all."[113] He stated this position in more than one major speech,[114] and it is seen in the continual efforts of liberals in Congress since the Vietnam War to pare down military budgets and stress domestic priorities. It is also suggested by the view they take of communism, which until recently—and this may actually be a premature conclusion—was the major international threat to the U.S. (as we shall see in the section discussing the new liberalism's view of communism).

The second purpose of government of the old liberalism is also shared by the new: protecting individual liberties. This is seen in McGovern's saying that there is "no better blueprint for healing our troubled land than is contained in the Declaration of Independence, the Constitution, and the Bill of Rights."[115]   (The first and last of these, especially the last, are concerned primarily about rights.) This is further confirmed by his speaking of "the equality of rights that is at the heart of our national heritage"[116] and his emphasis on the importance of "human freedom."[117] It is still further confirmed in the many judicial opinions of Justice Douglas that defended a fairly extreme notion of individual liberty.

The concern about human freedom is, of course, compatible with papal teaching. Extreme notions of liberty—i.e., illegitimate liberty, license, runaway individualism—are not, and such notions are seen clearly in some of the new liberals' specific applications of liberty in the next chapter. The new liberalism is incompatible with the popes' teaching also in that it fails to mention duties which, as noted, the popes always links up with rights. Similarly, although the new liberals speak about human dignity, it seems largely to be linked up with rights and with government providing things for people.[118] Nowhere do the new liberals speak of man, by his nature, having certain ends which the maintenance of his dignity requires him to aim for, possibly with the help of government.

Another purpose of government, according to the new liberalism, has already been noted: the promotion of equality, taking the form of equal results or outcomes. The new liberal rhetoric, as mentioned, often makes it clear that equality of results is what is specifically sought, even though sometimes the old rhetoric of equality of opportunity is still used.[119] It was mentioned that the promotion of equality, per se, accords with papal teaching, although the promotion of equal outcomes may not be or at least is not required and the focusing of remedies for inequality on classes, which may be largely abstractions anyway, instead of individuals clearly does not accord with it.

Another purpose of government that is perhaps subsumed in the purpose of promoting equality is shared with the old liberalism: to end prejudice, particularly racial prejudice.[120] This objective clearly accords with papal teaching, so long as government does not go about it by promoting what the popes call "group or class 'egoism.' "[121]

The old liberalism made the combating of economic privilege a prime purpose of government, and so does the new liberalism. In 1972, George McGovern was given a "populist" label by some, and his speeches make abundantly clear that he stands against economic privilege and wants to use government to end it.[122] This idea is expressed especially in terms of establishing a more just tax policy. This specific point will be discussed in Chapter Four.

The same comments made about the old liberalism's espousal of this purpose as regards its incompatibility with papal teaching are applicable to the new liberalism. The popes have promoted social justice and supported the cause of the poor, but have repudiated class conflict and insisted that social justice must be coupled with social charity. The new liberal sources examined do not state directly that the presence of some kind of class conflict is desirable—as the old liberalism did (seen with Schlesinger)—, but McGovern's rhetoric and his very status as a "populist" convey essentially that viewpoint. Nowhere do these sources speak of cooperation between economic classes as Schlesinger does; essentially they call for taking from the rich and giving to the less well-off. The following quote from a McGovern campaign speech is typical:

> The administration [Nixon's] tells us that we should not discuss tax reform in an election year. They would prefer to keep all discussion of the tax laws in closed rooms, where they, their powerful friends, and their paid lobbyists can turn every effort at reform into a new loophole for the rich. But an election year is the people's year to speak; and this year, the people are going to ensure that the tax system is changed so that work is rewarded and so that those who derive the highest benefits will pay their fair share rather than slipping through the loopholes at the expense of the rest of us.[123]

Again, there is no problem if McGovern is merely acting as an advocate for the cause of the poor and dispossessed, taking account of the basic conflict between the better and the less well-off of any political order, and seeking simply to vindicate the legitimate rights of the latter. It is our judgment, however, in light of the above, that he stresses a much more conflictual theme than Schlesinger, and so, we believe, deviates from papal teaching.

Elsewhere on economics, the new liberalism, like the old, sees government as having an important role. First of all, it favors regulation of the private business sector by government, which is seen "as a countervailing force," in order "to prevent abuses."[124] This is akin to what the old liberals said about combating economic privilege, mentioned above. The new liberalism's—and the old liberalism's—belief that government should not only regulate the economy to prevent abuses, but also should be heavily involved in spurring it on is well-known and is seen strikingly in McGovern's 1972 speeches.[125]

There are two other aspects of government's economic role, according to the new liberals: improving peoples' material welfare and insuring that they have employment. These objectives are not substantially different from those of the old liberalism, except that the new liberalism possibly puts greater emphasis on government's role and the necessity of "socially responsible" private investment, and is more willing to frame the idea of full employment in terms of a government *guarantee*. These differences are seen in McGovern's speaking of providing a "solid, socially useful investment opportunity for our business community," of a "marriage of social responsibility and an enlightened government,"[126] and of "[t]he highest priority of. . .[his prospective] administration. . .be[ing] to ensure that every American able to work has a job to do so"[127] (elsewhere he speaks of "guarantee[ing] a job opportunity").[128]

McGovern's objective here certainly conforms with papal teaching, but the manner he proposes does not because it seems impervious to subsidiarity and would tend to make government (especially the federal government) too powerful. One also wonders if this approach would not lean in the direction of or lead to socialism, which would definitely not be compatible with the Church. As it stands, however, it could not be said to be, per se, "socialistic" because it calls for a role for private enterprise in the undertaking.

One might further be tempted, by McGovern's speaking of a business-government "marriage" of sorts, to think of the pope's emphasis on cooperation among the various participants in the economy. We do not believe, however, that the new liberalism is deserving of such an accolade for conformity to papal teaching on this score for the following reasons.

First, it is a very inchoate notion of cooperation. McGovern is hardly calling for an economy built on the principle of cooperation and is not even putting forth the small point he makes as a full-blown theory. Second, the notion seems limited to business-government cooperation that the popes favor,[129] although it is not cooperation in the fuller sense that they call for. The new liberalism says nothing about labor-business cooperation, for example. Finally, McGovern's rhetoric about economic privilege makes it seem that he favors not cooperation, but confrontation, in economic affairs (again, of a sort that goes beyond what the old liberals had in mind or that the popes sanction when speaking of the role of unions and the right to strike).

There are two final purposes of government enunciated by McGovern that are without direct parallels in the old liberal literature: to advance democratic ideals and to make people more compassionate. McGovern says this of the former:

> From participatory democracy to women's liberation and citizens' conservation councils, we see an increasing assertion of the individual, a desire not simply to have things done, but to do them. The task of future leadership is not to rule people's lives. It is to change the institutions of our society so the citizens may shape their own lives.[130]

On the matter of "compassion," McGovern straightforwardly says this: "The most important goal of government should be 'the creation of a society where we truly care about each other.'"[131]

The old liberalism would not necessarily have disagreed with these goals, but it was too tough-minded and hard-nosed to put them forth as part of the purpose of the government or to express them in the way that McGovern does. It would have seen such conceptions as too naive, idealistic, vague, and motivated by fuzzy psychological notions.

As far as the comparison of these last two goals with the goals of the popes is concerned, the following can be said: The popes would only partially endorse the first. As mentioned, the popes favor people having the opportunity to participate in public affairs to shape the policies that affect their lives. They do not favor any particular form of government, however. (McGovern's comments clearly favor democracy.) Further, if letting "citizens shape their own lives" means that the individual is to view himself as totally in control of his life without the need for God, the popes would obviously oppose it. The popes would almost surely go along with the second goal, but would never hold it to be exclusively the province of government. Nor would they state the point as vaguely as McGovern does. They would spell out exactly what "care about each other" means.

What are the purposes of government according to the *neoliberals*? They agree with both the other new liberals and the old liberals that government must be involved in the economy. Their views on this are closer to the latter than the former, however. The state should encourage economic initiative by the private sector and should protect workers "on health and safety issues." They believe business should be encouraged to take a "long-term" view in its actions instead of a short-term one.[132] These positions would seem basically compatible with the popes'. Their strong emphasis on economic liberalism (the euphemism "free market" is usually used) is probably outside of papal teaching, although more specific ideas of theirs would have to be examined to say for sure. Their favoring of worker participation in the ownership of their companies[133] clearly promotes the cooperation the popes call for. (In general, they emphasize greater worker-business cooperation than we see in the thinking of either the old liberals or the other new liberals.)

The neoliberals are also clearly in accord with papal social teachings in their strong support for protection for the aged and other guarantees of people's material welfare (even though their seeming satisfaction with federal government control of such programs would not be required by the popes and might not be justified under the principle of subsidiarity).[134]

The neoliberals also see education as an important purpose of government.[135] Neither the old nor rest of the new liberals would disagree. The popes would not necessarily disagree, but would take issue with the fact that the neoliberals oppose making private education (i.e., parental choice in education) easier via some kind of voucher system.[136]

Finally, neoliberalism is compatible with the Church in regarding government as having the purpose of promoting social justice and ending racial, religious, and sex discrimination.[137] The source used does not spell out specifics and it cannot be said if the popes would support its specific solutions.

II. God, Religion, and the Natural Law as the Basis of the Political Order

In order to determine the new liberal thinking about God and religion as the basis for our political order, we would do best to turn to Justice Douglas. He addressed this matter, implicitly or explicitly, in both his judicial opinions and other writings.

Douglas' 1952 opinion on behalf of the Supreme Court in *Zorach v. Clauson*[138] makes it seem as if he would basically concur with the papal understanding of God and religion. He wrote that "[w]e are a religious people whose institutions presuppose a Supreme Being."[139] We should not take this passage as determinative of his views, however, because it was written before the time the liberal transformation occurred and because his later writing seems to dispute it. In 1961, he joined the Court's opinion, written by Justice Hugo L. Black, in *Torcaso v. Watkins*, which stated the following:

> Neither a State nor the Federal Government can constitutionally force a person "to profess a belief or disbelief in any religion." *Neither can constitutionally pass laws or impose requirements which aid all religions as against nonbelievers, and neither can aid those religions based on a belief in the existence of God as against those religions founded on different beliefs.*[140]

In his concurring opinion in *Engel v. Vitale*[141] the next year, Justice Douglas wrote the following:

> [He quotes the Supreme Court's *McGowan v. Maryland* opinion][142] "if a religious leaven is to be worked into the affairs of our people, it is to be done by individuals and groups, not by the Government. . ." By reason of the First Amendment government is commanded "to have no interest in theology and ritual". . .*for on those matters "government must be neutral"*[143]. . .*The First Amendment leaves the Government in a position not of hostility to religion but of neutrality. The philosophy is that the atheist or agnostic—the nonbeliever—is entitled to go his own way.*[144]

He reiterated this basic position in his 1963 concurring opinion in *Abington School District v. Schempp*.[145]

The emphasized lines above are the important ones for our consideration. They show that Douglas'—i.e., the new liberalism's—view is sharply at odds with the Church. The claim of state neutrality about any matters of religion contrasts with the popes saying that God and religion must be viewed as basic to all endeavors and to the social-political order. In effect, Douglas, the Supreme Court, and the new liberals endorse the contemporary secular humanist or secular humanitarian position that it is not only not necessary to assert that God and religious principles are the basis of government, but also that government should be based only on secular principles. Religion, for them, seems to have no place as a guiding force in our public life. (Indeed, what Douglas and the Court said, in effect, is that the American government is *forbidden* to base its practices and laws not only on sectarian ideas *but on any religious principles whatsoever.*)

The quotations above further conflict with the Church's teaching in that they insist that government view believers and nonbelievers in the same light, that belief and nonbelief are to be seen as equally valid. While the Church does not support the persecution or oppression of nonbelievers, she firmly rejects the idea that a person has any "right" not to believe.[146] As far as the Church is concerned, even though belief is not to be coerced, such a nonchalant attitude about the nonbeliever's being "entitled to go his own way" has no place.

This seems to confirm Hitchcock's assessment about the increasing secularization and open rejection of religion by the new liberalism—even while, as is seen in Douglas' quote—it professes no *hostility* to it. (If we were examining the New Left, we would doubtless find the kind of open hostility Douglas disavows. Even though Douglas claims his position is not hostile to religion, the fact that the new liberals have continued to insistently adhere to the "neutrality doctrine" when it seems to have led to greater hostility to religion and, in some cases, to the embracing of *anti*-Judeo-Christian moral norms in our public institutions—as in the case of public school sex education curricula—indicates at least an acquiescence in such hostility.[147])

The comparison of what was stated in the first section of this chapter with the above further confirms Hitchcock's view that the old liberalism, in contrast to the new, was much quieter about expressing whatever skepticism it had about religion. It did not seem to embrace the view—at least not directly— that religious principles were not important to the political order.

Douglas explains why the new liberalism, at least initially, endorsed this "neutrality" position:

> [D]isorder. . .[results from] the mixture of sectarian and secular authority. . .either disorder between the majority sect and minority ones, or disorder between the church and the government. . . .

School boards have been torn asunder by contests over whose prayer will be read in the public schools, whose catechism will be read. Religious contests over secular power have been among the bloodiest in history; though free of blood, they have no equal in emotional content unless it be a racial argument.[148]

He states this much more succinctly in *Engel*: "[I]f government interferes in matters spiritual, it will be a divisive force."[149] He also asserts a positive advantage to noninterference: "a government neutral in the field of religion better serves all religious interests."[150]

Even though the above is the "official" reason for the new liberals' position on religion in American public life, there is perhaps another more basic reason that is similar to the old liberals' skepticism: they believe that other, non-religious principles are more important. In his book *The Bible and the Schools*, Douglas speaks approvingly of pluralism—as the old liberal Commager does—and embraces a set of beliefs that he suggests is paramount to traditional religious beliefs for him. This might be called "American civic religion." Of this he says:

> [Our] heritage...is one that all sects, all races, all groups have in common. It is not atheistic nor is it theistic. It is a civic and patriotic heritage that transcends all differences among people, that bridges gaps in sectarian creeds, that cements all in a common unity of nationality. . .[151]

When the new liberals indicate that they *do* regard religion as important in public life, it is as a justification for an activistic stance in favor of secular liberal political objectives, such as civil rights, poverty, and peace. This is seen vividly in a speech George McGovern made at evangelical Wheaton College (Illinois) in the 1972 campaign.[152]

What is the new liberal view about natural law? The term "natural law" is not mentioned in the sources we used; this itself may tell us that the traditional notion of natural law—i.e., the Church's—is not promoted or accepted by them.

The new liberals are not pure positivists, however, since they make appeals to "justice,"[153] "moral decency,"[154] "national conscience,"[155] and to rights older than our Constitution and Bill of Rights.[156] Clearly, these demonstrate a belief in moral principles beyond those in human law or resulting from human decisions. Nevertheless, it seems that the new liberals see the roots of these moral principles in essentially human instruments or undertakings, such as our Constitution or American traditions. (The only thing indicating otherwise is McGovern's reference to "God given rights" that is made only once in the materials that were considered.[157])

For example, McGovern makes many references to "the enduring ideals of the republic," "our founding ideals," "the dependable values of the Declaration of Independence and the Constitution," etc., [158] and Douglas speaks of penumbras, or unenumerated (unstated) rights "formed by emanations" from "specific guarantees in the Bill of Rights."[159] It is *possible* that the new liberals see the latter notions as based on transcendent norms, but they give no indication of this. As such, we cannot assume that their notion coincides with the Church's anymore than that of the old liberalism.

What do the neoliberals say about God, religion, and the natural law in the political order? There is a chapter in the neoliberal book being examined, called "Values." There is some attention to God and religion by a few of the members on the "Values" panel at the conference it was noted the book was based on. Nicholas Lemann of *The Atlantic* laments that Jimmy Carter did not mention God in his nomination acceptance speech and that Ronald Reagan made a point of referring to Him, but Lemann says nothing about the role of God or religion in our national life. (His unhappiness may be for purely utilitarian reasons: Reagan was more successful at holding the support of evangelical Christians because he was willing more openly to espouse their belief in God.) Lemann suggests the importance of "personal values," but does not state their content.[160]

Kathleen Kennedy Townsend states that liberals can appeal to people if they take religion seriously, but says nothing more (again this may be merely a utilitarian position).[161] James David Barber seems to view "values" as synonymous with simply the traditional liberal notion of protecting the poor and minorities, nothing more.[162] Amitai Etzioni basically stresses only two values that he says are the only ones liberals share: "caring" or "commitment" (which is trendy language without particular substance) and civility.[163] He is not apparently concerned that important "values" which are outside of the traditional liberal consensus are neglected.

Thus, except for thinking, in a vague way, that God and religion should be brought into politics, the neoliberals are no closer to the papal teaching about the primacy of God, religion, and the natural law in the political order than the other new liberals.

III. The Thinking About Freedom

A very good, brief statement of the new liberal view of freedom is found in Justice Douglas' concurring opinion in the lesser-known of the two abortion cases decided on January 22, 1973, *Doe v. Bolton.*[164]

In this opinion, Douglas seeks to spell out the rights of the individual under the Ninth Amendment which provides that "[t]he enumeration in the

Constitution, of certain rights, shall not be construed to deny or disparage others retained by the people." He says that "many" of these rights "come within the meaning of the term 'liberty'. . .in the Fourteenth Amendment," which is why they are pertinent here. Included in this definition of "liberty" or "freedom" are the following: "the autonomous control over the development and expression of one's intellect, interests, tastes, and personality" (he states that these are the rights protected by the First Amendment's guarantee of freedom of speech and tells us "they are absolute, permitting of no exceptions,"[165] including, he tells us in another opinion, obscenity)[166]; "the freedom of choice in the basic decisions of one's life respecting marriage, divorce, procreation, contraception, and the education and upbringing of children" (he says this includes the right to marry a person of one's own choosing, to direct the education of one's children, and the right to use contraceptives); and "the freedom to care for one's health and person, freedom from bodily restraint or compulsion, freedom to walk, stroll, or loaf.[167] One thing which Douglas tells us violates all these general categories of putative rights is legislation barring abortion.[168]

It was mentioned that the old liberalism believed that freedom of inquiry, expression, etc. leads to the truth. That the new liberalism has a similar view is seen by Douglas' opinion (a concurring opinion) in another case, *New York Times v. United States*[169] (the celebrated "Pentagon Papers" case):

> Secrecy in government is fundamentally anti-democratic, perpetuating bureaucratic errors. Open debate and discussion of public issues are vital to our national health.[170]

Also, like the old liberalism, the new liberalism—as again seen in Douglas—believes in the primacy of individual conscience, not necessarily shaped in accordance with religious teaching. Douglas states the following in *Gillette v. United States*,[171] a case involving a draft deferment for a conscientious objector whose views on war were not shaped by religious beliefs:

> Conscience is often the echo of religious faith. But, as [Gillette's] case illustrates, it may also be the product of travail, meditation, or sudden revelation related to a moral comprehension of the dimensions of a problem, not to a religion in the ordinary sense.[172]

Our neoliberal source does not contain such philosophical comments about freedom, possibly because most of those writing in it are persons of practical pursuits. We get a glimpse of their thinking in certain statements, however.

Amitai Etzioni says that "we need to learn to balance self-interest with a commitment to the commons."[173] This may sound like the Church's notion of common good, but it is not clear that it is really not an expression of individualism.

The neoliberal espousal of an apparently excessive notion of self-interest is observed in its acceptance—a much more eager acceptance than is the case with other new liberals—of an economic order that makes self-interested competition its ordering principle.

A further indication of the neoliberal view on freedom is seen in Etzioni's endorsement of legalized abortion and his unwillingness to speak against pornography (since this would cause divisiveness among liberals).[174] Similarly, neoliberal Philip Stern favors easy, essentially do-it-yourself divorce.[175] Even though—as Etzioni indicates—the neoliberals view themselves as "middle-of-the-roaders," they are such, in some sense, probably only in economics. They are as extreme libertarians in moral questions as other new liberals are.

How does the above square with papal teaching? The new liberals' views about freedom of conscience and the likelihood of freedom leading one to the truth are subject to the same criticisms as the old liberals' views on these were. As far as the general philosophy put forth by Justice Douglas is concerned, the following observations can be made.

First, the Church obviously rejects the view that men are "autonomous." They are *not* autonomous; they must devote themselves to God and follow His laws and will. This is a basic truth of Christianity and what was said about rights having corresponding duties underscores it. It is because men are not autonomous that they do not have complete freedom over such matters as marriage, divorce, procreation, contraception, abortion, and child-rearing.

The Church treats marriage as relatively easy to enter, but, for good reasons, it will not permit certain persons to enter it—e.g., those who do not have the capacity to carry out its purposes—and attaches conditions to entering it. The Church acknowledges the right of persons to control procreation, but with conditions. For example, unmarried persons have no right to procreate since they have no right to engage in sexual relations. Married couples have this right, so long as they do not seek to use unnatural methods to regulate it and take seriously their obligation to approach it responsibly. No one has the right to bring about procreation by unnatural means, such as *in vitro* fertilization. No one has the right to divorce, contraception, or abortion.

While the Church holds that parents have the natural right to raise and educate their children as they see fit,[176] there are conditions that both Church and state can impose (e.g., the Church rightfully obliges Catholic parents to rear their children in the Faith[177] and the state may require parents to have their children educated in some manner[178]). Thus, the Church clearly rejects Douglas' absolute notion of these rights and, in the case of some activities, rejects the view that they are rights at all.

By and large, the Church would not have much problem with Douglas' third group of rights; most involve morally neutral activities. She would even say that caring for one's body is not only a right but an obligation. She would probably reject the idea of "loafing"—depending on what Douglas means by it—because sloth is a cardinal sin.

By addressing Douglas, we have also addressed some of the neoliberal dogmas which the Church opposes. Clearly, the implicit neoliberal view that competition is to be accepted as the ruling principle of economic life is rejected by the Church's social teaching as stated in Chapter Two. She would also look askance generally at the neoliberals' excessive emphasis on self-interest—which is observed especially in economics—because it comes close to endorsing selfishness, (despite their professed concern for carrying out certain moral obligations in the economic order).

V. The Thinking About Equality

Perhaps the major difference between the old and new liberalism is that the latter is clearly more egalitarian-oriented. The old liberalism, as mentioned, understood equality as essentially meaning equal political and legal rights and equal opportunity. The aim of the new liberals, by contrast, is equal results or equal outcomes. This is seen clearly in the second of the late Vice President Humphrey's books: examined *Beyond Civil Rights* (which is appropriately subtitled *A New Day of Equality*).

Humphrey indicates that the new notion of equality for the new liberalism may have first been formally promoted by President Lyndon Baines Johnson in a June 1965 speech in which "[h]e spoke of the importance of equal '*results*,' in addition to equal 'rights.'"[179] Humphrey calls this "the second stage" of the civil rights movement.[180]

In this second stage, Humphrey claims—and this notion has been widely accepted among new liberals—"affirmative action" is needed "to break down the remaining barriers of custom and inertia and disguised prejudice."[181] This means that we "must take account of race," that "[w]e must count the numbers of black or Negro apprentices or minority group members who are advanced—otherwise there is little or no change." Just stopping discrimination is not enough.[182] (This view, of course, was later extended to gender and other categories.)

The reason Humphrey gives for this radical change in liberalism's approach to civil rights and understanding of equality is that the *past* effects of racial discrimination must be remedied.[183] Reparation, he indicates, is necessary because racial prejudice "is built into the themes of our culture and the institutions of our society"[184] and—he does not explicitly state this but implies it—blacks will be unable to truly be elevated to the American mainstream without it.[185] He also mentions some of the specifics of what this approach entails: full employment, as well as fair employment, good education as well as integrated education, enough housing as well as fair housing.[186]

Clearly, the Church agrees with the new liberalism about the evil of racial prejudice and its concern that blacks and other minority groups be permitted to share fully in society. As was discussed in Chapter Two, the Church also rejects an extreme notion of equality that would deny the existence of legitimate differences among people and so, unlike the new liberals, she does not clamor for equal outcomes or results.

It is unclear if she would judge affirmative action efforts to be just or not. Probably it would depend on the content of such programs, exactly what they sought to do, and how they did it. If they sought to bring about an artificial equality or to disadvantage certain individuals or groups to benefit others— which some allege affirmative action does—it does not seem that they would be in accord with Church social teaching.

As mentioned in Chapter Two, the Church does not say that no preference may be given on the basis of criteria such as race, but only that no *undue* preference be given. It seems that affirmative action programs, then, would have to be undertaken *prudently* and with an eye to both social justice for all groups and social charity.

We come to these conclusions on the basis of, again, the popes' teaching about equality and their insistence that "group or class 'egoism'" must be rejected and ethnic minorities must not exalt themselves or view the advancing of their own interests as advantageous to all.[187] Also pertinent here is the popes' stress on brotherhood as the great need of today. If affirmative action programs would *genuinely* undermine brotherhood, we believe the Church would find them unacceptable.

The popes seem to be in sympathy with the specifics of equality that Humphrey mentions: employment, education, and housing. Chapter Two stated that these specifics are among the basic human rights the popes have identified. While the popes do not call for equal results here—i.e., that everyone be insured the same income, same level of education, or same type of housing—they at least want everyone to be able to have a sufficiency of basic goods. Although this position could be inferred to be really an endorsement of equality of opportunity (i.e., an equal chance to seek these things to the fullest extent one is capable of), we believe it is more. The popes are saying that justice demands at least a *greater equalization* of these basic goods. True human dignity and the respect of human rights requires this. So, there is a call for "equal results" in a certain sense. It is not, however, like the open-ended, egalitarian notion subscribed to by the new liberals.

Further, the Church has left matters even in crucial areas such as those mentioned in the preceding paragraph to the domain of prudential and expert judgment, when appropriate. To apply this to another specific question, we might say that while she insists that morality requires that everyone who wants to work be able to do so, she would not specify a particular public policy approach for achieving full employment nor would she attempt to completely define what "full employment" is (i.e., this would involve a statement of what an acceptable and realistic level of frictional unemployment is—the unemployment caused by the fact that some people choose freely to leave a job and maybe seek a different job—which even economists disagree about).

It was noted that the popes call for ending the disparity of wealth on the *international* level. They make clear that to do this necessitates going beyond "equal opportunity" and toward a *greater* equality of outcomes in the relations among nations in such matters as trade competition. The popes say that the gap in wealth between rich and poor nations must be *limited—not* absolutely and utterly equalized—because justice, brotherhood, and basic human rights require it. If the popes say this about international matters, it is further evidence that such a standard must also apply on the domestic level when basic human rights are involved. This is because the popes make clear in their social encyclicals that the natural moral law, which the Church has always taught binds individual men, applies also to nations, since they are collectives of men. *A fortiori*, a moral standard asserted for nations would then have to apply for individuals.

The new liberals' stress on equality of outcomes over equality of opportunity points the way to another principle they have adopted that, since it is unqualified and open-ended, is contrary to Christian moral norms. The focus on equality of outcomes has led to the idea that remedies for unequal treatment and discrimination should be applied to whole classes (i.e., with specific whole classes being elevated by them and certain others being disadvantaged) instead of individual cases of discrimination being dealt with. The reason this is contrary to Church teaching is, first, that it offends the basic Christian understanding of justice and responsibility—one is responsible for only what he knowingly and deliberately does and should not be deliberately advantaged or disadvantaged because of the actions of others. Second, it is not so clear that the classes which, say, present-day affirmative action seeks to (supposedly) elevate are genuinely distinct groups of people with common backgrounds, experiences, and interests.

For example, why should a person from a long-wealthy American black family be given special preferences aimed at elevating his economic status? These classes are thus perhaps unlike the working "class" that Pope John refers to in *Mater et Magistra* who has substantially shared the experience of inadequate wages for very hard, demanding work.[188] Certain "classes" are abstractions, conceived of in the theorizing of social engineers influenced, to some extent, by Marxist formulations.

Pope John thus addresses a situation more like traditional labor problems in America and not really like problems giving rise to affirmative action today: where classes or groups of people (such as blue collar workers) are not remunerated according to the worth of their work—are not even paid enough to meet "the necessities of life"—and others are paid much more than their work deserves.[189] What he speaks of is not elevating classes of people on the basis of accidental qualities of birth, irrespective of what they have done, but of elevating classes because they have not received a proper return for the work and efforts they have actually put forth.

Does the neoliberal branch of the new liberals differ from the other new liberals on the matter of equality? The neoliberal source examined indicates that it does not. In one section of the book, *A New Road for America: The Neoliberal Movement*, co-editor Charles Peters says the following:

> We are liberals. There are large areas in which we are in almost complete agreement with other liberals—from protection of the environment to opposition to any form of racial, religious or sexual discrimination.[190]

The last two lines of this quote *suggest* that perhaps the neoliberals oppose affirmative action (i.e., it says "any form of discrimination"). After the quote, however, Peters goes on to discuss the differences the neoliberals have with other new liberals (the neoliberals refer to the other new liberals as "old liberals" in the book. They would actually mean the Humphreys, McGoverns, and Douglases). Disagreement with their support for affirmative action (which is an important enough public issue to merit discussion in the book) and with the new liberal view of equality in general is nowhere mentioned in Peters' discussion,[191] or elsewhere in the book including his "Appendix: A Neoliberal's Manifesto."[192]

V. The View of Communism

As we shall now see, the new liberalism does not view communism as intrinsically evil and menacing as the Church and the old liberalism do. Let us survey the thinking of each of our new liberal sources about communism.

Humphrey, the "transitional figure" who in 1948 was the co-organizer (with Schlesinger and others) of the strongly anti-Communist liberal organization Americans for Democratic Action (ADA) (which is spoken about in Chapter Four) sang a different tune in 1976. Humphrey writes that the containment policy extolled by Schlesinger—and attacked as inadequate by postwar conservatives—"needs revision" because there is now "a very different

Communist world." He does not elaborate about this. He concedes that the U.S.S.R. still engaged—in 1976—in "interventionist and aggressive policies and practices," but is reluctant to endorse American military action as a response. He seems to put the primary emphasis on "political, economic, and technological power."[193]

Humphrey appeared to see the Soviet Union, not communism per se, as the threat. Such a position vaguely implies that he did not see the ideology of communism as dangerous. He also, obviously, favored a somewhat "soft" response to the U.S.S.R. since he wished to avoid the use of force. In short, the Soviet Union is a threat, but not one for military power—the strongest means of response—to counter.

While Humphrey appeared to change his views on communism somewhat late in his political career, George McGovern took a softer line on communism from a much earlier point. For example, McGovern believed America could trust the Communist powers—this was well before any of the developments of the late 1980s—to a much greater extent than she had and called on her to be conciliatory. He believed they will respond positively if we do this.[194] (It is worth noting, however, that the reduction of hostilities with the Soviet Union and the changes in Communist regimes in the late 1980s came about not after conciliatory policies by the U.S., but after relatively "hard-line" ones.) He believed that, to a substantial extent, our problem with communism and the Soviet Union is a "psychological" one: we have had an insecurity about them and "the scaremongers are playing upon the anxiety that the United States can take no chances."[195] Clearly, this was a much more optimistic assessment than the old liberals, by and large, had, and one which clearly turned the tables of responsibility for improving the East-West relationship from the Soviet Union to the United States.

McGovern's conception of the state of international communism was like Humphrey's and also diverges from that of the old liberalism. He puts down the notion of communism being "a monolithic world. . .conspiracy"[196] and, sharply at odds with Schlesinger, does not see Western Communist parties as necessarily totalitarian-oriented, lined up with the Soviet Union, or threatening to the West.[197]

McGovern's call for accommodation with Communist governments and Western Communist parties seems offensive to, at least, the spirit of the popes' repudiation of communism. The popes make it clear that Communist ideology cannot be accommodated to Christian belief since their basic premises are at odds. The popes say the same about socialism, about which McGovern, as judged by his discussion of it in Portugal, seemed not at all concerned.[198]

We believe that McGovern's willingness to accommodate communism was not just for the prudential reason of wanting world peace, but has more basic ideological roots. He seemed to believe that the very nature of communism has changed, as seen in his speaking about "the far more independent, professedly democratic Communist parties" in Western Europe.[199] Despite its traditional ideology, he did not see communism as an international effort. It seemed to him to be a new phenomenon. His extreme eagerness to trust Communist governments and find fault with the U.S. in relations with them lends further weight to this judgment.

McGovern's conciliatory attitudes were most emphatically confirmed, however, when he says about the Cuban Communist despot Fidel Castro, that "[t]hough we may wish that he would see the world our way, his own scale of values weighs social and economic equality far more than civil liberties."[200] He here indicates a willingness to treat the beliefs of the Communists as every bit as valid as our own; they choose to emphasize certain principles and we choose to emphasize others. He implies that their values are acceptable for them and ours are acceptable for us. This is, without question, qualitatively and substantively *at odds* with the Catholic teaching against communism which rejects it for its atheism, extolling of class conflict, commending of violence, repudiation of private property, and for the other reasons mentioned in Chapter Two. In other words, the Church rejects communism for its hostility to God and to the perennial principles of the natural law. Nowhere does McGovern mention these points or express alarm—or even mild concern—about them.

We can perhaps infer the new liberalism's ideological assessment of communism from McGovern's reticence on the above. If this inference is accurate, it demonstrates how sharply opposed to the Church the new liberal ideology is.

It is obvious also, upon reading McGovern's autobiography and considering his political career, that he has not placed the kind of emphasis on consensus and bipartisanship in foreign policy that the old liberals did. He made a point in the autobiography of discussing his efforts to oppose the foreign policy initiatives of presidential administrations from the time of his first term in Congress in the Eisenhower years. He was also, of course, a leader in the anti-Vietnam War movement.

The other new liberals being surveyed, as time went on, came similarly to the point of repudiating this consensus view of foreign policy and attacked administrations freely. (Humphrey perhaps came around to this position the most slowly, but he joined in the chorus of Democratic opposition to the Nixon war policies when he returned to the Senate late in his political career.) This constrast with the old liberalism possibly confirms Hitchcock's general point about the fact that the new liberalism is much less willing to seek political consensus than the old. Foreign policy has traditionally been the area of greatest consensus in American politics; domestic policy the area of most contention. The fact that *foreign policy* became an area of so much discord possibly shows the overall limited emphasis the new liberalism gives to consensus.

Justice Douglas also takes the view that much of our problem with communism has to do with our perception that our type of political order and theirs are "completely antagonistic," and that we have failed to recognize (again, this was well before the late 1980s) that communism is changing. He adds two different points from Humphrey and McGovern that have become, to some degree, standard new liberal beliefs. One is that our economic order and the Soviet's "seem to be converging." He explains that "[w]e have. . .moved from free enterprise to a sui generis form of socialism" and that in Communist countries "[t]he private sector is increasing."[201] (Exactly how little the latter was actually the case is being seen in the difficulties former Communist countries are experiencing in the early 1990s in shifting to basically capitalistic economies.) The other point is that we should retract from military entanglements around the world and downplay the military solution to world conflicts. Actually, Douglas' position on these latter points is probably more extreme than that of most new liberals (although we believe that most of them would agree with the direction and spirit of these views). This is seen when he says that "[o]ur...treaties of defense designed to make the world 'safe from communism' are relics of a barbaric and unenlightened age" and "[m]ilitary might is no longer a solution to world problems."[202]

Clearly, Douglas shows no awareness of the ideological irreconciliability of communism to the Western Judeo-Christian tradition, pointed to by the popes. This tradition undergirds, to a substantial degree, the American political and social order.[203] If he did, he could not have claimed that our orders were then converging and communism no longer need be feared.

The neoliberal source used does not say much about communism. The few remarks made are in the "Introduction" to the book by its co-editor Charles Peters. He is a main spokesman for the neoliberal movement and edits its journalistic mouthpiece, *The Washington Monthly*. He indicates that neoliberal views are not different from those above when he says "many of us differ little from traditional liberals [i.e., the other new liberals] on such matters as the insanity of the nuclear arms race, the importance of foreign aid to the Third World, and our antipathy to exercising our military power abroad."[204] They also apparently dislike military treaty commitments.[205] This suggests the same kind of new liberal soft approach to dealing with communism, in contrast to the old liberals. This also indicates the same inablility to appreciate the evils of communism as stated by the popes, but we cannot be sure of this. Neoliberal lack of attention to communism in a major work like this and the statement of agreement with "traditional" liberals (the other new liberals) on foreign policy suggest that anti-communism has not been a matter of major concern to them, however.

Conclusions

Since comparisons have already been drawn between the various points comprising the old and new liberalisms' general philosophy of government, this brief closing section of Chapter Three will simply make final general conclusions for each of the major points.

On the matter of the general purposes of government, it is a bit difficult to make a direct comparison between the old and new liberalism as regards the Church's teaching because they do not each assert the same specific purposes (and so we cannot determine which comes closest to what the Church says as far as satisfying the specific purposes). What we *can* compare, of course, is whether the purposes put forth by each accord with the Church's teaching.

Of the purposes put forth by the old liberalism, we can say the following in recapitulation. Protecting the state is a purpose that clearly concurs with the popes. Its emphasis on protecting individual liberties also accords with the popes, but its downplaying of individual duties obviously does not. Social control accords, but (while stating the importance of the reform of men internally in changing society for the better), the old liberal comments suggest that they place a greater faith on the reform of institutions than of men to accomplish this social control (against what the Church would hold).

Promoting equal opportunity and stopping unjust discrimination concurs with the popes' position; combating economic privilege concurs to an extent, but the old liberal belief in the necessity of some kind of economic class conflict or conflict between participants in the economy is in opposition. The concern for the general welfare is akin to the popes' emphasis on promoting the common good, but the old liberal focus was on too much material welfare and too little on spiritual welfare in the Christian sense. (The popes insist that both be promoted, but the spiritual is the more basic).

Assisting men to achieve their proper ends is related to the above and also the protection of human rights and dignity and the requiring of human duties to be performed. While this goal is stated by the popes as a purpose of government, it is not mentioned by the old liberals.

The following must be said of the new liberalism's purposes of government. Protecting the state is alluded to but deemphasized, and this deemphasis is against the papal teaching that sees this as the most fundamental purpose. Protecting individual liberties, the next new liberal purpose, is shared with the old liberals and, as mentioned above, accords with the Church, but the silence about duties and their extreme notion of individualism does not. Promoting equality is compatible in principle with the popes, to the extent that it means equal dignity and equal treatment under law. It is *incompatible* to the extent that it means an egalitarian levelling (a temptation to which we believe the new liberals fall prey) and the way of going about it may also be in opposition.

Ending racial prejudice accords with the Church; combating economic privilege, again, may be compatible, but the new liberals' exhibiting an even more intense notion of inter-class hostility than the old liberals is not compatible. Promoting economic development and regulating and working with business for socially good ends is in accord with the popes, especially since economic cooperation is suggested. There is perhaps, however, an implicit tendency in this to make government too powerful, which does not confirm to the popes' teaching). Further democratizing institutions ("letting people shape their own lives") *may* be among papal objectives—at least to the end of heightening citizen participation in the making of public policies—and would be supported by them unless it promoted an extreme individualism.

Finally, making people more "compassionate" would be encouraged by the popes in principle, but the specifics would have to be spelled out.

On balance, we can see that the old liberals are closer to the papal teaching on more of the purposes of government than are the new liberals. Further, none of their purposes are as clearly in opposition to the popes, as with the views of a few of the new liberals.

The neoliberal branch of the new liberalism, to the extent that their views are spelled out, has notions of government's role that are more in accord with the Church's than those of the other new liberals. These compatible views include involvement in the economy to bring development, protection of workers and encouraging their participation in the control of their firms, bringing about social security and economic welfare, securing social justice, promoting education (although not in the manner proposed), and ending discrimination. In these issues, neoliberalism compares favorably with the views of the old liberals. Their individualism, downplaying (like other new liberals) of government's role as protector, and inattention to peoples' spiritual welfare, however, requires the overall conclusion that the old liberals are closer to the Church than even the neoliberals.

On the matter of the view of the two liberalisms about religion, God, and the natural law as the basis of the political order, we can conclude that neither accords with the Church's teaching, although the old liberalism—because it at least gives a nod to the value of Christian norms, does not explicitly embrace the position of state neutrality as between belief and unbelief, and at least some of its thinkers stress moral norms above man—is not as far from it as the new. The neoliberals are not as far away from the Church as the other new liberals because they at least give some deference to God.

As far as the thinking about freedom is concerned, the new liberalism in comparison to the old is more extreme in its view, more individualistic (i.e., more supportive of the view of the individual as "autonomous"), and more openly in opposition to the Church's moral teachings (e.g., because of the belief that divorce, contraception, abortion, sloth, etc. should be choices for the individual). The neoliberals are not much better than other new liberals on these positions and may even be a shade worse with their promoting of an ethic of excessive self-interest in economics. The new liberalism is thus further away from the Church on this matter than the old.

On equality, the old liberalism comes closer to the papal teaching than the new because, with its flat-out emphasis on equal results or outcomes— which goes beyond the *greater* equality of results the popes call for in certain basic areas—, the new betrays an egalitarian "levelling" impulse that is close to socialism and risks the problems of prudence and racial and ethnic chauvinism the popes have warned against.

Finally, on communism, the old liberalism, which saw it essentially as evil and a threat, is clearly closer to the Church than the new liberalism, which either does not or does not to a great degree. There is no indication that neoliberalism is different than the rest of the new liberalism on this. Neither the old or new liberalism believes communism is evil because of its radical assault on spiritual principles.

As a general conclusion, we must say that neither version of liberalism accords fully with Church teaching, but that the old liberalism clearly did to a greater extent.

FOUR

COMPARING AMERICAN LIBERALISM AND CHURCH TEACHING, PART II: SPECIFIC PUBLIC POLICY PROPOSALS

In this chapter, the important specific policy proposals put forth at selected times by the old and new liberalism will be examined in light of papal teaching. The primary source used to examine the policies of liberalism are presidential election year platforms of the Democratic party, as mentioned in Chapter One. It was also mentioned there that, as the liberal party, the Democratic platform is a good place to look for the policy objectives that liberalism in each period was seeking to promote. The platform is a particularly good source because it contains the proposals that liberals most unite around, believe the most important, are putting forth most prominently before the public, and seek to promote through the efforts of government. The proposals would not have gotten into a national party platform if these things were not the case. Party platforms are where one will find, in one place, the greatest number of public policy positions of a predominant political perspective in American life.

We shall also examine, however, the positions on important issues of one prominent national liberal organization, the Americans for Democratic Action (ADA), to, in effect, confirm that the platforms are truly liberal documents (since some might doubt this because of the tendency for parties to represent coalitions among those of different perspectives, etc.). The treatment of this organization is relatively brief and is done only in a comparative context with the platforms (the same thing is done when examining conservative positions in Chapter Six). We do not build our study of liberalism primarily around the ADA's views (i.e., we do not make it the focus and basis of a comprehensive study of liberalism) nor do we attempt a comprehensive study of the nature, activity, or views of the organization.

In order to examine the policies of the old liberalism, the Democratic platform of the year 1948 has been selected. The new liberalism's policy proposals will be evaluated via the 1984 Democratic platform. 1948 was selected because it represents a year when the old liberal thinking was pretty well consolidated and its policy preferences established after its uncertainty of direction during the New Deal—when the old liberalism was just "feeling its way," so to speak—and after the changes and reevaluations that took place in it as a result of World War II and the rise of Soviet communism. The 1984 platform is a good one to examine because it apparently embodies ideas and principles from both the "mainstream" of the new liberalism, as represented by Walter Mondale and the neoliberal bloc, centered around Gary Hart (a third candidate going into the convention was Jesse Jackson). *The New York Times* reported the following on the shaping of the 1984 platform:

> The 1984 Democratic platform already carried the substantial imprint of both Mr. Hart and Mr. Jackson, added in the preconvention period by representatives on the platform committee. Leaders of the Mondale majority on the committee accepted thousands of words of new language from the other two camps...[1]

The neoliberal Hart found the platform acceptable enough that his forces pushed for only one minority plank after the Platform Committee completed its work, and this was accepted by the Mondale forces.[2]

The platforms will not be surveyed; only the proposals relating to points of the papal teachings that have been discussed will be gone into. Platforms, especially in recent years, are formidable documents, both in terms of length and detail, and much that is in them is irrelevant to our topic. There has been a trend of making Democratic platforms longer in the years since the New Deal. The 1948 platform examined here took up 6 1/2 pages in Johnson's *National Party Platforms*,[3] while that of 1984 one took up a full 34 *larger-sized* pages in *Congressional Quarterly Almanac*.[4] This greater length is probably due to two factors: the desire of the party to go into greater detail in its platform and its insistence that the national government involve itself in more and more activities.

Another reason may be that in 1948, the Democratic party held the presidency and did not have to go into so much detail because its positions were already pretty well known as presidential policy proposals. In 1984, the party had to spell out more precisely what it would do since it did not hold the presidency. This is probably not as good an explanation as the others, however, because in 1948, the platform of the Republicans—the "out" party—was only 4 1/2 pages long (in *National Party Platforms*),[5] while that of the Democrats in 1980, when they held the Presidency, was 30 1/2 pages long.[6]

The pertinent points (i.e., those which address the important points found in papal social teachings) in each of the two platforms studied fall into six categories: economic and social welfare policy (this includes both domestic and international economic policy), agriculture and the environment, education, civil rights and civil liberties, defense and disarmament, and foreign policy. This chapter will be organized in the same manner as the last: the old liberal proposals (in the 1948 Democratic platform) in each area will be stated and compared with the Church's teachings, as stated in Chapter Two. Then the same will be done with the new liberal proposals (in the 1984 platform). Then some general conclusions will be drawn.

The Old Liberalism: The 1948 Democratic Party Platform

I. Economic and Social Welfare Policy

The first part of the 1948 platform makes more than one reference to the party being at "the service of all and not to a privileged few."[7] The popes, as said in the last two chapters, are supportive of the poor and lowly in their attempts to overcome injustices perpetrated by the wealthy and powerful. To this extent, the Democrats' thinking coincides with the Church. Again, however, depending on the full meaning of the above and their perspective about the rich, the Democrats seem to be in opposition to the Church if there is an endorsement of inter-class conflict and an ignoring the necessity of social charity.

Let us consider economic policy first, then social welfare policy. First, the platform says this about taxes:

> We favor the reduction of taxes, whenever it is possible to do so without unbalancing the nation's economy, by giving a full measure of relief to those millions of low-income families on whom the war-time burden of taxation fell most heavily.[8]

It states further that the Democrats "endeavor to remove tax inequities."[9]

Fairness in taxation, as noted, is emphasized by the popes. The old liberals are thus in accord with them on this point, so long as the former are not implying that by lessening the burden on low income people they wish to raise it to an *unfair* level against high income people.

The platform "pledge[s] a positive program to promote competitive business" and "support[s] the right of free enterprise and the right of all persons to work together in cooperation and other democratic associations for the purpose of carrying out any proper business operations free from any arbitrary and discriminating restrictions."[10] There is no problem with promoting competition and enterprise based on private initiative as far as the popes are concerned, but it is entirely unclear—especially in light of their concommitant emphasis in the platform on vigorous antitrust law enforcement—whether the old liberal Democrats do not see it as the ruling, organizing principle of economic life. Their call for cooperation and "democratic associations" for business purposes is permissible under papal teaching since the popes have stressed the rights of all to form private associations.

The 1948 Democratic platform says much on labor matters. It calls for the repeal of the long controversial Taft-Hartley Act,[11] which established for the first time certain union actions to be "unfair labor practices," banned the "closed shop," and gave states the authority to enact "right to work" laws (i.e., laws banning even the union shop). The platform also states the following:

> We advocate such legislation as is desirable to establish a just body of rules to assure free and effective collective bargaining, to determine, in the public interest, the rights of employees and employers, to reduce to a minimum their conflict of interests, and to enable unions to keep their membership free from communistic influences.[12]

First, the proposals about securing the rights of both employees and employers clearly accord with the popes, but the opposition to the Taft-Hartley Act—which essentially sought to give some legal protection to employers' rights and to curtail excesses in the exercise of employee or union rights—casts doubts on how completely the Democrats embrace this papal principle. We have said that the popes strongly support the rights of workers to unionize and to bargain collectively. Clearly, the 1948 platform agrees with the popes in seeing the danger of communism and in seeking to minimize the conflict between employees and employers.

One past party objective, since realized, is referred to approvingly and is definitely endorsed by the popes: the "outlaw[ing of] child labor and the sweatshop."[13]

The platform also calls for legislation assuring "equal pay for equal work, regardless of sex."[14] The popes say that women should not be discriminated against or kept out of jobs for which they are suited by nature. Presumably, unequal pay for genuinely equal work would be discrimination and would be disapproved, and so this proposal is in accordance with the popes' teaching. The popes' concern about a "family wage" being earned by the head of the household—usually the husband—makes one think, however, that the popes do not *rigorously* and uncompromisingly adhere to the principle of "equal pay for equal work." It does not seem that the popes would be eager to endorse such a principle if it meant that a man with a family to support had to receive less than a family wage in order to insure that a single woman doing the same work receives an equal wage. If this is the interpretation the Democrats have of this principle, they may actually run afoul of papal teaching.

Interestingly, the Democratic platform supported the Equal Rights Amendment (ERA) as early as 1948.[15] The aforementioned papal teaching about women and work shows why the ERA would be incompatible with Catholic teaching, including the teaching on abortion.

According to the thinking of most ERA proponents, such views as special recognition for women in their family role, the undesirability for women with a family working outside the home, women having a different nature than men, the notion that there may be jobs for which women are unsuited (all of these appear in *Laborem Exercens* and *Familiaris Consortio*) and that it is morally wrong for women to destroy their offspring by abortion, are to be rejected. So are the legal manifestations of these views which are supported by the popes, such as protective labor laws for women, exclusion by law of women from certain jobs which would be harmful, and the prohibition of abortion. Indeed, the reason its proponents push the ERA is because they believe it will accomplish the opposite legal positions—and many legal experts agree with them.[16] (It must be acknowledged, in fairness, however, that it was not believed in 1948 that the ERA would have results like these and, if it were so believed, virtually no one then would have endorsed it.)

Let us now turn to the social welfare planks of the 1948 platform. The Democrats say they "favor the extension of the Social Security program" by, among other things, "[i]ncreases in old-age and survivors' insurance" and expanding "unemployment insurance." They also "favor the enactment of a national health program," programs to "aid...handicapped persons to become self-supporting," and "efforts to expand maternal care, improve the health of the nation's children, and reduce juvenile delinquency."[17] They say that "[e]mployment and economic security must be afforded all veterans."[18] Virtually all of these ideas are supported to at least some extent by the popes—even though they may not have spelled them out in their encyclicals until after 1948. The difference is that while the Democrats are proposing these as programs or extensions of programs run by the national government, the popes do not say they must be done this way. In fact, *Laborem Exercens* indicates, in its discussion of the responsibilities of the "direct" and "indirect" employer, that they are preferably to be provided by the company or organization employing the person.[19] However, it is the government, the "indirect" employer, which sets the requirements that must be met on some points by the "direct" employer. The encyclical indicates this as follows:

> [T]he indirect employer substantially determines one or other facet of the labor relationship, thus conditioning the conduct of the direct employer when the latter determines in concrete terms the actual work contract and labor relations.[20]

Interestingly, the 1948 platform speaks only of employment for all veterans and not, more widely, for all able-bodied men or persons seeking work. This comes even after the U.S. Congress, with a Democratic majority, passed legislation in 1946 to make the striving for full employment a policy of the U.S. government. (It did not, however, promise a government-created job to anyone who could not find one in the private sector; its purpose was to commmit the government to stimulating the private sector.) The popes would have no problem supporting a policy of stimulating veterans' employment, but would favor the wider stimulation stated above.

The platform also pledges to "enact comprehensive housing legislation, including provisions for slum clearance and low-rent housing projects initiated by local agencies." It also says that war-time rent control "must be continued" until there is adequate housing for Americans.[21]

II. Agriculture and the Environment

The 1948 platform says much about agriculture. The old liberal Democrats clearly put themselves forward as the party of the small farmer. The platform says that they "pledge...[their] efforts to maintain continued farm prosperity, improvement of the standard of living and the working conditions of the farmer, and to preserve the family-size farm."[22] All of these except the last are said by Pope John XXIII in *Mater et Magistra* to be required; the last is something he says is desirable.

Other policy proposals the 1948 Democrats put forth on agriculture involve such ideas as a permanent system of flexible price supports, an extended crop insurance program, continued expansion of the rural electrification program, and strengthening of agricultural credit programs. These positions would seem to be clearly endorsed by the spirit of *Mater et Magistra*, even though they may not be specifically mentioned by it. The difference here again, however, is that the Democrats are proposing these as national government initiatives. The popes do not necessarily say they should be undertaken by this level of government or by government at all. The Democrats do not appear to have kept the principle of subsidiarity in mind, although we cannot make this judgment for certain without considering the history behind these ideas. An historical analysis is necessary to tell us if the private sector or lower levels of government had failed to take the initiative, or, if they did but were unsuccessful.

Another point made by the Democrats about agricultural policy clearly echoes something which John XXIII essentially favored. They "strongly urge the continuance of maximum farmer participation" in the programs they propose.[23]

Finally, relating to agriculture and interior policy, the Democrats say that "[o]ur natural resources are the heritage of all our people and must not be permitted to become the private preserves of monopoly."[24] This, in essence, conforms to a teaching of the Church that stands behind her social teachings: that, as *Rerum Novarum* puts it, "God has given the earth for the use and enjoyment of the *whole human race*."[25] This is essentially reiterated in Pope John Paul II's 1989 environmental statement. This conformity exists even though it is highly unlikely that Democrats derived their position, at least consciously, from any traditional Christian religious teaching.

In 1948, there was not much national stress on environmental questions. Such problems were not then as serious and threatening as they would become twenty or so years later. The greater concern of the Democratic platform—and the nation—was natural resource development. There is some indication of awareness of the need to preserve the integrity of the environment in the above passage quoted and in the pledges of improving national waterways and harbors—although the main concern with this was doubtless to improve their navigability—, to improve flood control efforts, and to expand forestation efforts. We really cannot evaluate the old liberals on the environment very well, however, because it was not much of an issue in their time. Indeed, we have to wait till the 1980s even for direct *papal* statements about the problem.

III. Civil Rights and Civil Liberties

On the subject of civil rights and civil liberties, one proposal has already been discussed: the Equal Rights Amendment. It was pointed out that this Amendment, at least as it has come to be understood in the present-day, has had the effect of promoting ideas and practices that are contrary to the Church's teachings. Again, it is difficult to fault the 1948 Democrats for endorsing the Amendment, however, because certain of its likely results were then unforeseen. Nevertheless, they were responsible for considering its constitutional and legal implications and the dangers of its vague wording ("[e]quality of rights under the law shall not be denied or abriged...on account of sex").

Let us now consider the other civil rights and civil liberties statements in the 1948 platform. First, the party takes credit for "the great civil rights gains made in recent years in eliminating unfair and illegal discrimination based on race, creed or color." It also opposes "economic discrimination."[26] The platform goes on to mention specific aims with respect to ending discrimination:

> [R]acial and religious minorities must have the right to live, the right to work, the right to vote, the full and equal protection of the laws, on a basis of equality with all citizens as guaranteed by the Constitution.

and

> We...[must] guarantee...these basic and fundamental American Principles: (1) the right of full and equal political participation; (2) the

right to equal opportunity of employment; (3) the right of security of person; (4) and the right of equal treatment in the service and defense of our nation.[27]

Finally, the Democrats declare: "We pledge ourselves to legislation to admit a minimum of 400,000 displaced persons found eligible for United States citizenship without discrimination as to race or religion."[28]

There is no question that the proposals to end discrimination based on race, creed, or color concur with the Church. Ending economic discrimination concurs too, depending on the definition of such. Clearly, the popes seek to elevate the poor and eliminate the extremes of wealth and poverty (we have explained how this is indicated by the papal teaching). The popes do not call, however, for a socialistic type of levelling. The Democrats probably were not insisting upon this—they were not socialists in 1948 and are largely not today—but there is a trace of redistributivist sentiment present here. As stated, however, redistributivism is not per se against Church teaching, although the extent and manner of it may be. We have no indication that the latter would be a problem here. Thus, we must conclude that this point about ending economic discrimination would not offend the Church's teaching.

The popes would not take issue with any of the other specific rights called for, even though they, of course, would view them as being grounded primarily in the natural law, rather than in a secular document like the Constitution.

The Democrats' contention that displaced persons be admitted to the U.S. without discrimination somewhat parallels Pope John Paul II's later emphasis on the rights possessed by political refugees in *Laborem Exercens*.

IV. Education

The national or federal government was just getting involved in education around 1948, so the platform does not say much about it. There is only one paragraph, the pertinent part of which states: "We advocate federal aid for education administered by and under the control of the states...We insist upon the right of every American child to obtain a good education."[29]

Pacem in Terris, as noted, affirms "the right to a basic education and to technical and professional training" according to the standard in a particular country, so the last statement above seems to accord with the Church. This, of course, does not mean that the national government would have to fund it; here again the subsidiarity principle applies and must be taken into account.

V. Foreign Policy

There are several statements about foreign policy in the platform that raise points relating to Church teaching. First, however, there is another attack upon communism, which clearly accords with the popes. The 1948 Democrats say, "We condemn Communism and other forms of totalitarianism and their destructive activity overseas and at home."[30]

The platform pledges support for "a sound, humanitarian Marshall Plan" and takes the then-Republican controlled Congress to task for allegedly being reluctant to fund it.[31] It also extols the U.S. government's leadership under Democratic President Truman for having "demonstrated its friendship for other peace-loving nations and its support of their freedom and independence."[32] It also supports "economic cooperation with the countries of the Western Hemisphere"—this would probably involve, in part, foreign aid—and the "regional arrangements within the United Nations Charter, such as the Inter-American Regional Pact and the developing Western European Union."[33] Further, the platform calls for "immediate determination by the people of Puerto Rico as to their form of government and their ultimate status with respect to the United States; and the maximum degree of local self-government for the Virgin Islands, Guam and Samoa."[34]

All of these proposals concur with the Church's teaching, most of which on these points was put forth by Pope John XXIII. They compare favorably with the teachings regarding well-endowed nations helping those in less fortunate straits, nations respecting the rights and preferences of other peoples and nations, colonialism, and the need for international cooperation.

The Democratic platform of 1948 also "support[s] the United Nations fully" and "approve[s] continued and vigorous efforts within the United Nations" to bring to fruition disarmament proposals advanced by the U.S. It says adopting these proposals "would be a vital and most important step toward safe and effective world disarmament and world peace under a strengthened United Nations which would then truly constitute a more effective parliament of the world's peoples."[35]

The matter of disarmament will be discussed in the next sub-section. The point to note here is that the stress on the United Nations is definitely in accord with Popes John XXIII, Paul VI, and John Paul II's speaking of the need for international cooperation, international organizations, and an international public authority to address concerns about the universal common good. The Democrats are not specific about what shape a "strengthened" U.N. would take and do not define the term "parliament." If the U.N. they hoped for was to be like national parliaments, it would be a legislative and governing body. This would be a world government, which the popes do not call for and which *would* offend the principle of subsidiarity. If they are basically uncritical in their attitude toward the U.N. (whereas Pope John Paul II is not, as seen by his calling for changes in international organizations), it is perhaps because in 1948 the experience with the U.N. and international organizations generally was very brief.

Finally, the 1948 Democrats pledge their support for "the efforts of subjugated countries to attain their independence, and to establish a democratic form of government" and say they "look forward to development of these countries as prosperous, free, and democratic..."[36] If this means merely the promoting of the end of colonialism and of the development of more opportunities for citizen participation in public affairs and governmental institutions, this statement is in accord with the popes. If on the other hand, it indicates the desire to spread democratic republican government as the form for all countries around the world because of the belief that it is the best form of goverment for them all, it is not. We must remember that the Church holds that no form of government is the "best," declaring instead that different forms will be suitable for different peoples depending on their particular history.

Somewhat related to this issue is the platform's proposing the following:

We urge the vigorous promotion of worldwide freedom in the gathering and dissemination of news by press, radio, motion pictures, newsreels and television, with complete confidence that an informed people will determine wisely the course of domestic and foreign policy.[37]

This espousal of freedom to the media demonstrates part of the Democrats' faith in the people. The Church would basically agree with the objective of promoting such freedom,[38] but, as pointed out in Chapter Three, would not have this same smug confidence—typical of both the old and new liberals— that freedom to gather and discover news and the providing of full information to people will always result in the truth winning out.

VI. Defense and Disarmament

The first thing the platform states in connection with defense policy is that the Democrats were the party "under which were conceived the instruments for resisting Communist aggression."[39] This is another strong statement against communism.

As far as America's national defense is concerned, the Democrats state the following:

We advocate the maintenance of an adequate Army, Navy and Air Force to protect the nation's vital interests and to assure our security against aggression.[40]

and

We pledge to maintain adequate military strength...sufficient to fulfill our responsibilities in occupation zones [set up over previously Axis-held territory after World War II], defend our national interests, and to bolster those free nations resisting Communist aggression.[41]

It also makes a clear statement about the important worldwide military role the U.S. must play, saying that "the United States has become the principal protector of the free world" and that "it is imperative that we maintain our military strength until world peace with justice is secure."[42]

The platform also favors the collective security arrangements of the Rio Pact which it says "implemented the Monroe Doctrine and united the Western Hemisphere in behalf of peace."[43]

Nothing in the above quotations seems contrary to Church teaching since they appear to take a genuinely defensive posture against Communist expansion and do not advocate any military actions that could be judged as unjust under the just war doctrine. The only question that might be raised is about the Rio Pact and the "implementation of the Monroe Doctrine." Collective security presents no problem for the Church, so long as the legitimate rights and preferences of all nations involved are respected and so long as the U.S., as the most powerful nation involved, would not try to intimidate the others. Moreover, if the U.S. sought to "impose" its preference of keeping communism out of a country or used military force against it to stop its supporters from taking over another country—whether the country wanted the U.S. to do this or not—, it is not clear that this would be against Church teaching since communism is an evil force in itself. In a case such as this, the moral principles governing intervention would perhaps come into play. Intervention by one nation in the affairs of another—even military intervention—is not against Church teaching, per se; there are, however, certain conditions which have to be met. This isssue is discussed in Chapter Six.

Lastly, as to disarmament, the proposals the 1948 Democrats wanted adopted by the U.N. concerned "the effective international control of weapons of mass destruction, including the atomic bomb."[44] Clearly, this position accords with the popes who have repeatedly and urgently advocated multilateral disarmament.

The New Liberalism: The 1984 Democratic Party Platform

I. Economic and Social Welfare Policy

The discussion of the new liberal 1984 Democratic platform will proceed from topic to topic as they appear in the text. The first broad objective put forth—which is followed by specific proposals which spell out how it is to be achieved—is that "[a] Democratic Administration will pursue economic policies which provide the basis for long-term economic growth and will allow us to fulfill our commitment to jobs for all Americans who want to work."[45] The patform is also critical of any governmental policy which makes "recession—deliberate high unemployment" a means of controlling inflation.[46] Since the popes have called unemployment an "evil," this perspective clearly accords with their teaching.

The endorsement in the 1984 platform of the policy of "ensuring that meaningful job training is available" and of the *federal government* developing a major comprehensive national job skills" program (especially for "the chronically unemployed and underemployed")[47] further underscores the Democrats' commitment to ending unemployment, but may involve a conflict with the principle of subsidiarity.

Two specific applications of this objective in the platform are not necessarily included within the papal teaching. The platform makes much of the unemployment rate among young people, particularly teenagers and especially minority teens.[48] This may be a problem, but in discussing unemployment the popes have spoken primarily about heads of families, and they make it generally clear that they mean husbands-fathers. Male heads of households—the majority of the major breadwinners in American families are male—are *nowhere* mentioned specifically by the platform. It also speaks of the unemployment problem among "the over age 50 worker and the displaced homemaker," saying that "education, training and retraining" are needed for them.[49]

The popes do not address the problems of the older worker except to say that his age should be taken into account in the "whole labor process."[50] This could be implicitly saying, as the Democrats do, that their "special needs" should be taken account of. The problem of "displaced homemakers" (wives forced into the workforce because of broken marriages) is substantially due to divorce and desertion by their husbands. The 1984 platform, however, does not endorse the one thing that could most directly affect and help correct this problem (and would squarely promote an important teaching of the Church): namely, the enacting of laws that would make divorce more difficult to obtain. The platform does not explicitly state its support for a "right to divorce," although we have already seen with Justice Douglas that the new liberalism does believe in such a "right" and sees the choice for divorce as entirely up to the individual. As we saw, its neoliberal wing is in agreeement.

Interestingly, nowhere in the 1984 platform's discussion of employment or workers' rights is there mention of such rights emphasized by the popes as the right to rest and the right of the worker to be given time for his religious duties. There is also no commitment made to insuring that Sundays not become like other business days and no expression of concern for the general spiritual well-being of workers. (The old liberal 1948 platform does not mention these either, but perhaps it can be excused to some extent since it does not go into such detail and specifics.)

The 1984 platform asks for tax reform. It says that "America needs a tax system that encourages growth and produces adequate revenues in a fair, progressive fashion" and insists that "every American...pay his or her fair share." The way it proposes this be done is by eliminating loopholes, preferences, exemptions, deductions, etc., for the rich from our tax code. It contends that "[w]ealthier taxpayers will have to shoulder a greater share of...tax burdens" and that [t]here must be a fair balance between corporate and personal tax increases."[51]

Mater et Magistra, as mentioned, calls for a "just and equitable" tax system based on "ability to pay," which is apparently a principle derived from the natural law. *Rerum Novarum* says that taxation cannot be unfair or excessive. The 1984 Democrats are probably within these papal guidelines, so long as 1) they would not expect the wealthy to share what is, even for them, an excessive burden and 2) tax policy is not seen as a way of punishing them (thus having overtones of class hatred and conflict).

The 1984 Democratic platform strongly endorses our current Social Security system and opposes reducing funding for it. The platform also goes so far as to call Social Security "an essential element of the social compact that binds us together as a community."[52] While concern for a social insurance structure may be a commendable expression of national solidarity, the above seems to be overkill and nothing more than campaign hype, especially when one considers that our Social Security program did not exist until our country was one hundred thirty-six years old and this particular program—which was set up under FDR—is by no means the only viable or workable one. Such rhetoric also indicates that the new liberal Democrats will not accept any social security program not run by the national government.

The popes clearly have promoted the concept of social security, but have never said it has to be a national government program. By so insisting (implicitly, but without much doubt), the Democrats appear impervious to the subsidiarity principle and to the direct-indirect employer distinction. The same criticism of the 1948 Democrats made with regard to this program is thus applicable to the 1984 Democrats, except that the latter appear even more clearly to ignore subsidiarity.

The 1984 platform is also concerned about another social welfare matter: health care. It supports private initiatives such as HMOs, PPOs, and "social HMOs" and "competition in health care delivery" and says that "[t]he states must be the cornerstone of our health care policies." It goes on to promise that "a Democratic Administration will provide the leadership at the federal level to assure that health care is available to all who need help at a cost we can afford."[53]

This objective is one that the popes certainly favor and the above seems to show an attention to subsidiarity questions. One wonders, though, if the comment about "leadership at the federal level," especially when coupled with the promise that "[w]e will limit what health care providers can receive as reimbursement" (it is unclear from the context if the platform is speaking here of just Medicare or all health care costs) is still not too much of an emphasis on federal efforts.[54] Whether subsidiarity would be violated by increased federal involvement in this area depends, of course, on whether the matter has not been effectively dealt with otherwise. That may be the case with spiraling health care costs—a major point of the platform's focus—although probably is not with the quality of American health care. This is obviously not an issue that can be resolved here, however.

The 1984 Democrats, like those in 1948, can also be questioned on the subject of competition in the economy. Whether it be in health care delivery (in spite of wanting federal involvement, they also laud alternative private arrangements and insurance programs) or the general economy, they stress competition. The Democrats say that "[i]n general, competitive markets are more likely to restrain sudden surges of prices than are markets dominated by a few large firms" and emphasize the value of antitrust policy.[55] Again, the popes have said that competition has a place, but it cannot be the organizing economic principle. The Democrats here make it sound as though they view it as the organizing principle, by the fact that they are decrying this situation because of the loss competition instead of a concern about human dignity.

The platform's means of dealing with the economy also leans away from papal ideas on another point: government regulation. The popes clearly acknowledge and emphasize the need for state involvement in economic matters, of course. They prefer that the regulation be done by industry councils and vocational groups voluntarily entered into by the participants, however. The Democrats, on the contrary, indicate they see government regulation as more of a solution than the popes do. For example, they are critical of the fact that "[t]he 1980's brought...a wave of deregulatory decisions by financial regulators....These changes raise serious threats to our traditional financial goals."[56] This is similar to the position of the 1948 Democrats, although the drift of liberalism since then has been toward the fostering of more and more regulation.

To its credit, the 1984 platform—obviously reflecting the views of the neoliberals—emphasizes greater worker participation in company decision-making and more labor-management-government cooperation:

> Partnership, cooperation and participation are central to economic growth. We need new cooperative institutions, and a steady definition of how labor and management, universities, the private sector, and state and local governments can work together.[57]

and

> We support greater employee participation in the workplace...The government should encourage employee participation and ownership, particularly as an alternative to plant shutdowns.[58]

The Democratic platform goes on to make a number of specific proposals pursuant to bringing about greater employee participation: 1) the creation of a national Economic Cooperation Council "to collect, analyze, and disseminate economic data...to create a forum where the gap between business, labor, and government is bridged, where all three develop productivity...and...to identify national priorities, make recommendations on how best to reach those goals, and help build consensus for action"; 2) "government financial and technical assistance programs should give preference to viable worker and/or community-owned or run businesses, especially as a response to plant shutdowns;" and 3) worker participation in management decisions and representation on corporate boards. It also emphasizes that "[e]ssential to fairness in the workplace is the basic right of workers to organize collectively."[59]

A second part of the platform's call for cooperation concerns public-private partnerships. This seems from the context to pertain to the delivery of public and quasi-public services and programs. The platform says that in delivering these, "[c]itizen involvement in governance should be as great as possible" and "[t]he reponsibility...should be with the level of government that is closest to the citizenry and that can still discharge those responsibilities effectively and efficiently." It also calls for a "partnership" between the federal, state, and local governments in developing and delivering these programs, and also "cooperation between states and the private sector."[60]

The first part of this cooperative program will be commented on first. When reading this part of the platform, one could almost think it is a page out of *Quadragesimo Anno*. Clearly, the new liberal Democrats are going in the right direction here, as far as the Church is concerned. Nevertheless, one might easily be led to conclude that their initiatives are doomed to failure. There are two reasons for this: First, they apparently believe that *government* can make this cooperation and these changed structures in the economy come about. (Even though they speak of government "encouragement" in one place, the fact that these ideas and proposals appear in a national political party platform and government "preference" is urged for firms that put them into practice suggests that they would be, in some sense, governmentally imposed. Platform proposals are suggestions for government policy, which, by its nature, almost always means initiatives backed by coercion. Also, the experience in the U. S. with government using the carrot has shown that, sooner or later, it becomes a stick. Whenever governments have tried to impose these cooperative arrangements and institutions—the popes insist they must be voluntary to succeed—they have failed (as in Mussolini's Italy).

Second, as was shown in Chapter Three and as is further confirmed by the fact that the 1984 platform makes no reference at all to God, the new liberalism does not believe a social order or a program of social reconstruction requires God and religion as its basis. The popes, of course, have emphasized that the truth is otherwise.

The second part of the cooperative program is almost a classic statement of the principle of subsidiarity. How much the 1984 Democrats truly are committed to this principle, however, is doubtful in light of some of the other criticisms made above. The emphasis on federal action being in the forefront, in spite of concommitant claims of respect for subsidiarity, is vividly summarized elsewhere in the platform when it speaks of the need for investment in the nation's physical infrastructure: "The federal government must take the lead in putting...[people] back to work, and in doing so, providing the basis for private sector investment and economic growth."[61]

In comparison with the old liberalism on the matter of promoting a cooperative economy, we might say that the new liberalism fares better in that it presents a more detailed and definite program. The old liberalism basically just endorsed the idea. Both seem to embody the flaw, however, of putting too much stress on governmental initiative or leadership to accomplish cooperation and to guide the economy (which augurs poorly for its success).

Interestingly, the platform does not say that much specifically about the rights of labor or unions. At one point it mentions, with obvious strong support, "the collective bargaining power and rights of working men and women."[62] At another, it contends that "[e]ssential to fairness in the workplace is the basic right of workers to organize collectively" and attacks the "union-busting" which it claims was "inspired" by the Reagan Administration.[63] Also, as mentioned in the section on "Agriculture and the Environment" below, the platform calls for protecting workers from workplace environmental hazards. The fact that more specific points do not appear does not indicate, in my judgement, a weakness in Democratic support for the cause of labor. The general points above more than encompass various other specific rights of workers and the twentieth century Democratic party has a consistent and admirable record of strong support for labor.

Child care is a social welfare program the Democrats say "must...be a top priority." As such they propose "[h]elping communities establish after-school care programs" for "latchkey children," encouraging the private sector "to provide quality, affordable child care," and "setting up centers for child care information and referral" to help parents locate "quality" child care.[64] They go even further than this, calling for "universally available day-care with federal or business funding."[65]

They Democrats say that "[p]reventing child abuse must be at the forefront of Democratic Party concern" and call for federal challenge grants to "encourage states to make local prevention efforts a real priority." On a related subject, they speak of "the alarming rate of increase in teenage suicide" and "commit" themselves "to seek out the causes [and] formulate a national policy of prevention."[66]

The way the Democrats view the above social welfare policy matters gives a good initial picture of their perspective on the family and shows it to be in conflict with the Church's. As mentioned, the popes clearly believe the woman's natural role is in the home as mother and, it follows, that children are best raised in the home environment. The platform clearly wants to avoid any suggestion of the idea that women should refrain from entering the workplace or pursuing careers. Instead of trying to make child care outside of the home easier, the Democrats, in order to conform to the papal teaching, should be discouraging it. They should also seek to do something about the following conditions that lead to the purported "need" for such programs: economic need (which may be a less frequent reason than some contend), which could be met by providing family allowances and the like so the mother does not have to leave the home; materialism, which motivates both parents to work so they can have more luxuries and conveniences; and divorce, by making it harder to get (which is something, as has been mentioned, the new liberals are not likely to do). Actually, many new liberal Democrats want more readily available child care to make it easier for mothers to leave the home to work in order to be able to "fulfill" themselves. All this is the opposite of the way the popes have said the economic order should be structured.

Regarding child abuse and teenage suicide the Democrats' insistence on federal action again subverts the principle of subsidiarity. They also fail to see the confict with their child care plank above. The accounts in recent years of child abuse in day care centers suggest that expanding out-of-the-home child care may aggravate the problem of abuse. Teenage suicide is likely to become a more serious problem, not lessened, by the absence of parents from the home. Further, the Democrats show no concern anywhere for the possible violations of the natural rights of parents, consistently defended by the Church, that can result—and a growing body of evidence indicates *does* result very frequently—

from an overzealous enforcement of child abuse laws. There are a great many cases of false and unsubstantiated reports of child abuse or neglect against parents; in fact, it may be that *most* reports in recent years have proven unreliable.[67] The Democrats show themselves lacking in concern about this not only by their silence but also by their insistence that "[p]rompt intervention efforts...be provided for children in crisis."[68] What this means, essentially, is a sanction to state authorities to take children away from their parents with few questions asked.

These views on child care and the family demonstrate part of the difference between the old liberalism and the new, and thus provide additional confirmation of Hitchcock's position. It will be noted that the old liberal Democratic platform of 1948 had nothing at all to say about matters such as these. The old liberals accepted the traditional view that they were matters largely outside of government's domain and, for the most part, genuinely believed they should be.

On housing, the Democrats accord with papal teaching in calling for "adequate and affordable" housing for all Americans.[69] They call for an expansion in "public" and "publicly-assisted housing programs" to shelter the homeless and generally want to strengthen their "commitment" to such housing for the needy. Despite calling for "a comprehensive" housing policy to address "the totality of our...need," the platform section on housing indicates respect for subsidiarity (e.g., it speaks about government acting to help those "not served by the private market," and its "tak[ing] a leadership role where others cannot or will not participate" and working in conjunction with lower levels of government).[70]

In short, on social welfare matters the 1948 and 1984 Democrats both compare favorably with the popes as far as objectives and proposals go, but seriously shortchange subsidiarity.

The Democrats also emphasize "economic self-sufficiency" and say that "individual empowerment must itself be an operating philosophy" in "the welfare system, in education, and in the laws affecting everyone from shareholders to the average voter."[71] This agrees with the popes to a certain extent, since the latter emphasize the importance of individual initiative, worker participation in enterprises, and individual participation in government. "Individual empowerment" is a vague notion, however, and when it is framed in terms of a "philosophy" (and seen as a part of a platform which includes many other questionable manifestations of individual liberty) one is motivated to think that it may be an expression of excessive individualism at odds with the Christian perspective.

What the platform says about international economics, particularly as relates to the relationship between the U. S. and the so-called "Third World," is pertinent to our inquiry. First, it acknowledges a reality the popes point to: that the world economic order is interdependent ("America is very much a part of the international economy").[72] The party commits itself to "pursue international negotiations to open markets and eliminate trade restrictions, recognizing that the growth and stability of the Third World depends on its ability to sell its products in international markets." It also asserts that "the growth and development of the Third World is vital both to global stability and to the continuing expansion of world trade, and seeks American efforts to solve an international debt crisis which both threatens the "social and political stability" of the Third World and "threatens the foundation of the international financial system."[73] These are definitely similar themes to those sounded in the encyclicals of John XXIII and Paul VI.

Although there was nothing about international economics in the 1948 platform, Chapter Three revealed that the old liberals, like the new, believed that the prosperous U.S. has obligations to our less fortunate fellow members of the community of nations. On another important international question, however, the new liberalism fails to measure up to the old (as we shall see in a forthcoming subsection): it does not mention, and so apparently does not see, the threat communism poses to these "Third World" countries.

II. Agriculture and the Environment

The key points that the platform makes about agriculture are its pro-family farm stance, its support for "humanitarian aid programs abroad," its stress on improving farm income, and its call for the use of federal programs to achieve stated objectives.[74] Again, the family-scale farm is *recommended* by the popes; help to needy nations by rich ones, however, is a *moral obligation.* Improving farm income is seen at least as desirable by the popes. The stress on federal action is a further example of the downplaying of subsidiarity. Their views on all these points are very similar to those of the old liberal Democrats of 1948 and thus, with the exception of the subsidiarity question, are in conformity with papal teaching.

While the 1948 platform says almost nothing about the environment, the 1984 says a great deal, devoting twenty-five paragraphs to it—a respectably-sized section in the overall platform. It calls for "sound resource management, careful planning, and strict pollution control enforcement" in order to have "a healthy environmnent."[75] The platform seems to want to avoid suggesting that maintaining a clean environment means retarding economic growth.[76] Among the topics it takes up are the following: cleaning up hazardous wastes; controlling toxic air pollutants; reducing water pollution and insuring that drinking water will be free of contaminants; protecting workers from hazardous contaminants in the workplace; guaranteeing that pesticides will not be dangerous to health and food supplies; maintaining governmental control over current public lands and protecting natural endowments in "the public interest"; resuming allegedly lost leadership in the international effort to control pollution; protecting wilderness areas, endangered species, and wetlands areas; and a renewed effort to develop water resources of adequate quality (which are especially important west of the Missisippi and Missouri Rivers.[77]

In all of these environmental matters (except possibly the regulating of pesticide use), the platform calls for federal action. (It does not state the level of government which should deal with pesticides, except to say that dangerous pesticides should not be permitted to be exported—something the federal government would have to do.)[78] Surely, the concern about addressing these environmental problems—and the clear sense of obligation to do this—concur with papal teaching. Again, however, subsidiarity remains the problem. The platform says nothing about the private sector or lower levels of government addressing the above environmental problems. Of course, if they have not been shown to be unsuccessful or incapable of doing so, federal assumption of responsibility cannot be justified. It also does not go as far in addressing the environmental problem as Pope John Paul II when he speaks about promoting respect for the environment by restraining unnecessary technology, excessive "lifestyle," etc. Indeed, its emphasis on economic growth suggests it would not be likely to go that far.

III. Civil Rights and Civil Liberties

It is on the subject of civil rights and civil liberties that the new liberal 1984 Democratic platform diverges most from both the 1948 old liberal one— which had limited its condemnation of discrimination to "race, creed, and color"—and papal teaching. Several points, which we shall consider now, are pertinent.

First, the platform says "[t]he Democratic Party affirms its support of the principles of religious liberty, religious tolerance and church-state separation and of the Supreme Court decisions forbidding violation of those principles."[79] Clearly, the Church supports religious liberty and tolerance and a separate control and governance of state and Church bodies.[80] As discussed in Chapter Three, however, the extreme view of church-state separation present in the Supreme Court decisions and in the new liberalism generally (which treats belief and non-belief equally and does not believe religious principles must be at the root of the political order) is fundamentally incompatible with the Church's teaching. It is also, as noted previously, at odds with the old liberalism (as Hitchcock asserted).

Second, the platform holds that "all our government processes should be open to all Americans, and that no essential right should be denied based on wealth or status" and all have "dignity" and "the right.. to equal access to and participation in the institutions and services of our society."[81] Obviously, this is in conformance with what the Church has said. The platform also generally commits the federal government to strong civil rights enforcement, including protecting voting rights.[82] The Church, of course, strongly supports government assuming as one of its basic roles the protecting of its citizens' legitimate rights. However, the particular proposals of the platform for doing this are irrelevant for our purposes, since the Church leaves particulars to those in political life.

Third, the party seeks the "eradication of discrimination in all aspects of American life through the use of affirmative action, goals, timetables," etc., and the "placing [of] women as well as minorities in positions of power in government" by recruiting them to run for office and spending "maximum resources" to elect them. It also strongly supports the Equal Rights Amendment.[83]

The same problems with Church teaching discussed before on related points are applicable here. The Church opposes unjust discrimination, but refuses to sweep so broadly that the unique nature and role of women are denied. Affirmative action and, even more, the clear preference given to women and minorities for election support may raise problems of prudence and of racial ethnic, and gender chauvinism. While seeking to promote some notion of social justice—it may be an extreme and distorted notion—the platform possibly runs afoul of social charity. The strong emphasis on achieving political power also seems to conflict with the Church's concern that things of this world not be our major objectives. All these aims are also well beyond anything the old liberalism advocated.

The 1984 Democrats' zeal for "women's rights" leads them perhaps to their greatest conflict with the Church, and gets us to the heart of Hitchcock's critique of the new liberalism. The Democrats say they "recognize reproductive freedom as a fundamental human right" and oppose "any constitutional amendment to restrict or overturn" the 1973 Supreme Court decision legalizing abortion on demand. They also favor public funding of abortions for poor women.[84]

The 1984 party goes almost as far in clashing with Church teaching on the matter of homosexuality or, as it calls it, "sexual orientation." While this section of the platform calls for "dignity for all"—a laudable objective as far as the Church is concerned—its insistence that "discrimination" on the basis of "sexual orientation," in the workplace, in the military, and as a criterion for emigration, suggests a desire to be neutral as regards practicing homosexuals and others.[85] This indicates an unwillingness to view homosexual activity as morally wrong and—even if not actually intended—is likely to result in a social and moral acceptance of it. It is on these last two points that the opposition to the Church is most apparent.

The old liberal Democrats, of course, never supported positions such as these.

The 1984 new liberal Democrats' concern with the various forms of discrimination mentioned leads them to specifically condemn what are some-times, in contemporary pollitical-legal parlance, called "hate crimes": "[v]iolent acts of bigotry, hatred and extremism aimed at women, racial, ethnic and religious minorities, and gay men and lesbians."[86] Two comments are in order to indicate how this statement betrays a perspective conflicting with Church teaching.

First, implicitly the platform seeks moral acceptance for homosexual activity. Second, what is omitted is telling: There is no mention of the hateful assaults occurring against children used for pornography or by adult homo-sexuals who exploit them for their own sexual satisfaction (as seen by the activities of an organization such as the North American Man-Boy Love Asso-ciation [NAMBLA]). Nor is any mention made of the massive killing of the unborn by abortionists, nor of the hateful assaults on anti-abortion protestors and "rescuers" by pro-abortionists (which had already begun by 1984, even though they became more frequent later on).

The platform's condemnation of the Ku Klux Klan and the American Nazi party are laudable as far as both the Church and the old liberalism would be concerned. It mentions other "hate groups" also, but does not single out or mention the American Communist Party, which always had a pro-Soviet orien-tation and thus defended or, at least, glossed over the totalitarian brutalities and ontrages committed by the U.S.S.R. and her allies against millions, including certain whole ethnic groups.[87] This omission seems to be another example of the downplaying of the threat of communism and of the unwillingness to acknowledge its evil nature (factors which set the new liberalism apart from both the Church and the old liberalism).

The Democrats also say they are "committed to the principle of forbidding *any* discrimination on account of age against the elderly, either in holding a job or obtaining one."[88] This objective has its laudable aspects if rea-sonably applied. The sweeping condemnation of all such "discrimination," however, is both unrealistic and contrary to *Laborem Exercens*, as mentioned before. Would it not, for instance, possibly be unfair to both the individual and the employer to expect an older worker to do physical labor that is too strenu-ous for his body?

The platform's statement that we should seek "to meet the special needs of the disabled" accords with the admonition of *Laborem Exercens*, but its failure to emphasize that on the matter of employment at least the work made available to them should be work "suited to them," indicates its reluctance to acknowledge reasonable limits as the encyclical does. The stress of the platform on only federal efforts in this area also neglects subsidiarity.[89]

In being concerned about protecting the rights of these latter groups, the new liberalism perhaps makes an advancement over the old. Its tendency to take an extreme, uncompromising, and unrealistic stand, however, discredits it as against the "hard-headed" old liberalism.

Next, the platform seeks "to prevent housing discrimination against minorities, women and families with children."[90] Certainly, as a basic principle, the Church favors this. Different racial, ethnic, etc. groups should have equal opportunity to get good housing. Nevertheless, depending upon what is meant by this platform provision—and it is quite broad and unspecific—there could be problems as far as the Church teaching is concerned.

For example, does non-discrimination against women here mean that all-male rooming houses or all-male dorms at YMCA's should be mandated by law to provide residence facilites to women, even with the moral implications this could raise? What is meant by "minorities"? Does it include a legal requirement that landlords rent their apartment to cohabitating heterosexual couples or homosexual men who are sexually active with each other? If so, then this is a position that would be on a collision course with the Church (since there is every reason to believe the 1984 Democrats would include such groups of people in their definition of "minorities" in light of what they say above about protecting homosexuals). The call for non-discrimination against families with children seems to be pro-family, and this would be in agreement with the Church. The Church would not insist, however, that the objective in question be carried out necessarily by means of a legal stricture.

A further aspect of civil rights protection that echoes the concerns of the popes is the Democrats' calling for upholding the rights of aliens, in addition to U.S. citizens. One of their particular concerns is ending policies that "subvert the basic principle of family unification." They also seek to change the immigration laws to insure "a balanced, fair, and non-discriminatory...policy consistent with the principle of affording all applications for admission equal protection under the law."[91] All this seems to accord with the popes' insistence that the rights of emigres be protected. The Democrats' saying that discrimination on the basis of ideology should be prohibited,[92] however, raises difficulties as far as papal teaching is concerned because it carries with it the implicit suggestion that all ideolgies (including, say, communism, socialism, and Nazism) are equally acceptable and that none are potentially dangerous. Finally, the platform's opposition to "workfare" for welfare recipients[93]—in which they are required to do some work as a condition of continuing their benefits— possibly comes into conflict with Church teaching because of its betraying a willingness to accept and foster idleness as a way of life.

IV. Education

On education, the 1984 Democrats say that the following are their "four key goals":

> [S]trengthening local capacity to innovate and progress in public education and encourage parental involvement; renewing our efforts to ensure that all children, whatever their race, income, or sex have a fair and equal chance to learn; attracting the most talented young people into teaching and enabling them to remain and develop in their profession; and ensuring that all American families can send their children on to college or advanced training.[94]

They go on to insist that "every child be afforded an equal opportunity to fulfill his or her potential" and that "educational equity [be provided] for all children."[95]

The popes and the old liberals would emphatically endorse equal educational opportunity for all and non-discrimination in education, although "educational equity" sounds like it goes beyond this to embrace equal outcomes. "Educational equity" may also imply that there be no distinctions made between boys and girls in education. This would possibly challenge the bias against co-educational instruction still held by many Catholic schools and diocesan school systems in the U.S. The point about "parental involvement" is at least a mild recognition of the parents' rights and obligations as primary educators of their children which, of course, is defended by the popes. What was said before about child abuse laws, however, indicates that the new liberals are selective and inconsistent in their defense of parental rights.

The platform seems to maintain respect for the principle of subsidiarity when speaking about elementary and secondary education, affirming that it "is the responsibility of local government" and calling for "a partnership for excellence among federal, state, and local governments" and "new ties between business and schools" [i.e., between the private and public sectors.][96] It insists further on increased federal educational funding—at least a restoration of funds cut during the first Reagan term—and "incentives to local school districts" to strengthen science and technology areas.[97] While subsidiarity sounds as if it is being upheld, one can doubt that it is because the platform puts so much emphasis on federal funding. Such funding characteristically carries conditions and restrictions with it. Indeed the Democrats' awareness of this reality—and support for it—is suggested by the platform's saying that, "[w]e will *insist* that every child be afforded an equal opportunity to fulfill his or her potential."[98]

The popes would laud the platform's commitment to taking pariticular care of the needs of disadvantaged and handicapped youth.[99]

The concern of the Democrats about the availability of higher education opportunities ("mak[ing] certain that higher education does not become a luxury affordable only by children of the rich"; funding of black and Hispanic colleges; and funding grant programs for the training of scientists and engineers, and promoting "the arts and humanities"[100]) also would be supported by the popes, although again, the stress on the role of federal government funding raises the issue of subsidiarity.

The platform has this to say about private and parochial schools:

> Private schools, particularly parochial schools, are also an important part of our diverse educational system. Consistent with our tradition, the Democratic Party accepts its commitment to constitutionally acceptable methods of supporting the education of all pupils in schools which do not racially discriminate.[101]

This seems to be an endorsement of private and parochial education, but when we consider how few "constitutionally acceptable methods" of support there are (this obviously refers to Supreme Court decisions which have been extremely restrictive[102]) we realize that it is half-hearted. It is indicative of the 1984 Democrats' lukewarm support for private and parochial school aid that they do not in their platform endorse specific programs for such aid that as far as anyone knows—since they have not been constitutionally adjudicated — are constitutional, such as vouchers (which we mentioned the neoliberals, at least, oppose) and tuition tax credits. The Democrats' general endorsement without specifics may be mere political jargon aimed at carrying the Catholic vote while not offending their sizeable number of supporters who oppose any aid. Basically, we must say that the 1984 Democrats support government schools and federal aid to such schools; for all practical purposes, they do not support aid, or significant aid, for private and religious schools. This is in obvious opposition to a natural law mandate for such aid which flows from the basic right of parents to educate their children.[103]

V. Foreign Policy

The 1984 Democrats do see the Soviet Union as an "adversary" of the U. S. They also seemed concerned about the "totalitarian nature" of the Soviet regime. Nowhere, however, in the section of the platform on foreign policy—or anywhere else—do they speak of the evil nature of communism as an ideology.

As far as the spread of communism is concerned, the main worry of the Democrats seems to be—on the basis of their singling this out for criticism—"the Soviet willingness to maintain communist regimes against the opposition of their own people."[104] The suggestion that having a Communist regime is acceptable if a people want it, indicates that the Democrats definitely find nothing especially evil about this ideology. The Democrats' underplaying of the inherent malignity and danger of communism is further seen in such statements as "we must ...never fear the outcome of any competition between our systems" and "[w]e must...[avoid] exaggerating the strength of a Soviet regime beset by economic stagnation and saddled with a bankrupt and sterile ideology." It is also seen in their cautioning against our "fuel[ing] Soviet paranoia," and in their general suggestion that negotiation will somehow make everything turn out right (e.g. the platform contends that "[o]ur security and their security can only be strengthened by negotiation and cooperation ").[105]

While developments proved the platform to be partially correct in the years ahead, it was not so clear in 1984 that the weak Soviet economy would lead to its becoming less of a threat to the West or that its leaders did not still take its ideology seriously. Gorbachev was not even yet in power.

The foreign policy section of the platform contains a notable emphasis on negotiation, cooperation with other countries (including our adversaries), and deemphasis on the use of force as a means of solving international problems. It says, for example, that a Democratic president will not commit troops to combat "[u]ntil all instruments of diplomacy and nonmilitary leverage, as appropriate, have been exhausted...[and w]here our objectives threaten unacceptable costs or unreasonable levels of military force."[106] This all clearly accords with what the popes seek and the latter point seems to be in conformnity with the Church's age old just war teaching, as discussed in Chapter Two. It is also not unlike the preference of the old liberals.

Running through this discussion is a distinct optimism about the results of the negotiation approach, which borders on the unrealistic. For example, it says that a "Democratic President will encourage our European friends to resolve their longstanding differences over Ireland and Cyprus" and that "we and our allies should employ active diplomacy to encourage the earliest possible end to the Iran/Iraq conflict" (the eight-year-long Iran-Iraq war).[107] This wording makes the solution of these conflicts—some of the most embittered, impassioned, and long-term in the world—seem easy if we can only get the parties talking and negotiating long enough. This betrays a starry-eyed naivete about international affairs and, for that matter, human nature which does not afflict either the popes or the old liberals.

On international aid and cooperation, the 1984 new liberal Democrats, like the 1948 old liberals, are clearly in agreement with the popes on two important points. They call for the making of "major advances at limited cost in the health and survival of the world's poorest people—thus enabling more people to contribute to and share in the world's resources..."[108] They strongly stress the need for promoting development, saying that their party "will pursue policies for economic development, for aid and trade that meet the needs of the people of the developing world and that further our own national interest."[109] As noted above, they also call urgently for solutions (and provide some proposals) to the international debt crisis that has caused "[t]he social and political stability of...developing countries...[to be] seriously challenged."[110] Of these points, the only question of tension with papal teaching that arises is with the platform's insistence that American assistance be given only when our national interest is furthered. The popes, it will be recalled, have said aid should be "disinterested." (At the same time, however, the popes do not show themselves to be impervious to the reality of international life that nations pursue their self-interest.) In any event, there is not much question about their belief that wealthy nations should assist poor nations.

The 1984 Democrats also say they "will work to see the power and prestige of the U. S. fully committed to the reform and strengthening of the United Nations and other international agencies in the pursuit of...peace, economic and social welfare, education, and human rights"[111] and call for regional cooperation, especially in the Western Hemisphere.[112] This emphasis on international cooperation and the use of international bodies clearly accords with the popes, as does their awareness of the need for reform of bodies such as the U. N.

On another point in this subject area—international population policy—the Democrats are in conflict with the Church. This is indicated in the following:

> Recognizing that unrestrained population growth constitutes a danger for economic progress and political stability, a Democratic President will restore full U. S. support for national and international population programs that are now threatened by the policies of the Reagan Administration.[113]

As mentioned in Chapter Two, Popes John XXIII in *Mater et Magistra* and John Paul II in *Sollicitudo Rei Socialis* addressed the subject of population control. While Pope John acknowledged that in some locales and countries there could be an imbalance between increases in population and the means of subsistence, he contended that the facts about it were inconclusive. In any event, if the problem of overpopulation were genuine and had to be addressed, he said that it had to be done in a way which upheld the natural law and human dignity. Thus, contraception and abortion were ruled out. John Paul, of course, condemns "systematic campaigns against birth" as against "true development". The international population programs the 1984 Democrats sought to restore had as their essential components contraception and abortion.[114] The Democrats placed themselves clearly on a collision course with the Church here.

Finally on foreign policy, the 1984 Democrats concur with the popes in their stress on human rights[115]—a subject about which they clearly outshine the old liberals since the latter do not mention it (probably because not enough international attention had yet been turned to it). They would also seem to be correct (as far as the Church is concerned) in not wanting to draw distinctions between "authoritarian" and "totalitarian" regimes in this regard (as they state the Reagan Administration did).

Clearly, the Church says all men must have their basic rights respected, regardless of the type of regime. This is not to say, however, that for reasons of prudence, governments like the U.S. may not deal with human rights violations differently in different types of regimes, even while opposing and condemning them in all regimes. Indeed, this may have been the essence of the policy of the Reagan Administration, as opposed to one which simply ignored human rights violations in authoritarian regimes. Actually, in spite of the 1984 Democrats claim to treat violations of human rights the same no matter what the nature of the regime—e.g., they say that "Soviet harassment of the Sakharovs is identical to South African house arrests of political opponents of the South African regime,"[116]—the emphasis of the platform does not really bear this out. Only one paragraph and an additional sentence in another paragraph criticize human rights violations in the Soviet Union,[117] one of the most populous countries in the world and one known for the systematic denial of basic human dignity and rights because of its Communist ideology. In the meantime, a full two pages are directed to spelling out proposed sanctions against South Africa—a much less populous country with a regime that, while not benevolent, cannot have been said, even at the height of apartheid before the recent changes, to have been totalitarian—for human rights violations and political oppression.[118]

The second problem with the 1984 Democrats respecting human rights is that, unlike the Church, they nowhere mention human duties in connection with rights.

VI. Defense and Disarmament

The section on defense in the platform is surprisingly short—only one page out of fifty-eight. One cannot say, simply on the basis of this, that the 1984 Democrats do not concur with Pope Leo XIII's teaching that "the safety of the commonwealth...is government's whole reason for existence." This fact, however, along with the underwhelming stress on defense seen in its comment that it "seeks prudent defense based on...a realistic assessment of threats,"[119] its opposition to every weapons system it mentions, and its pledge to "[c]ancel destabilizing or duplicative weapons systems,"[120] make one wonder if this is not the case.

None of the other points made about defense policy raises questions involving papal teaching, except, at least one implicitly. The platform says it "[o]ppose[s] efforts to restrict the opportunities of women in the military based solely on gender."[121] This possibly—again we do not know what is included here because they do not get specific— conflicts with the point emphasized by John Paul II and previous popes that some kinds of work are not suitable for women. The platform seems to acknowledge that women should not be in combat—though it does not specifically state this—,[122] but there are other types of employment in the military, aside from combat duties, that also would seem to be unsuitable for women.

The platform endorses collective security arrangements, speaking specifically about "the Atlantic Alliance" (NATO), the Rio Treaty, and the OAS (Organization of American States).[123] There is nothing offensive to Church teaching in this, so long as the conditions of a just war are always upheld and, again, the U. S., as the most powerful nation in these alliances, does not seek to dominate the others and threaten their sovereignty or refuse to accord recognition of their rights as nations. The fact that the platform emphasizes "consultation" in these alliances and "acting in concert *with*" other nations in this hemisphere—and not, acting out of with "paternalism" "*for*"—them indicates that it respects the latter papal teaching.[124]

The 1984 platform says much about arms control and disarmament. It lists a number of specific proposals in a section longer than the one on defense policy. The section and the ones that follow it express a strong concern about avoiding nuclear war. The platform takes these positions: it favors ultimately "abolish[ing] all nuclear weapons"; it supports negotiations to cool the arms race; it supports "a verifiable and Comprehensive Test Ban Treaty" and the previously negotiated SALT II, Threshold Test Ban, and peaceful Nuclear Explosions Treaties; it endorses "a comprehensive, mutual and verifiable freeze on the testing, production, and deployment of all nuclear weapons"; it seeks "significant mutual and balanced reductions" in NATO and Warsaw Pact conventional forces and "effective international agreements to limit and reduce the transfer of conventional arms"; it opposes chemical weapons; and it promotes other joint disarmament efforts. These positions echo those of the popes.[125]

The question that comes up, however—especially in light of the easy confidence the 1984 Democrats seem to exhibit about solving difficult international problems and in dealing with sworn enemies of the U. S., and their dizzying endorsement of so many arms control ideas—is whether they have the realistic understanding the popes do about the difficulties of achieving *mutual* disarmament and peace and how true peace must come from within people, based upon what one might call a proper ordering of the soul.

What can be said about the comparison between the 1948 and 1984 platforms on defense and disarmament? The fact that the latter devotes more space to and has more specifics about disarmament than defense policy suggests that it places more stress on disarmament than does the former. The 1948 Democrats, while unquestionably concerned about disarmament and arms control, are more concerned about a strong defense. The converse is true for the 1984 Democrats.

The greater emphasis on disarmament possibly puts the 1984 Democrats—the new liberals—closer to the popes than the old liberal 1948 Democrats, particularly in light of the heightened concern of recent popes about disarmament and the arms race. It should be emphasized that the popes do not deny nations their right to self-defense and do not pronounce a conventional or even nuclear deterrent immoral. They have been increasingly insistent about the need for disarmament, however, because each passing year has brought a more dangerous world situation.

Reference to Another Source to Confirm the Liberalism of the Democratic Platforms

Although it has been explained why platforms are a particularly good source of liberal (and conservative) policy ideas in a particular period, some may question these conclusions because of the tendencies of platforms to forge accommodations among different elements in a party and because American parties have historically tended to be less ideological than those in many other countries and to move toward the "center." This possible criticism, in our judgment, downplays the ideological distinctness of our two major parties. Nevertheless, we shall briefly point to another recognizably liberal source for each of the years in question whose positions correspond substantially with the platforms. This will give further evidence of the platforms' being accurate indicators of the policy views of "mainstream" liberalism.

As mentioned, the other source we shall look to, both for 1948 and 1984, is the Americans for Democratic Action (ADA). This is an obvious source to examine if one wants to find the "liberal" position on important public questions. In his 1962 book on the ADA, Clifton Brock—who says he is in "general agreement" with its objectives but is not and has never been a member of the organization—calls it "a conspicuous liberal organization" and "a major voice of organized liberalism."[126] In a 1962 statement, the ADA called itself "the only independent liberal organization operating on a nationwide scale."[127] The ADA was formed, according to Schlesinger, as a "new liberal organization excluding Communists and dedicated to democratic objectives."[128] It favored expanding New Deal programs in the domestic arena, the anti-Communist containment policy of Truman in foreign policy, and, unlike the "Doughface progressives" of Henry Wallace, refused to have any association with American Communists.[129] Obviously, the ADA does not address every single point that the platforms do, but, as we shall see, considers most of them.

First we compare the ADA with the 1948 old liberal Democratic platform. Our source material for the ADA positions are Clifton Brock's book *Americans for Democratic Action*, essentially a history of the organization from its founding in 1947 to 1962, and the ADA's rating of Congress for 1948. Each year, the ADA selects key votes it believes have resulted in basically a liberal-conservative division of the U.S. Senate and House of Representatives and rates the members according to how they voted on them. It determines the percentage of times each member voted "liberal" (i.e., supported the ADA position) and publishes the rating annually. Many interest groups now rate members of Congress in a similar way (the source we use to compare against the Republican platform positions is another such group, the American Conservative Union), but the ADA was the first one to do it (in 1947). We shall simply mention the different ADA positions—mostly on bills before Congress in 1948—as they relate to the different parts of the platform. We do the same thing with the 1984 platform.

How do the ADA and the 1948 platform compare on economic and social welfare policy? First, the ADA has showed that it agrees with the general thinking of the 1948 platform of being against privilege and for creating what it says is a fair tax structure that requires the wealthy and big corporations to pay more and the average citizen to pay less.[130] This is seen in the ADA's support for a Congressional attempt to reimpose an excess profits tax in 1948, opposition to 1948 Republican attempts to reduce income taxes for people in the higher brackets, and support for an attempt in the House to give tax relief to lower income groups. On labor, the ADA supported various pro-organized labor initiatives in 1948, including bills to raise the minimum age and maintain tough enforcement procedures in labor legislation and to stop a reorganization of federal labor agencies which the labor movement opposed. The ADA has worked closely with organized labor from its beginning and has even received funds from it, although at times the latter has regarded the ADA as "too liberal" even on economic matters.[131] A major initiative it worked closely with labor on, which the platform was committed to, was a repeal of the Taft-Hartley Act. The materials examined do not address the equal pay for equal work issue or speak about the ERA at this early stage. The ADA began to support the ERA at least from the time it became a major political issue in the early 1970s in the new liberal period.[132] We can also presume that it supported equal pay for equal work.

On social welfare matters, the ADA has been distinguished for its support of governmental programs—especially, but not exclusively, federal—in such areas as housing, social security, unemployment compensation, medical care for the aged and for all in need, nutrition, and aid to depressed areas.[133] It has also promoted government efforts to maintain "full employment and rising standards of living,"[134] using such policies as wage, price, and credit controls.[135]

It has placed particular emphasis on the federal role in this matter of economic regulation and stimulation. Its position on various 1948 bills illustrates these points: it opposed a Republican effort to stop the extension of war-time controls to control inflation, it supported the Truman effort to extend Social Security, it supported a comprehensive federal housing funding and planning program, it supported efforts to tighten anti-trust laws and it supported bills both to provide health care to the needy and comprehensive health insurance.[136] Many of these ideas are specifically supported in the platform, as we have seen, or else—in the case of the federal government guaranteeing full employment, economic controls, and anti-trust legislation—were pushed by Truman and the liberal Democrats in Congress.

In the area of agriculture and the environment, we see a close parallel between the ADA and the platform. The ADA supported bills maintaining the government agriculture appropriation programs of the New Deal and price support programs of World War II. A number of these programs are mentioned, it will be recalled, in the platform. Like the platform, the ADA singled out the family farm for particular praise, favored federal aid to family farmers, and also opposed attempts to tax farm cooperatives (an idea it claimed was "inspired" by "big business").[137] The ADA does not mention the rural electrification program as the platform does, but its support for legislation aiding the Tennessee Valley Authority and setting up other similar authorities and its opposition to other legislation restricting public power indicates its support for such government efforts. That the ADA has a similar position as the platform about natural resource development is seen by its opposition to legislation that makes it easier for "private business" to develop—and "exploit"—oil reserves in tide-lands areas.[138] In short, there is a clear parallel between the ADA and the platform in this area.

On civil rights and civil liberties, there is a very close correspondence. In fact, the platform plank on civil rights was drafted and marshalled through the 1948 Convention by the ADA and its supporters.[139] The platform's position on displaced persons is also shared by the ADA, as seen by its support of two bills aimed at lessening or eliminating discrimination against displaced persons of certain nationalities seeking to enter the U.S.[140] It is apparent from what has been said about its position on taxes, as well as from the ADA's 1947 "statement of principles and policies" (in which it says that "[c]ivil liberties must be protected from concentrated wealth"),[141] that it shares the platform's opposition to economic discrimination. The platform does not speak about civil liberties much; it speaks mostly about civil rights. From what I have said when discussing Schlesinger, however, we know that one of the biggest civil liberties issues for old liberals at this time was protecting the civil liberties of Communists, Communist sympathizes, and other leftists under fire from government loyalty programs or being singled out for attack by government officials.

Brock discusses the significant role the ADA had in supporting civil liberties in such cases, even though it refused to permit Communists to become members of it.[142] This is seen in the 1948 ratings in the ADA's opposition to the Mundt-Nixon subversive activities bill. The ADA has pushed a strong civil liberties agenda on matters such as this, and free speech and assembly generally, for years.[143]

On education, the ADA was clearly in the platform's corner. The ADA was an early supporter of federal aid to education.[144] Its support for the platform's belief that every American child has the right to obtain a good education is demonstrated by the very fact that the reason liberals wanted aid in the first place was because they believed that in various states not enough money was being put into education to make this possible. This is also evidenced by the ADA's opposition to economic discrimination, by its clamoring for equal opportunity before the platform Committee,[145] and by its later opposition to discrimination in federal aid programs.[146]

In foreign policy, the ADA also was close to the platform. As stated, a major part of the reason for its creation was to be an anti-Communist liberal force. Like the platform, it has sought to promote freedom in other nations.[147] At the time of its founding it called for "political and economic support to democratic and freedom-loving peoples the world over."[148] Its 1948 ratings show support for Truman's Marshall Plan and other major post-war foreign economic assistance.[149] Over the years, it has been a strong and consistent supporter of foreign economic aid bills, especially to underdeveloped countries.[150] The ADA materials used do not mention support for the United Nations, but Brock's telling us that the ADA "has been whole-heartedly internationalist" seems to suggest its on-going support of an organization like the U.N.[151] The ADA also supported both the Truman Doctrine—the military and political program to contain communism after World War II—and, as already indirectly indicated, the Marshall Plan, two points specifically present in the platform.[152]

The latter shows how the ADA also parallels the platform's defense and disarmament provisions. It has supported regional alliances, like the platform.[153] As has been indicated, it was a strong supporter of the anti-Soviet Communist foreign policy of the Truman Administration.[154] It represented the hard-nosed Cold War anti-communism associated with people like Schlesinger, one of its founders. It supported the military build-up that went along with the new anti-Communist foreign policy; this was part of the post-War bipartisan foreign policy consensus. At the same time, they were giving at least a brief nod to the ultimate objective of multilateral disarmament—the same as the platform gave it—by calling for the international control of atomic energy—as the platform did—and, at least in the years that followed, by enthusiastically embracing Adlai Stevenson and his disarmament ideas. At one of their major gatherings, he spoke on the topic of "Science, Disarmament and Peace."[155]

All told, then, there is little doubt about the correspondence of the ADA's positions with the 1948 platform. There is thus little reason to doubt that the 1948 platform was indeed a liberal one.

Now we compare the stands of the ADA with the 1984 new liberal Democratic platform. The primary ADA source material consulted for this is its 1984 ratings of Congress (although some other ADA materials will be referred to on a few points). First of all, as far as the ADA is concerned, there is no question about its agreement with the platform, in a general sense, on unemployment. None of the bills in Congress it took a position on directly sought to cut unemployment, but it did support an effort to secure federal funding for health care benefits for the unemployed and opposed a change in the immigration laws to permit a temporary foreign worker program that could have threatened Americans' jobs. It took a position on only one tax bill, which imposed additional corporate taxes. It supported this. The ADA also favored two other budget bills which cut military spending while generally raising taxes.[156] This shows conformity, in general, with the platform's thinking about taxes: a willingness to raise them, especially to balance the federal budget, and a belief that corporations are not paying a fair share. This corresponds with the ADA's long time view that the wealthy should be taxed more heavily.[157]

The above position on health care and its support for a general increase in spending for programs in the Departments of Health and Human Services, Labor, and Education indicate its closeness to the Democratic platform's basic thinking on health care, education, support for the cause of labor and, again, unemployment. The ADA's agreement with the platform's guarantee of health care assistance for all who need it, while not addressed in any of the 1984 votes, is seen in the fact that it first expressed support for "comprehensive national health insurance" way back at the time of the Truman Administration.[158] Its emphasis, with the platform, on more social welfare programs is seen further in its support for the two military-cutting budget bills above (which would have freed up more funds for domestic purposes), its opposition to two other budget-cutting bills which would have either not cut defense spending while cutting domestic spending or not cut it enough,[159] its opposition to a line-item veto bill for the president (which Ronald Reagan undoubtedly would have used to cut down mostly on domestic spending),[160] as well as in the health care and three-department spending bills above. The ADA's corresponding position with the Democratic platform on labor is seen further in its opposition to a bill to curb the use of union dues for political activity and its support for allowing union contracts to be rejected by companies filing for bankruptcy.[161] None of the 1984 votes focused on government regulation of the economy, but, as we have seen, a few in 1948 did and throughout its history the ADA has tended to favor an active government interventionist approach to the economy involving, *inter alia,* wage, price, and credit controls.[162]

On child care and welfare, the ADA comes out close to the platform in supporting federal aid for after-school child care programs and for child nutrition programs.[163] The same questions pose themselves (as with the platform) about conformity with papal teaching, especially on the point about outside-of-the-home care of children. The 1984 ADA ratings do not directly deal with any housing bills, although the general opposition to cutting federal domestic program spending obviously includes this. The ADA support for federal housing assistance has been seen since the earliest years of its existence and was noted in the 1948 ratings.[164]

There is nothing in the 1984 ratings about international economics, but the ADA has been a supporter of foreign economic aid.[165] As far as I have been able to discern, the ADA has not put forth statements about the matter of cooperation in the economy (which is prominently featured in the platform). Overall, however, we can see that on social welfare and economic questions the ADA conforms closely with the 1984 platform.

There is nothing in the 1984 rating about agriculture, although, as noted, the 1948 rating supported federal efforts and money to aid American agriculture, a position taken by both platforms. That the vigorous federal effort in environmental matters called for by the 1984 platform is desired also by the ADA is seen in its advocacy of the "superfund" program to clean up toxic wastes and of a bill to permit citizens to sue dumpers of hazardous wastes.[166]

On civil rights matters, the ADA has long championed the cause of blacks and opposed unjust discrimination for reasons of race, religion, or national origin, as the 1948 discussion indicates.[167] The similarity of its views on sex discrimination and affirmative action with the 1984 Democratic platform is seen in its support for the so-called "Civil Rights Restoration Act" which overturned a narrow Supreme Court interpretation of Title IX regarding sex discrimination in educational institutions.[168]

On two other matters, the ADA also takes positions which are in line with the platform and, it has been noted, are sharply at variance with the Church. The ADA clearly supports legalized and readily available abortions, as seen in its 1984 support of expanding federal payment for abortions for poor women to cases of conceptions due to rape or incest and the inclusion of abortion in federal employee health insurance.[169] The 1984 ratings do not involve any bills concerning "discrimination" against homosexuals, which, as we have pointed out, really involves, for the most part, an endorsement of homosexual practice as morally acceptable. The 1988 ratings of the ADA, however, show the ADA's support for this position by the fact of their opposing a prohibition on funding for AIDS educational programs which promote or encourage sexual activity and their opposing efforts to exempt religious institutions in the District of Columbia from an anti-homosexual discrimination ordinance.[170] (Indeed, the latter demonstrates an unwillingness of the ADA—and the new liberalism, in general—to fully respect religious freedom.)

The ADA materials examined do not address discrimination on the basis of age or disability. The general ADA emphasis on broad civil rights notions makes one think, however, that it would have the same views as the Democratic platform. The 1984 ratings do not speak of "workfare," but a look ahead again at the 1988 ratings shows that the ADA, like the platform, opposes it.[171] Again, what we have already said about the ADA and civil liberties indicates that the platform and the organization, in the specific areas of this subject addressed by both, are very close.

On education, there is also similarity. We have already stated that the ADA was an early supporter of federal aid to public education. Brock's book leaves some question, however, whether—like the 1984 platform—it is concerned enough about the principle of subsidiarity.[172] The ADA has strongly opposed government aid to parochial and other private schools.[173] As we have argued, this is essentially the position of the 1984 platform.

Next we consider foreign policy. As noted, the ADA was started as a strongly anti-Communist liberal organization with a hard-nosed, realistic view of the Soviet Union and her intentions in the world at a time when she pursued aggressive policies under Stalin. How anti-Communist it remains is somewhat in doubt, if we can judge by the Congressional ratings.

The ADA came to betray a much greater confidence in Communist intentions—well before any of the dramatic changes of the Gorbachev period—as seen by its opposition to every weapons system development bill it rated Congress on and its strong belief that Communist regimes can be trusted and relatively easily negotiated with. The latter is seen in its supporting the following: the conditioning of funding for an anti-satellite weapon defense system on the president's "certifying" his willingness to seek limitations of such arms with the U.S.S.R.; the call for an agreement with the Soviet Union for a ban on underground nuclear tests; the claim that a "mutual and verifiable" nuclear freeze could be seemingly readily gotten; and bills to deny military aid to El Salvador (fighting Communist rebels) and military or military related aid to the Nicaraguan contras challenging the Communist government.[174]

As noted, the ADA has favored foreign assistance, especially of an economic kind, and also indicates the desire to promote international human rights progress by tying this to continued American aid for other nations.[175]

Like the platform, we can infer—without being able to be conclusive—that there may be a downplaying of human rights abuses in Communist countries and an excessive emphasis on such in non-Communist, authoritarian countries. This is seen by the fact that human rights problems are mentioned in the 1984 ratings and again in the ADA ratings and presidential election material in 1988 only in conjunction with South Africa and non-Communist Central America.[176] Like the 1984 platform, too, there is no memtion of human *duties* in association with human rights. There is thus a definite corespondence between the platform and the ADA on foreign policy.

On defense and disarmament, what has already been said shows the closeness of the ADA of the 1980s and the 1984 platform. Indeed, we can also see the same difference between the old and new liberal ADA (the ADA in the 1940s as opposed to the ADA of the 1980s) on this subject as we have seen between the old and new liberal Democratic platforms.

All told, then, there can be little doubt about the fact that, as measured against the positions of the avowedly "liberal" ADA, the 1984 Democratic platform is clearly a liberal one as, in the period of the old liberalism within the meaning of the term at that time, the 1948 platform was.

Conclusions

Let us now draw some conclusions about the comparison between the old and new liberals on the six specific areas examined in the two platforms.

First, we consider economic and social welfare policy. On the matter of competition as the organizing principle of the economy, both the old and new liberals are guilty of diverging from the popes. The new liberals of 1984, however, have a better conception of the kind of cooperation needed as a fundamental aspect of a just economy (as seen especially with the neoliberal wing). The new liberals are closer to the popes on unemployment; the old liberals, at least in the 1948 platform, do not go far enough (even though their other actions at the time show them to be almost as close to the popes). Both concur with the popes about concern for the rights of labor and the material needs of workers, but neither addresses their spiritual needs.

The 1948 platform betrays a seeming obliviousness to the rights of employers, however, so 1984's is more acceptable in this area. Both seem to accord with what the popes say about fairness in taxation, but it is unclear if both would not subject the wealthy to somewhat excessive taxation that may even go beyond the popes' "ability to pay" principle. On welfare matters, both concur with the popes on social security, but the new liberals are ahead of the old in their expressed concern about housing. Further, the new liberals seem to run into no subsidiarity problems on this. On health care, both versions of liberalism accord with the popes, with the new perhaps better respecting the principle of subsidiarity. Both are concerned about the economic welfare of other countries, but the new liberals translate this into specific policy ideas, so they must be judged as better.

When we consider all of the above, we would probably be inclined to say, on balance, that on economic and social welfare policy the new liberals are closer to the Church. Two other matters are sufficiently *at odds* with the Church, however, to lead one to conclude that *overall* the old liberals—even if weaker or less explicit and detailed on some points—are closer to the Church's teachings. These are the subsidiarity question which has been repeatedly mentioned and the new liberals' views on the very thing that Hitchcock said separated them from the old: social policy relating to the family. With regard to women and the economy, child care, proposed programs to help problem children and the like, the new liberals seem too eager to displace the family and turn such matters over to government. They seem less concerned about keeping families intact and providing financial support to families (e.g., like the family allowances the popes call for, so mothers will not have to work) than about making it as easy as possible for married women to become independent of their families.

On agriculture, both the old and new liberals take positions that accord with the popes. On the environment, of course, the new liberals are closer to the Church because the old liberals do not address this question at all. Even the 1984 platform, however, does not go as far as Pope John Paul II has in his statements about the environment.

On civil rights and civil liberties, the contrast between the old and new liberals, as far as their compatibility with Church teaching is concerned, is seen most starkly. The old liberals' opposition to unjust discrimination based on race, religion, and economic status (while not promoting socialism) accords with the Church. The new liberalism ostensibly opposes this also. The fact that it carries the notion of opposition to discrimination to an extreme and establishes new "rights," not part of the natural law, result in its coming into conflict with the Church. Its endorsement of a levelling view when speaking of sex discrimination (even though the old liberals also supported the ERA, without understanding its likely consequences as the new liberals do), its extreme notion of church-state separation and willingness to treat belief and unbelief alike, its support for affirmative action despite the questions of prudence and group conflict it raises, its support for abortion "rights," and its call for special protections for homosexuals (which can result in the ignoring of the evil of homosexual acts)—all demonstrate its conflict with Church teaching. Even in areas where it supports ideas endorsed by the popes, as in its opposition to unjust discrimination against older persons and the disabled, it sweeps so broadly that it seems to run afoul of the parameters of Catholic teaching.

The same may possibly be the case with housing discrimination and is likely the case regarding discrimination in emigration. On non-discriminatory access to political processes and institutions, the old and new liberals seem to be equally in conformity with the popes. It is thus on the subject of civil rights and civil liberties that the new liberals, as noted in effect by Hitchcock, show themselves to be so much less compatible with Catholic teaching than the old. Indeed, on some points the new liberalism proves itself to be utterly hostile to the Church.

On education, the new liberals, all in all, are less compatible with the Church's teaching than the old. This is because of the neglect of subsidiarity created by insistence on too much national government involvement in education and the fact of the new liberals' lukewarm support (really, virtually no support at all) for state aid for parochial schools.

On foreign policy, the main point that separates the new liberalism from both the old liberalism and the Church is its view of communism. The new liberals are also at odds with the Church on the approach that international population policy should take (the old liberals do not address this).

On points such as the emphasis on negotiation to solve international problems, the need for international cooperation, promoting the economic development of less advantaged nations, and respecting the rights and preferences of other nations as well as aiding those that are poor, the new liberalism compares favorably with the old liberalism and the Church. It also agrees with the Church on human rights, a subject the old liberal 1948 platform did not address (although it was part of the old liberal agenda). On balance, however, the old liberals must definitely be said to be closer to the Church's teaching than the new.

Lastly, on defense and disarmament, it was observed that the old liberalism stressed defense and the new liberalism stresses disarmament. This fact does not necessarily bring the latter closer to the Church, however, because disarmament was also a stated objective of the old liberalism (although it is stated much more vigorously by the new liberalism which puts forth many more specific proposals for it). Whatever advantage this greater insistence on disarmament and specificity about it gives the new liberals over the old liberals in their comparison with the Church, however, is lost by obliviousness of the point made strongly by the popes that a truly effective peace must first be internal (issuing forth from the human heart), and by their excessive optimism about the ease with which peace can be secured. Also, if the new liberalism, as a matter of principle, has downplayed defense as a responsibility of the state, this would be a serious criticism. (Though there are suggestions it may be doing this, it is far from clear). The pro-collective security positions of each version of liberalism do not offend the Church. Overall, in this area, the old liberalism is a bit closer to the Church, but only *a bit*.

The general conclusion after these comparisons of the two liberalisms' specific policy proposals is essentially the same as after the comparison of their views about the purposes of government in the previous chapter: neither completely accords with the Church's teachings but the old liberalism is closer. On specific policies, however, we must say that this state of its being closer is much more manifest and certain than on the general principles of government. What is also clear here, which may not have been in the previous chapter, is that some elements of the new liberalism, in contrast to the old, are *hostile* to the Church's teaching. This latter conclusion essentially confirms Hitchcock's thesis, especially when it is seen that the areas on which the greatest hostility occurs pertain to sexual matters and the family.

FIVE

COMPARING AMERICAN CONSERVATISM AND CHURCH TEACHING, PART I: THE GENERAL PHILOSOPHY OF POLITICS AND GOVERNMENT

This chapter does with American conservatism what Chapter Three did with liberalism: it seeks to discern the broad political philosophy of American conservatism—its view of the general role of government, its basis for political authority, and its view of the rights, duties and place of the individual in the political order—and to evaluate it in light of papal teaching. Chapter Six will then undertake a similar evaluation of specific conservative policies and program ideas by looking at Republican party platforms.

Again, as with the examination of liberalism, the areas of thought that will be considered in this chapter (distilled primarily from our discussion of the papal encyclicals) are the following: conservatism's views on the purposes of government; its understanding of the role that God, religion, and the natural law have as the basis for the political order; and its views on freedom, equality, and communism.

Different Perspectives Within American Conservatism

As with American liberalism, we shall focus our attention on American conservatism in the post-World War II period. Also, as with the former, the latter has different perspectives within its camp that must be taken account of in trying to determine precisely what the content of "conservatism" has been in this period. Just as there were good reasons to take 1945 as the year that roughly marked the point at which contemporary American liberalism took definite shape, there is a good reason for saying it marked the point of the emerging contemporary American conservatism. George H. Nash, one of the leading chroniclers of the latter, writes the following:

In 1945 no articulate, coordinated, self-consciously, conservative intellectual force existed in the United States. There were, at most, scattered voices of protest, profoundly pessimistic about the future of their country. Gradually during the first postwar decade these voices multiplied, acquired an audience, and began to generate an intellectual movement. . . .the need for consolidation of the conservative camp [among its different, but not unrelated, elements] was urgent by the mid-1950s. Through the medium of various journals and organizations, this task was gradually accomplished.[1]

Although Nash speaks specifically of intellectual conservatism—not of conservatism as a political movement—it is correct to go along with his starting point because in this chapter we wish to assess the broad philosophy, which begins with and substantially involves intellectual reflection. In spite of the fact that we have to be careful about viewing conservatism as an ideology, as discussed in Chapter One, the fact is that a significant part of this postwar conservative intellectual reflection led to practical political ideas and programs and a certain number of the conservative intellectuals have sought actively to promote these, in one way or another, in the political arena. As Nash says:

[C]onservatives were by no means constantly preoccupied with internal, theoretical issues and controversies. For in the 1960s a momentous transformation of the Right began to occur: a transition from minority to potentially majority status in American politics and culture. . . .Right-wing critiques of liberal foreign and domestic policies were expounded with increasing sophistication and effectiveness, while conservatives strove to develop intellectually serious and practical alternatives. . . .[T]he 1960s. . .generated new alignments that facilitated the emergence of conservatism as a powerful intellectual and political force.[2]

Thus, it is correct for us to discuss postwar conservatism as a *political ideology* (in the sense we have been using the term).

Unlike liberalism, we do not believe we can divide postwar American conservatism into "old" and "new" phases or types. There does not seem to have been any significant, qualitative shift in the nature of mainstream conservatism. Mainstream intellectual conservatism (i.e., what is generally accepted as being part of that political perspective in America that goes under the banner of "conservatism") is made up of a number of different groupings or elements, each of which has different points or perspectives that it stresses— aspects of or interpretations of social or political life it believes especially important—and which share certain basic principles (as we noted in Chapter One).

In a noteworthy article entitled "Varieties of Conservative Experience," which appeared in 1971 in *Modern Age*—"the principal quarterly of the intellectual Right"[3]—conservative editor, journalist, and commentator M. Stanton Evans identified a number of perspectives within mainline conservatism which are the ones we shall largely follow here (with some deviations).[4] Nash also divides intellectual conservatism into distinct but related groupings.[5] The way to study mainline American conservatism, then, to determine what are its major tenets is to examine the groupings that make it up. Our analysis in this chapter will focus on the works of one or two representative thinkers or figures in each of the perspectives or groupings identified. Some of these sources will address only certain of our five areas of concern, others will address them all. Then, at the end of the chapter, the points and strains of thought discussed in the various areas will be brought together to determine the general thinking of conservatism, per se, on each area and a comparison with Catholic social teaching will be made. There will be some limited discussion of which individual conservative groupings or perspectives are closest to Catholic teaching, but no substantial comparison between each of the groupings and the teaching is made. The objective, it will be recalled, is to determine where conservatism *overall* stands in relation to the Church.

This chapter is considerably longer than the corresponding chapter on liberal thought (Chapter Three) simply because these many different perspectives have to be examined, which involves looking at representative writers within each of them in order to make a fair overall assessment of conservatism. Thus, the greater length of this chapter does not suggest that conservatism is examined more carefully than liberalism; it is just a matter of not being able to determine any three or four thinkers as representative spokesmen for all of conservatism which possesses a greater complexity because of the various schools of thought within it.

The first grouping that shall be examined is the theological-natural law-cultural conservatives, or what Evans lumps together into the category of "traditionalists."[6] We shall here call them simply "cultural conservatives." These cultural conservatives are concerned about restoring secularized, confused Western man to the traditional precepts of Christianity (or Judeo-Christianity)— i.e., where these precepts stood before they became infected with liberal theology and skepticism—and/or the notion of a higher law not made by man (either in its Classical or specifically Judeo-Christian conception). Their thought is also characterized by the following: a rejection of moral relativism; a realization of the imperfect, fallen state of man which precludes utopian schemes, and generally a respect for tradition, authority, order, and virtue.[7]

Different individual thinkers among these conservatives emphasize different aspects of these principles, hence the specific designations of theological, natural law, and cultural conservatives. The writers in this general grouping of cultural conservatives who shall be considered are the following: Russell Kirk, perhaps the leading intellectual conservative in America, and author of twenty-five books, who Evans says "has done more than any other single individual to restore the term 'conservative' to the vocabulary of American scholarship"[8] (Kirk's 1953 book, *The Conservative Mind*, which has gone through seven editions, "dramatically catalyzed the emergence of the conservative intellectual movement", according to Nash)[9]; Willmoore Kendall, Yale and University of Dallas political scientist, one-time extreme leftist, and a man well-known for his difficult and contentious character who became a leading figure in postwar conservative circles; the late John Courtney Murray, S.J., well-known Catholic theologian and Vatican II *peritus* whose ideas on religious liberty were said to be an inspiration for the Council's document *Dignitatis Humanae* (*Declaration on Religious Liberty*); and John Eidsmoe, an increasingly well-known evangelical Protestant writer on government and law who is also a law professor.

These three writers will give us a good picture of the different areas of emphasis within "cultural conservatism" (i.e., avowedly theologically-based political ideas from the two great branches of Christianity and ideas which do not have such an origin, but are based on philosophical or other formulations not directly grounded in Revelation). The works of Kirk's that have been selected for this study are *The Conservative Mind*,[10] *A Program for Conservatives*,[11] and an article he published in *Modern Age* in 1981 entitled "Libertarians: the Chirping Sectaries."[12] Kendall's main longer work, *The Conservative Affirmation*,[13] will be a source, as will Murray's and Eidsmoe's main political works, *We Hold These Truths: Catholic Reflections on the American Proposition*[14] and *God and Caesar: Biblical Faith and Political Action*,[15] respectively.

The second grouping within conservatism that will be considered is the "fusionists." They accept many of the positions and perspectives of the cultural conservatives, but are less concerned about the stress on tradition and more eager to stress the need for sound general philosophical/metaphysical principles, the importance of individual freedom, and the limited role of the state.[16] The thinker who, by far, is most closely identified with this particular grouping is the late Frank S. Meyer, another one-time radical who became a well-known figure in conservative intellectual circles in the 1950s and 1960s. We here examine his major work, *In Defense of Freedom* (which carries the subtitle *A Conservative Credo*).[17]

The next grouping that will be considered are the economic libertarians. Unlike Evans, we omit the general libertarians, or what he calls the "extreme libertarians" and related writers (e.g., the Ayn Rands and Murray Rothbards). This is because the general libertarians do not seem to have been a part of the postwar conservative mainstream.[18] Indeed, this element seems closer to the far left than to conservatism at times.[19]

The economic libertarians *are* part of the conservative mainstream, however.[20] Evans says the following about the "free-market economist" libertarians (as he calls them): "the[ir] major preoccupation is with personal liberty as such, with limitations on the state, and with the deleterious social consequences of governmental intervention. A chief concern. . .is the danger of state intrusion in matters of economics."[21] Some of the leading names associated with this grouping have been Ludwig von Mises, Friedrich Hayek, Wilhelm Roepke (all Europeans who either lived in or had a long association with the U.S.), and the man whose thought we examine primarily, Nobel Prize-winning economist Milton Friedman. Friedman's leading work, *Capitalism and Freedom*,[22] which he wrote with the assistance of his wife Rose D. Friedman, is our source here. Also, although he is not an American, some brief attention will be given to Roepke's *A Humane Economy*[23] because he has been influential in American conservative circles and because it will give a fuller, broader picture of the social outlook of these economic libertarians. (Parenthetically, it should just be pointed out that what puts these economic libertarians in the mainstream and the "extreme libertarians" out of it is that, while both share the views noted just above by Evans, the latter exhibit also "an active hostility toward conservative and religious philosophic themes."[24])

There are three other groupings we shall examine which are not discussed by Evans.[25] Of these, only two are additional distinct perspectives within contemporary American conservatism. These are the "neoconservatives" and the "new right."[26] (These groupings are no doubt not mentioned by Evans because they had not yet appeared at the time he wrote his article in 1971.[27]) The other grouping is not a distinct perspective but should be included, we believe, to gain a more complete picture of what conservatism stands for. This is the viewpoint of active conservatives in national politics, as discerned from their leading spokesman who have reflected in their own right on conservative political philosophy. (It is additionally appropriate to do this because a number of the liberal sources examined were people in active political life.)

Neoconservatism, first of all, emerged in the late 1960s and the 1970s and most of its early key figures were formerly on the left.[28] The "godfather" of neoconservatism, Irving Kristol, whose writings we examine here as representative of its overall perspective, describes neoconservatism as having "no lingering hostility" to the welfare state in the area of social and economic policy, but seeks to eliminate its "paternalistic orientation" and remake it along the lines of a " 'social insurance state' that provides the social and economic security a modern citizenry demands while minimizing governmental intrusion into individual liberties."[29] Following the pre-modern perspective, they see "politics

[as] always tak[ing] some degree of priority over economics," even in foreign policy where national interest and aspirations must take precedence.[30]

Neoconservatism believes that human nature is not perfectible, so men need social restraints. It also tends to believe, however, that the economy should be subject to less social or governmental restraint, however, because "within limits, the notion of the 'hidden hand' has its uses in the marketplace."[31] This brief discussion, given to provide a definition of neoconservatism, will serve as the basis for our more in-depth discussion of it in the rest of this chapter. Kristol's main work—at least the one which gives us the most comprehensive insight into his thought—is probably *Reflections of a Neoconservative*,[32] which is the one we focus on here. It is a compilation of his essays over the years.

The new right did not grow from intellectual roots, but is a "populist movement" comprised, most typically, of conservative Catholics and evangelical Protestants,[33] who have reacted especially against "the concrete breakdown of the community." In the parlance of the post-1970 period, this phase has come to mean the "social issues": the disintegration of and state interference in the family, the increase in crime, pornography, abortion on demand, the "drug culture," "gay rights" (which involves the carving out of special legal privileges for homosexuals with the aim of making sodomy a morally and socially acceptable behavior), and the secularizing of the public schools and society generally. The new right has developed a general dislike of the secular welfare state and the bureaucratization that is part of it because it sees it as eroding principles it treasures, such as self-reliant individualism. They want to secure individual rights, but realize that this must be done within a social context.[34]

There has been quite a range of people and groups within the new right, from Rev. Jerry Falwell's Moral Majority (now defunct, which had a base built substantially on an evangelical Protestant element) to such long-time conservative activists and political action committee (PAC) leaders as Richard Viguerie and Howard Phillips, to intellectual conservative and capitalism proponent George Gilder. As the sources for our examination of the new right here, we have chosen a couple of works compiled by the Free Congress Research and Education Foundation, a leading Washington D.C. "think tank" identified with the new right and headed by a generally acknowledged new right leader, Paul M. Weyrich. We have done this because we believe Free Congress is a good representative of the various elements in this new right grouping.[35] These works are Future 21: *Directions for America in the 21st Century*,[36] edited by Weyrich and Connaught Marshner, and *Cultural Conservatism: Toward a New National Agenda*.[37]

(In spite of the name and the fact that "cultural conservatism," as defined in the latter book, says it has "intellectual roots" in two of the Russell Kirk books we are examining in this chapter, and the fact that Kirk endorses this new effort to promote such "cultural conservatism," it is surely correct to include the latter book in the new right grouping and not in what we have called "cultural conservatism."[38] This is because it is associated with new right figures and was put out by the Free Congress Foundation—which houses the Institute for Cultural Conservatism, set up to promote the ideas contained in the book—and because it is much more programmatically-oriented than the thinkers in our cultural conservative grouping are. Indeed, the book notes that "[c]ultural conservatism has other roots in recent American experience. These...include the New Right and the Religious Right.")[39]

We shall not cover any writers from the so-called "Religious Right" because its thought—the thought of much of the more directly and distinctively religious element of the new right—is seen in Eidsmoe's book which is best placed in our "cultural conservative" category.

Finally, two books by active political conservatives are considered: former Senator Barry M. Goldwater's well-known *The Conscience of a Conservative*[40] and an anthology of essays on different national issues by conservative Republican members of the U.S. House of Representatives entitled *Liberal Cliches and Conservative Solutions* (edited by Rep. Philip M. Crane of Illinois).[41] Goldwater, from Arizona, was, of course, the 1964 Republican presidential candidate and the man generally viewed as the political embodiment of conservatism from the early 1960s until the emergence of Ronald Reagan as a national figure fifteen years later. In selecting these two works, we have been able to get, to some extent at least, an overview of the ideas of active political conservatives on fundamental political questions over the past generation. The Goldwater book, we believe, pretty well captures the conservative outlook during the 1960s and into the 1970s. (It was first published in 1960 and went through many printings into the early 1970s. This latter point and the fact that his 1970 book, *The Conscience of a Majority*,[42] reveals no basic changes in the political perspective of the previous book, make one think that it represents well the views of self-identified conservatives in politics well into the 1970s.) The Crane book gives a good picture of the thinking of conservative politicians from the late 1970s to the present.

As mentioned, we believe it is desirable to examine the thinking of this group because some of the liberal spokesmen we looked at were most noted for being active political figures. Space precludes our speaking in great detail about each grouping's or perspective's thinking on each of the five areas focused on. What is done is simply to take a small number of passages from the writings of our representative figures which give us a good idea of each grouping's views about each area. Then, a conclusion is drawn about the view of contemporary American conservatism *overall* for that area, and a comparison with Catholic teaching made. Within each area, the views of each conservative grouping are stated *first*, before we move to the conclusion and the comparison. We have just introduced, of course, the broad positions that distinguish these groupings; in the remainder of the chapter we will focus on them more thoroughly and closely. Although the works above are the sources used, occasionally citations from other works by the above authors will appear.

I. The General Purposes of Government

The Cultural Conservatives. There seems to be a measure of ambiguity in the role of government put forth in the writing of the cultural conservatives. On the one hand, they state that a sharply limited role is appropriate. Russell Kirk says, for example, that "[t]he primary function of government. . .is to keep the peace: by repelling foreign enemies, by maintaining the bed of justice domestically"; securing order, "the first need of all," is paramount.[43] The theologically-based cultural conservatives concur. Eidsmoe says the following: "God established human government—to restrain sin and to organize society." The former involves "the authority to restrain and punish crime;" the latter is needed because "[e]ven if man had no sin nature, he would need leadership and organization."[44]

Cultural conservatives argue that government may not run a planned economy or a socialized or communized economy (i.e., may not have too great of a role in economic life.)[45] They oppose anything resembling a collectivized social welfare state (i.e., centrally-controlled government welfare programs which compel citizens to pay for or take part in them).[46] They do not favor government fashioning a program specifically for the restoring of "the ethical system and the religious sanction" as a means of social control. Among their objections are that these must always be viewed as worthy in and of themselves, not as mere instruments;[47] that the Bible does not assign such a role to the state;[48] and that religious teaching cannot be applied to political life without considerations of prudence.[49]

In eschewing the notion of such a governmental program, they are *not* saying, of course, that God's law is not to be the basis for political and social order.[50] Further, they say that governmental power by its nature must be limited; they insist that this is especially mandated by our American tradition.

As Willmoore Kendall states, the federal or national government in the U.S. was "constitutionally excluded from concern with certain major spheres of human endeavor."[51] Murray echoes this thinking about political society being natural and necessary for man—stressing that nature as understood by reason (i.e., the natural law) holds this—and about it being limited (which he says is both dictated by nature and the American tradition, which is grounded in natural law).[52] One major limiting factor in the natural law, which he mentions, is the principle of subsidiarity—discussed in previous chapters—which undergirds

American federalism.[53] The further specific ways in which Murray says that the state is limited is that its power to regulate and sanction can touch only activities, not ideas. Even when it comes to activities, its reach is not unlimited. A well-ordered state is constantly struggling to maintain a balanced policy of regulating or restricting those human activities that are more private by nature (e.g., those involving sex or the reading of erotically-oriented materials), realizing that social order and health must be protected but also realizing that legitimate freedom cannot be intruded upon lest perhaps greater evils develop.[54]

On the other hand, the cultural conservative writings in places state or suggest a much broader role for government. "Organizing society" may well demand considerable governmental initiative and assumption of responsibility. The same is true even with "maintaining the bed of justice" (Kirk also uses the terminology of "restrain[ing] the passionate and the unjust").[55] Another point Kirk makes about the role of government suggests that, contrary to the above, the cultural conservative really does seek to have the state strengthen "the ethical system and the religious sanction":

> The conservative finds that the state is ordained of God. In Burke's phrases, "He who gave us our nature to be perfected by our virtue, willed also the necessary means of its perfection.—He willed therefore the state. . .[56]

The way Kirk reconciles this seeming inconsistency is to say that "the state" and "government" are not the same thing. *Government* is needed to satisfy human wants, among the more important of which is—Kirk again quotes Edmund Burke—"'a sufficient restraint on their [men's] passions.'"[57] This seems to be more in line with the more restrictive view of government mentioned above.

Kirk is surely correct that there is a distinction between "the state" and "government." As Fr. Higgins tells us, the former is the unity among a people derived from a common social bond and a common authority, the latter is the "officially accepted and legitimate person, individual or moral, to whom the function of actual sovereignty is entrusted."[58] It is not clear, however, that this general-specific distinction between the two is precisely the one Kirk draws; even if it is, however, the particular government is just the one set up to carry out the purposes of the state. The state possesses political authority (i.e., "the legitimate power to direct and compel its members to co-operate toward the attainment of the common public good").[59] Thus we must say that, for all practical purposes, the purposes of the state and of government are the same. (Indeed, we are treating the terms as interchangeable in this section of the chapter.) Moreover, even if Kirk seeks to draw a further distinction, the supposedly more limited task of *government* of restraining human passions in practice might require its taking on substantial responsibilities.

Actually, Murray does not believe it necessary to make any such distinction. He says that the "state" has an "ethical...function"; its laws have an "educative character" which is "directive of man to 'the virtuous life.'" It thus must seek to promote the common good in the fullest sense of the word—the good of the community and of the individuals in it—"and not simply be protective of particular interests."[60]

We must say, then, that the cultural conservatives want government, in at least some sense, to help shape human virtue. They do not limit its role just to restraining certain behaviors.

Also, while the cultural conservatives do not favor programs like Social Security—because of its coercive, centralized, and collectivist nature—they do not object to the principle behind it. As Kirk puts it, "modern industrial society has grave cause for restoring economic security...to the mass of men; and doubtless government is sometimes the most convenient instrument."[61] He even indicates that the government should plan on supporting people who failed to save when they should have, when they finally reach "their hour of need." However, we should not "compel" them to save as our present Social Security system, in effect, does.[62]

So, it must be said that the cultural conservatives see government as having a definite social welfare function, depending on how it is done. Murray indicates that this social welfare function of government (at least of affluent nations like the U.S.) reaches beyond our borders. He suggests that our foreign aid program should provide assistance for basically altruistic reasons—because people need it, not just because it will further foreign policy or geopolitical objectives.[63] Other cultural conservatives might not agree with this.

In summation, the cultural conservatives favor a basically limited government and prefer that whatever governmental activity is carried on be done, if possible, in a more localized fashion. Government's primary task is negative—to restrain both foreign and domestic enemies of order—but it has a positive function as well. Although wary of government programs specifically aimed at promoting virtue, they believe that contributing to the development of individual virtue, in some fashion, is clearly within goverment's purpose. Government can also rightfully be relied on to insure the social and economic welfare of its citizens, even if there are limits to its use of coercion and to its authority to actually run economic enterprises.

The Fusionists. The fusionists, per Frank S. Meyer, also say that the state is limited. It has only two basic functions (he calls them "natural" functions, so he sees them as derived from the very nature of what the state is): to maintain order while at the same guaranteeing to each person in its area of government the maximum liberty possible to him short of his interference with the liberty of other persons."[64] Meyer also states this somewhat differently and more precisely: the state "protect[s] the rights of citizens against violent or fraudulent assault and. . .[it is] judge in conflicts of right with right. It has a further third function, which is another aspect of the first...to protect its citizens from assault by foreign powers."[65] The fusionist view about the purposes of government reflects its determined effort to reconcile the problems of freedom and order, which it sees as the central political problem.

Freedom is of central importance to the fusionist—his view of freedom will be discussed in more detail later in this chapter—so much so that Meyer says that the "criteria" by which the state and *all* human institutions should be judged is "their adequacy. . .to the achievement of the best possible circumstances in which human beings may work out their destiny."[66] Nevertheless, of course, there must be order lest no one be able to truly act in freedom. He says that the state is "natural," "necessary and inescapable,"[67] but its being evaluated always in light of the aforementioned criteria leads one to wonder how or why this should be. Although he believes the "achievement of virtue" to be "[u]ltimately...the most important of problems," he completely rejects the idea that it is a *political* problem.[68] The state can have no role in *enforcing* virtue—this is not to say it cannot be concerned about it since it is, after all, man's proper end,[69] or perhaps cannot promote it in other ways—because the freedom of the individual means that he must be able to have "control over his destiny" and to be free "to search for and to choose virtue." Otherwise, he "is absorbed into the destiny of society. . .[whose] virtue must be his virtue. . .the central tenet of totalitarianism."[70]

The fusionist somewhat deviates from the natural law ethician's definition of "state" given above: he sees it simply as a "group of men, distinct and separate from other men. . .possessing the monopoly of legal coercive force."[71] It is because of this understanding of the state that it cannot be invested with the power of enforcing virtue. The dangers to the citizens, to their freedom, would simply be too great, even in a democratic political order. By its nature, this kind of state would be characterized by excesses; that is why the state must be limited by its nature.[72]

In short, then, the fusionists believe that the role of government must be restricted to maintaining internal order and providing security from external threats, protecting individual freedom, and acting as a referee in conflicts between citizens.

The Economic Libertarians. The economic libertarians have a similar restrictive view of the role of government, perhaps even more so. Their emphasis is, as noted, on the maintenance of a free market economy, where individual free choice is preeminent. This is what Milton Friedman says about government:

The existence of a free market does not of course eliminate the need for government. On the contrary, government is essential both as a forum for determining the "rules of the game" and as an umpire to interpret and enforce the rules decided on.[73]

He also says, elaborating on the latter purpose and adding an additional obvious aspect, that "protection of the individual and the nation from coercion...prevents exclusive reliance on individual action through the market."[74]

The sum total of the activities this would involve are listed by him: maintaining law and order, defining property rights and providing a means to modify them and other "rules of the economic game," adjudicating disputes regarding the rules, enforcing contracts, promoting economic competition, providing a solid framework for monetary control, countering "technical monopolies" and serious "neighborhood effects" (such as pollution), and supplementing private charity and the family in protecting people who are "irresponsible" (such as children and the insane).[75] The latter would include supporting such policy as the giving of subsidies to parents for their children's schooling.[76] These are limited functions, perhaps not as limited as the fusionist perspective, however. (This judgment is made on the basis that the above cataloging seems to suggest both a very limited social welfare function and some degree of government involvement in the economy—to insure the functioning of a truly free market—that is not found in Meyer's discussion.) Like the fusionists, the economic libertarians seem to see government as something which, while necessary for certain functions, is essentially a threat to the freedom of people, an inevitable adversary to be kept at a distance. Friedman goes so far as to say that relying on government "tends to strain the social cohesion essential for a stable society" (quite a damning indictment). Thus, it should be turned to "only on a limited range of issues."[77] The economic libertarians' underlying view of freedom invites the same observation as that of the fusionists: they see an "invisible hand" motivating free men to virtue (although they are not so ready to spell out the acquiring of virtue as man's proper end).

.   One cannot so readily make the same observation about Wilhelm Roepke. He asserts that any society, including one with a free market, needs a solid spiritual and ethical base, already in place, and a leading group of virtuous citizens—a natural aristocracy—to be active in an on-going way as a guiding light for social ethics, public spirit, and high standards of taste. As far as the welfare state and social security are concerned, he is close to the cultural conservatives and more supportive of them in principle than of economic libertarians like Friedman. He supports a governmental role in this area, but prefers voluntary private efforts. If government is to be involved it must be in a decentralized manner, generally non-coercive, and in a way that does not become on-going for the individual or the normal form of satisfying his needs.[78]

In sum, then, the economic libertarians see a minimal role for government, but betray a willingness to let government play some limited role in the economy and even in social welfare.

The Neoconservatives. Like the other versions of contemporary American conservatism examined so far, neoconservatism favors limited government. Unlike the others, however (as already suggested), it is less inhibited in supporting a positive role for government in social welfare matters. In taking this position, it insists that it is just taking account, as must be done, of the desires of modern Western man. As mentioned, it strongly promotes the free market economy believing that the "hidden" or "invisible hand" has its place, at least within limits. Just as with social welfare, government has some role with respect to the functioning of the economy. As Irving Kristol states: "In economic and social policy. . .[neoconservatism] seeks not to dismantle the welfare state in the name of free-market economics but. . .[to] mak[e] it over" into the "social insurance"-type state of the sort demanded by "a modern citizenry," which can be done while preserving individual liberties.[79]

Neoconservatism is more sanguine about the possibility of success in accomplishing the latter than the other types of conservatism. There is no question that neoconservatism supports the other very basic purposes of government mentioned by each of the other types discussed; it is apparent that its difference is that it goes beyond them in its acceptance of government's social welfare role and, probably, its role in the economy. Moreover, Kristol's criticisms of a cultural "liberation," of the freeing of the individual from social constraints, and of the "hidden hand" working in areas other than economics; his belief that the "destiny" of the political order "is finally determined by the capacity of its citizenry to govern its passions"[80]; and his acknowledgement of his being influenced by political philosopher Leo Strauss[81] all make one think that the neoconservatives would differ from the above groupings, including the cultural conservatives, in one further respect: they would favor government acting to promote, even enforce, virtue.

Finally, the neoconservatives go out of their way to stress government's role—speaking here specifically of the U.S. government, as an economically and militarily powerful nation—not only to provide security to its people from external threats—a "myopic national security"—but to plan an active role as a world power, pursuing its interests around the globe.[82]

The New Right. A combination of general statements and principles and policy ideas from our two new right sources enables us to determine its thinking about the role of government. (Policy ideas are necessary to consult here because, although we generally ignore them in this chapter to take them up in the next, they make up a substantial portion of at least one of the books.)

The new right tells us that government's "tasks and duties" at all levels include not only helping "protect individuals against risks imposed against their will by others" and "upholding public order but also promoting the general welfare and the common good." Government can and must be limited in spite of this, however, and this is especially done through subsidiarity or federalism and reliance on mediating institutions.[83] They say they "generally prefer the free market to governmental action" because it is usually more effective at addressing needs. Government (preferably local government) can and must enter the picture when the market would not be effective, or would not normally be appropriate (e.g., police functions), or would yield "excessively cruel" results.[84]

As with Roepke, the new right says that the market works properly only if certain preconditions exist (i.e., "a community of values" must be in place) and government must help foster this.[85] They state that they favor a "governmental activism" which "would seldom take the form of legislation or massive spending," but "would be leading by example and using the government's 'bully pulpit'" especially "to point out the virtues of our cultural traditions" (in the manner, say, of a William J. Bennett, President Reagan's second Secretary of Education). They want government to respect and acknowledge the value of religion and to work with religious organizations for socially important purposes. Where they propose legislation, it mostly is to reform Federal government structures or practices or to promote "[e]mpowerment—providing people the means with which they can solve their own problems."[86]

At one place in the book *Cultural Conservatism: Toward a New National Agenda,* a "Cultural Conservative [i.e., "new right", as we are using the terms here] Bill of Rights" appears. It lists a number of "cultural rights" which give us a further insight into the new right's view of government: "the right to a government that respects traditional values...in its actions as well as its words"; "the right to active government support of the family"; "the right to an education...[and] a government that understands...[that] education...is important [because] it is the only means by which the culture can continue itself generation after generation...[it] is more likely to perform its cultural duties when it is controlled by parents than...by a central state apparatus"; "the right to effective protection against crime...[by] government"; "the right not to be confronted with pornography"; and "the right to assistance in the preservation of our communities."[87]

Upon examining new right policy proposals, one finds that they essentially go along with the general statements of government's purpose above— i.e., they support government "giving example" or encouraging or "goading on" certain types of actions—but some are different and give us a further picture of their view of government. For instance, they propose that as condition of receiving federal funds, that colleges and universities "should be required to include a core curriculum reflecting a classical education in their undergraduate program" and that public school districts not use textbooks with a bias against religion (in spite of their "Bill of Rights", then, they do not want *parental* control of education exclusively—they prefer some governmental control); they favor government (including the federal government) spending to help public housing residents buy their own homes, and to establish education vouchers;[88] and they favor restricting access, to at least some extent, to divorce and marriage (in order "to ensure reasonable fitness" for it and to hold down the number of divorces).[89] The restrictions here are seen as justified because the state must bear certain burdens and costs because of divorce.

We can see from these proposals that the new right believes it appropriate, in certain cases, for government to fund and to use coercion for desirable social and cultural purposes. Their *general* desire to have a limited, noncoercive government puts them in agreement with the other conservative groupings. Their desire to have, concommitantly, a generally *active* government makes them like the cultural conservatives and the neoconservatives. In their greater willingness to use coercion, the new right is really close only to the neoconservatives, but it is probably accurate to say they support the notion of the welfare state less than the neoconservatives.

What conclusions, then, can we make about the new right's view of the role of government? For them, it clearly has a positive role and not just a negative one, and this positive role is especially focused on restoring a solid moral and cultural situation ("traditional values"), even by coercively enforcing moral norms. They also want government to actively support and help strengthen the basic units of society, such as the family and local communities and their constituent parts, and to help struggling people to help themselves. Government clearly has a social welfare role, especially in helping the needy, but the preference is to have private institutions carry this out and the aim is to serve people only until they can achieve self-sufficiency.[90] The new right concedes a larger role for government than perhaps any other grouping except the neoconservatives, but, like all the others, at the same time it wants to try to limit government and (like all but possibly the neoconservatives) is suspicious of it.

Active Political Conservatives. The active political conservatives examined do not have, as would be expected, the depth to their thought that we see with major conservative scholars. Their discussion is on a much more basic level, sometimes sounding simply like a speech they might make. Their approach is essentially empirical, discussing why certain policies have failed and why others might succeed, and giving a sprinkling of statistics and references; they seldom provide broad, profound statements of political philosophy. Nevertheless, there are points made that demonstrate a definite, if not thoroughly articulated or comprehensively developed, political perspective. For the most part, the active political conservatives do not really challenge the basic conception about the role of government prevalent in the American political order since 1933, but dispute the degree to which it has expanded and extended itself and the precise aims it has sought (i.e., they support a social welfare role for government, a notion of government that goes beyond simply maintaining order, insuring liberty, and acting as a referee).

Goldwater's book contains a number of key statements about government's role, even while he focuses many of them specifically on the role of the *federal* government. Like many active political conservatives (and, as we have seen, intellectual conservatives), he favors handling matters at lower levels of government. In his political career, he particularly stressed states' rights, the notion, supported by the Tenth Amendment to the Constitution, that matters not specifically delegated to the federal or national government by the document were reserved to the states.[91] This, in his judgment, included certain matters affecting blacks' civil rights, such as whether states should be required to integrate their schools. He objected to the notion that the federal government had any role in education at all, including integration. More broadly, on the subject of civil rights, he believed that not every basic natural law-based right or "human right" was a civil (i.e., legally-protected) right. It could not be made into one by judicial action, but only by the common law, statute, or the Constitution.[92]

As mentioned, the active political conservatives accept government's social welfare role to some extent. On a subject like federal aid to education, Goldwater, in 1960, took what was perhaps an extreme position in opposing it entirely.[93] Even today, this group generally is not enthusiastic about federal involvement in education and seeks to limit it. Their view about the federal social welfare role, if we can judge from their actions in Congress over time, seems not to be substantially different from that of the new right: programs should be oriented to self-help and people should not be allowed to become dependent on government in the long term. The way they see people really being helped in the long-run is through the free market. As one of the Congressmen in the Crane anthology states: "Instead of just giving fish to the needy, they should be taught how and given an opportunity to catch their own fish." The way government can best aid the free market in doing this is simply to let it "continue creating jobs by minimizing. . .its [government's] interference."[94]

As far as government regulation of the economy generally is concerned, this group essentially opposes it like the other conservative groupings. Its rhetoric against it, however, is perhaps most like what would be expected of the most anti-government ones: the fusionists and economic libertarians. It sees it as simply resulting in bloated, "elitist" Washington bureaucracies.[95] Government has the role of providing a good economic environment for the free market to flourish in, but not to control or tightly regulate the economy. This seems in part what conservative politicians mean when they say, as the Congressman above does (in line with the new right), "the role of government" is "more limited" than the liberals see it, "though not necessarily less active."[96]

It seems that another part of what is meant by this (also in line with the new right) is the promotion of solid morality and good family life, especially by advocacy and noncoercive means.[97] The active political conservatives place perhaps their strongest stress on the most fundamental role of government: to defend against foreign adversaries. As another of the Congressmen in Crane's book states: there is a need "for a military policy second to none."[98] On the matter of the American role in the world generally, they believed the U.S. should play a major role in defending, militarily and politically, non-Communist nations from Communist take-over or influence and, at least when Goldwater's book was published, to even take prudent steps to reverse Communist control where it existed. They are reluctant, however, to support American economic aid to help improve the domestic welfare of foreign nations. As Goldwater starkly put it: "The American government does not have the right, much less the obligation, to try to promote the economic and social welfare of foreign peoples." Accordingly, they supported the foreign aid program mostly to promote American Cold War objectives.[99]

The Conservative Perspective Overall on the Purposes of Government. From our above examination of the various perspectives within conservatism, we must now come to some overall conclusion or consensus, if you will, about conservatism's view about the role of government. We will then evaluate it in light of papal teaching.

The following statement seems to be a fair summation of the conservative view: All the conservative groupings want limited government. They stress most the most basic functions of government: to defend the state, maintain order, punish crime, and preserve liberties. On balance, however, conservatism—thanks largely to the views of the cultural conservatives, new right, and neoconservatives—wants to go beyond a minimal role for government, but prefers that wherever possible, governmental functions be carried out more on a local or state level. It wants government to assume some social welfare role, while not generally wanting to be coercive. It dislikes the massive modern welfare state. Conservatives also favor limited governmental control over economic matters. They believe the governmental role should be primarily to help the free market work better and to promote equal opportunity and self-help. Also, on balance, they want government to promote morality—"traditional morality" or that implicitly based on the natural law—but more by example and encouragement than coercion.

Conservatives do not seem to give any particular emphasis to the state having a role to promote or foster religion. Most of the groupings would agree that the laws and life of the state should embody religious principles (i.e., Judeo-Christian principles in a Western state like the U.S.) and that the state should respect religious groups and not interfere with their efforts. Only the new right wants the state to play a definite, open role in emphasizing the value of religion, but even their ideas are mildly expressed. Conservatism's view toward religion appears based on the fact that it simply sees religion as the churches', not the state's, function, and that promoting religion is incompatible (in its view) with the notion of a limited state. They also believe that a positive state promotion of religion would threaten individual freedom. Finally, conservatism seems to acknowledge virtually no role for the state in the area of promoting international welfare, except possibly to further its own objectives (which may be entirely good ones, like stopping communism).

Evaluation of Conservatism's View of the Purposes of Government in Light of Papal Teaching

How do the above perspectives square with Catholic teaching? Certainly the popes stress limited government: e.g., freedom for individuals and families, the state being limited in what it can do by the natural law, and the principle of subsidiarity. On these points, conservatism compares very favorably. Its stress on the most basic functions of government, such as defense, the maintenance of order, and insuring that everyone's rights be respected corresponds with points made in encyclicals like *Rerum Novarum* and *Pacem in Terris*. As the next section makes clear, conservatism stresses the maintenance of the common good—"public well-being and private prosperity," in the words of *Rerum Novarum*—and the various aspects of its thought seem to generally advance this (i.e., it is concerned about morality, good family life, respect for religion, general material benefits—all factors that *Rerum Novarum* says advance the common good). It will be recalled that *Pacem in Terris* says that the common good involves both the material and spiritual well-being of the citizenry; also, the classic definition of the common good involves both the promotion of the welfare of the community and every individual.[100]

On the other hand, keeping this definition in mind, it is unclear exactly how far conservatism actually *goes* in advancing the common good. This is because, as noted, while it supports the rights of religious groups and respects the contributions of religion, it does not go far in promoting it. The emphasis of many of its groupings on economic matters (the cultural conservatives and the new right are an exceptions; the neoconservatives, despite their saying the political takes precedence over the economic, would be included among the groupings stressing the economic because of their extolling of the "invisible hand"), the clearly stated preference of all of them for the free market (plus the fact that *morality* is not even stressed—at least not as a public concern—by the fusionists and the economic libertarians) makes one think that material concerns, on balance, come out ahead of moral and spiritual ones. The latter certainly do receive some attention, however, and are, in fact, stressed more than with liberalism. Moreover, they are stressed as essential in and of themselves without having essentially a material concern behind them (as with liberalism). An additional problem results from the conservative stress on economic freedom and on such a substantial degree of freedom generally. This leads one to think that maybe conservatism downplays the *community* side of the common good. (The cultural conservatives are perhaps the exception here; writers like Kirk have gone out of their way to describe community as something intrinsically and utterly important to man.)[101]

Part of the promotion of the spiritual well-being of man involves, according to the popes, promoting the individual's dignity and helping him to be a *better* person. We noted that both the old and new liberalisms did not and do not want to be involved in making men better. Here conservatism—typified especially by the cultural conservatives, new right, and neoconservatives—definitely is closer to Catholic teaching in the latter's concern about promoting morality (which by definition involves seeking to make men better) and helping make men virtuous. The other conservative groupings which do not want to involve government in this area are nonetheless concerned that morality and virtue be furthered in some private way (economic libertarians like Friedman *may* be considered an exception here).

The social welfare role that conservatism assigns to government and its willingness to let government act to correct problems caused by the free market, at least to some extent, would be welcomed by the popes. Its unwillingness to let such government action be more than limited, however, would be a point of some difference. First, conservatism's stress on the market is laudable from the point of view of the Church, to the extent that she favors individual economic initiative. Second, its support, by and large, for the governmental social welfare role (with the particular caveat that it not be coercive) accords with Church teaching. The Church does not say that such a function necessarily has to be carried out coercively, like U.S. Social Security (which people must pay taxes to support). While it may be true that conservatism (because of its pro-market, pro-economic freedom emphasis) may at times have been lax in acknowledging that individuals sometimes need assistance from the community and that private sources cannot always provide it, it supports, in principle at least, a social welfare function for the state (which the popes call for).

We shall wait until our consideration of conservatism's specific policy proposals in the next chapter before determining if it supports such specific elements of this role as providing unemployment and old-age insurance and relief (which are supported by the popes). Enough has been stated, however, to indicate that it would be reluctant to concede to the state the kind of on-going, possibly substantial role suggested by the popes (although, again, the latter do not endorse the activities of the modern, bureaucratic, centralized Western welfare state with its ignoring of subsidiarity).

On state activity with respect to the economy on other points, what we have said about conservatism seems to indicate that it would not support papal teaching. The popes support for the state's acting to preserve an appropriate balance between the sectors of the economy (by providing credit and insurance and addressing prices, etc., and providing for "overall planning" to avoid unemployment) go well beyond what conservatism finds acceptable. In fact, any kind of a government planning role in economics is something from which the conservative seems to instinctively recoil. More generally, while conservatives would support, in principle, the state helping secure social justice and social charity, their reluctance to have it actively promote morality and their emphasis on the free market suggest they would not be happy with the state actively and vigorously implementing these functions.

Finally, the conservatives also reveal a blind spot with regard to the Church's teaching in recognizing the role of rich nations like the U.S. to provide economic and developmental assistance to poorer nations (irrespective of whether this aid benefits the former or helps promote their policies). This further suggests that conservatism tends to be too nationalistic and is inadequately concerned about, or at least unwilling to pursue on the level of governmental policy, efforts at world brotherhood.[102] Conservatism is definitely further from the Church than both versions of liberalism on this point, although, as we shall see, on one dimension of the international question (the view about communism) it is definitely closer to Church teaching than either the new liberalism, or the old.

II. God, Religion, and the Natural Law as the Basis of the Political Order

The Cultural Conservatives. In the cultural conservative writings being surveyed, there are many references to the centrality of God, religion and the natural law in the political order. We shall be able to note only a few of them. Kirk tells us that "[p]olitical problems, at bottom, are religious and moral problems."[103] As already noted, he says that the state is "ordained of God." We also saw his belief that there is a need for spiritual restoration, *for its own sake,* and he makes clear that if faith in God, and certain other factors are lacking, the state will grow oppressive.[104] Kirk even insists that the role of Providence must be acknowledged when change, which is inevitable, occurs in society (this seems to be a call for recognizing that God has a plan for individual societies).[105] This follows from his basic belief that "[o]ur real wants. . .are those of the spirit."[106] Kirk's comments are a strong endorsement of the notion that God must be at the basis of the political order.

Not surprisingly, the same idea is conveyed by the religious wing of the cultural conservatives. We saw this in the comments of Eidsmoe already discussed. We also see it in the closing statement in Murray's book in which he says that the "dynamic order of reason in man. . .has its origin and sanction in an eternal order of reason whose fulfillment is the object of God's magestic will"[107] and in another place where he approvingly notes the Supreme Court's one-time position that "[w]e are a religious people whose institutions presuppose a Supreme Being."[108] Kendall is not quite so direct about this, but he speaks very favorably about the Great Tradition of political philosophy of the West that was based on Greek philosophy, the teachings of the Bible, and "the rapidly-developing corpus of Christian theology." The American Founding Fathers essentially emerged from this tradition.[109]

Kirk's views about the natural law are also unmistakable. He says that "the essence of social conservatism is preservation of the *ancient moral traditions of humanity*."[110] He insists that, for both "the religious man" and "the philosopher," a notion of a "*just society*" governs.[111] He also speaks of "*ancient beliefs and customs*," "*the natural world*," and "*the immortal spark in. . .[one's] fellow men*."[112] We previously saw that Kirk includes among the purposes of government "maintaining *the bed of justice* domestically" and, although he does not want *government* to do it, speaks of the need to restore "*the ethical system*."[113]

Kendall and Eidsmoe write in a similar way. In his discussion of the "Great Tradition," Kendall speaks about the "'law of nature,' 'law of reason,' 'law of God,' and 'divine law,'" which the Tradition acknowledges as governing all men. For the Tradition, "the true purposes of society. . .[are] those of *justice* and *right*."[114] He indicates, as Kirk does, that conservatives understand that one "cannot talk meaningfully about politics in the absence of the idea of Natural Law. . .a standard of justice to which questions of right and wrong may ultimately be appealed."[115]

Eidsmoe, in spite of his Calvinist background (Calvinists have often seen the standard of nature as a challenge to God), endorses the idea of natural law. He does this by identifying it, as the Catholic Church does, with the "law of God" (which he says is the typical "Christian conservative" position).[116] Like Kirk and Kendall, he says that this law is essential if the state is to remain limited and non-threatening to men.[117]

Murray's whole thesis is that the natural law tradition, developed to its greatest extent in the Catholic medieval world, is the only reasonable basis for political life and, in fact, squarely undergirds the principles of the American Founding.[118]

In short, the principles of the cultural conservatives assert that God, religion, and the natural law must be at the very heart of a political order.

The Fusionists. The belief in the centrality of religious belief and natural law principles for the fusionists is seen in M. Stanton Evans'—who puts himself in this grouping—statement that they hold that "the ends of life must be given axiomatically through religious truth conducted in accordance with the dictates of the higher law."[119] Meyer makes clear in his book that he endorses "the Western and Christian tradition." At one point, in a footnote, he says "that Christianity, which informs Western civilization, is the highest and deepest relationship to the Divine that man can attain, I am. . .certain."[120] He also speaks about the reality of good and evil. He maintains that a sound metaphysics and the "disciplined philosophical establishment of criteria by which political societies should be judged" are crucial. He says there are "absolute truths and absolute values towards which men should direct themselves," and "good ends" that men have a "duty. . .to pursue." He says there is a "moral law [which] remains the same," and contends that "[d]uties and rights both derive from. . .the moral ground of man's nature" and are based in "objective value."[121] This is doubtless an emphatic statement of affirmation of the Christian/natural law framework.

Clearly, too, Meyer wants political society to be structured around natural law principles, even though he does not want men forced to follow them. He says that a truly good political order must both guarantee freedom and, through the persuasive efforts of its "intellectual and moral leaders...maintain the prestige of tradition and reason, and thus...sustain intellectual and moral order throughout society."[122] Even though he says that acting rightly or virtuously must be voluntary, by very necessity it is, to some degree, nevertheless coercive because of the purpose of government partly being to maintain order. The principles of order (essentially laws) must have some moral content, and it is quite apparent that this, for Meyer, would be from the natural law (and perhaps also from the Judeo-Christian tradition). We come to the latter parenthetical conclusion because, although Meyer does not specifically say the political order should be based on God and religion, his emphasis on "the Western and Christian tradition" makes it seem correct. (He observes, for example, that "[t]he Great Commandment...is the cornerstone of the structure of Western moral thought,"[123] and the above indicates that Meyer believed that this is responsible for shaping political society's principles of order).

One point on which there is some divergence between fusionists, such as Meyer, and the popes is on the former's minimalist conception of the state, a conception that is perhaps too limited as far as the natural law is concerned. The fusionists may also downplay the need, stressed by the popes, to have natural law principles permeate the institutions and whole way of life of a society. This is because of their almost exclusive focus on the individual. Meyer, for example, says: "The institution, the association, the community, is neither virtuous nor unvirtuous, and cannot itself inculcate virtue. Only individual persons can do this."[124] While the popes hold it is true that evil issues primarily from the hearts and minds of individuals, they make it clear that the community and institutions can encourage evil. The fusionists seem unaware of the impact of "sinful social structures."

The Economic Libertarians. It is a point such as the one being examined which justifies my decision to consider not only a Friedman—who may be closer to a pure "libertarian"—but also a Roepke in order to get "a fuller, broader picture of the social outlook" of this grouping.

First of all, they have obviously different views of the role of God, religion, and the natural law in the political order. Friedman does not mention God or religion. The thrust of his thought would doubtless indicate that these are strictly up to the individual. As far as the natural law is concerned, he gives us no statement that definitively indicates that he believes it exists or, if he does, that it should be the basis for the norms of political society (or, for that matter, play *any* role in shaping these). In fact, there is considerable evidence that his thought is both positivistic and relativistic. In speaking about property rights, he does mention they stand for "[t]he notion of property, *as it has developed over centuries and as it is embodied in our legal codes*" and that they also embodying "*generally accepted social rules.*"[125] The emphasized phrases could obliquely be referring to natural law. They could also refer, however, to an historical tradition or merely man-made legal and social norms which have become a customary part of Western or American political society over time.

Expressions and examples of Friedman's relativism are: 1) his writing that "bad" and "good" people "may be the same people depending on who is judging them"[126]; 2) his speaking approvingly of how the free market is impervious to the goodness or badness of a thing produced or the moral beliefs of a person producing it (in the case of the latter, he provides the example of a Communist engaged in producing)[127]; 3) his saying that the family is the basic unit of our society (not because God deigned it to be such, as the Church and the sound philosopher hold), but only, "in considerable part," because of "expediency rather than principle"[128]; and 4) his contention—completely in contrast to the papal social encyclicals and in line with the relativistic Enlightenment view—that an "invisible hand" will direct the self-interested efforts of business and labor to desirable ends for society (with the corresponding conclusion that they need not view themselves as having any social responsibility).[129] It seems fair to conclude, then, that natural law is not upheld by Friedman.

Roepke's thinking is, in many ways, opposed to Friedman's. He says that the "most important aspect" for a political and economic order is "the spiritual and moral one." He says that individualism, utilitarianism, and legal positivism "must be counterbalanced by all the imponderables which ultimately are the basis of the nation. . .the immutable standards of natural law, continuity, tradition, historical awareness, love of country. . ."[130] He also says that before people can compete in the market, they must already possess, *inter alia*, "a sense of justice. . . fairness. . .respect for human dignity, firm ethical norms."[131]

Elsewhere, Roepke says that his "picture of man is fashioned by the spiritual heritage of classical and Christian tradition" and that he is "attached to a humanism which is rooted" in this perspective and "regards man as the child and image of God."[132] He also says we err in "thinking only of bread and never of those other things of which the Gospel speaks."[133] It seems fair to conclude then, without making any judgment at this point as to whether Roepke's thinking corresponds in every instance to the ethical mandates of the natural law or the Gospel, that he accepts, in principle, that both are supposed to guide man and the political order.

What the above means is that serious philosophical differences characterize the views of these two leading economic libertarians. When one considers the writings of some of the other leading lights that would be placed in this grouping, such as Ludwig von Mises and Friedrich A. Hayek, a perspective similar to Friedman's is found.[134] This leads us to conclude that, on balance, the economic libertarians do not agree with the Church's teaching that holds that the political order must be *understood* as having its basis—because, in truth, it *does*—in God, religion, and the natural moral law. Roepke is probably not representative of the views of this grouping here, and it does not seem easy to reconcile his views with Friedman's or the others.

The Neoconservatives. Irving Kristol, speaking supportively of the "Anglo-Scottish Enlightenment" thought which he says underlies the American Founding, contends that it had a "respectfulness toward moral beliefs as a part of. . .[our] spiritual heritage." These were "traditional moral values hitherto associated with church and synagogue" that "might become more secular, less theological. . .but would still have the power to 'civilize' the individuals in the new, liberal community."[135] This suggests, essentially, the importance of the natural law background for a civilized political community.

The problems which are indicated by these quotes, however, is first, that it is irrelevant for the neoconservatives whether the principles of the natural law have their origin in God—as opposed to just, say, an ungoverned "nature"—and, second, that they believe these principles retain their force for men even when divorced from religion. This, of course, is opposite of what the Church holds—i.e., that God is Author of the natural law and without Him men will not abide by it for long.[136] Elsewhere, Kristol *does* stress the vitalness of religion when he says, "[n]eoconservatives look upon family and religion as indispensable pillars of a decent society,"[137] but he puts it in the context of a more general statement about the need for "intermediate [i.e., mediating] institutions...[to] reconcile...community with liberty."[138] Thus, it cannot be said that the neoconservatives see religion as truly important *by itself* for the political order or as being at the heart of it. There is also a troublesome uncertainty, prompted especially by the latter quote, as to whether religion acts on the individual merely as something which commands his loyalty and thereby, in a purely natural way, helps secure order in the commonwealth, or whether it also acts supernaturally through grace to order the soul with all the good results that come from this. Interestingly, many of the other sources, both liberal and conservative, tend to speak about religion in this same manner.

We must add a caveat to our conclusion that the neoconservatives advocate the need for the natural law. Kristol does not use the term "natural law" and, although his references in some of the above quotations clearly indicate that there is a transcendent standard of right and wrong, he does not appear to have a good understanding of the highly-developed Christian notion of natural law. Following the Classics which he so admires, he may not even understand standards of natural justice as having the character of law as St. Thomas Aquinas and the Church see them. One gets a sense of this when Kristol discusses "autoerotic activities" in an essay in his book about pornography and obscenity. While stressing its undesirability, he nevertheless says that masturbation is "a perfectly natural autoerotic activity."[139] He seems to betray a somewhat confused notion of "nature" here, seeing what is "natural" as what is commonly done by people instead of what accords with the nature and ends of man.

Overall, it appears correct to conclude that the neoconservatives do see natural law, or at least norms of natural justice, as the basis of the political community. They see God and religion as essential, too (although not necessarily as part of the community's basis or origin and in a way inadequate and unsatisfying from the Church's perspective).

The New Right. The new right literature examined expressly espouses the natural law notion of the Judeo-Christian tradition, making it clear—as the great Catholic philosophers consistently have—that one needs to be neither a Jew nor a Christian to accept it. As Connaught Marshner writes in *Future 21*:

> The natural law is independent of divine revelation, since its first principles are common to mankind as a whole, accessible to reason. The most articulate scholars who have studied and written about the natural law have, however, been Christian, since the teachings of revelation coincide with natural law.[140]

In a similar vein the authors of *Cultural Conservatism: Toward a New National Agenda* write:

> Cultural conservatism [i.e., the new right] is the belief that there is a necessary, unbreakable, and causal relationship between traditional Western, Judeo-Christian values, definitions of right and wrong, ways of thinking and ways of living—the parameters of Western culture—and the secular success of Western societies. . ."[141]

People will be drawn to this perspective, whether Western or not, who believe that "the most basic political issue is the nature of man, and who believe man's nature to be a constant." It "does not exclude the agnostic, the atheist, someone who follows a non-Western religion or philosophy...provided that he shares the basic insight that traditional values are functional values."[142]

It is crystal clear, then, that the new right both accepts the natural law and views it as the very basis of the political order. In fact, they perhaps accept it more specifically in its traditional Western conception as natural *law* than do any of the other conservative groupings.

There is, however, a point about natural law on which the new right deviates from the Church. This is suggested by the latter part of the last quote above, but is spelled out more explicitly when *Cultural Conservatism: Toward a New National Agenda* notes that some will want to view the origin of natural law principles "as purely secular, a matter of what mankind has learned about itself over many generations"[143] and when Mrs. Marshner contends that "[w]ith or without the premise of God, nature does have design and order. . ."[144] Again, it is true that the natural law applies to and can be grasped by all men, believers or not, because it is discernible through human reason irrespective of Revelation—even though existing in a religious framework makes certain of its principles easier for reason to derive. The Church makes clear, however, that God is at the root of it and that, ultimately, there cannot be ethics without God. The criticism here is the same as that directed against neoconservatives.[145]

On the matter of God and religion, the criticism is also the same as that made of the neoconservatives. The new right says that "[o]ur position is pro-religious" ; that "religious belief can be and often is a social force, with objective effects on society's behavior"; and that "religion makes a massive and positive contribution to the well-being of our society."[146] The new right, then, clearly favors religion and wants political society to favor it, but, in light of the positions that we have noted, we must say that they do not see it—at least they do not *say* they do—as absolutely *necessary* for man or as being the very foundation of society. It is possible they are silent about this and that they fail to assert the presence of God behind the natural law because they are trying to

build coalitions in a secular society (it is very clear from *Cultural Conserva-*
tism: Toward a New National Agenda that coalition-building is very much on
the authors' minds[147]). Perhaps their ultimate hope is even to make people more
disposed to religion by getting them first to accept natural law thinking. Nevertheless, one must judge their theory according to the way it is stated; thus, we
believe these conclusions are justified.

Active Political Conservatives. The writings of the active political
conservatives we are considering say very little about the subject of this section. The few indirect references suggest a belief in natural law and even its
importance as a guide for public policy, but the discussion is not so deep or
involved as to address the notion of government being based on it. Usually,
God and religion are not alluded to at all. The absence of any mention of the
latter itself perhaps indicates a secularization of thought. One is led to think that
this group has given this question little thought or that they do not regard it as
important. That is not to argue that they may not be religious themselves, or
believe religion to be important for the individual, or even believe about its role
what the neoconservatives and the new right do, but this is not the same as the
Church's teaching that God and religion are the necessary basis of and essential
to the political order.

As far as the role of the natural law is concerned, Goldwater gives a
nod to it—or at least some version of a theory of it—when he says, "[t]here
may be some rights—'natural, human,' or otherwise—that *should* also be civil
rights" (even though he does not want the courts to just proclaim them as such,
as we noted).[148] He also admits that society should take care of the less fortunate in a way—not relying on the welfare state—"that is conducive to the
spiritual as well as the material well-being of our citizens. . ."[149] In my judgment, the latter is less a statement about religion than about higher principles of
right which, if followed, help make one a better person.

Similar oblique or roundabout references that appear in our other
source are the following. In his Introduction to *Liberal Cliches and Conserva-*
tive Solutions, former Congressman Jack Kemp says that for "[t]he conservative Republicans" contributing to it, "the moral principles of freedom and
democracy are universal truths and dependable guides for all people everywhere."[150] In his chapter on family policy, Congressman Tom Bliley speaks
about the "difference between right and wrong" when discussing sexual activity,
and comments that *"[m]oral neutrality is a myth."*[151]

Both Congressmen are expressing a belief in natural law principles
and both obviously want to see them reflected in political life. Kemp, however,
is not speaking about specific requirements or constraints of the natural law—it
is true that freedom is required by the natural law, but this is a broad thing as
opposed to a particular human behavior called for or forbidden, which is

generally what a *law* does—so much as inclinations that are present in human nature. Further, the popes, as noted, teach that there is no natural law mandate for any particular form of government. If Kemp, in speaking about "the moral principle of democracy" claims it is a "universal truth," he is incorrect. If, on the other hand, he is implying that the political participation of the people in a nation is required and/or universally desired, he is correct. Nevertheless, Kemp affirms his belief in the notion of a universal natural law.

In short, then, the active political conservatives can be said to endorse the natural law as existing and being needed to guide political societies, even though their notion of it is unfocused and unspecific. They do not, however, specifically emphasize that political societies must be built around God and religion.

The Conservative Perspective Overall on God, Religion, and the Natural Law as the Basis of the Political Order. In general, it must be concluded, when putting the various conservative perspectives together, that conservatives per se believe in the natural law and that it should direct political affairs. Only the economic libertarians are not in accord with this, but such a prominent representative of this grouping as Roepke deviates to strongly endorse natural law. Clearly, some of the groupings have a better developed notion of the natural law than others.

As far as God and religion are concerned, most of the perspectives acknowledge their significance and support religion in some way, and, for the most part, conservatism does view them as being absolutely essential to the political order (with God as the foundation on which it is erected).

Evaluation of Conservatism's View About God, Religion, and the Natural Law as the Basis of the Political Order

We have criticized conservatism for diverging from Church teaching in its understanding of the following: the character of natural law, how central/essential it sees religion as being in society, and the almost utilitarian role some conservative groupings see religion as playing. Nevertheless, we must judge conservatism to be not far from the Church. Conservatism is notably closer to the Church on the subject of natural law than with regard to an explicit affirmation of God and religion in the political order. Ultimately, we would judge that cultural conservatism and the new right are closest to the Church on the natural law point, cultural conservatism definitely closest about God and religion, and cultural conservatism closest on both taken together.

III. The Thinking About Freedom

The Cultural Conservatives. Russell Kirk gives us some good general statements about the cultural conservatives' thinking about freedom. He says that "[l]iberty and justice may be established only after order is tolerably secure. . .true freedom can be found only within the framework of a social order. . ."[152] (This explains why he emphasizes the keeping of order as a main purpose of government.) Neither individuals nor political orders can have unlimited freedom. "[T]he conservative. . .knows that people cannot be 'autonomous' without roots or principles" which provide "some sanction. . .and some regular discipline of their intellect." Kirk insists that "[t]he most 'autonomous' persons who ever existed, the Christian gentlemen whom Burke eulogizes, were free" because they were "secure in an order, attached to which were very high privileges and very great duties."[153]

In the political order, Kirk says, "[t]he conservative will not tolerate ravening liberty. . .he knows that those who commence with absolute liberty will end with absolute tyranny." The more sensible idea of liberty holds that genuine rights are "developed slowly and painfully in the civil social order" becoming "sanctioned by prescription."[154] In other words, then, freedom goes hand in hand with duties and means nothing if a strong social order is not present to protect it. Rights—which represent the social order's granting legitimacy to a certain exercise of freedom and acknowledging that it will protect freedom—are not abstractly formulated and grafted on a political society, but, as noted, emerge from its tradition after struggle.

Kirk and Kendall single out some examples of alleged freedoms or the degree to which they are exercised, thereby giving us a further statement of the cultural conservative view. Kendall speaks in opposition to the notion that freedom of thought and speech and academic freedom are absolute and that the former two—as many "civil libertarians" claim—are to be seen as "the society's ultimate standard of order."[155] He also speaks approvingly of the idea that freedom ultimately comes from and is based on the natural law, which is really the divine law.[156] Both also contend that economic freedom (the term is loosely stated here) is an essential part of overall freedom. Kirk, speaking specifically about property rights, says that "property and freedom are inseparably connected" and that if a society "[s]eparate[s] property from private possession...liberty is erased."[157] (Note that he does not say "private use," which perhaps suggests his awareness that private property must always be used for the common good.) Kendall specifies that he is approving of a more sweeping notion of "economic freedom": freedom to choose one's profession, to compete "at all levels," "to grow rich, or go broke," to make unlimited profit, and to acquire, bequeath, and inherit a fortune.[158] Kirk would probably agree with these putative freedoms, except perhaps for the making of unlimited profit. I make the judgement about the latter because he says (quoting Burke) that "'[s]ociety requires. . .that. . .the inclinations of men should frequently be thwarted, their will controlled, and their passions brought into subjection.'" He also states that "[t]he conservative will not tolerate ravening liberty," that government needs "effective power...to restrain...the unjust," and (again quoting Burke) that "'[m]en of the intemperate mind can never be free.'"[159]

With regards to those cultural conservatives who come from more avowedly theological premises, their positions are not markedly different. Murray and Eidsmoe both speak of freedom relating to belief, which is not just related to religious belief. Murray speaks approvingly of "the freedom of the individual conscience" which was acknowledged as the proper source of man's understanding of principles of justice by the early modern political philosophy which shaped America (it was understood, however, that these principles were absolute ones, dictated by "the transcendental order of justice").[160] Freedom of belief, according to Eidsmoe, means that the jurisdiction of civil rulers extends only to actions; thoughts are to be entirely free, to be dealt with only by God.[161] Murray, as noted, holds the same. They both hold, not surprisingly, that freedom of the church from state interference is an essential element of freedom.[162] Eidsmoe thus defines freedom as "the liberty to make one's own decisions before God without restraint by government."[163] As would be expected, these writers stress, with the other cultural conservatives, that freedom cannot be unlimited.[164]

At the same time, government is limited in its power to intrude upon individual freedom. Eidsmoe catalogues, as examples, the traditional rights of the common law and those found in the first ten amendments of our Constitution.[165] Murray poses concerns about governmental censorship of speech and publications, but acknowledges that there are circumstances in which such is necessary.[166] Both espouse the principle of subsidiarity; Eidsmoe says that the excessive concentration of power in the national government in the U.S. has illegitimately restricted individual freedom.[167]

On the question of economic freedom, there appears to be a division between the theological cultural conservatives, much as there is between Kirk and Kendall. Eidsmoe unabashedly endorses the "free enterprise system," although he seems to mean by it essentially the economic liberalism of the John Locke-Adam Smith school. He espouses a notion of the "invisible hand": that society will benefit when individuals pursue their self-interest in economics.[168] He calls for considerable economic freedom, as Kendall does, but says it must be restrained by "the biblical ethic" and condemns "the tooth-and-claw, survival-of-the-fittest Social Darwinist capitalism of Herbert Spencer."[169] Murray does not say a great deal about economics, but he is critical of "Manchesterism and the *laissez-faire* state" and the "economic privilege" of the nineteenth century—which, he says, introduced "new chains" on men—that was spawned by Lockean individualism.[170] This reaction is an expected from a thinker coming out of the Catholic and pre-modern natural law traditions. Even while, as just noted, Eidsmoe rejects Manchesterian, Spencerian capitalism also, the tone of the two authors indicates that Eidsmoe endorses a much less restricted kind of economic freedom than Murray. They epitomize the difference between Catholic and Protestant, especially Calvinist, thinking on the subject.

Both Eidsmoe's and Murray's understanding about freedom is based on Christian and natural law notions. As Eidsmoe says, "men have rights...because God has created man with human dignity and has bestowed upon him certain basic rights as part of that human dignity."[171]

In summation, the cultural conservative position on freedom is characterized by the following: 1) freedom is understood as grounded in transcendent truths—either from nature or Revelation—and not simply human opinion or abstract theoretical formulations 2) it is limited; 3) it is not the same thing as license and cannot survive without a framework of order; 4) it grows up with a political society organically over time, instead of being grafted on it suddenly; 5) it includes essentially traditional Western rights, not novel or ersatz ones; and 6) property and economic rights are part of the corpus of rights which must be guaranteed in order for men to have true freedom. While agreeing that the latter rights are not unlimited, the cultural conservatives disagree as to how expansive they must be. Probably, on balance, we can say that they want economic freedom to be fairly broad and that at least some of them do not fully appreciate the dangers of individualism in this area.

The Fusionists. The whole point of Frank S. Meyer's book is freedom, and the fusionists' central theme is its preservation. For the fusionists, man must be free to make moral choices because if he is not, making the right choice will be without merit.[172] More than any of the other groupings of conservatism, the fusionists see freedom as a means, an instrument, as relating to an act of the will; it must not be confused with the thing finally chosen. It is like power: morally neutral. It can be used for good or bad ends. For the fusionist, it is not bad for the individual to have even absolute freedom, as long as it is used rightly.[173]

It may seem only a matter of semantics, but this point is the one on which fusionists diverge from cultural conservatives, such as Kirk, who judge the nature of freedom as good or bad, acceptable or unacceptable, *only* if it is used to achieve the right ends. Basically, fusionists reject the notion that there is any such thing as license because, again, freedom does not itself have a moral content. As previously noted, this does not mean the fusionists reject "absolute truths and absolute values" or a higher law; on the contrary, they affirm these.[174] They clearly reject the claim that freedom is the end for man,[175] a position that, essentially, is taken by libertarians of various stripes. Man has a duty to pursue good ends, to pursue "intellectual and moral order throughout society," to pursue virtue.[176] As already stated, however, fusionists reject the argument that the state should enforce virtue. Pursuing virtue, they say, is strictly up to the individual. Only individuals themselves can decide to become virtuous or can inculcate virtue. No association, including the state, can do this. Coming into association can "make the movement of human beings towards virtue easier or more difficult," and in working to acquire or inculcate virtue individuals must draw upon the heritage of "a moral and intellectual order" which is bequeathed to them in a common civilization, but that is all.[177] It was noted before that fusionists tend to see the state simply as a group of men distinct from other men. One gets the sense, that, for them, society more broadly is also understood merely as a grouping of individuals, not unlike the way it is seen in the liberal tradition of Locke and the Utilitarians. We say this even while realizing that the fusionists' emphasis on moral absolutes, right ends, and the obligation of the individual to pursue virtue clearly separate them from this tradition. Moreover, one wonders if there is not also something of Adam Smith's "invisible hand"— another aspect of the Lockean-Utilitarian tradition—in fusionist thought: they admit that virtue and right order are necessary, but since they discount any role for the state or voluntary associations to enforce it they seem excessively optimistic that individuals will use their freedom wisely on their own to achieve them.[178]

In his book, Meyer singles out economic freedom for particular atten- tion. This is the only specific area of liberty he addresses at considerable length. He strongly opposes the contemporary liberal, Keynesian economic order, which he believes is really socialistic. The great danger with the latter, or of a Marxist economic order, or any economic order which puts greater control in the hands of the state, is simply that it is destructive of freedom. Meyer says that "an economic system cannot of itself be a source of virtue," but by suppressing freedom it can, following his general theory of freedom, "inhibit the possibility of virtue" (just as it can "indirectly conduce to virtue" if it respects men's freedom).[179]

The Economic Libertarians. The economic libertarians, of course, focus their attention on economic freedom. Friedman says the following:

> Economic arrangements play a dual role in the promotion of a free society. On the one hand, freedom in economic arrangements is itself a component of freedom broadly understood, so economic freedom is an end in itself. In the second place, economic freedom is also an indispensable means toward the achievement of political freedom.[180]

This quote suggests again what was indicated previously: that for the economic libertarians—or at least most of them (Roepke is an exception)— freedom is the end in itself. Even when Friedman speaks above of freedom as a means and not an end, he regards it is a means to simply another aspect of freedom.

He gives examples of what he regards as the denial of economic freedom even when political freedom is not at stake: the current U.S. Social Security scheme, which compels a citizen by law "to. . .purchase. . .a particular kind of retirement contract, administered by the government"; occupational licensing laws; "fair trade" laws, which make illegal the selling of goods at a price below that set by the manufacturer; and laws and regulations limiting the amount of a particular crop that a farmer can grow.[181]

Friedman says that the kind of economic order that "provides economic freedom directly"—competitive capitalism—is the one that best protects political freedom. This is because capitalism "separates economic power from political power"—i.e., does not permit both to be concentrated in the same people or institutions—"and in this way enables the one to offset the other."[182] He insists that "[h]istory suggests that capitalism is a necessary condition for political freedom."[183] He says that there is no question but that central economic planning, which has increasingly characterized Western "mixed economies" as well as Communist states, when carried to the logical extent necessary to make it work, would intrude directly on traditional liberties by centrally allocating individuals to occupations (which was actually briefly tried in Great Britain).[184]

A further way that the lack of economic freedom harms political freedom is that it squashes dissent and unpopular opinion. The obvious way a government which controls significant portions of the economy does this is by denying its opponents newsprint to publish, postal rights to send out publications, and access to meeting halls and organs of the media to get out their message.[185] Friedman, despite opposing communism and believing it "would destroy all of our freedoms," nevertheless insists that freedom includes the right even to promote totalitarianism. One should not even be economically penalized for doing so.[186] Actually, if government controlled all or most of the economy, the obvious way it would suppress someone who challenged the status quo would be to deny him employment. The great advantage of an "impersonal market" is that it "separates economic activities from political views and protects men from being discriminated against in their economic activities" because of them or for any "reasons that are irrelevant to their productivity."[187]

Roepke demonstrates that there is a difference of opinion within economic libertarianism about whether freedom is an end or a means. He places his libertarianism distinctly within the context of Judeo-Christian principles and the concern for solid morality, family, community, public spirit, tradition—all matters usually associated with the cultural conservatives.[188] As Roepke puts it:

[W]hat I reject in socialism is a philosophy which. . .places too little emphasis on man, his nature, and his personality. . .My picture of man is fashioned by the spiritual heritage of classical and Christian tradition. . . .These. . .are the reasons why I so greatly distrust all forms of collectivism.

It is for the same reasons that I champion an economic order ruled by free prices and markets…this is the only economic order compatible with human freedom, with a state and society which safeguard freedom, and with the rule of law. For these are the fundamental conditions without which a life possessing meaning and dignity is impossible for men of our religious and philosophical convictions and traditions.[189]

To summarize, our economic libertarian sources are divided about whether freedom (most of their focus is on *economic* freedom) is a means or an end. Friedman sees it as the latter, but Roepke sees it as a way of preserving man's dignity which is grounded in his spiritual nature. Whatever its character, the discussion in the section on "The General Purposes of Government" makes it clear that the economic libertarians believe that freedom, especially economic freedom, should be very broad. They want something approaching a *laissez-faire* state—one largely in the image of nineteenth century Britain or America— whose basic function is to preserve individual freedom.

The Neoconservatives. Kristol's thinking on freedom in his book is most directly spelled out in the 1971 essay (referred to previously) entitled "Pornography, Obscenity, and the Case for Censorship." The first statement he makes which indicates his rejection of the notion that freedom is the primary purpose of life or of political society is this: "The purpose of any political regime is to achieve some version of the good life and the good society."[190] He makes the suggestion that the "good life" to be strived for, as the cultural conservatives indicate, must be one promotive of human dignity and decency:

> An older idea of democracy—one which was fairly common until about the beginning of this century…puts the matter more strongly and declares that if you want self-government, you are only entitled to it if that "self" is worthy of governing. There is no inherent right to self-government if it means that such government is vicious, mean, squalid, and debased. Only a dogmatist and a fanatic, an idolater of democratic machinery, could approve of self-government under such conditions.[191]

This last sentence particularly shows a rejection of freedom for its own sake, or freedom as an end.

Kristol further shows that he rejects the Millian-Utilitarian view of society as being merely the sum total of its parts—with the implication that what the parts do privately cannot affect the whole—when he observes that under the modest censorship ("liberal censorship," he calls it) that prevailed in the U.S. until the 1960s, the "quality of public life was only marginally affected" because only a small number of adults wanted to go to the trouble to read pornography.[192] In other words, public life *can be* and *is* affected by what individuals do in their private lives, and if it is easy for most people to do an undesirable thing privately, society will suffer more than if it were not.

We do not believe Kristol can be completely identified with the cultural conservatives in noting this. True, he believes in decency, community, and the need for public morality, but other comments suggest that he places himself on the "freedom spectrum" closer to the "license end" than they do. His comments also suggest that he is more concerned about how pornography affects society than how it affects the individual (in the way of spiritual harm). He also apparently does not judge pornography to be intrinsically wrong in itself. For example, he says that "many people were able to read" *Fanny Hill* and the Marquis de Sade under a regimen which publicly banned such works ("which is as it should be under liberal censorship").[193] What he sees as people's rightful freedom was not infringed on because society's moral tone was kept relatively high when only a small minority indulged. Elsewhere, as noted, he speaks of masturbation, saying nothing about it being an intrinsically evil act, but only that it has rightfully been traditionally discouraged because it can possibly lead to a "regression toward the infantile condition." (His unwillingness to see it as intrinsically evil is further confirmed by his regarding such "autoerotic activity" as "perfectly natural.")[194]

It would be excessive to suggest that neoconservatives do not have any sense of the *intrinsic* worth or lack of worth of different things—this is apparent from the upcoming discussion on equality—or that freedom in one context is as intrinsically valid as in some other. For example, Kristol rejects the view which holds that "obscenity and democracy" (or the freedom of political speech) are to be "regarded as equals."[195]

The other area of freedom that Kristol addresses is economic freedom. As indicated, the neoconservatives do not espouse the minimalist state that the economic libertarians do; they are not for laissez-faire, but, as noted, they do extol "liberal-democratic capitalism" and believe, in some sense, that the "invisible hand" works in economics where it does not in other areas. They reject the "current version of liberalism's preference" for "massive government intervention in the marketplace." They believe that "a predominantly market economy...is a necessary if not sufficient condition for a liberal society." Their rationale for stating this is as follows: A capitalistic economic order satisfies the need for economic growth, which in turn insures the social and political stability necessary to sustain a liberal political order.[196] The way this happens is that economic growth results "in a huge expansion of the property-owning middle classes," which is always a source of moderation and, hence, stability.[197] In short, what was said about the neoconservatives favoring the "invisible hand" indicates they believe that freedom should be greater in economics than in other areas.

The New Right. Our two new right sources make a number of scattered references to different aspects of freedom. First, they discuss freedom as a moral principle, i.e., freedom of the will to choose morally right or wrong actions.[198] Second, they, like the cultural conservatives and neoconservatives, stress the need for limits to freedom. They say such limits are needed for the sustenance of healthy societies, and continually contrast themselves with "cultural radicalism" which rejects limits and espouses, in effect, "immediate gratification of instinctive desires." [199] Like the cultural conservatives, they recognize that the destruction of limits in the name of freedom—seen in all areas of society from morals to politics to intellectual work—ends up resulting in no freedom at all.

For example, this cultural radicalism has led to new "'orthodoxies'" that seek "to control thought and speech," finding "any autonomy in the cultural order intolerable." Cultural radicals want to censor newspaper columns, control the content of novels, films, and historical works, and restrict the subjects of scientific research. "[T]he only effective barrier against totalitarianism," according to the new right, is "traditional culture" with its traditional limits.[200] As mentioned, they see Western, Judeo-Christian principles as the source of these limits.

It has been noted that the new right prefers the "free market" to governmental action, unless the latter is clearly necessary. Like especially the cultural conservatives—and most especially the theologically-based cultural conservatives—they stress the principle of subsidiarity as a way of preserving freedom, and they particularly emphasize that government should respect and encourage "mediating institutions" which in "a healthy society" deal with many more "public problems" than government does.[201] Like the cultural conservatives and Roepke among the economic libertarians, they state that there must be "preconditions" for the appropriate exercise of economic freedom; it is necessary that "a sense of community, especially a community of values," be fostered. Unlike Roepke, the new right believes that government should play an active role in securing these preconditions. This new right view is shared by the cultural conservatives and the neoconservatives, but is rejected by the other groupings. Furthemore, they are the *only* grouping which stresses the "effectiveness" of the market in meeting needs as their reason for defending it.[202]

The other conservative groupings agree that the market does the latter, but make other reasons—such as the necessity of a market economy for preserving political freedom—their prime basis for defending it. Presumably, the new right believes the market does this, too, even though our sources do not mention it. More than any of the other groupings (it is almost certain that Murray, coming out of the Catholic natural law tradition would be sympathetic, however) they stress "the social function of property." They insist that "[p]opular property rights do not mean approval of an individualistic search for self-gratification through greed. They imply a commitment to community, charity, and capital formation."[203] None of the other groupings would likely agree with this completely. All *would* say that if "self-gratification through greed" means destroying others to attain one's wants or objectives, it is wrong.

The cultural conservatives, especially concerned about the need for limits, would be critical of creating conditions in which a vice like greed can control people, and they would be especially eager to promote charity and community. Kirk and Murray are especially troubled about the danger of self-gratification, however. Other cultural conservatives and the other groupings continue to believe that society would ultimately benefit because of the invisible hand. The economic libertarians would almost certainly reject any idea of the social function of property. Friedman makes it clear, for example, that business should not see itself as having social commitments but should just be concerned about profitmaking (it is *that* which will redound to society's good).[204] Further, the new right is alone in stating that its views of economics are shaped by a belief in the *dignity of work* grounded, in turn, on the "Western belief in the dignity of all human beings."[205] It is also the only grouping that stresses employment as a *central* economic objective.[206] The new right is in *agreement* with all the other groupings on having a preference that whatever action the state undertakes in the economy, it be voluntary and in the nature of incentives.[207]

Active Political Conservatives. Many, although not all, of the points made about freedom by this last grouping involve or relate to economic freedom. One of the Congressmen in Crane's book argues that the Democrats [i.e., the liberals] "tend not to trust...the free marketplace....Republicans [i.e., the conservatives] tend to believe that government can best help the free market...by minimizing government interference."[208] An unimpeded free market, he says, will will create more and more jobs.[209] Another says that the free market is the best way of expanding the pie.[210] The active political conservatives, then, clearly believe in the invisible hand.

Goldwater lines up squarely on the side of the classical liberal theorists of economics by speaking about "the natural law of economics" and "the laws of competition."[211] Clearly, for him, there are economic laws which work dependably and with certainty if only government does not interfere and monopoly does not develop (he favors anti-trust laws and thinks they should be applied to unions as well as corporations).[212] He favors letting the free market rule in all areas of the economy, including agriculture. Those who are "inefficient" should just be forced out of business or off their farms—by the market— and he says it is hardly "heartless" to advocate this.[213] He is especially opposed to industry-wide schemes for negotiating labor contracts, setting prices, etc.[214] This would seem to make him utterly opposed to both the industrial codes of the early New Deal and the functional group ideas of Catholic solidarist economic thinkers.[215]

The active political conservatives also see the welfare state as restrictive of freedom by creating on-going dependency on government and limiting freedom of choice, as in the case of public housing programs which require those eligible to live in government-owned projects with all the problems present in them.[216] They also see many liberal-sponsored welfare programs as restrictive of the freedom of the family by having government assume more and more of its responsibilities and interfering in its relationships (e.g., by requiring that families send their children to day-care centers as a condition of receiving government child-care benefits.)[217] Further, these active political conservatives, like the other groupings we have looked at, see economic freedom and private property as necessary for political freedom.[218]

Goldwater speaks of two other aspects of freedom tied up with property rights/economics. The first is the right not to have one's property rights infringed on by excessive taxation (he speaks particularly about the federal government and says that the 30% tax rate figure of the early 1960s is excessive). Each individual has "an obligation to contribute his fair share to the legitimate functions of government," but the problem is that government has gone well beyond its "legitimate functions" and takes more than its "fair share" by graduating tax levels instead of making them equal.[219] The second additional aspect of freedom is freedom of association, which Goldwater says is infringed on by compulsory unionization (he favors unions if they are not compulsory). He also sees the use of dues by unions for political purposes as violating political freedom.[220]

In Crane's book, Congressman Jack Kemp speaks about the general commitment of Republican conservatives to freedom. Hearkening back to the party's early years with Lincoln, he speaks about its "commitment to equality and liberty" and says the conservative Republican Congressmen in the book "have restored the idea of enlightened popular consent respecting basic human rights to its central place in policymaking."[221] Moreover, these conservative Congressmen, as already noted, see freedom and democratic government as universally valid and deserving of promotion overseas by U.S. foreign policy.

Kemp has been previously quoted to the effect that "the moral principles of freedom and democracy are universal truths and dependable guides for all people everywhere."[222] One of the other Congressmen in the volume says that our foreign aid programs should have the purpose of "promot[ing] freedom."[223]

The Conservative Perspective Overall on Freedom. By bringing together the various points expressed above, we come to the following conclusions about what post-war American conservatives think about freedom.

First, freedom must by understood as a means and not an end (except for many of the economic libertarians). It is not unlimited; freedom is not to be confused with license. Its limits are found in traditional Western and Judeo-Christian principles. Secondly, freedom is always conjoined with duties. Men should not regard the political arrangements suggested by a proper understanding of it—self-government—to be automatic; this is something they have to show themselves capable of. Freedom is impossible without a framework of order (otherwise, of course, there would be no way of enforcing it). What individuals do can affect society, so freedom must be limited in order to protect society (even where this freedom involves what seem to be essentially private actions such as reading pornography). This shows a rejection of the utilitarian notion of a society as being nothing more than the sum of its parts, not an entity in its own right.

Thirdly, the conservatives regard the principles of freedom that they enunciate as universally valid because they follow from man's nature. They have mixed views about whether government can restrict freedom explicitly to promote virtue. They do make clear, however, that actions alone—and this would seem also to include open advocacy—are within the reach of government's power of restraint or control, though thoughts are not.

Finally, conservatives stress the interconnectedness of economic and political freedom—it is not possible to have the latter, in any meaningful way, if the former is not present. Economic freedom is singled out for discussion possibly more than any other area of freedom. While rejecting individualism and the idea that unhampered (or relatively unhampered) individual action redounds to society's benefit in other areas, they argue that it is essentially the case in economics. In this area, conservatives, by and large, believe in the "invisible hand."

Evaluation of Conservatism's Thinking About Freedom

There is no question that conservatism corresponds with the Church in holding that freedom must not be viewed as an end in and of itself. Obviously, the end of man for Christianity is not freedom; it is the Beatific Vision. God gives men a free will, so they can freely choose courses of action that will lead them either toward or away from this rightful end. At the same time, freedom is needed so men can be capable of doing the things that lead them to that end. Also, it is only because men cooperate freely with God that their actions have merit and can help them to achieve their proper end. There could be no merit gained by man if he were a mere puppet on a string, with no control over his will.

Clearly, too, the Church rejects the notion that freedom, per se, is unlimited. (We have noted, however, that conservatives do not apply this idea of freedom being limited to all areas.) What has been said in previous chapters leaves no doubt about that. So, the conservatives stand with the Church here (although the Church more consistently applies this belief). As noted about *Pacem in Terris*, there are corresponding duties to all rights; conservatism conforms with the Church in believing this also. The Church would not generally state, say, that the limits to freedom are found in "traditional Western and Judeo-Christian principles." This language might be seen in certain Church statements—e.g., for the purposes of taking note of the fact that the moral truths the Church stands for have long shaped the thinking of even religiously diverse cultures—but the teaching would be expressly held to be based on the "natural law" or "God's law" or "the tradition of the Church" or "the Magisterium's teaching." The latter are the source of the Church's teaching about the appropriate limits of freedom—i.e., about which actions are forbidden or obligatory—as they are of all her specific moral teachings.

Nevertheless, when one analyzes what conservatism regards as the content of "traditional Western and Judeo-Christian principles," he would largely find it in conformity with the Church's teachings.[224] So, we must say that conservatism, especially in light of the fact that it upholds the notion of natural law, is in conformity with the Church about what the basis is for limiting freedom.

We must next take up the question of conservatism's conformity with Church teaching specifically on the matter of the relationship of men's freedom to society and the political order. On the matter of self-government or the people being, directly or indirectly, in control of their governmental institutions and the making of public policy, we are unable to render a clear decision about conservatism's conformity with the Church. It depends on how far conservatism goes with its position on this.

If it is saying, merely, that there is no right to the political order we call liberal, or representative, democracy, it is correct. The Church, as noted, does not have an unconditioned preference for any particular governmental institutions or forms, nor is she opposed to any so long as the common good is upheld. There is some basis in the encyclicals for conservatism's argument that a people must show itself worthy of self-government. This is perhaps inferrable in the linking up of rights with duties in *Pacem in Terris* and its affirming that man's "right to a decent manner of living [is correlative] with the duty of living it becomingly," etc.[225] Agreement with conservatism on this point is also seen in *Pacem in Terris*' noting that the "manner" in which a people should expect to be able to take part in government—which it befits their dignity to do—depends on their political order's "level of development."[226]

On the other hand, if the conservatives contend that the people in general have no right to participate even minimally in government or that government does not need to take their thinking into account (because most men do not have the skills to govern or are inclined to excesses in freedom), they run afoul of the recent line of social encyclicals. As stated, *Pacem in Terris* calls for allowing citizens to "participate in government" so the civil authority can more readily learn what the common good truly requires, as well as because, simply, their human dignity requires it.[227] *Sollicitudo Rei Socialis*, it will also be recalled, says that "*democratic* and *participatory*" political institutions should be permitted to emerge.[228] This is because, as noted, states must accept the fact that popular consent is an important part of the foundation of their legitimacy.

It is also clear that the conservatives correspond with the Church in rejecting an atomistic, Utilitarian view of man in society. This latter position results in an expansive view of freedom because men then believe that their "private" actions (such as in the area of sex or in any area that does not result in overt, immediate harm to someone else) have no import for the community. That the Church disagrees with this line of thinking is seen in its age-old espousal of the notion of the common good, as previously discussed. Disagreement is vividly seen in recent American history in the opposition of the Church in the U.S. to the spread of pornography and attempts to decriminalize homosexual practice or enact "gay rights" bills. Such matters—which substantially involve private, consensual activity—nevertheless have profound effects on the community in lessening its moral tone and creating an ambiance which holds immorality to be perfectly acceptable.

The conservative notion that freedom is impossible without order seems to be confirmed by, again, the popes' linkage of rights and duties. The conservatives say that a framework of political and social order is needed in order to protect the legitimate exercise of freedom (i.e., the individual's acting upon certain rights and prerogatives). *Pacem in Terris*, similarly, says—to return to the quote previously given—"to one man's right there corresponds a duty in all other persons: the duty, namely, of acknowledging and respecting the right in question. . .A well-ordered human society requires that men. . .each contribute. . .to the establishment of a civic order in which rights and duties are...acknowledged and fulfilled."[229] A *civic order*, in other words, is needed to accomplish this. Further, the chief purposes of the state as set forth by the popes—insuring the safety of the commonwealth and preserving the common good—presuppose the need for order.

As we have seen, the popes stress *legitimate* freedom. So, in speaking about the state having to also insure safety, freedom must exist within the context of the order that the state must secure. The common good, as Fr. Higgins states, is "made possible only by co-operative effort" and brings forth "benefits produced by institutions like the family, the local community, the State, the community of nations, and a variety of associations based on freely chosen ends."[230] The common good thus implies order: to have any "co-operative effort" and flourishing institutions there must be order.

On the question of government being able to restrict freedom expressly to promote virtue, it was said that the conservatives had no widely-shared position. On balance, we would judge that those among them who favor the idea of government taking a role in shaping individual virtue are closest to the Church's position. This is because, as *Rerum Novarum* teaches "the end of society is to make men better." The encyclical goes on to say, that "the chief good that society can possess is virtue."[231] Even though in Catholic thought a distinction is made between "society" and the "state" or "political order,"[232] this passage of the encyclical makes it fairly clear that the type of society Pope Leo here refers to is the state, as the governmental organization of the political society.[233]

It is true that the Church does not reserve the shaping of virtue exclusively or even predominantly to the state, but those conservatives who believe this is included in the proper role of the state, do not do so either. They do not propose the enforcement of something like the "civic virtue" that would be identified with the Jacobin or totalitarian state, but rather true virtue (which is, of course, what the Church stands for). That it is *true* virtue they envisage is seen in their support for natural law and religion. That they believe the state cannot have the total or primary responsibility for inculcating virtue is seen in their belief that its power must be limited and in their endorsing the principle of subsidiarity, which provides a substantial role for intermediary bodies and the family. The Church, of course, sees the family and herself as being the prime teachers of virtue.

As far as the reach of the state in restricting freedom or in promoting virtue is concerned, both the conservatives and the Church see it as not being able to restrain thoughts or beliefs. That the Church holds this position—contrary to what some might think—is seen in the fact that even the medieval Inquisition did not punish belief, but actions pursuant to belief, which, in the context of the time, had the added effect of threatening the social order.[234]

On the point of economic freedom the conservatives can be judged to diverge from the popes. They agree with the Church in seeing the connection between economic liberties and the right of private property, on the one hand, and political and other liberties, on the other. Their sympathy for something moving in the direction of *laissez faire* in this area and their belief in the "invisible hand" suggest that they would essentially make competition the controlling principle in the economy. Also. they would not realize—or at least not fully accept—that ethical principles must be always operational in economics so that it is not enough to simply let the "market" operate on its own.

Finally, it is clear that freedom, rightly understood, is something that is possessed by, and should be exercised by, all men; on this, the Church and the conservatives agree. This is because both are committed to the natural law. There is disagreement between the Church and some conservatives, such as the active political conservatives discussed, as to whether freedom should necessarily be equated with the form of government we call "democracy"—i.e., representative government, a constitutional republic—and whether the latter should be actively promoted around the world. This is because, once again, the Church favors no one form of government as appropriate for all peoples.

IV. The Thinking About Equality

The Cultural Conservatives. The cultural conservatives take considerable pains to spell out what constitutes true and false notions of equality. First of all, Kirk tells us that true equality is not "uniformity and equalitarianism," aspects that characterize radical thought.[235] Unlike the latter's notion of it, true equality rejects "political levelling"; it does not support "*total* democracy, as direct as practicable." All political distinctions across the board are not condemned. There are natural distinctions among men which make leadership possible.[236] Cultural conservatives reject Marx's notion that superior natural endowments must be suppressed and so "we must treat the strong, the energetic, and the intelligent unfairly, that we may make their natural inferiors their equals in condition."[237] This view of equality as equal conditions or results has substantially influenced twentieth century thought in the West as well as in the Communist East (as the many Western efforts at social engineering attest. Kendall speaks about the latter as being motivated by "the egalitarian principle."[238] It is because of the basic, inherent differences among people that "civilized society requires orders and classes."[239] All it can insure, then, is "merely an equal right to compete. . .with. . .[one's] fellow men in the race."[240]

This is not to say that, for the cultural conservatives, equality should not include a rightly understood notion of political equality, and legal equality as well. They endorse the equality principle of the Declaration of Independence—"all men are created equal"—which, Kendall tells us, means that all human beings "are created with an equal claim to be treated as persons. . .with an equal right to justice, and an equal right to live under a government limited by law."[241] Although the cultural conservatives do not believe that men are entitled to equal political *power* nor are all necessarily entitled to the vote (that would afford them political equality in a sense), they would agree that a relative political equality, in which most people would have the vote and be permitted to carry out the full prerogatives of citizenship, is to be sought. This is seen by their espousal of the principles of *The Federalist*.[242] Murray spells out further what putting people on this "'footing of equality'" politically means: according to the definition of a democratic republic, it means all citizens are able to take part in the collective "judg[ing of] the prince and the legislative act."[243]

There is another, more profound way in which the cultural conservatives' view stresses the equality of men: their equal human dignity and their moral equality. Murray speaks approvingly of the fact that the "American consensus"—i.e., the traditional principles undergirding our political order—"has its ultimate root in the idea of the sacredness of man, *res sacra homo*. Man has a sacredness of personal dignity which commands the respect of society in all its laws and institutions."[244] Our political order has been distinguished for its protection of human rights because of this. Kirk says that "[t]he only true equality is moral equality,"[245] which means that all men are bound to follow the same moral law and will reap the same consequences if they violate it, both here and *certainly* in the next world. All this is ultimately grounded in the fact that, as Eidsmoe says, "[M]en are to be considered equal in the sight of God."[246]

The *res sacra homo* that Murray speaks about suggests another aspect of equality, which would probably not be agreed to at all by some conservative groupings and perhaps not even by cultural conservatives such as Kendall and Eidsmoe. It concerns not the equality of man himself, but his equal right to make certain claims on government: "[H]e may. . .utter certain prohibitions in the face of society and state" (this involves the respecting of human rights above) and "[h]e may make certain demands upon society and the state which require action in their support" (which would be the controverted by other conservatives).[247]

Also relating to human dignity is Murray's rejection of the Jim Crow "separate but equal" principle that characterized the racially segregated Old South. (Murray mentions this because he is writing in the midst of the 1950s-1960s "civil rights revolution.") "Separate but equal," he indicates, was not equal at all (all the other groupings of conservatives would surely agree with him) and was immoral because it violated human dignity.[248]

The final aspect of equality that our cultural conservative sources address is the economic. Kirk attacks the egalitarian position here—issuing forth from the French Revolution and given its latter-day momentum by Marx. This position essentially claims a right of the less well-endowed "to appropriate the goods of their more prosperous neighbors." What it really is advocating "is a vice—the vice of covetousness." It represents a false notion of social justice, "which would treat all men alike," like the other distorted aspects of the notion of equality. On the other hand, "true justice," to which the cultural conservative subscribes, "secures every man in the possession of what is his own, and provides that he will receive the reward of his talents." The "abstract equality" of the egalitarian is not the same thing as the Christian virtue of charity. The latter "does not command the sacrifice of the welfare of one class to that of another class" or call for levelling; rather, it calls for a kind of *noblesse oblige*: it "looks upon the rich and powerful as the elder brothers of the poor and weak, given their privileges that they may help to improve the character and condition of all humanity."[249]

As Eidsmoe summarizes, for the cultural conservative "certain inequalities in the economic sphere are not only inevitable but even just and desirable."[250] Certainly in this economic area the previously stated point of Kendall's that a proper notion of equality includes the equal right to compete, is pertinent.

How can we summarize the cultural conservative position on equality? It flatly rejects egalitarianism—i.e., an insistence that people be equal in every way the state would be capable of making them equal—and denies the belief that equal results in life must be assured to everyone. The cultural conservatives hold that a proper equality means equality before the law and a relative political equality, at least as far as voting and citizenship go, and certainly an equality of human dignity, grounded in the fact that all people are children of God, face the same moral obligations, and incur the same basic results for their moral actions. The cultural conservatives also insist that economic equality is folly in light of innate human differences.

The Fusionists. The fusionists echo exactly what the cultural conservatives Kirk and Kendall had to say above by way of criticism of egalitarian notions. Meyer says this about the correct understanding of equality:

> The only equality that can be legitimately derived from the premises of the freedom of the person is the equal right of all men to be free from coercion exercised against their life, liberty and property. This is the touchstone of a free society. For the rest, the capabilities of men, specific and inherited, should determine their position, their influence and the respect in which they are held.[251]

The only other kind of equality that Meyer endorses is also seen in the cultural conservative writers: equality before the law. He says that this principle is "based upon the innate and incommensurable value of each individual created person" and "is essential to the moral functioning of a limited state."[252]

The Economic Libertarians. Our economic libertarian sources do not provide a direct, in-depth analysis of equality. What they think about equality is grasped mostly indirectly. They are staunchly opposed, of course, to collectivism in all "its guises, whether it be communism, socialism, or a welfare state"[253] and are firm supporters of an essentially unencumbered market. The latter is known especially for bringing basic inequalities to the surface—different talents, capabilities, strengths, etc.—which result in different outcomes for different people. Roepke deplores the "intellectual egalitarianism" of contemporary life, "aiming at the leveling out of 'mental income inequalities.'"[254] They thus clearly reject the egalitarian principle. It can also be clearly inferred—from Friedman's chapter about education, in which he shows concern for "equalizing opportunities" among children (presumably so all can get ahead in life)— that the economic libertarians also agree with the cultural conservatives about equality including an equal right to compete.[255]

The economic libertarians also seem to favor political equality in essentially the same sense as the cultural conservatives do. This is seen in Friedman's endorsement of the support nineteenth century ("classical") liberals (he considers himself one) gave to "the development of representative government and parliamentary institutions."[256] Roepke implies a preference for "the original concept of the modern democratic state," which, from his description, seems to have been something like what prevailed in the early American Republic or in early nineteenth century Britain (both characterized by representative institutions, a restraint on the standardizing and homogenizing danger of extreme majoritarianism, civic-minded political parties oriented to the common good instead of narrow material interests, and the prevalence of mediating groups and institutions which played the role "of defending themselves and their rights against the power of the state and the claims of other groups represented therein").[257]

The economic libertarians' inclusion of the principle of equality under the law in their conception of equality—also seen with the cultural conservatives—is seen in Friedman's approval of classical liberalism's concern with insuring "reduction in the arbitrary power of the state, and protection of the civil freedoms of individuals."[258] Friedman also states that one of the basic purposes of government, as previously noted, is to be an umpire so that generally accepted rules are complied with by all and *everyone* will then be able to truly carry out his freedom to pursue his chosen objectives.

On the matter of the more basic equality of human dignity, we can say that it is endorsed by the economic libertarians but apparently only those, like Roepke, who have an acute realization of the spiritual and moral dimensions of human existence, bother to discuss it.[259] Roepke, as noted, "see[s] in men the likeness of God"[260] and subscribes to the "classical and Christian tradition," so he implicitly acknowledges both this aspect of equality and the related moral equality of men, both of which the cultural conservatives stress. As part of this, the economic libertarians oppose racial segregation, the implication being that this should be done because it violates equality (although Friedman, at least, was unwilling, due to his notion of freedom, to enforce *integration* with the civil law). (He did not favor the law enforcing segregation either, as with the old Jim Crow statutes.)[261] This illustrates the opposition of the economic libertarians to the use of government, generally, to enforce equality.

The Neoconservatives. Basically this grouping opposes economic and (what Kristol calls) "cultural egalitarianism" and endorses what Kristol calls "social and legal egalitarianism."[262] The neoconservatives' view about economic egalitarianism is the same as that held by the other three groupings surveyed thus far. Kristol sees the economic egalitarianism which has influenced American thinking and public policy for most of this century as having been given its original impetus by "socialist, quasi-socialist, or 'progressive' critics" in the 1920s.[263] Economic egalitarianism has influenced Western European states even more profoundly. They have reshaped themselves as "social democracies," which are *"inherently unstable,"* creating "a momentum for equality—in the bizarre sense of special privileges for all." This normally has disastrous consequences, "creat[ing] an overbearing, bureaucratic state confronting a restless and 'ungrateful' citizenry."[264] These states have "degenerated into a fierce internal struggle between proliferating interest groups for particular advantage, a struggle usually fought under the banner of 'equality.'" They have also witnessed a "rate of taxation that frustrates economic incentives, and an inexorable decline in productivity and economic growth."[265]

Kristol never provides a definition for cultural, social, or legal egalitarianism. We can assume that the latter refers to legal equality, which we have seen characterizes the other conservative groupings also. What he means by cultural egalitarianism is probably explained in his essay discussing pornography. As stated previously, Kristol is not particularly troubled by the fact that when a stricter control of pornography was in effect, only a small number could have access to it under rather circumscribed conditions. He acknowledges further that under the "liberal censorship" he calls for, "the rich will have privileged access to obscenity and pornography."[266] Certainly it bothers some people—"egalitarian maniacs,"[267] Kristol calls them—that the rich and the poor do not have, in effect (he does not state it this way, but it is the upshot of this point), the equal right to do morally wrong things and thus do spiritual and moral harm to themselves (so such critics make an equality issue out of it).[268] Cultural egalitarianism seems to mean, then, at least in part, that people must have an equal access to even the lowest, most corrupt forms of "culture" and moral practice.

There is possibly another dimension of Kristol's understanding of cultural egalitarianism, however. This is that all sorts of things are supposed to be treated as equally good "culture," for example, a pornographic and a nonpornographic novel. As he says (writing in 1971): "A pornographic novel has a far better chance of being published today than a nonpornographic one, and quite a few pretty good novels are not being published at all simply because they are not pornographic."[269] As already noted, the neoconservatives have an intrinsic notion of excellence and want it to take precedence over freedom, at least if the type of freedom claimed is not a particularly legitimate one.

As far as social egalitarianism is concerned, Kristol considers it as something akin to the political equality which has been discussed with regard to the other groupings; no person or group is to have excessively undue political power. There cannot be an hereditary aristocracy which would accumulate excessive political power because of its social superiority. That this is probably his meaning is borne out in his declaring that "social...egalitarianism [is]...essential to a viable democracy."[270]

The New Right. The new right's thinking about equality is, like that of the economic libertarians, expressed, by and large, indirectly in the writings examined. In this fashion, they address almost all of the aspects of equality that have been discussed above. They have essentially the same views we have seen with the other groupings.

The new right holds that all have an equal human dignity. This is seen in the following: their statements about our culture's rightfully viewing the impoverished homeless as "human beings who deserve our concern, rather than as sub-human outcasts or objects of contempt," "[t]he immutability of human nature," and the dignity of all labor[271]; their belief that there must be equality under the law (i.e., they insist that "[c]ourts...provide justice to *all* parties")[272]; and their affirmation of a right to political equality, as indicated by their allusion to America's traditional "civil rights" (which include the right to vote, the source of political equality).[273] The new right also *rejects* the notion of their being an equality of moral standards (i.e., that all acts are equally good morally). This is seen in their rejection of the attempts of cultural radicals to make it morally imperative to eliminate such things as "sexism" and "homophobia."[274] They also oppose economic egalitarianism, as seen in their stress on the market and rejection of "comparable worth" (i.e., government deciding that certain typically [predominantly] male jobs and typically female jobs are "comparable" so that wage rates can be required to be made equal under the federal civil rights laws).[275] The latter also, implicitly, shows their endorsement of an equal right to compete, but a rejection of equal results.

There are two points about equality which are suggested by the new right but not found in the other conservative groupings. The first concerns "cultural equality," or what might be called its version of social equality. Although the new right would probably accept what the neoconservatives say about this, they enunciate another dimension of it which would seem likely to put it at odds with the other groupings (except possibly for cultural conservatives like Kirk and Murray). It says that Americans have "cultural rights" which are not found in our Constitution but are "simply there" (i.e., indicated by man's nature) and are "embodied in lived experience during most of our nation's history.[276] These include the right to an education, the right to literacy, and "the right to effective protection against crime."[277] The other groupings would likely oppose all except the last of these rights, along with the whole *idea* of "cultural rights," since they would necessitate affirmative demands on government.

The second point concerns the new right's expression of a kind of "equality of attitude" that exists among the American people which they say we must take account of and be willing to accept. "One of the things all Americans have traditionally had in common...is a belief that life would get better....Prosperity—steadily increasing prosperity—has always been an important component of this 'better.'"[278] This is a position that the cultural conservatives, particularly, would find problematical because it seems to cater to mass tastes or desires and places too great an emphasis on acquiring wealth, without any particular purpose and in place of higher things.

Active Political Conservatives. The active political conservatives state their commitment, in general terms, to equality. Congressman Kemp speaks about liberty and equality both being traditional principles our nation and his Republican party have defended.[279] Their opposition to an egalitarian notion of equality, in the various ways it has been discussed (setting aside here the social and legal "egalitarianism" of the neoconservatives), is made clear by their support for the market; their rejection, per Goldwater, of a graduated income tax[280]; and Goldwater's saying the following: "We are equal in the eyes of God [i.e., equal dignity, as above] but we are equal in *no other respect*. Artificial devices for enforcing equality among unequal men must be rejected" because such an effort "does violence both to the charter of the Republic [our Constitution] and the laws of nature."[281]

Like the cultural conservatives (explicitly) and the other conservative groupings (implicitly), they reject uniformity or standardization. This is seen in Goldwater's rejection of giving all children the same education.[282] Their notion of equality also means equal opportunity (but not equal results); this is seen in in the comment on welfare by a Congressman-commentator that "[i]nstead of just giving fish to the needy, they should be taught how and given an opportunity to catch their own fish"[283] and by their general commitment to the market (which, by definition, means an acceptance of unequal results).

The Conservative Perspective Overall on Equality. The conservative thought on equality, first of all, rejects levelling of human differences and unwarranted uniformity or standardization. It opposes any attempts at economic egalitarianism—in which all economic differences are sought to be swept away—and cultural/moral egalitarianism—in which all cultural and moral positions and ways of living are regarded as equally valid and desirable. All men are equally bound by the same principles of morality and justice, which have their origins beyond man.

While economic egalitarianism is rejected, the conservatives *do* support the right of everyone to compete equally, a sort of ethic of equal opportunity. They reject the notion of absolute political equality. They would favor most people having the vote and would reject any kind of hereditary, politically all-powerful aristocracy, but would not carry political equality to an extreme. The ways we can rightfully say men are equal, according to them, are that men have an equal human dignity (i.e., because they are all children of God) and are equal under the law (i.e., all people are entitled to the same rights and protections under the law). In accordance with the latter, the old, racially segregationist "separate but equal" standard is rejected.

Evaluation of Conservatism's Thinking About Equality

The above makes clear that American conservatism has been an unremitting opponent of egalitarianism. This corresponds with what the popes have said.

In the encyclical *Quod Apostolici Muneris (On Socialism)*, as noted, Pope Leo XIII *condemned* the thinking of those ideologies which declare that men possess a complete political equality (such that those with authority, including hereditary monarchs, are not entitled to respect), and that there is generally meant to be an equality of all rights (i.e., political rights, as opposed to basic human rights) and political power. We also noted that in the encyclical *Divini Redemptoris (Atheistic Communism)* Pope Pius XI restated the Church's condemnation of an extreme version of political equality, referring specifically to communism. There can be no question that the popes oppose a political egalitarianism.

Again, the development of teaching in recent encyclicals makes it clear that in spite of this, men do have the right to wide participation in government. If conservatism carries its notion of political egalitarianism so far as to not acknowledge this—which we have suggested may be the case—it is in tension with Church teaching.

That the Church opposes economic egalitarianism is also seen in its flat-out rejection of socialism and communism and in what we said (when comparing the new liberalism to her teaching) about how she does not, essentially, support equality of wealth or equal outcomes. (She merely favors equal opportunity and the avoidance of too great a gap in wealth among different groups). The latter point (as well as the emphasis the popes place on the social obligations of those with private wealth and property) indicates that the Church would not accept the position taken by some of the conservatives that one has an unlimited right to accumulate wealth or profit. Nor would she accept the argument of the economic libertarians that economic enterprises should not use any of their wherewithal to deal with social problems. The opposition to a graduated income tax found among the active political conservatives would probably not square with the social encyclicals, as seen from our previous discussion. It should be noted that these latter points are not necessarily reflective of all American conservatism, but only of these particular groupings.

In the areas of equality *favored* by conservatives, we see that their view of equal human dignity is clearly upheld by Church teaching. So, of course, is the notion of moral equality discussed. Equality under the law and racial equality, also stressed by conservatism, are likewise in conformity with the Church.

Overall, conservatism's understanding of equality, with the possible exception of certain points regarding political and economic equality (depending on what various conservative writers seek to emphasize), is in agreement with the Church's teaching. The Church would dispute some of the positions on equality taken by certain conservative thinkers, however.

V. The View of Communism

The Cultural Conservatives. This grouping is very pointed in its statement of the evils of communism and the reasons for these evils. Murray, like virtually all the other conservatives examined in this chapter, is aware of the realities of life in Communist states.

The Soviet Union, he said (writing in 1960), is a "gigantic police state" where "there is no such thing as the 'rule of law'" and "no concern for justice and no sense of human rights."[284] "[O]rganized and guided in accordance with a revolutionary doctrine," this is the first nation ever to "erect. . .an atheistic materialism into a political and legal principle that furnishes the substance of the state and determines its procedures."[285] If the Soviet Union does not seek "world domination," it surely seeks a "Communist world revolution."[286]

It is for all these reasons that Murray saw communism as a profound philosophical and moral threat to the West. Most basically, "Communist doctrine is an affront to the Western tradition of reason and the manner of empire that it sustains" (as with the expansion of the Soviet domain and sphere of influence) "is a further affront to the liberal tradition of politics and law that was born of the Western tradition of reason."[287] What Father Murray means by this "Western tradition of reason" is seen in his writings about natural law and also in the following discussion by the other cultural conservatives, Meyer and Roepke.

Kirk condemns Marxist communism's turning "strife," instead of co-operation, into "the governing influence in the state" (that is, Marxism promotes class conflict and validates the "seiz[ing of] the property and the rights that belong to other classes and persons").[288] It is an extreme version of egalitarianism and all his previously stated criticisms of egalitarianism apply to it.

Eidsmoe says that "[c]onservatives find themselves philosophically opposed to Communism on every point: the improvability of human nature, the role of government, the theory of the state, government power, economic equality, individual freedom, property rights, radical change."[289] He also takes to task both communism and its ideological first-cousin, socialism, for the economic failure they engender (something which became completely obvious to the world as the 1980s came to a close):

> Socialism and Communism tend to be economic failures because they are based upon a false understanding of human nature, the view that man is basically good or improvable. Such systems would have men work and produce at their jobs, not for any direct benefit to themselves, but for the benefit of the commune, or for the benefit of society as a whole. The individual quickly realizes that how hard or how well he works has little to do with any benefits he enjoys, and that if he slacks off a little in his work he takes home the same paycheck as before.[290]

He goes on to say that "Socialist and Communist leaders"—he fails to define his terms or distinguish between the two ideologies—"have to choose between two options. First, they can allow their economies to stagnate. . .Or second, they can supply an artificial incentive by governmental force—work or be shot!. . .[S]uch compulsion. . .[is] inimical to human freedom; it also doesn't work nearly as well as the profit incentive of the free enterprise system."[291]

Kendall perhaps sums up the cultural conservatives' reason for opposing communism. Criticizing an author in one of his book reviews (reprinted in *The Conservative Affirmation*) for his defense of alleged Communist subversives in the U.S. on civil liberties grounds, Kendall says that "[a]ny time the 'constitutional order' gets in our way, as regards combating the evil of Communism, we shall seek a change in the constitutional order—not. . .for. . .'reason of State'. . .but for reason of God."[292] It is probably the assault on the truths and the things of God by communism that forms the cultural conservatives' most fundamental reason for opposing it. They thereby see communism as intrinsically evil.

Finally, the urgency with which the cultural conservatives view the confrontation of the West with communism is observed in Murray's observation that the West's loss of understanding of its own traditions "might lead to downfall."[293] The nature of what they believe the West's response must be— besides recovering an understanding of its own intellectual and moral foundations—is seen in Kendall's call for "'tough' anti-Communism."[294]

The Fusionists. Frank S. Meyer echoes the cultural conservatives: communism is an evil and a threat because it "bases itself on a set of values radically hostile in their very foundation to the Western view of man."[295] It has based itself, like "Nazism, socialism, [and] the milder theories of the welfare state," on the erroneous view "that individual men are secondary to society."[296] As such, there can be "no common ground" with it and everything "projected" in his book "presupposes the defeat of this monstrous, atavistic attack upon the survival of the very concepts of moral order and individual freedom."[297] Communism thus vehemently repudiates the two principles which are the very essence of fusionism, as well as of Western society (as understood by Meyer). What's more, Communism "advances with a messianic zeal and cold scientific strategy toward domination of the whole world."[298]

Meyer insists that the Western response—in an era when communism was at its height—must be every bit as vigorous as the cultural conservatives believe: "[R]esurgent conservatism in America. . .must organize the power of the consensus of Americans. . .to direct. . .the rightful power of the state against the ravening drive of the armed and messianic collectivism of Communism."[299]

The Economic Libertarians. Friedman's stated opposition to communism is confined to two reasons: its opposition to human freedom and its hostility to the market. We have already seen the substantial threat he sees communism representing to the former and also—consistently, yet contradictorily—how he believes that a commitment to freedom requires permitting people to freely advocate it. (This is, of course, *consistent* with his theory because people must be free to advocate all other sorts of things and *contradictory* because communism seeks—and, all the evidence indicates, it *will* do this if given the opportunity—to destroy all freedom.)

Roepke's thinking on the reasons for opposing communism is more thoroughgoing, much like that of the cultural conservatives. Certainly, he opposes it on economic grounds: it rejects the market, crushes political freedom because it crushes economic freedom, and fails to satisfy material needs and produce a decent standard of living. He does not believe this is the most basic ground for rejecting it and, in fact, insists that we err by thinking that the likelihood of it successfully taking root is mostly contingent on poor material conditions in a particular country.[300] Rather, Communism and other totalitarian doctrines prosper to the degree that a people have "lost the true, pre-eminently non-material conditions of human happiness." He says that "the decisive battle between Communism and the free world will have to be fought. . .on the field of spiritual and moral values."[301]

Communism, for Roepke, is a surrogate religion, something which has moved into the void caused by "the dissolution of our traditional Christian and humanistic conception of man," and threatens the whole way of life built upon it.[302] Like Eidsmoe, Roepke stresses communism's false and dangerous belief in the perfectibility of man.[303] Indeed, perhaps the most threatening aspect of communism, according to Roepke, is "the violation of the human soul," the "remaking of man," the preposterous belief that the realities of human nature can be changed—forcibly if necessary.[304] He also mentions the utter repressiveness associated with Communist regimes—the "revolting" nature of their "internal police power"—and the fact of their military might and their being "a dictatorship bent on world conquest." Like Meyer and the cultural conservatives, he saw the stakes as being as very high: it was a battle "for our own existence which Communism has forced upon the free world."[305]

The Neoconservatives. Kristol's book does not demonstrate as deep an analysis of communism as the cultural conservatives', but he criticizes communism on more grounds than Friedman and thus seems to have a greater appreciation of the range of its dangers. Kristol certainly does speak of Communism's, and socialism's, economic failures. As he puts it, "[c]entral economic planning of a rigorous kind has demonstrated a radical incapacity to cope with a complex industrialized economy and urbanized society." (This of course, has now become starkly clear to the whole world.) This is because "[t]he immense bureaucracy involved in such planning simply cannot compete with the free market as an efficient mechanism for allocating resources, nor is bureaucratic caution able to substitute for entrepreneurial risk-taking as a mechanism of innovation and economic growth."[306] This failure is related to the fallacious idea of socialism—in both its Communist and less extreme versions—"that we do not need that human incentive we call self-interest, that we can rely on altruism, on the pure spirit of fraternity." Human experience shows this to be utopian, especially when tried "in a large heterogeneous society" and/ or for a long period of time. To increase wealth and better people's material condition, materialistic incentives simply are needed.[307]

Communism has a religious character for Kristol, as it does for Roepke (and would almost certainly for Meyer and the cultural conservatives, even though they do not mention it in these writings). This is seen, Kristol suggests, in its stated aims to create—in the Russian context—"'the new Soviet man'" from "'the Soviet experiment.'" He goes on to say that "Soviet Communism is a pseudoreligion, and the Soviet government is a pseudotheocracy," which, like any religion, has tried zealously to make converts (but failed miserably, as seen in the widespread disinterest in Marxist-Leninist ideology in the Soviet Union).[308]

The category of religion, according to Kristol, that communism falls into is gnosticism. Like any gnostic movement, it has a three-fold structure: leadership group (i.e., the party elite), believers (i.e., the party), and the masses. Only the leaders have the *gnosis*, the truth, which is "the arcane knowledge of how to reorganize the world, so as to make it a perfect place." In spite of this high-minded idealism, they then use—and feel justified in using—"the most Machiavellian means" to achieve this aim.[309]

Perhaps the greatest reason why Kristol sees communism as a threat is that he remembers the heyday of the Cold War when the Soviet Union "engaged in a world-wide campaign of ideological belligerency against liberal [i.e., Western or Western-oriented] nations, liberal values, and liberal institutions."[310] He no longer seems to see it engaging in such a belligerent campaign, but he does not think it any less hostile to these things.

The New Right. Much of the thinking of the new right about communism is found, in our sources, in Charles A. Moser's article in *Future 21*. He says the struggle between the West and communism is simply one between "freedom and tyranny" and it "is currently being fought at the levels of conventional warfare, economics, and political ideology all at once."[311] He clearly sees communism as against "American principles," but he does not discuss the nature of these except to indicate that they involve freedom.[312] When we examine the discussion in *Cultural Conservatism: Toward a New National Agenda*, we can infer that the new right understands these principles further to include the Judeo-Christian tradition and the great cultural traditions of Western Civilization. There is thus a further basis for its opposition to communism.

Communism is also rejected in the latter book because its economic theory "exalt[s] conflict rather than cooperation as the heart of economic activity." This, it says, is "inimical to Western culture." (The new right also rejects other economic theories, such as "social Darwinism" and *laiss ez-faire* capitalism, which do the same thing.)[313] *Cultural Conservatism: Toward a New National Agenda* also shows an awareness of the brutality which has characterized Communist regimes.[314] The new right also sees communism as utterly imperialistic, as is stated by most of the other conservative groupings. As Moser puts it: "The communist purpose [he writes before the developments of the late 1980s and early 1990s] is gradually to take one country after another across the globe, usually employing the device. . .once called 'international civil war'. . .sometimes using surrogates. . .or their own troops.[315] It is because of this and the fact that "[t]he communists are our declared enemies, explicitly reject" our principles, and "are consciously working for our destruction, and will settle for nothing less" that we must say that "[t]he hostility between" us and them "is not based on misunderstanding that can be cleared up through improved communication." As some of the other conservatives also say, ". . .it is pointless even to discuss. . .'compromise.'"[316]

The new right also joins other types of conservatives in calling for a tough Western foreign policy stance against communism (again, in the era of undisputed Soviet power). Moser calls for an offensive, and a defensive, strategy for the U.S. to deal with it, not just militarily but in the other areas mentioned above as well.[317]

Active Political Conservatives. The reason why the active political conservatives surveyed see communism as dangerous is starkly put by one of the Congressmen in the Crane book: "The advocates of communism do not share our basic goals and values of peace, freedom and human dignity."[318] Goldwater further says that it is "a ruthless despotism." He states what he believes is the extent of the threat: "We are confronted by a revolutionary world movement that possesses not only the will to dominate absolutely every square mile of the globe, but increasingly, the capacity to do so."[319]

Also, like many of the other conservatives considered, Goldwater sees a weakness of Western will as being a major liability in facing communism. Writing in the early 1960s, he says that "it has now reached the point where American leaders, both political and intellectual, are desperately searching for means of. . .'accomodating' the Soviet Union as the price of national survival." Our Communist enemies, he goes on, "are determined to win the conflict, and we are not."[320] Further, we are naive about the meaning of the struggle between East and West (e.g., the reasons why communism is a threat, the stakes involved, and Communist intentions). "Our enemies have understood the nature of the conflict, and we have not."[321]

The appropriate response, Goldwater and the other active political conservatives tell us, is resistance. As the Congressman above says about the significance of the 1983 Grenada invasion:

> Grenada...served as a strong signal to America's enemies that...Moscow and Havana will no longer subvert nations of this hemisphere without meeting strong resistance on our part.[322]

Goldwater declares the following:

> Peace, to be sure, *is* a proper goal for American policy—as long as it is understood that peace is not all we seek. For we do not want the peace of surrender. We want a peace in which freedom and justice will prevail, and that—given the nature of Communism—is a peace in which Soviet power will no longer be in a position to threaten us and the rest of the world. A tolerable peace, in other words, must *follow* victory over Communism.[323]

He says, however, that a resort to arms is not preferred. "Overt hostilities should always be avoided" because of the danger of nuclear destruction.[324] The avoidance of war, however, cannot be "our chief objective" or we would be "committed to a course that has only one terminal point: surrender." We must not view war as "unthinkable," for, as has been said by others who have studied Communist military doctrine, it is not seen as such by the Communists.[325]

One aspect of our foreign policy, the foreign aid program, is singled out for particular discussion in these sources. The writers say, as already noted, that it should be used essentially only to further American foreign policy interests, which must fundamentally include resistance to communism.[326]

The Conservative Perspective Overall on Communism. Conservatism opposes communism for many reasons: political, economic, social, philosophical, and religious. It emphasizes, particularly, communism's attack on human freedom, individuality, and dignity, ideas that are based on the Western and Judeo-Christian traditions, and which communism is at war against.

Communism's repudiation of human dignity is seen in its unrealistic and dangerous attempt to achieve the perfectibility of man on earth. Its tendency to sow conflict between classes is pointed out. That Communist regimes have been so brutal and ruthless, is another point stressed by conservatives in their opposition to it. Conservatives also have seen communism as driving for world domination and as implacably hostile to the West. It represents a genuine military threat to the West, which should not compromise with it at all. Conservatives insist upon a strong, determined, and multi-faceted American foreign policy stance against it, including the willingness to use military action if warranted.

Evaluation of Conservatism's Thinking About Communism

On this subject, the conservatives are in close conformity to Church teaching. The encyclical *Divini Redemptoris*, as noted, attacks Communist doctrine on all of the same grounds conservatism does: its atheism; radical materialism; suppression of freedom, individuality, and human dignity; brutality; and repudiation of Judeo-Christian truths. Like the popes, the conservatives see communism as intrinsically evil, bent on spreading its false perspective around the world (the popes do not, however, address the aspect of world-wide Soviet military domination).

Divini Redemptoris and the much later *Instruction on Certain Aspects of the "Theology of Liberation"* of the Congregation for the Doctrine of the Faith agree with the conservative idea that communism and Marxism cannot be compromised with. The Church, however, has said this mostly in reference to the realm of ideology: Church teaching and Communist doctrine are simply incompatible. The conservatives mean this in reference to the ideological dimension, but also, apparently, to the military and other dimensions. It is on this point that we perhaps see some divergence between the popes and the conservatives (this difference especially applies to certain conservative groupings). The former, both by their emphasis on negotiating solutions to international differences and their advocacy of ending the arms race and achieving a general disarmament, can rather obviously be inferred to oppose any rigid, uncompromising military postures. They favor negotiations and compromise in this area—at least, on the matter of immediate problems and tensions in order to avoid the outbreak of war—even while, they realize, that communism affords no possibility of justice and that there can be no true or lasting peace unless justice universally prevails.

A final point worth mentioning is that while conservatism opposes communism partly because of its hostility to the Judeo-Christian tradition, the writers examined—except for the theological wing of the cultural conservatives—do not say much about communism's ruthless suppression of religion and religious people and institutions, as the popes do. They are certainly against this, but one wonders if their limited attention to this and their *primary* stress on other points, as valid and good as they are, does not reveal a rather secular attitude and a disagreement with the Church in basic priorities. This perhaps follows from the utilitarian kind of role some conservatives see religion as playing (as noted earlier).

Post-World War II American conservatism is clearly much closer to the Church than the new liberalism in its understanding of communism and its preferred posture toward it. It is probably also closer than the old liberalism because of its more thoroughgoing critique of communism (i.e., its opposition is more thorough especially because of its more profound recognition of communism's assault on human nature).

Chapter Conclusion

As we look back in summary over the five areas on which post-War American conservatism and Church teaching have been compared, we come to these brief conclusions.

Of all the areas, there is perhaps the most divergence on the role of government. It was stated in that section that conservatism does not seem to see the state's full role in shaping the common good, it does not accept the full range of the state's domestic social welfare role, it does not concede to the state a sufficiently large prerogative in the economic realm, and it is not aware enough of the international obligations of states growing out of the virtue of charity. On the subject of God, religion, and the natural law as the basis of the political order, much of what conservatism says echoes the Church, except that there is some evidence of a utilitarian view of religion and a secular motivation in the shaping of its principles and priorities. Also, conservatism does not have, for the most part, the fully developed notion of the natural law of the Church's tradition.

There is substantial conformity on the subject of freedom, except in the realm of economic freedom. On equality, there is substantial agreement with the Church, except possibly on some aspects of the understanding of political and economic equality (as regards at least some conservative groupings). On the view of communism, there is overwhelming agreement except on the willingness of some conservative spokesmen to be too uncompromising militarily with Communist regimes.

Overall, we can say that there is substantial correspondence between conservatism and Catholic teaching. The areas of disagreement, except for economics, tend to involve an *insufficiency* on the part of conservatism. Perhaps because of the *laissez-faire* background (ironically a *liberal* idea, originally) of conservatism, the latter is particularly deficient with regard to the proper role of the state in the lives of men.

SIX

COMPARING AMERICAN CONSERVATISM AND CHURCH TEACHING, PART II: SPECIFIC PUBLIC POLICY PROPOSALS

In this chapter, we evaluate conservatism's important specific policy proposals with reference to papal teaching. As with liberalism, the sources relied upon consist of platforms of the major party connected with the political ideology under discussion, in this case the Republican. The reason given in the discussion of liberalism as to why a party platform is a particularly good source for determining the policy ideas of those with a certain political perspective, applies here too: it contains the most important proposals in the minds of conservatives that should be worked for politically.

The Republican party platforms of 1952, 1964, and 1984 have been selected for this analysis. Three platforms instead of two are examined for the following reasons.

First, unlike liberalism, there is no need to choose one "very good" platform to represent each of the two major expressions of the ideology in recent decades (broken down by chronological period). We explained in Chapter One that contemporary conservatism has not had such distinctly different expressions changing over time. Second, it was thought that whatever variations in conservative thinking as manifested in public policy proposals has occurred in recent times—apart from the sharp ideological shifts which we do not believe have occurred—could be accounted for by examining a platform from each of the different periods since 1945 when avowedly conservative perspectives were preeminent, or at least influential, within the Republican party. Differences that occur on subjects in these different platforms are duly noted. As we see, though, the perspectives expressed are overwhelmingly alike.

In 1952, the Republican presidential nomination contest was largely between Senator Robert A. Taft and Dwight D. Eisenhower. The supporters of Taft, the pre-convention frontrunner—historian Clinton Rossiter in his 1955 book *Conservatism in America* called him "surely the key figure of the modern Right.'"[1]—had the majority on the Platform Committee.[2] This suggests that the platform that emerged was likely to be a quite conservative document. Even if the usual compromises occurred on the Committee, however, the fact that the Taft supporters backed it with little dissent further illustrates its likely conservative orientation.

Actually, the supporters of *both* Taft and Eisenhower on the Committee seemed satisfied with the document[3] and Eisenhower himself may also have wanted a conservative platform. He was possibly a conservative himself, although there is considerable disagreement about this.[4] It is likely, at any rate, that Eisenhower supported a platform as conservative as the preeminently conservative Taft wanted in 1952 since in the pre-convention campaign they differed little with each other on the issues.[5] For these reasons the 1952 platform is a good one to choose for our purposes.

In any event, the 1952 platform seems to be an especially good choice for our purposes. The 1964 platform bears the distinct imprint, of course, of Senator Barry M. Goldwater and those in the party that called themselves "conservatives."[6] This was the year in which the "conservatives" finally took control of the Republican party and is an obvious platform to choose for our purposes.

The final platform examined is that of 1984. This is a good platform to choose because it represents the mature political thinking of a president, Ronald W. Reagan, who has been a strong, long-time supporter of conservative principles. Indeed, many think that he has been the only genuinely conservative president since before the New Deal. One, of course, could choose the 1980 Republican platform as an appropriate one to examine on these grounds also. 1984 is preferred, however, because it enables us to select one platform of the conservative party when it already held the presidency. This enables us to be able to get an even broader picture and to evaluate conservative public policy positions not only when proposed as an alternative, but also when tempered with the prudence and realism that quickly shape the approach of a president who has been trying to get his program approved.[7]

As with the Democratic platforms, we see a considerable increase in length as time passes. The 1952 Republican platform spanned 9 1/4 pages in *National Party Platforms*. The 1964 platform took up 13 1/2 pages in the same book. The text of the 1984 platform ran 30 comparable-sized pages in the *Congressional Record*, where it was inserted by then-Senate Majority Leader Howard H. Baker, Jr. Again, we see the increasing tendency to go into greater detail in these documents as time has gone on. This further illustrates (paradoxically for the Republicans, since their platforms frequently emphasize, as we shall see, the private sector and lower levels of government handling problems instead of the federal government) how much greater the area of activities has grown to which the parties believe at least *s o m e* national attention must be given.

An examination of the platforms enables us to conclude that it is appropriate to divide our analysis into the same specific categories as we did with the Democratic ones. These are economic and social welfare policy (which includes both domestic and international economic policy), agriculture, education, civil rights and civil liberties, foreign policy, and defense and disarmament. Within these various categories, we see discussed the various subjects that were addressed by the papal teachings surveyed, even if the encyclicals do not always use the same category titles. As with the Democratic platforms, we do not examine all of the provisions, but focus only on those that relate to the papal teaching discussed.

Besides these categories of policy, we also note the statements that appear at the beginning of each of the platforms on four of the subjects that were addressed by the conservative thinkers surveyed in Chapter Five: the purposes of government; God, religion, and the natural law as the basis for the political order; freedom; and equality. Unlike the two Democratic platforms considered, the Republican ones devote some attention, albeit brief, to these matters of general political philosophy.[8] It is for this reason that it is appropriate that we have noted them in this chapter, even though we did not when examining the Democratic platforms. As we shall see, these statements concur with the thought of most of the writers previously surveyed.

The general purposes of government are referred to in some fashion by each of the platforms. The 1952 platform says the following in its first paragraph:

> We maintain that man was not born to be ruled, but that he consented to be governed; and that the reasons that moved him thereto are few and simple. He has voluntarily submitted to government because, only by the establishment of just laws, and the power to enforce those laws, can an orderly life be maintained, full and equal opportunity for all be established, and the blessings of liberty be perpetuated.[9]

The platform goes on to say that government and those in it "should set a high example of honesty, of justice, and unselfish devotion to the public good" and insists that they "labor to maintain tranquility at home and peace and friendship with all the nations of the earth."[10] Another pertinent observation made is that "local self-government is the cornerstone of the freedom of men."[11]

The platform, then, at least *expressly* seems to view government as an artificial construct of men, not something natural to them (although, as we see, it implicitly suggests quite the opposite). It is something men created and they conferred political authority on (i.e., gave it the right to rule over them) voluntarily and knowingly. They did this for the purposes mentioned above—liberty, order, and equal opportunity—and only because of the realization that these purposes are most attainable when there is a means of making and carrying out just laws (i.e., when there is government).

The latter position seems to contradict the social contract notion of government being a mere human creation given earlier in the passage. If it is only by means of government that these crucial purposes can be attained, then man by his *nature* would seem to require government (i.e., government, then, is natural not artificial). This would seem especially to be the case when one considers that one of the purposes of government is "an orderly life." This is the very essence of what men need government for; how men could have lived in some pre-political state where there was no government and still maintained public order is hard to imagine. It is difficult also to see how men could have sought to enter political society to secure "just laws" if they did not have some prior conception of justice. Since justice is the supremely *political* virtue,[12] this would have required men to have already been living in political society. So, we must conclude there is considerable ambiguity on this point in the platform.

Another point about the purpose of government that is seen in the above quotations is that it must promote justice and the public or common good. Also, it must assume the responsibility for establishing amicable relations among the peoples of the world, or at least among the people who are governed by some particular government and all other peoples. Finally, it should be noted that the quotation about local self-government above reinforces the one purpose of government stated in the longer quoted passage, that of promoting liberty or freedom.[13]

There are two general references to the purpose of government in the 1964 platform. By asking, in the first paragraph, "[A]re men in government to serve, or are they to master, their fellow men?",[14] it suggests a broad purpose: to be of service to its citizens. Without trying to read too much of a meaning into this, it at least is saying that government must respond to its citizens' wishes and may even obliquely be referring to its need to promote the common good. A second reference appears when the platform says the following:

> It is for government to foster and maintain an environment of freedom encouraging every individual to develop to the fullest his God-given powers of mind, heart and body; and beyond this, government should undertake only needful things, rightly of public concern, which the citizen cannot himself accomplish.[15]

In other words, government must promote individual freedom and play a minimal role in other unspecified areas, depending on demonstrated public needs.

A third purpose of government mentioned—"a high mission of government"—is "to help assure equal opportunity for all, affording every citizen an equal chance at the starting line but never determining who is to win or lose."[16]

The 1984 platform makes references to the purposes of government in the context of speaking about other broad questions. In a section entitled "Free Enterprise, Democracy, and the Role of Government" (referring here primarily to the role of government in economic matters, not its role generally), the platform speaks of our "nation"—and, implicitly our government—being "dedicated to individual freedom and human rights."[17] This phraseology suggests, of course, that promoting the latter is a purpose of government.

In another section, the platform says, "every generation has relearned the art of self-government."[18] What this states, obliquely, is that government—following the 1964 platform— has the purpose of being responsive to its citizens. In another section entitled "A Free and Just Society," the 1984 platform says that the American people "want government to foster an environment in which individuals can develop their potential without hindrance"(this is very much like the quote above from the 1964 platform). It terms this an "opportunity society." It then goes on to say that "our common goal [is] a free and just society."[19] We see other purposes of government expressed here: it should help create individual opportunity—it does not clearly define "opportunity," but the context of this part of the platform makes one think it concerns mostly economic achievement—and, echoing the other platforms, it should promote freedom and justice. The stress on promoting freedom is present, as we see, in all three platforms. In order to help people pursue opportunity and maintain "a safety net of assistance for those who need it," three other specific governmental purposes are set out: protecting property rights, providing a sound currency, and "minimizing...intrusions into individual decisions to work, save, invest, and take risks." (This latter purpose, of course, involves, once again, the protecting of freedom [specifically economic freedom]).[20]

On the subject of God, religion, and the natural law as the basis of the political order, we see scattered references in the platforms. The 1952 platform closes with a theistic reference to its efforts being "under the guidance of Divine Providence" (i.e., this is an acknowledgement of the on-going role God plays in human affairs).[21] The 1964 platform makes the strongest statement about the importance of religion, and how ignoring it has created problems in America:

> Much of today's moral decline and drift—much of the prevailing preoccupation with physical and material comforts of life—much of today's crass political appeals to the appetites of the citizenry—can be traced to a leadership grown demagogic and materialistic through indifference to national ideals founded in deeply held religious faith.[22]

The 1964 platform goes on to declare that the Republican party is "determined to reaffirm and reapply" this "heritage of faith and high purpose." It expresses the belief that men owe their very selves and abilities to God when, in the passage where it speaks about government's role in promoting freedom, it says that every individual has "God-given powers of mind, heart and body." A further theistic reference is seen in the platform's first paragraph when it rhetorically asks, "[I]s man to live in dignity and freedom under God or be enslaved[?]"[23] Similarly, near the end of the platform an appeal is made for "the help of Almighty God" to enable the party to defend America's interests and warn our adversaries of our strength.[24]

The 1984 platform contains two brief references to God and religion. In one place, the platform speaks of "the divine command to help our neighbor"[25] and in another, it says that "America was built on the institutions of home, family, religion, and neighborhood."[26] There is thus a nod to the importance of religion, but it is little more than that. These are the only *explicit* references (two lines in thirty-one pages of text).

The above references to "justice" and "just" laws (1952 platform), a "just society" (1984 platform), and "national ideals founded in devoutly held religious faith" and "high purpose" (1964 platform) are all oblique references to the natural law. So is the 1984 platform's reference to "traditional morality."[27] At no point, however, do the platforms speak about natural law in explicit terms or say that it must be the *basis* of the political order.

We have already seen references to the notion of freedom in the platforms. All have held it to be of crucial importance and a duty of government to promote. The quotes already given about freedom will not be repeated, but the following additional ones will be noted which further reinforce this strong emphasis on greater freedom. The 1952 platform speaks of Republican foreign policy, especially *vis-a-vis* the Communist countries, as "reviv[ing] the contagious, liberating influences which are inherent in freedom." This obviously refers to a dynamic being created among the populations of these countries which will lead their rulers to grant them more freedom, eventually "mark[ing] the beginning of their [the Communist regimes'] end."[28] The nature and content of these "liberating influences" are not specified and how such influences are different from freedom itself is left unsaid.

The 1964 platform contains the most direct references to freedom. Besides the ones we have already noted, the platform speaks of our nation being "the beacon of liberty" and laments the fact that "individual freedom" is retreating in the face of heightened governmental power. It says that "[t]o Republicans, liberty is still today man's most precious possession" and insists that "[e]very person has the right to govern himself...with a minimum of governmental interference."[29] In addition to those mentioned, there are five other general references to freedom.[30] The 1984 platform makes two other general references to freedom besides those mentioned, and both are very prominently placed in the Preamble:

> The Republican's Party's...basic premise [is]: "From freedom comes opportunity; from opportunity comes growth; from growth comes progress."

and

> If everything depends on freedom—and it does—then securing freedom, at home and around the world, is one of the most important endeavors a free people can undertake.[31]

On the subject of the view of equality, we have already seen that all three platforms firmly and insistently express the belief that government must help secure equal opportunity, but, as the 1984 platform puts it, must not "attempt to dictate results."[32] The 1964 platform, as already noted, says essentially the same thing.

The view of communism expressed in the platforms shall be discussed when we speak about the foreign policy positions taken.

Public Policy Positions in the Conservative Platforms

I. Economic and Social Welfare Policy

The first point we should take note of on this subject is the platforms' discussion of private property, free enterprise, and capitalism. The 1984 Republican platform provides a clear statement of the fundamental nature of the right of private property. Echoing the conservative thinkers examined, it calls it "the cornerstone of our liberty and the free enterprise system" which "safeguards for citizens all things of value," including "their religious convictions, their safety and liberty." It is a "God-given and inalienable right."[33] All three platforms give a ringing endorsement to free enterprise,[34] with the 1984 one being the most pronounced and profound:

> Free enterprise is fundamental to the American way of life. It is inseparable from the social, religious, political, and judicial institutions which form the bedrock of a nation dedicated to individual freedom and human rights.[35]

As was noted in Chapter Five, the Church and conservatism concur in seeing that preserving political liberty and other legitimate human liberties necessitates liberty in the economic and property realms. The 1984 platform goes beyond the teaching of the Church in its seeming belief (expressed in the quotes above) in how *utterly* fundamental the latter are to the former, and in seeing them basically as underlying all other rights and the good life. One can almost infer from these passages the distinctive belief of modern political philosophy that there is a certain primacy of the economic realm over other realms. In spite of affirming—as the Church would also—a "God-given right" of private property, the impression can easily be gotten that economics is the foundation for the other realms of human thought and ideas, instead of religion and philosophy (as the Church and the Western tradition has held). This reinforces what was said above about how the platforms do not seem to outrightly acknowledge that God, religion, and the natural law are at the base of the political order (even while making reference to them directly and indirectly). The platforms are not as close to papal teaching as the conservative thinkers surveyed in seeing the centrality of God, religion, and the natural law in politics.

In line with the above, the Republican platforms strongly endorse two corollaries of the "capitalist"-free enterprise thinking: the great value of competition and free trade. The 1964 platform features an entire page-long (out of fourteen pages) subsection entitled "Faith in the Competitive System."[36] Various planks in that sub-section make clear the advantageousness of competition in an economy.

This viewpoint is not incompatible with papal teaching. As noted, the popes have mentioned the "right of free commerce" and have said that competition is valuable. It is not competition that Church teaching opposes, but uncontrolled competition, competition unregulated by anything. Momentarily, we shall consider what the platforms say about this.

The platforms demonstrate apparent agreement with the popes' belief that property should be spread around to as many people as possible. For example, the platforms emphasize the importance of small business and of assisting small businesses, and of making home ownership possible for more people.[37] The platforms' consistent stress on private sector initiative and control whenever possible, along with their frequent mention of preferring state and local government action over federal, shows an endorsement of the principle of subsidiarity (even though they never mention the term).[38] This position also demonstrates agreement with *Mater et Magistra* in noting that "where private initiative of individuals is lacking...much stagnation occurs in various sectors of the economy."[39]

There is also demonstrated a basic acceptance in the platforms of the undesirability of monopoly which, as stated, is affirmed in the encyclicals (this does not mean that either outrightly opposes all monopoly, however). *Quadragesimo Anno* notes that "unrestrained free competition" results in a "concentration of power" because the strongest are permitted to prevail and then to squash all others.[40] The 1952 and 1964 platforms support anti-trust laws and other means of restoring and strengthening competition. (The 1984 platform does not mention anti-trust legislation).[41]

It is clear that the platforms favor competition in the economy. The question is: Do they want it to be restrained? We have already seen the bias in favor of an extremely broad notion of economic freedom in the writings of the conservative thinkers surveyed. It is difficult to come to any conclusive judgment about that from a study of the platforms. They clearly stress *more* private economic freedom and want to limit government's interference and regulatory activities in the economy, but they also clearly do not seek to eliminate them or even to bring them down to a nominal level as might be expected in a truly *laissez-faire* state.

We might be able to make two at least tentative conclusions about the conservative thinking as embodied in the platforms. As with both visions of the liberals, they see competition as the ruling principle of economic life, in conflict with the popes. On the other hand, their dislike for government regulation, while accepting and even embracing it when they are convinced it is definitely needed, perhaps puts them closer to the popes than the liberals, since the popes, while pointing to a role for the state, prefer voluntary submission of enterprises to industrial and vocational groupings. Liberalism, as noted, has pushed increasing amounts of government economic regulation.

It should further be said, however, that the focus of the platforms is not necessarily the elimination or reduction of government regulations, but of *federal* government regulation. This is what most of their pertinent planks are directed toward. Perhaps this is to be expected, since national party platforms concern programs which a presidential administration is supposed to address, and not necessarily ones that state governors or local mayors would be running on, in an off-presidential year; and so any call for limiting government in them is going to be a call for limiting the *national* government. Nevertheless, even in the direct statements of political philosophy, where all three platforms speak about limiting government, only one (1952) speaks about it at all in a generic way. The other two discuss only the restraint of the federal or national government. This possibly illustrates the tendency that is often observed, at least in some sectors of American conservatism, to concern itself almost exclusively with restricting *national* government power and not turning to the *national* government to solve problems or develop programs (while oblivious to the fact that state and local government can also be oppressive).

The next subject we consider is employment and labor-management relations. The importance of having people employed is seen in all three platforms. The 1952 platform states that "regular and adequate income for the employee...[is] essential to a sound national economy."[42] The 1964 one pledges the Republican party to "enlargement of employment opportunities for urban and rural citizens."[43] In 1984, the platform proudly claimed that, because of

President Reagan's economic policies, six and a half million more people were working. It also says that the small businesses the Republicans want to help have been an important factor in economic recovery (because they provide over fifty million jobs) and it criticizes standing Democratic-enacted minimum wage legislation for keeping youths from getting jobs.[44]

Unlike the new liberal 1984 Democratic platform, the Republican platforms do not commit themselves to provide jobs, by some means or other, to everyone who wants to work. This latter, as indicated, is a position closer to that of the popes. The impression given is that while the Republicans stress employment, they probably do not do so to the same extent as the new liberals, or as emphatically. While none of the platforms makes it an explicit governmental policy objective to increase employment or attain or maintain a certain low level of unemployment, each sets forth many other broad economic policy priorities, such as balancing the federal budget, combatting inflation, controlling the public debt, cutting taxes, establishing a sound monetary policy, and reducing government spending and regulations.[45]

The platforms *do* commit themselves to (or mention favorably) federal efforts in, specfically, job training and vocational rehabilitation.[46] Nevertheless, the lack of overall stress on eliminating unemployment suggests that they do not regard it as so central an economic problem and perhaps not much at all of a moral problem (as the popes do who, it will be recalled, call it an "evil"). Though unemployment is an implicit concern behind the other economic policy objectives mentioned , it is seemingly not the Republicans' *major* concern. Embodied in the platforms is the notion that it is up to the private sector to provide the jobs—which the platforms certainly concede is an essential undertaking—and what government can best do is to create the economic conditions that will best make that possible. This is a perfectly acceptable approach as far as papal teaching is concerned. Still, the lack of a specific stress on the problem makes one think that there is indeed a lesser appreciation of it and not just a different view about to how to deal with it.

All three platforms uphold the right of working men to join unions, bargain collectively, and strike.[47] This is certainly in keeping with the Church's teaching. Two of the three platforms make a point of saying that these things should be able to be undertaken without government or "third-party" involvement.[48]

Even though it is clear from other provisions that the Republicans do not oppose all legislation regulating the employer-employee relationship—for example, they reaffirm their long-standing support for the Taft-Hartley Act[49] and give implicit support for the idea of minimum wage laws, (as seen above)—the fact that they want the government to stay out of the picture is something which does not accord with papal teaching, for the latter emphasizes that the state should eliminate potential labor problems by proper legislation beforehand. It is fair to say that the statements about government non-involvement indicate a Republican lack of enthusiasm for a key principle asserted by the popes.

The 1952 platform actually lists a set of rights of working men and unions. Such a list does not appear in the later platforms; but there is no indication the party's position is any different about these. They are probably listed so prominently in the 1952 platform because that was drafted during the period when the nation's basic labor legislation, starting with the 1935 Wagner Act and culminating with the 1959 Landrum-Griffin Act, was still being hotly debated, developed, and refined. The fact that the rights of each worker are stressed like this—and this is the only place where the rights of *any* groups are spelled out in the platform—indicates an agreement with the popes that the laboring classes are in a position of weakness in an economy, so that government must be particularly concerned about protecting them. Those with wealth and greater economic power do not need government's help. The platform seeks to protect workers not only from abusive employers, but also from unjust practices and demands by their unions. (The Democratic platforms are silent about the latter.)

The question is legitimately raised as to what the Republican platforms believe the nature of relations between labor and management, and also government, should be. In other words, what do they say about cooperation, a persistent theme of the popes?

Two of the platforms explicitly reject the idea of class conflict, so fundamentally characteristic of Marxism.[50] This is not the same thing, however, as saying that in the context of a liberal democratic political society such as America's, which rejects Marxist principles, that the essential relationship between labor and management should be a non-conflictual one (in which structures and practices are set up to consciously promote interdependence and cooperation. There is not a single statement in any of the platforms that alludes to such a cooperative ideal or depicts it as a desirable objective.

Other types of cooperation *are* mentioned. The 1952 platform supports "bona fide farmer-owned, farmer-operated cooperatives."[51] The 1964 platform speaks about a relationship between private enterprise and *government* "in advancing the balanced use of the nation's resources."[52] The 1984 platform pledges the federal government to help restructure farm and ranch debt procedures, included among which would be "the establishment of local community farm and ranch finance committees, which will advise borrowers, lenders, and government officials" regarding such restructuring.[53] The latter also features a number of planks which commit the federal government to aid lower levels of government in their efforts to better provide certain services and programs, such as in the area of education.[54] It thus stresses *intergovernmental* cooperation quite a bit.

All these forms of cooperation either are very limited and isolated to a few areas of the economy or else, again, they are essentially of a different sort—e.g., intergovernmental cooperation—than that discussed by the popes. The platforms in no way speak of the kind of worker-management joint action stressed by the 1984 Democratic platform.

What has already been said should be enough to indicate that the Republican platforms have respect for the principle of subsidiarity, which liberalism—especially the new liberalism—frequently neglects. Actually, the platforms are replete with statements about the essentiality of letting the lower levels of government—states and localities—address problems, direct programs, etc.

Let us now turn to the matter of social welfare programs which are mentioned in the platforms. All three support the Social Security system to financially aid elderly Americans.[55] Both the 1964 and 1984 platforms also indicate support for medical assistance programs for the elderly, the former calling for support for such programs for the "needy" elderly and the latter endorsing Medicare (which provides benefits irrespective of need and which did not come into existence until after 1964).[56] This is certainly in keeping with the teaching of *Mater et Magistra*.

Let us now consider further the matter of health care. Two of the three platforms support better delivery of health care to the entire population, but all object to it being done in a compulsory way by the federal government directly.

The 1952 Republican platform states that "[t]here should be a division of responsibility between government, the physician, the voluntary hospital, and voluntary health insurance" and that it is "opposed to Federal compulsory health insurance" which it sees as expensive, inefficient, and promotive of "debased standards of medical care," but does "support those health activities by government which stimulate the development of adequate hospital services without Federal interference in local administration."[57] The 1984 platform features a sizeable section on "Health" in which the party supports federal help for medical research, nutrition, and educational programs, non-discrimination in health care, and respect for the rights of parents and the family in dealing with health problems of children and the elderly. It also states emphatically that "[w]e reaffirm...our opposition to any proposals for compulsory national health insurance."[58] The party insists that it has a "commitment to assure a basic line of high quality health care for all Americans," but believes that this can and has been handled best by private health care deliverers.[59] Except for the Medicare (elderly) and Medicaid (poor people) programs and V. A. hospitals,[60] government should not be running health insurance or health care programs and can best help in the above mentioned ways and by controlling inflation.[61]

The above thinking about health care seems to better conform to what the popes have said than do either the old or new liberalism. Both the latter groups and the present platforms emphasize the need for providing good health care to everyone and support government assistance for it. The Republicans (i.e., the conservative party) are much more cognizant of questions of subsidiarity, however. Indeed, the 1984 Republican platform stresses this in more than one way in its discussion of health care. (We suggested in Chapter Four that perhaps a good case could be made for "federal involvement in health care." Both parties advocate this, although it should be pointed out that endorsing such involvement is not necessarily the same thing as advocating compulsory, federally mandated and administered health insurance.) The very fact that the Democrats specifically pledge themselves to "federal leadership" in this area (their 1972 and 1980 platforms specifically called for national health insurance) while the Republicans make a point of opposing a federal imposition of health insurance in favor of private sector responsibility—indicates that the Republicans are more in line with Church teaching on subsidiarity.

Regarding the Republican platforms' views about welfare programs (i.e., programs for the poor), there are only two brief references to this subject in the 1964 platform (there are none in 1952's). At one point there is a critical reference to "the 42 existing Federal poverty programs" in a way that seems accepting of them, since the Johnson Administration's "War on Poverty" is spoken of as duplicative of them. In this same passage, there is a clear approval expressed of other, non-federal poverty programs: the "War on Poverty," it says, "would dangerously centralize Federal controls and bypass *effective* state, local and private programs."[62] Another passage calls for federal, state, and private cooperation for vocational rehabilitation to help "the mentally and physically handicapped, the chronically unemployed and the poverty-stricken."[63]

The 1984 platform explicitly makes clear the obligation society has to those in critical need: "Helping the less fortunate is one of America's noblest endeavors...Aid should be swift and adequate to ensure the necessities of a decent life."[64] It makes equally clear that there are distinct limits to welfare: "The American people want an opportunity society, not a welfare state. They want government to foster an environment in which individuals can develop their potential without hindrance."[65] Particular concern is expressed about previous federal welfare programs creating dependency on government, not truly meeting the poor's needs, aiding the undeserving, damaging family cohesion, and being self-servingly directed to keeping a welfare bureaucracy operating. The belief is also expressed that programs should be "self-help" oriented and should be administered by state and local governments, even if the funds come from Washington (like the 1964 platform says). The platform also sees economic improvement as the best solution.[66]

This all appears to concur with papal teaching. There is, first, the recognition of the duty to care for those in need, but at the same time not to let those who do not have a need to benefit. Certainly the popes say the former; the latter is also the essential point that is made when *Quadragesimo Anno* says that people must "not...become burdensome to others" if they "are able to provide for" themselves.[67] The fact that the platforms are ready to have the state, even the federal government, provide welfare, if necessary, concurs with the popes. So does the belief that the federal government ought not to do it if the lower governmental levels can (here is subsidiarity again).

Interestingly, the only thing said about a private role concerns the partnership for vocational rehabilitation; there is nothing about private relief efforts. The fact that this issue is not even mentioned by these platforms suggests that, implicitly, the conservative party joins the liberal one in deviating from the Church by regarding welfare as primarily a governmental responsibility. The popes believe the relief effort, at minimum, should be a cooperative one and actually prefer that it should be essentially a private one (performed by the Church herself). They also want to see the need for relief averted by undertaking prior initiatives to alleviate the plight of the poor. This would seem to be met by the 1984 platform's stressing that government policy should be used to cure inflation, thus helping the economy.

The importance of the family is obviously stressed above, and also is in other parts of the 1984 Republican platform.[68] The "Welfare" section of this platform speaks about "the maternalization of poverty" caused to some degree by the welfare system but "worsened by the breakdown of the family and accelerated by destructive patterns of conduct too long tolerated by permissive liberals."[69] Among the factors at work here (the platform is almost certainly implying) are divorce and sexual licentiousness. Yet, the fact that the platform will not spell them out directly and will not call for an end to divorce or legal restraints on various types of immoral sexual behavior, suggests that these concerns do not have a high priority—and that possibly the breakdown of the family itself does not either.

This deemphasis surely does not agree with the concerns expressed by the popes.[70] On the other hand, the platform's endorsing of "programs to assist female-headed households to build self-sufficiency" conforms to the popes' insistence that there not be unjust discriminations against widowed, divorced, and separated women. Its speaking of the term "breadwinner" in the normal context of a male—a husband—is certainly in keeping with the natural family arrangement the popes have underscored.[71]

Overall on the welfare or relief question, we must say that the platforms argee with what the popes have taught. The platforms do not mention unemployment compensation—which is strongly stressed by the popes—but that is probably because the principle has for such a long time been accepted, that the drafters probably figured that it did not have to be mentioned. The welfare question is a somewhat different issue and one that has continued to be the subject of much public debate.

Another area addressed by the Republican platforms is tax policy. 1952's attacks "confiscatory taxes." It also calls for a "minimizing of double taxation"—the same types of taxes being imposed by different levels of government—and "[a]dministration of the tax laws free from politics, favoritism and corruption."[72] The 1964 platform is critical of "overly regressive taxation and the unfairness of forcing the poor to finance...programs for the rich."[73] It calls for federal "fiscal discipline" so tax rates can be reduced, and for "credit[ing] against Federal taxes...specified State and local taxes paid."[74]

Taxes are highlighted in the 1984 platform, reflecting the fact that cutting taxes was a central part of President Reagan's economic program. As far as tax fairness is concerned, the following passages seem the most pertinent. There is a concern about "oppressive tax rates" and about insuring that "tax burdens are not shifted to the poor." It "support[s] tax reform that will lead to a fair and simple tax system" and says it "believe[s] a modified flat tax—with specific exemptions...is a most promising approach." It opposes "taxation of churches, religious schools, or any other religious institutions," except for "any business income unrelated to...[its] religious function."[75]

These provisions are in agreement with the Church, except possibly for the flat tax proposal, which would seem to violate the encyclicals' "ability to pay" principle (this is not, however, certain; it depends on how it would be set up and how extensive the exemption structure would be and whether it would be aimed at reducing the burden on the poor). The platform provisions endorsing the Reagan Administration action of "virtual[ly] eliminati[ng] the 'widow's tax' which had jeopardized retirement savings of senior women" and seeking the ending of "discrimination against homemakers with regard to Individual Retirement Accounts," seem to accept the above papal teaching that unjust treatment of different classes of single women be ended. The support for the Reagan Administration's action of "rais[ing] the maximum child care tax credit" per family might be said to be doing this also, but it could also be viewed as something that has the effect of hurting the family by encouraging more mothers in intact families to work outside of the home.[76]

The final topic in this realm of policy to be considered is trade policy. What can generally be said about these platforms is that they heartily endorse free trade. The 1984 platform addresses this by saying: "We are committed to a free and open international trading system."[77] They state caveats to this, but they essentially concern preserving American national interests or pressuring certain tyrannical regimes.

For example, the 1952 platform says it supports "reciprocal trade agreements...to safeguard our domestic enterprises...against unfair import competition"[78]; and the 1984 one insists that the Republicans "will not tolerate the loss of American jobs to nationalized, subsidized, protected foreign industries."[79] Also, the latter platform calls on American "trading partners to join us in reviewing trade with totalitarian regimes" (i.e., Communist ones).[80] In summary, the Republicans favor negotiated free trade arrangements so long as a sense of fairness and respect prevails for the interests of *both* trading partners and attention is given to the furthering of American foreign policy objectives. Free trade is the norm, but is not absolute.

The position on trade does not compare favorably to the Church's. As noted, the Church says that free trade internationally can no more be the ruling principle than free competition can be in domestic economics. There is no discussion of social justice being involved with trade or of the need to let free trade give way to some degree of preference for underdeveloped nations, as is called for in *Populorum Progressio.*

II. Agriculture and the Environment

The three Republican party platforms have a number of pertinent points to make on this topic. First, both the 1952 and 1984 platforms stress the essentiality of agriculture for the country. The former says that "[a] prosperous agriculture with free and independent farmers is fundamental to the national interest."[81] Similarly, the latter platform declares that "[w]e recognize that a prosperous agriculture is essential to the future of America and to the health and welfare of its people."[82]

Furthermore, there is sentiment expressed is in favor of the family farm. The 1984 platform says the following: "Family farms and ranches are the heart, soul, and backbone of American agriculture; it is the family farm that makes our system work better than any other."[83] Many of the farm proposals in the platform are directed at family farms and ranches, specifically.[84]

There is concern expressed about farm labor, both from the perspective of aiding the owner-employer and of protecting the hired farm worker. On the former, the platform wants to insure that there will be enough farm labor available for owners who need to bring on hired help[85] and that self-employed family farmers and ranchers will be able to handle costs associated with the providing of such essential personal and family needs as hospitalization insurance premiums.[86] It also seeks to insure that non-owner farm employees are protected adequately by the law. On the latter point, the platform says it "support[s] comprehensive farm-labor legislation, fair to workers *and* employers."[87]

There is much stress on the independence of farmers. The 1964 Republican platform says that farmers must have "the maximum opportunity to exercise their own management decisions on their own farms" and so it opposes "all efforts to impose upon them further Federal controls."[88] The 1984 platform claims that "[t]he primary responsibility of government with respect to agriculture is to create the opportunity for a free and competitive economic and policy environment supportive of the American farmers' and ranchers industrious and independent spirit and innovative talent,"[89] and insists that "[e]xcessive federal regulations...have been a crushing burden."[90]

Nevertheless, as already indicated, the 1984 platform does not believe government should take a *laissez-faire* attitude toward agriculture. It says that in the case of "well-managed and efficient farms and ranches" that "are temporarily unable to make a profit...it is in the public interest to provide reasonable and targeted assistance."[91] Among the federal programs the three platforms support to aid farmers and ranchers are the following: full parity prices, farm credit, a soil conservation program, agricultural research and education programs, assistance in rural electrification programs and distribution facilities, a program to provide supplemental farm labor for production and harvesting, aid in restructuring debt procedures, a program to reduce reserve stocks of agricultural commodities, water programs, and changes in tax and bankruptcy laws.[92] The emphasis, of course, is on privately-run agriculture and, in areas where the states have traditionally dealt with agriculture problems, such as water policy, the aim of not superseding them is stated; thus, subsidiarity is respected.[93] Another point mentioned about agriculture has already been noted: the encouragement of co-operatives.

On the matter of the environment, the following appears in the platforms. The 1952 and 1964 platforms pre-date the contemporary "environmental movement," but they contain provisions that seek, to some extent, to address environmental problems. The former says that "[f]lood control programs should include the application of sound land use reforestation and water-management practices for each watershed," and it includes a section called "Natural Resources"—only a minority of which deals with conservation — which calls for "a full and orderly program for the development and conservation of our natural resources." Indeed, most of this section concerns either natural resource or economic *development*, state land and resource rights, and the fishing industry.[94]

The 1964 platform has a section entitled "Neglect of Natural Resources," but it is exclusively devoted to deploring government obstacles to

development and its alleged failure, under Democratic adminstrations, to protect the fishing industry. Elsewhere, it seeks cooperation among all levels of
government and the private sector "in advancing the balanced use of the
nation's natural resources" and "comprehensive water-resource planning and
development,"[95] and calls for other avenues of resource development. Again,
we see mostly a discussion of the need for development. (Even this much
discussion, though, is at least a *shade* more than we saw with the old liberalism
in a pre-environmental consciousness era.) It has already been mentioned that
the 1984 platform speaks of soil and water conservation and water policy. It
also contends that some federally-owned land should be sold to make development possible.[96] There is a section on "Environment" elsewhere in the platform
which addresses pollution and other environmental problems most directly. Its
first paragraph says the following: "The environment is not just a scientific or
technological issue; it is a human one...We assert the people's stewardship of
our God-given natural resources. We pledge to meet the challenges of environmental protection...conservation of our nonrenewable resources, and preservation of our irreplaceable natural heritage." The platform endorses "a strong
effort to control and clean up toxic wastes," to implement "meaningful clean air
and clean water acts," "to reduce the threat...from acid rain," and the elimination of "the dumping of raw sewage." It insists that "the health and well-being
of our citizens must be a high priority." It quotes early Republican "environ-
mentalist" Theodore Roosevelt to the effect that, " 'Conservation means development as much as it does protection.' "[97]

Having stated the Republican platforms' positions about agriculture
and the environment, how, then, do they square with the social encyclicals?

They square pretty well with them. Clearly, the platforms do not seek
to leave agriculture behind in the push for economic development, as warned
against by the popes. They specifically endorse the family farm concept. Their
concern for farm earnings clearly corresponds with the encyclicals' call for
insuring a decent level of farm income. The 1984 provision seeking farmer
involvement in the establishment of new general debt restructuring plans indicates
that they are open to farmers and ranchers being prime shapers of rural policy
(although they do not stress this as much as the Democratic platforms), and
their endorsement of co-operatives shows support for farmers organizing. These
positions were both papal admonitions, although not stressed as moral mandates.

The general willingness of the Republican platforms to have government assist farmers and ranchers when, despite strong and sincere efforts, they
are still struggling economically, is certainly in conformity with the thrust of
the encyclicals. The call for federal help with electrification and distribution
facilities concurs with Pope John's contention that efforts should be made to
aid in rural modernization. The environmental concern expressed in the plat-

forms agrees with John Paul II's statements in *Sollicitudo Rei Socialis* and his December 1989 statement, but probably do not go as far as he does. He does not reject development, but calls for a recognition that natural resources are not inexhaustible, that pollution has become a serious threat, and that man does not have *"absolute dominion"* over natural resources (i.e., he is but a steward). These points *do* appear in the Republican platforms.

Nevertheless, the latter do not echo John Paul in attacking indiscriminate applications of technology, the mentality that puts production over human dignity, and a wasteful or excessive "lifestyle." The platforms are not necessarily *f o r* these things, but their silence about them and, more, the strong emphasis of especially the 1984 platform on economic growth, suggests an obliviousness to them.

III. Civil Rights and Civil Liberties

Civil rights and civil liberties is a large, multi-faceted category, as was seen when treating it in the liberal platforms. What is included here is an examination of the Republican platforms' position on individual, family, and group rights protected by law and the rights of racial, ethnic, and other minority groups as well as women.

The first point that should be noted here concerns equality. As has already been pointed out, the Republican platforms, like the conservative thinkers examined, favor equal opportunity, but oppose the notion that government must guarantee equal results. As part of this position, they oppose such notions as quotas to achieve racial, ethnic, and gender balance, "reverse" or "inverse discrimination," and affirmative action (called "preferential treatment" by the 1984 platform).[98] As stated before, the Church agrees with the notion of equal opportunity, but does not require equal results. In fact, what was said before about the encyclical *Socialism, Communism, Nihilism* indicates that the Church would be critical of the idea because it goes against human nature. What was stated before about affirmative action applies here (see Chapter Three): at the very least, if such programs are not undertaken prudently, they can create a group or class egoism harming brotherhood, and would be morally unacceptable.

This general thinking about equality leads to its particular applications in the area of civil rights. The platforms strongly oppose bigotry and discrimination in employment and other areas based on race, ethnicity, religion, or class.[99] This includes rejecting racial segregation and any unreasonable impediments to the exercise of voting rights.[100] They also reject unjust discrimination based on gender. The 1952 platform supports the Equal Rights Amendment (it was not realized at that time, as with the 1948 Democrats, what far-reaching and undesirable implications it would have), and "equal pay for equal work."[101] The 1984 platform insists that "women have equal opportunity, security, and real choices for the...future" and also stresses support for "equal pay for equal work." It extols the Reagan Administration for a project to identify sex discrimination in federal and state statutes and for filing a substantial number of sex discrimination—in employment—cases. In line with its opposition to affirmative action, it rejects "comparable worth."[102]

There are other ways, not so much legal as public policy in nature (and thereby not pure civil rights matters), in which the 1984 platform endorses advancement for women (at least in the particular way of opening up new career horizons). For example, it opposes restrictions on in-home work, which it says "limit economic opportunity, especially for women and the homebound;"[103] seeks to help women business owners "become full partners in the economic mainstream of small business" by means of legislation and more government contracts;[104] encourages, female access to "the traditionally higher paying technical, managerial, and professional positions;"[105] wants to bring more women into government service[106] and extols the fact that "the United States leads the world in integrating women into the military...serv[ing] in a variety of non-combat assignments."[107] The 1984 platform addresses another "equal rights" area, discrimination against the handicapped (this is not mentioned by the earlier platforms, but was not then an important public issue). It calls for government to "seek out disabled persons and their parents to make them knowledgeable of their rights" and to "prompt[ly] and vigorous[ly] enforce...the[se] rights."[108] It says further that "[a]ll Americans stand to gain when disabled citizens are assured equal opportunity" and that efforts should be made "to remove artificial barriers...so that disabled individuals may reach their potential and participate at the maximum level of their abilities in education, employment, and recreation." The latter includes removing, "insofar as practicable," physical, transportation, communication, and "attitudinal" barriers.[109]

Clearly, the insistence upon ending all of the above types of discrimination—all other things being equal—is in agreement with the Church, as we have already seen when discussing liberalism. The passages about the handicapped are, of course, in accordance with *Laborem Exercens*, probably more so than with the new liberals. This is because the 1984 Republicans realize—as seen in their speaking about the particular "potential" and "level" of the disabled person's abilities and doing what is "practicable"—that there are genuine limitations and what must indeed be aimed at is that which is best suited to the disabled in their particular situation, and not an absolute, abstract notion of "equal access."

As far as discrimination against women goes, especially in employment (which is the focus of most of the platforms' provisions on this subject), the Church, as has been said, requires that qualifications be made which are not made by the platforms. First, the same problem with accepting the rigid notion of "equal pay for equal work" (noted in Chapter Four) applies here. Second, the Republican Party dropped its earlier support of the ERA. In Chapter Four, we noted the problems with the ERA from the standpoint of the Church, once it was fully understood amidst the changed climate of the neo-feminist period. It must also be recalled that the popes oppose discrimination against women in employment *they are suited to by nature.* The 1984 platform seems essentially oblivious of this limitation; there is nothing raised at all about how some jobs simply might not be suitable to women. The only implied limitation is that women should not be in combat roles in the military, but this may not even be much of a limitation since so many supportive roles in the military could embroil women in combat and, in fact, many non-combat roles (because of the physical demands and psychological relationships they thrust upon women and the threat to their morals they present) are probably not suited to them.

Moreover, for all the concern expressed in the 1984 welfare planks about damage to the family and the maternalization of poverty, there is a surprising neglect of the point emphasized by the popes that women have a unique family role. While the aim of eliminating restrictions on in-home work surely respects this point, the emphasis placed on opening up—and, even more, strongly encouraging—women in a full range of careers in the job-world may actually make proper respect for recognition of this family role in society more difficult (as well as damaging further the family which working married women will be increasingly neglecting as they pursue their careers).

One final point needs to be made. Just as the1984 Democratic platform seemed to elevate the things of this world by stressing the acquisition of political power for women above almost anything else in achieving their "equality," so the 1984 Republican platform does similarly by stressing pri-marily the achievement of economic success and wealth. In both cases, of course, material concerns are placed in the overriding position; there is, essentially, silence about the *spiritual* welfare of women.

There is also discussion in the Republican platforms of other, more traditional Western and American rights: rights to citizen security, religious freedom, a free press (i.e., media), voting and family protection. On the first of these, the 1984 platform speaks about the right of innocent citizens to be protected against crime, a right neglected under Democratic administrations. They criticize the most recent of the latter for having "had more concern for abstract criminal rights than for victims of crime," and declare that the Republican Reagan Administration "has redressed that imbalance."[110]

In stating this, it does not seem that the Republicans are opposing traditional Bill of Rights guarantees for criminal suspects. Instead, their speaking of "abstract rights" suggests they are concerned about illegitimate rights claimed for the accused which have little basis in our Bill of Rights or legal traditions. The platform holds, in effect, that individuals have a right to security which the state has an obligation to protect. It says that "[o]ne of the major responsibilities of government is to ensure the safety of its citizens."[111] This is obviously akin to *Rerum Novarum's* contention that the primary reason the state exists is to protect "the safety of the commonwealth," and so is supported by papal teaching.

Religious freedom is both a traditional American right and strongly defended by the Church, most forcefully in *Dignitatis Humanae (Declaration on Religious Liberty)* of Vatican II. Religion freedom is upheld, implicitly, in the Republicans' rejection of discrimination based on religion, opposition to taxing churches and religious institutions (both already mentioned), commitment to make appointments to federal positions irrespective of religion,[112] and support for constitutional amendments to overturn Supreme Court decisions nullifying voluntary prayer in the public schools.[113] The latter proposal has been supported by the U. S. Catholic bishops.[114]

Press and media freedom are mentioned by the 1964 platform. It says it is "dedicated to freedom of expression for all news media" and "independence of...news-gathering media from excessive government control," and supports the media's having "the right of access...to public proceedings."[115] Press freedom, of course, is guaranteed by the U. S. Bill of Rights and basically supported by the Church, so the Church and the Republicans concur on this.

The right to vote is mentioned in the Republican platforms in connection with minorities being protected or helped in their attempts to exercise this right.[116] The right to vote is, of course, defended by the Church in light of what she has said about governments permitting their citizens to take an active part in public life. Concern about the rights of minorities that we have seen expressed in different ways by the platforms is something that is particularly stressed in *Pacem in Terris*, it will be recalled.

Finally, let us consider family rights. We have already alluded to the platform's thinking about the family in some of the points made above. We here mention some additional statements in the platform which specifically address legal rights and issues affecting the family. Additional points about family/parental rights are discussed in the "Education" section below.

The platform's concern about family rights is seen, first of all, in the fact that it has an entire half-page section on "Family Protection." There are also three noteworthy general statements about support for family life in the 1984 platform; two expressed in a positive context and one in a negative. The first is as follows:

> Republicans affirm the family as the natural and indispensable institution for human development. A society is only as strong as its fami-

lies, for they nurture those qualities necessary to maintain and advance civilization.[117]

The second statement alludes to the 1980 Republican platform, which the 1984 version says represented "a renewed vision...based upon home, family, and community as the surest guarantees of both individual rights and national greatness."[118] The final statement attacks the "Washington, liberal experimenters" for "attack[ing] the integrity of the family and parental rights."[119] The essentiality of the family for civilization, sound family life as a basis for national prosperity, the necessity of the state respecting family integrity and parental rights—these are all points the Church has stressed.

Although it has been pointed out that the Republican platforms do neglect some obvious things that could legally protect the family (such as advocating the restriction or prohibition of divorce), the 1964 platform seeks to check pornography by excluding it from the mails.[120] (Besides infringing on family rights and integrity, Pope John Paul II, as noted, tells us pornography is an "offense against women."). The 1984 platform seeks only to ban *child* pornography, but it also speaks against sex and violence in the media (even though it seeks no legal restraint on them). It concurs with John Paul in singling out women and children specifically as victims of the media exploitation (although he, at least, would not confine this "victim-status" just to them).[121]

Parental rights are defended mostly on educational issues (see below), but the 1984 platform insists also that parents be permitted to participate in health care decisions for their children.[122] What especially seems to be in mind here are efforts to provide birth control and abortions to minors. Clearly the Church agrees here, both because of its concern about parental rights and because it teaches that abortion and artificial birth control are against the natural law and thus immoral in all cases.

Another point manifesting respect for the integrity of the family in health care is the 1984 platform's call for letting people as much as possible have medical treatment in their homes so they can be with their families, and with its giving approval to the notion of the hospice.[123]

The 1984 Republican platform's opposition to legalized abortion and federal abortion funding (it was not a public issue in the 1950s or for most of the 1960s) and support for constitutional and statutory protection for the unborn child are the points in which it most starkly deviates from the 1984 Democratic platform. As stated above, the new liberals clearly oppose the Church on these points. The 1984 Republican platform further underscores its commitment against abortion by commending President Reagan for appointing federal judges who support "the sanctity of innocent human life."[124] Twice it expresses support for his appointments of federal judges who respect "traditional family values."[125]

An additional way in which the 1984 Republican platform distances itself from the 1984 Democratic one on family issues—and, also, refrains from placing itself at odds with the Church—is that it does not say anything about homosexuality. It refuses to endorse special discrimination protection for homosexuals, essentially equating them with racial and ethnic minority groups, as the Democratic platform does.

IV. Education

The education planks of the Republican platforms—especially 1984's, which by far contains the most comment of any on the subject of education—can be divided into two categories: the federal role in education and parental rights. We examine the former first.

In brief, the platforms' thinking about the federal role in education involves advocating the following: federal financial assistance to public schools and higher education generally, tax breaks to parents, a minimum of federal control and regulation, and respect for maintaining education as a state, local, and private function. In this way (and in what we see later about parental rights), the platforms clearly respect the principle of subsidiarity.

The 1952 platform's statement about education is terse. It simply endorses the system of free public education and the fact that responsibility for it "has always rested upon the local communities and the States."[126]

The 1964 platform supports tax credits, but apparently only for people paying the expenses of college education.[127] It takes the Democrats to task for "always preferring the route leading to Federal control over our schools."[128] It calls for "selective [federal] aid to higher education" (without saying how it should be "selective").[129]

The 1984 platform, like the corresponding Democratic one, supports equal educational opportunity. This is indicated when it says it supports "protecting civil rights" in education and also in the strong emphasis placed on "excellence" in educational quality throughout the country (because to be denied a good quality education is to be denied later opportunities that education makes possible), and in the particular mention of "revitaliz[ing]...inner city schools."[130] On this point, it particularly stresses a return to the "basics."[131] It says "[t]he federal role in education should be limited" since it "is a local function," and spends much time commending states for recent, positive educational reforms. The federal role discussed is limited to enacting tuition tax credit and parental voucher legislation, enforcing federal handicapped education laws, making block grants (which carry wide state authority to decide their use), and reducing federal regulations. The need for strong academic standards and discipline in schools is stressed and concern expressed about federal interference in private colleges and universities.[132] Vouchers, tuition tax credits, and aid to private colleges and universities are seen as having the effect of increasing educational opportunities and choice; they especially can be helpful to religiously-affiliated institutions of education.

The above would seem to be closely in conformity to papal teaching because of the respect manifested for the principle of subsidiarity, the respect and support for private and religious educational institutions, support for more widespread educational opportunities, and the support for equal educational opportunity regardless of race and the like.

On the subject of parental rights in education, the 1984 platform begins by saying: "Parents have the primary right and responsibility for the education of their children."[133] This statement, of course, coincides with the teaching of the Church. It is also what the sound ethician would say is a mandate of the natural law (even without reference to Divine Revelation).[134] The platform goes on to say that the school systems and educational institutions "have the primary responsibility for supporting that parental role."[135] The proposals above are promotive of parents controlling the choice of institution and the type of education to be given to their children.

Two other important platform statements concerning parental rights in education affecting children already enrolled in public schools. One calls for "aggressive enforcement" of the Hatch Amendment, which "prohibits requiring any pupil to reveal personal or family information" as part of any federally-supported program without prior parental consent. The other concerns sex education, about which the platform declares: "We...urge...schools to evaluate their sex education programs to determine their impact on escalating teenage pregnancy rates....[And w]e urge that school officials take appropriate action to ensure parental involvement."[136] Both of these statements are in keeping with the Church's concern about the state respecting the independence and integrity of the family institution. The latter echoes *Familiaris Consortio* in its cautioning about sex education and implicitly expresses a concern about maintaining a sound sexual morality such as is taught by the Church.

V. Foreign Policy

Thr Republican platforms seem to express three general ideas about the direction American foreign policy should proceed in and the basic goals it should have. The first is not surprising, as it characterizes any nation-state and is part of the nature of international relations in any era: the U. S. must seek to promote her self-interest. The second is expressed very directly by the 1964 platform: advancing freedom, and thereby justice, around the world.[137]

These ideas/goals contain three implicit corollaries. They may be an extreme application of them, or at least have been carried out with a crusading zeal in the course of American history (not solely by Republicans). They are the beliefs that: 1) democracy is for everybody and should be actively promoted around the world; 2) human rights should be promoted worldwide; and 3) (related to the second goal) communism must be stopped. These ideas/goals, to be sure, are not always compatible with each other, but a thorough analysis of such is beyond the scope of our concern here. The important thing for our purpose is simply to *identify* the ideas /goals and, like the other points mentioned, to evaluate them in light of Church teaching.

First, regarding national self-interest, it must be said that our previous discussion indicates that papal teaching does not forbid its pursuit. Indeed, the popes implicitly acknowledge that the pursuit of self-interest is expected and acceptable for nations, when they say war is legitimate for self-defense, that a nuclear deterrent may be possessed, and that nations *must* give up only their *superfluous* wealth. (This implies, of course, that nations may keep and use what they truly need for themselves.) Moreover, when they endorse competition, the popes acknowledge the necessity of men, pursuant to seeking their self-interest, to be able to satisfy their needs and reap legitimate benefits (so long as this pursuit does not push beyond respect for social justice and social charity which, of course, insures that respect for human dignity will be the ruling principle in economic life). This directive would apply to nations— collectives of men—as well, since the popes generally hold that the ethical norms governing individuals should govern nations also.

As far as advancing freedom and justice and stopping communism are concerned, these objectives certainly would not be opposed by the popes. Nor would the Popes object to the promotion of human rights everywhere (which the Church herself has been involved in doing), or the furtherance of democracy (if this meant stimulating citizens' public participation and seeing consent as an essential element in governmental legitimacy). The question would be how these objectives would be pursued—a matter addressed next in our examination of the 1984 Republican platform's discussion of communism.

The platforms, by and large, saw communism as do most of the conservative thinkers surveyed. First of all, they viewed it, especially when linked with the military might of the Soviet Union, as seeking genuine world domination and as a grave threat to the West.[138] The 1952 platform calls communism "a world conspiracy against freedom and religion."[139] 1964's—which devotes more discussion to communism in proportion to its length than any of the three—refers to Communist "imperialism" and "Communist leaders remain[ing] ideologically fixed upon ruling the world."[140] 1984's speaks of the Soviet Union's globalist ideology and its leaders' obsession with military power "mak[ing] it a threat to freedom and peace on every continent," and of its arms build-up of the 1970s through which it sought "to achieve an intimidating advantage over the Free World." It refers to "Communist expansion" in Central America "inspired and supported by the Soviet Union and Cuba."[141] The 1984 platform also sounds like the conservative thinkers in stressing "that there is a profound moral difference between the actions and ideals of Marxist-Leninist regimes and those of democratic governments."[142]

The repressiveness of Communist regimes, as manifested in their suppression of human rights and human dignity, denial of liberty, and their intimidation toward other nations, general aggressiveness, and spreading of subversion and terrorism, is noted.[143] The papal encyclicals have not specifically assessed the military threat of the Soviet Union and her allies, but they have noted the spread of communism around the world—thus recognizing its international, expansionistic character—and have condemned its tendency to use subversion and terrorism. Subversion is obviously rejected by the Church's declaring that nations have a right to their integrity and security, which mandates nonintervention by other nations. The same rights of integrity and security added to the Church's teaching that only defensive (never aggressive) war can be moral, indicate that Communist threats to other nations would be rejected by her. Her endorsement of human rights everywhere has already been emphasized. All of this means that the above platform positions are in keeping with Church teaching.

The Republican platforms attacked the Democrats for being weak in dealing with the foreign threat of Communist nations and domestic Communist subversion (the 1952 platform addresses the latter since it was written in an era of great concern about such subversion), and for not understanding the evil nature of communism.[144] The 1952 platform is critical of the Democratic-initiated policy of "containment." It does not specifically oppose the policy, but its tone is unenthusiastic, since in Republican opinion it did not wholly contain communism. (Many Republican politicians of the time opposed containment as grossly inadequate.)[145]

The 1952 platform also boldly called for "repudiat[ing] all commitments contained in secret understandings such as those at Yalta" which aided post-World War II Soviet expansion.[146] Although levelling these criticisms and saying they have "never compromised with Communism"[147] and pledging to "take the cold war offensive on all fronts,"[148] the Republicans made it clear they would negotiate with the Communist nations but only from a position of strength, insuring that any agreements made would be fair and carried out by the Communists,[149] and that they would "never abandon insistence on advantages for the free world."[150]

Both the 1964 and 1984 platforms talked of arms reduction agreements, as we shall see shortly. These later two platforms seem more willing to negotiate than 1952's. This possibly reflects the fact that the Stalin period had ended by then and the post-World War II Soviet power grabs were farther behind. There was probably also not as much domestic pressure for a hard line against communism in the later periods.

Some brief observations can be made about the above statements in light of Church teaching. First, it might have been good rhetoric to oppose containment, but if the cost of a more aggressive anti-Communist military policy were heightened conflict and large-scale war, such would not have been practical and the Church could not have supported it. Next, the Church would probably not support the idea of simply repudiating international agreements, even when retrospectively they may seem unjust or burdensome. It is worth recalling that Pope Pius XII's encyclical *The Function of the State in the Modern World* stated that if such were the case, discussion among nations about modifying a treaty should take place; one party cannot simply take it upon itself to unilaterally rescind it. Even though Yalta and the other post-World War II agreements were not formally "treaties" in the international law or U. S. constitutional law sense, they would seem to be within the ambit of the encyclical's concerns. However, a nation, it will be recalled, may void a treaty if the other party or parties have failed to live up to their obligations under it.[151] This may have been the case here, since many of the Soviet promises in these agreements were not lived up to.[152] It is possible, therefore, that repudiating such agreements could have been morally justifiable.

As we shall shortly discuss more thoroughly, the Church would applaud the platforms' willingness to negotiate with the Communist countries in the interests of world peace (being fully aware that the Communist ideology is fundamentally unjust and so genuine peace, in the full sense, is impossible with it still controlling other nations). She would be troubled, probably, by the uncompromising rhetoric sometimes found in the Republican platforms. As we have said, the popes have stressed that there is no alternative to negotiation in view of the potential for international destruction which exists today.

The platforms speak favorably about international organizations, especially the U. N. All endorse the U. N., the 1952 platform noting that it was a "good" development in U. S. foreign policy "accomplished with Republican cooperation."[153] They give their endorsement with qualifications, however. They all suggest that changes are needed in the U.N.'s operation which will help it to "revitalize its original purpose"[154] of being "a place where differences would be harmonized by honest discussion and a means for collective security under agreed concepts of justice."[155]

The thrust of the 1984 platform's unhappiness with the U. N. and other international organizations is that they have been pro-Soviet or pro-socialist/Marxist and have acted against American interests and principles.[156] The 1964 platform favors two specific changes at the U. N.: "a change in the method of voting in the General Assembly and in the specialized agencies that reflect population disparities among the member states and differing abilities and willingness to meet the obligations of the [U. N.] Charter," and denying votes to members "which refuse to meet properly levied assessments" so the U. N. will "more accurately reflect the power realities of the world."[157] Other noteworthy points in the 1984 platform are these: 1) international development agencies that promote "state-dominated" and Marxist economic systems or which favor nations pursuing policies of austerity will not be supported by the U. S.; 2) the U. S. will "eliminate all...funding for organizations that in any way support abortion or research on abortion methods;" 3) the U. N. is rebuked for having been used "to foster anti-semitism; 4) U. N. initiatives on control of the seas, Antarctica, and outer space are rejected; and 5) there is a commitment that the U. S. will "monitor...[the] votes and activities of international organizations, "and particularly the votes of member states which receive U. S. aid" (presumably to pressure them).[158]

With reference to Catholic teaching, we can make the following assessments of these points. The Church certainly agrees that international organizations like the U. N. are important as forums for discussion and resolving differences. *Sollicitudo Rei Socialis* acknowledges that changes are needed in them, however, because they have been misused. In this sense, she would understand the desire of the Republican platforms to reform them.

Her doctrine about communism and socialism would also motivate her to agree that international organizations must not promote these ideologies or economic systems based upon them. The fact that this encyclical was disturbed about international organizations being used to further "political rivalries" and manipulated by nations indicates that the Church would not want them to have the pro-Soviet bias the U. S. sees—or a pro-American one either. She might thus be bothered, likewise, about the platform's seeming desire that the organizations the U. S. participates in should further U.S. interests (even while accepting, as noted, that nations per se can rightfully seek to further their interests). It seems very likely the Church would oppose any "weighted voting" in the U. N. of the type proposed, both because it would violate her teaching on the equality of nations and because it would be to the disadvantage of the poorer nations for which she has especially sought to be an advocate. She would probably look askance upon the implicit promise to pressure nations voting against the U. S. in these organizations (and who are aid recipients) because this offends the principles of equality and integrity of nations. It also violates her call for "disinterested aid." (It should be noted that even while there seems to be a willingness to intrude upon free decision making by other countries here, the 1984 platform *does* explicitly acknowledge the principle of national self-determination, a principle applauded by the popes.)[159] The Church, of course, would support the U. S. in opposing the promotion of abortion by these organizations. She would likewise support the opposition to their fostering anti-semitism, which she has strongly spoken against.[160] It may be suspected that the Church would not support the platforms, at least in principle, on the subjects of control of the sea, Antarctica, and space because of her stressing that creation is the common inheritance of all mankind. The particulars of the U. N. treaties and initiatives in question involve factual matters and prudential judgments. She would probably not comment on these.

It should be noted that there seems to be a difference in terms of intensity of support for the U. N. between the 1952 platform and the later ones. All express support for international organizations and continued U. S. involvement in them, but 1952's is the most glowing in its endorsement of the principle behind the U.N. The later two platforms spend more time criticizing it and other international organizations than supporting them. This may not reflect a philosophical shift, but just the experience over time of the serious problems associated with them (some of which have been noted above).

The 1964 and 1984 platforms both support foreign aid. The lack of mention of it in the 1952 platform perhaps reflects a greater commitment to foreign aid over time; Republicans, especially conservative ones, were generally not known for their support of it in the 1950s and 1960s.[161] The 1964 platform commits itself to "overseas sales of surplus farm commodities to friendly countries" through the Food for Peace program, and supports foreign aid to "serve the cause of freedom," making sure that it does not "bolster and sustain anti-American regimes." In the same paragraph as its discussion of foreign aid (although it does not explicitly link up the two), it opposes the expropriation of American property in foreign countries "without prompt and adequate compensation as contemplated by international law."[162]

The 1984 platform has quite a bit to say about foreign aid. First, it extols the Reagan Administration's "increased food assistance and agricultural export financing programs" which it says have climbed to "a record level."[163] It supports "continuing humanitarian aid "to refugees of the Afghan war.[164] It supports continued "necessary security and economic assistance to African nations with which we maintain good relations to help them develop the infrastructure of democratic capitalism."[165] It insists that all American bilateral economic assistance "be directed at promoting economic growth and prosperity in developing nations." Such assistance should be "reduce[d] or eliminate[d]...to nations with foreign policies contrary to our "interests." Thinking no doubt of the increasingly coercive dimension of the U. S. AID population programs, it says that aid programs should respect the principle that "[d]ecisions on family size should be made freely by each family." The 1984 platform also contends, more broadly, that "those who are responsible for our programs...[be] more sensitive to the cultural needs of the countries to which we give assistance." Finally, it endorses "[f]oreign military assistance," claiming that it "strengthens our security by enabling friendly nations to provide for their own defense."[166]

We can say the following about how the provisions on foreign aid square with Church teaching. First, of course, the *support* for economic, food, and various forms of humanitarian assistance clearly concurs with the Church. Certainly, too, protecting family rights in planning family size and respect rendered for each country's unique culture are what the Church would favor. What can we say about the various conditions the platforms call for? Insisting that aid promote American interests presents a probable conflict with the Church because of her contention that aid should be disinterested. This seems likely to be the case even though she, as mentioned, recognizes the legitimacy of nations' pursuing their self-interest within limits. (One of these American interests, to repeat, is the stopping of the expansion of communism, and that would not be judged adversely by the Church.)

With respect to aid being aimed at promoting freedom, economic growth, and democratic capitalism, we can say the following. The Church would probably prefer aid to be given simply because charity is to be sought. She would not, however, condemn nations for extending it primarily for other reasons (no more than she condemns men for having only imperfect contrition and not perfect contrition for their sins). Moreover, she recognizes that nations are going to act self-interestedly; that is simply the reality of international life. Furthermore, the imposing of certain conditions for aid is not necessarily evil; much depends, of course, on precisely what is meant by them. Such conditions could be beneficial to underdeveloped countries. Indeed, seeking specifically to promote nations' development and doing it with a self-help emphasis is endorsed by the popes, the former directly in the internationally-oriented encyclicals and the latter by application to the international realm of principles stated in the domestically-oriented social encyclicals.

The popes would likely say, however, that the notion of development being limited just to the economic and political realms is not broad enough. The platforms' argument that aid should not help anti-American regimes would be understandable to the popes because of their awareness that nations act in their self-interest and of the realities of international politics, as well as because nations are permitted to act in their self-defense. The Christian teaching that one must love his enemies is not entirely inapplicable to relations among nations, however (since, after all, they are made up of human persons). Thus, the popes would probably urge nations not to let the fact of adversarial status preclude their giving aid. The people of the other nation, most of whom are not involved in governmental decisions, may need such aid.

Papal teaching does not forbid military assistance—nations, after all, may send aid to other, weaker nations to help them protect themselves or may assist them directly with their own forces—but the popes almost certainly would be troubled by it in light of what they have said about the regrettable spread of arms. They would at least exhort nations against it. An adverse judgment would depend on whether it makes the likelihood of war breaking out in an individual case more or less likely. Finally, since the popes accept expropriation in some circumstances, but say that just compensation is needed, this point in the 1964 platform would conform to their teaching.

We have already mentioned the pro-democracy and pro-human rights planks in the Republican platforms and stated how they accord with Catholic teaching. We can note a few additional points about them here. The 1984 platform has a broad definition of "human rights," including in it not just respect for basic human dignity, but political rights (such as voting), the existence of free institutions (such as a free press, free political parties, and free unions), and economic freedom.[167] This broad treatment is in accord with what is said in *Pacem in Terris*. It opposes, like the Church, the racial injustice of South African apartheid.[168] It states the following about their overall policy of encouraging international human rights: "A well-rounded human rights policy is concerned with specific individuals whose rights are denied by governments of the right or left, and with entire peoples whose Communist governments deny their claim to human rights." It picks up "the cause of human rights for all the world's peoples," and stresses that Communist totalitarian regimes "violate human rights in an organized systematic fashion."[169] Such insistence on respecting human rights in all kinds of political orders is certainly endorsed by the popes.

In doing this, however, the platform draws a distinction between the attitude about human rights in totalitarian and traditional authoritarian regimes, and establishes a basis for a different policy in *dealing* with each type on the issue. (The former type of regime is more total, systematic, and severe in its denial of human rights than the latter. It also usually feels justified in this because it is motivated by a morally relativistic, pseudo-religious ideology which is indifferent about the need to respect human rights.) Thus, the U.S. might be more open and vocal when condemning a totalitarian regime, but go about trying to reshape the human rights policies of a friendly authoritarian regime in a quieter, more behind-the-scenes fashion (because of fear that treating it the same way might undermine its government and pave the way for Communist-type totalitarian elements to take over and create a much worse situation, as has often happened). This would not offend the Church's teaching. The nature of the policy and approach a government might choose to promote respect for human rights in another country is in the realm of an acceptable prudential policy judgment (so long as human rights violations everywhere are condemned and sincere efforts made to address them all).

The 1984 Republican platform seems to favor the promotion of democracy (i.e., a democratic republic, a representative regime with constitutional safeguards) as a political arrangement around the world. It extols the

Reagan-created National Endowment for Democracy, "and other instruments of U. S. diplomacy" as ways of doing this. The Republicans say they are motivated to do this by their human rights concerns. Although the creating of democratic governments is not suitable everywhere in the eyes of the Church, the *principles underlying* democratic forms of government (e.g., respect for funamental human rights, participation by people in public decisions affecting them) are endorsed by the Church as universally valid (cf. *Mater et Magistra* and *Pacem in Terris*).

VI. Defense and Disarmament

There are several statements made by the Republican platforms on this subject which explicitly or implicitly address moral questions and so are particularly suited to evaluation in light of Church teaching.

All the platforms, not surprisingly, stress the importance of sufficient and dependable military strength. *How much strength* is a question they all take up and differ about. The 1952 platform simply says the U. S. needs military power sufficient "to deter sudden attack [by the Soviet Union] or promptly and decisively defeat it."[170] 1964's is the most emphatic about maintaining military superiority over the Soviets. It says that, if in power, the Republicans "will maintain a superior, not merely equal, military capability as long as the Communist drive for world domination continues" and pledges to "end 'second-best' weapons policies."[171] This probably refers to an across-the-board military and weapons superiority.

The 1984 platform seems a bit more restrained, saying just that "technological" and "qualitative superiority" are "essential" for deterrance purposes.[172] It says nothing about quantitative superiority. From the perspective of international defense policy, maintaining a superiority of power (i.e., not just military power) over likely adversaries is wise (nothing in 1984 suggested that the Soviet Union was no longer an adversary) because it is always better to have more than a nation thinks it needs or thinks the other nation has (because there is always uncertainty about how great the other's power is).[173] The 1984 platform expresses this latter point in saying that President Reagan was seeking to achieve "an effective margin of safety."[174] The popes might raise some concern about this because of the fear of fueling an on-going arms race, with each side constantly trying to outdo the other. Such a policy might accept it as moral, however—especially as needed for deterrence (as both the 1964 and 1984 platforms claimed it was)—so long as sincere efforts were being made at the same time to achieve lasting peace.

This point about the need of a deterrent is stressed strongly and repeatedly by the 1984 platform. It says that "[o]ur military strength exists for the high moral purpose of deterring conflict, not initiating war. The deterrence

of aggression is ethically imperative."[175] Our nuclear deterrent must be "sufficient to deter attack against the United States and our allies" and is "the
ultimate military guarantor of America's security and that of our allies."[176]
President Reagan is spoken of favorably as having built up our deterrent "while
pursuing negotiations for balanced, verifiable reductions of nuclear weapons
under arms control agreements" which the party pledges to continue to do.[177]
These points conform to the papal teaching that the building up of a nuclear
deterrent is normally acceptable so long as efforts at arms control and reduction
and the ultimate abolition of nuclear weapons are being made. The criteria
stated here for reduction essentially concur with papal teaching that arms in
general (nuclear and non-nuclear) be reduced *equally and simultaneously in
various countries* and that negotiations be carried out to secure *mutually verifiable* nuclear arms control agreements with the aim of *complete progressive
nuclear disarmament* and *effective* control of such arms.

Moreover, another platform and Reagan proposal would also seem to
have the effect of furthering the papally-stated goal of complete abolition of
nuclear weapons if it indeed could work in the manner promised: the Strategic
Defense Initiative (SDI), a space-based nuclear missile defense system.[178] If such
a system indeed could make nuclear missile attack impossible, and if the major
nuclear powers each adopted it (the Soviets have been working on such a
system also[179] and, even if the U. S. developed it first, President Reagan declared
during the 1984 campaign that he would share the technology with them so
they could employ it too[180]) it *could* have the effect of motivating them to destroy their nuclear stockpiles because they would no longer be able to effectively build national security strategies around them. The Church, of course,
would have no illusion that an SDI-type system or any weapon could end all
war. Peace, she insists, comes only through internal change. She would have
reservations, moreover, about even a thoroughly defensive weapons system
whose cost would likely be enormous and thus divert resources away from
other human needs.

An arms control point in the 1984 platform that clearly would be
supported by what the popes have said is the endorsement of effective nuclear
non-proliferation.[181] There is clearly a more favorable attitude toward arms
control negotiations and initiatives conveyed by the 1984 platform than is
found in either the 1952 platform (which does not mention arms control at all)
or in the 1964 one which, while accepting the limited nuclear test ban treaty of
1963, does so only skeptically, while insisting that the U. S. have "full readiness" to violate the treaty if undesirable "consequences" come about.[182] This
perhaps suggests that conservatism, as embodied in the Republican party, has
moved closer to the Church in this area as time has gone on.

On the question of nuclear arms, the platform opposed the long-
standing American nuclear deterrent strategy called "Mutually Assured De-

struction" (MAD). MAD was the strategy of targeting nuclear missiles at Soviet population centers with the idea that the threat of having a massive number, if not most, of that country's innocent civilians wiped out by an attack, would be enough to deter the Soviet leadership from deciding to attack first. Besides being of very dubious reliability and based on a highly questionable assumption (i.e., that the Soviet leaders would never sacrifice a substantial portion of their civilian population)[183]—MAD is assuredly immoral because, as Higgins says, "Killing noncombatants in air raids [which a missile attack would surely be considered] may never be directly willed...To bomb a purely civilian area for the sake of terrorizing the enemy into subjection is merely mass murder."[184] So, the platform is clearly in agreement with the Church here.

The 1984 platform, in a philosophical passage, states when the use of force in general is justified. Echoing President Reagan, it declares that "there is a profound moral difference between the use of force for liberation and the use of force for conquest and territorial expansion."[185] This agrees with what the Church has taught about just versus unjust wars.

The platform also applauds American financial and arms support for anti-Communist rebels or "freedom fighters" in both Nicaragua (during the period of Sandinista rule) and Afghanistan.[186] This raises an important question: Is this kind of assistance in the use of force justified, according to Church teaching? We have alluded above to the answer. The same analysis about foreign military assistance given earlier would apply here. It cannot be said that, per se, one nation's aiding elements within another to throw off a genuinely oppressive government is immoral. As the leading Catholic natural law text on social ethics says, "[T]here is no absolute sovereignty, but only sovereignty in conformity with the order of individual state and of international sovereignty...there is a right of intervention against a state which seriously offends against this order."[187] Three of the cases in which the text says another state can intervene would seem pertinent to the situation in Nicaragua (as seen by the platform) and one also to Afghanistan's situation (as seen by the platform). The platform clearly charges that the governments of both countries were oppressing their people. One of the cases which would justify intervention (which may be carried out either by a state directly offended by another state's conduct *or* by other states) is when the state is "guilty of gravely injuring the natural rights of large groups of citizens, such as those belonging to a particular political party or national minorities."[188]

The other two cases which the platform's assessment would make us think could apply to Nicaragua are when a state "encroaches on the right of freedom of another state (e.g., by supporting a party's preparation for or attempt at revolution)"[189]—the platform says that Nicaragua had been "exporting terror and arms" throughout Central America and has supported Communist

guerrillas trying to overthrow the democratic government of El Salvador[190]—
and when "a state directly or indirectly offends seriously against international
regulations in matters such as the drug traffic"[191]—the platform claimed that
Nicaragua was guilty of "smuggling...illegal drugs into the United
States...[which is] a crime against...international law.[192]

Whether, of course, the Nicaraguan situation actually falls into one of
these cases, as the platform claims (thus justifying intervention), is a factual
question. It is beyond the scope of this analysis to confirm the factual correct-
ness of the platform's assertions about Nicaragua. The important point for our
purposes is that the principle of intervention does not violate traditional Catholic natural law ethics. The manner in which a legitimate intervention may take
place can vary— military assistance to rebel elements would be an acceptable
means.[193]

Finally, the 1984 Republican platform speaks in a number of places
about terrorism, which it calls "a new form of warfare waged by the forces of
totalitarianism against the democracies" used "to weaken democracy and undermine world stability."[194] It is sponsored and/or carried out by a number of
Communist countries and their allies. The platform calls for appropriate action
against terrorists, including (it is suggested) military action.[195] This condemnation of terrorism has been seen in such leading papal encyclicals as *Divini
Redemptoris*—where the use of terror by Communists is also noted—and
Sollicitudo Rei Socialis.

Reference to Another Source to Confirm the Conservatism of the Republican Platforms

As with the Democratic platforms, the objection may be raised that
the Reublican platforms really are not the best source of conservative public
policy positions. Although we have argued why we believe they are (and that
the particular Republican platforms chosen would seem appropriate, because
they are from years when conservatives were in control of the party and shaped
the platform), we shall, as with the Democratic platforms, "cross-check" the
matter by examining the positions of a leading avowedly conservative organization, the American Conservative Union (ACU).

Like the liberal ADA, ACU annually rates members of Congress on
the basis of selected key votes on which there can be expected to be a liberal-
conservative division. The ACU was organized in the wake of the Goldwater
defeat of 1964 to continue the conservative political effort on the national level.
Its founders included such conservative luminaries as William F. Buckley, Jr.,
Rep. John Ashbrook, William Rusher, and J. William Middendorf. They have
built their program around four basic "goals": 1) upholding the original intent of
the American Founding Fathers; 2) asserting that capitalism is the only eco-

nomic system compatible with personal liberty; 3) opposition to communism and Communist expansion; and 4) the belief in the need for a strong national defense. Their activity has included lobbying, education, political organizing, litigation, and attemping to build public support for conservative policies. It is known for its organizing of the annual Conservative Political Action Conference, which brings conservative activists from around the country together to exchange ideas, take part in education sessions, and stimulate continued enthusiasm. It also puts out a number of regular publications, including, since 1971, its ratings of Congress. It is one of the leading and most influential conservative organizations in Washington today.[196]

First, we shall consider the ACU's economic and social welfare policy positions. It should be recalled that the major positions taken in this area in the platforms were the following: private sector initiative; the value of competition; the limitation of government economic regulation (especially from Washington); free trade (except with totalitarian regimes); a sub-minimum wage for youth; balancing the federal budget; the usual rights of labor (but support for the Taft-Hartley Act, which included "right to work" laws); a seeming lack of almost any stress on cooperation in the economy; arranging programs so as to strictly uphold federalism; support for the Social Security system; support for Medicare; opposition to compulsory federal health insurance; intergovernmental and government-private sector cooperation in welfare programs and a general limitation of the governmental role in this area to assist only when necessary; opposition to excessive taxation; and tax fairness so the poor and groups such as widows and homemakers are not disadvantaged. The following indicates how the ACU compares with the Republican platform policies. (Most information is from the ACU's 1984 ratings of Congress).[197]

The ACU opposed all attempts, in the votes focused on, to restrict private economic interests with government regulation and to let the government instead of the private sector handle activities. It opposed requiring the steel industry to invest in worker development; favored airline deregulation; favored government contracting out of Job Corps programs; and favored the cutting of funds for public broadcasting. It supported efforts to eliminate protectionist provisions in the Trade Remedies Reform Act of 1984 and efforts to restrict trade with Hong Kong, Taiwan, and South Korea, all strongly anti-Communist allies of the U.S.[198]

In 1986, the ACU opposed easier trade for Communist totalitarian Romania.[199] There were no votes in 1984 for a sub-minimum wage for youth, but in 1988 the ACU opposed a general hike in the minimum wage.[200] We were informed by the ACU national office in Washington that it has never taken a formal position on the former, but would probably favor it if it did.[201]

A sense of the ACU's position on labor matters is further seen by its support for a funding cut for the Departments of Labor, Health and Human

Services, and Education, and its *opposition* to union use of dues for political purposes in 1984, to the expansion of powers of construction unions in 1986 and 1987, and to plant closing notification requirements in 1988.[202] There was nothing in the ACU materials reviewed about cooperation in the economy. The stress on reducing and perhaps ultimately balancing the federal budget was seen in its support for a 10% across-the-board budget cut, a $19.5 million cut in the Legislative Appropriations bill, and the restrictions on social program spending mentioned below.[203] The support for federalism—i.e., for avoiding the "Washington solution" if government must be turned to at all—is seen in ACU's opposition to the Civil Rights Act of 1984 (the "Grove City" bill) because it insisted it would be "absurdly expanding federal power" and in its opposition to a 1987 bill which it said would "federalize the problem of the homeless."[204] There were no votes in the ratings on Social Security.

ACU says that it has taken no stand on the Social Security system, except that it did oppose the 1984 changes that made Social Security tax deductions mandatory for 501(c)(3) non-profit organizations.[205] The ACU's 1987 opposition to a drastic expansion of Medicare and a compulsory premium to pay for it best shows where it stands on the Medicare program and on compulsory national health insurance generally.[206] Its general opposition to a substantial federal social welfare role is seen in its opposing a large public health funding bill and another bill which would have enabled people with more assets to get welfare.[207] There were no votes dealing directly with the issue of tax fairness, but there were votes showing a preference for reducing federal taxes. One was on a bill delaying tax indexing, another was on the 1984 Tax Reform Act which would have raised taxes over three years, and another was on a deficit reduction package which also would have raised taxes. ACU opposed all three.[208] Also, ACU says that it had once favored a flat tax instead of the graduated income tax approach, but was no longer pushing this position.[209]

In short, it is fair to conclude that the ACU, on the subjects delineated, was close in outlook to the Republican platform positions. It must be noted, in fairness, that just because the ACU opposed certain measures—such as those dealing with social welfare programs—this does not imply that it did not favor addressing the problem, or even necessarily opposed the particular program. It may have just opposed a governmental approach to it or objected to *expanding* a particular program or adding additional programs. This observation applies to all six issue areas.

We cannot say a great deal about the ACU's position on agriculture because there was only one vote on it covered in its ratings. In this vote (in 1986), it opposed considerable additional spending on federal farm programs.[210] This seems to concur with the platforms' thinking that government's role should be primarily to provide a good environment for competition and take a restrained—but sometimes necessary—role in providing financial assistance.

On the matter of the environment, the ACU somewhat deviates from the platforms. It opposed each environmental bill it considered for the ratings in different years. In 1984, it opposed a citizen lawsuit provision in the Superfund program.[211] In 1985, it opposed a reauthorization of the Clean Water Act.[212] It seems that on this issue, the platforms are more willing to support federal initiatives than the ACU. The platforms do not say *expressly* that the effort should be federal, but this can easily be inferred.

Although the ACU materials examined do not cover the breadth of subjects in the civil rights-civil liberties area that the platforms do, the subjects they do cover show a similar perspective as the former. This is seen in the following: support for a proposed constitutional amendment to permit voluntary school prayer and related legislation (in 1984 and 1985)[213]; opposition to the "Grove City" bill, with its affirmative action dimension (in 1984 and 1988)[214]; support for the Equal Access Act to try to stop educational institutions from denying facility use for voluntary student religious meetings (in 1984)[215]; support of every initiative to protect the lives and rights of unborn children by opposing abortion in different years (these all involved the barring or restricting of federal abortion funding)[216]; support for legislation removing jurisdiction over school prayer cases from the federal courts (in 1985)[217]; opposition to minority quotas for Pentagon contracts (in 1986)[218]; and support for 1988 legislation protecting religious liberty by absolving religious institutions from a District of Columbia statute requiring non-discrimination against homosexuals.[219]

On education, again the Republican platforms address several more issues than the ACU materials examined do, but we see a clear correspondence on the common issues. This is seen in the above noted support for reducing funding for the Department of Education—evidencing a common desire to reduce the federal educational role—and the equal access bill.

The three basic ideas about the objectives of U.S. foreign policy seen in the platforms are also essentially (though implicitly) found in the ACU ratings: promoting American interests, promoting "freedom and justice" around the world, and stopping communism (the latter, of course, has also been one of its basic organizational goals).

On a number of votes in the latter part of the 1980s, the ACU supported military and other aid to the Nicaraguan contras and the government of El Salvador.[220] In 1984, it also opposed Congressional moves that would have undermined Taiwan and reduced military assistance aid for thirty "friendly" (i.e., non-Communist, anti-Communist) countries.[221] It also, as noted, opposed the attempt to alter trade relations in an unfavorable way for anti-Communist Hong

Kong, Taiwan, and South Korea. In 1985, it supported repeal of the Clark Amendment to permit U.S. military aid to the anti-Marxist rebels in Angola (and supported the actual provision of such aid), opposed economic aid to Marxist Mozambique, and opposed sanctions against South Africa for its apartheid policies. The sanctions included restrictions against the sale of American computer goods and nuclear materials, the sorts of items the U.S. will permit transfer of only if its national interests dictate.[222] Besides promoting the general objectives mentioned above, many of these specific ideas are found in the 1984 platform. There are a number of other foreign policy points from the platforms which are not addressed by the ACU.

Finally, on defense and disarmament, while the ACU does not go into the philosophical dimensions of this question the way the platforms do—especially 1984's—it clearly shares with them a belief in the need for military strength as the best guarantee of security. While the ACU's ratings do not go into as many specific points as the platforms do, this conclusion is warranted by the points it *does* go into (as well as by considering, again, its organizational goals.) For example, in 1984 the ACU supported the anti-satellite defense system (SDI), supported the MX missile, supported the deployment of cruise and Pershing II missiles, and opposed "a mutual and verifiable freeze and reductions in nuclear weapons" (presumably because the ACU believed it would be neither mutual nor verifiable).[223] These *specifics* are all in conformity with proposals in the 1984 platform.

In summation, the only one of the six issue areas in which there is a seeming disagreement between the Republican platforms and the ACU is the one concerning the environment. On all the others, and in the other part even of that one (agriculture), the correspondence is close. The Republican platforms selected, it must be concluded, are definitely conservative in nature and are good examples of conservative policy positions.

Chapter Conclusion

We come to the following brief conclusions about the public policy positions of conservatism—discerned from the three Republican platforms—as considered in light of Church teaching. On economic and social welfare policy, the platforms of the Republican party (and, thus, conservatism, since the party is held to embody it) are, on most questions examined, close to Church teaching. The most noteworthy exceptions are on employment and the need for cooperation in the economy. They have some weak points regarding the role of women. On agriculture and the environment, the conservative *platforms* take positions which conform well with Church teaching. The ACU's deviation from the platforms' commitment to the environment, however, suggests that conservatism really is not so close to the Church. On civil rights and civil liberties, the conservative position also agrees with the Church, and this is most notable in its stands about the family, parental rights and abortion.

The rights of women are, again, an area where conservatism is shaky. On education, the platform conforms to papal teaching; its position on parental rights in education is particularly good. Foreign policy is the area in which there are the most ambiguities in the conservative (Republican) thinking when evaluated against Church teaching. The conservatives balance a general willingness to negotiate, with an uncompromising rhetoric against dealing with the Communist powers. They support international organizations, but want them to further American interests. They want international spaces not to be governed by international authorities. There would probably be some papal reservations about their views on foreign aid, even though there is overall conformity. They do not always seem respectful of the principles of the equality and integrity of all nations. The conservatives promote ideas of human rights that the Church endorses, but they also seem to want to promote essentially *one* form of government—democracy—as an absolute good for all peoples. Finally, on defense and disarmament, the positions stated are clearly within Church teaching.

What remains to be done now is to compare post-World War II conservatism with the old and new liberalism of the same period and to see which, of the three, is most in harmony with the Church's teaching. This is the subject of the final chapter.

SEVEN

CONCLUSION

In this chapter, on the basis of the analysis of the previous chapters, we shall attempt to determine which of the three political ideologies examined—the old liberalism, the new liberalism, or conservatism—is most in conformity with Catholic teaching, especially regarding its general perspectives about government and major public policy positions. After this, we attempt to explain the reasons why liberalism and conservatism stand as they do in relation to Church teaching. Finally, the chapter reflects briefly on the direction American Catholics might take in politics if they are concerned about upholding their Church's teachings and working to put them into effect in our political society.

Which is Closer to the Church: Old Liberalism, New Liberalism, or Conservatism?

In this first section, we make the conclusions as to which of the three political ideologies is closest overall to the Church's teaching. We shall not again compare the two versions of liberalism with each other; we already did this in Chapters Three and Four. We shall simply take each perspective and finally conclude how each ranks in terms of conformity to Church social teaching.

First, we give our conclusions in the five areas involving the general philosophy of politics and government. On the role of government, conservatism and the old liberalism, in our judgment, come out almost even in the comparison with the Church, with the old liberalism just a little ahead. The new liberalism is behind both. *None*, of course, is fully in conformity with the Church. Both versions of liberalism are better than conservatism in accepting a fuller role for government, especially in such areas as the economy, social welfare, and international aid obligations. On the other hand, their notion of the role of government is corrupted by too eager of a willingness to strengthen the national government at the expense of the very important principle of subsidiarity (this tendency intensifies with the new liberalism).

In addition, the new liberalism seems less concerned with the perennial and most fundamental purposes of government such as defense or security and seeks rather to have it promote freedom and equality beyond the bounds of what Church social teaching indicates is legitimate. Perhaps, on balance, the new liberalism has the greatest orientation of the three to promoting some version of the common good (in the sense of promoting the community's needs, and not just those of individuals). It does not have as valid of a conception of common good as certain conservative groupings do, however.

All three ideologies, in different ways, extol individualism to an excess, showing that they share a common, basic modern outlook. Of the three, conservatism is probably the least given to individualism, if only because it stresses duties as well as rights. In terms of government promoting religion and spiritual concerns, conservatism and the old liberalism are about equal (the new liberalism is far less sympathetic). All betray deficiencies regarding the role of religion in public life.

None of the ideologies, then, goes as far toward fostering religion as the popes indicate the state should. Conservatism tends to have a more materialistic focus in some ways, but it also stresses the need for religion more. The old liberalism talks about "spiritual" principles and concerns, but is quite secular-oriented. Both are with the Church in stressing the state's most basic role of self-defense, whereas the new liberalism seems to lose sight of such while preferring to focus on other roles (which are often quite legitimate). Perhaps of the three, the old liberalism possesses the fullest overall picture of the state's role, which makes it closest to the Church. Besides emphasizing this basic role of self-defense and other legitimate roles, the old liberalism holds that the state must help secure social justice. Conservatism is weak on the latter.

Conservatism is undoubtedly closer than either the old or new liberalism in its understanding about the role of God, religion, and the natural law in the political order. It stresses natural law ideas more directly and emphatically and, by far, stresses the importance of religion more. Most of the conservative perspectives or groupings examined emphasize the importance of religion, even though a few speak of it mostly in a utilitiarian way.

By contrast, both versions of liberalism are secularized—noted for their failure to stress the centrality of God and religion to the state (although the new liberalism is clearly more so). The old liberals gave at least some deference to God and a nod to the value of Christian norms. Also, unlike the new liberals, they did not take up the cry for state neutrality between belief and unbelief. We *do* see some willingness of the neoliberal wing of the new liberals to speak about the importance of religion, but it is tepid.

As far as the natural law is concerned, conservatism clearly has a more well-developed notion of this and a stronger belief that the political order must be shaped in accordance with it. The old liberal writers tend to make references to moral norms above men, but do not enunciate a clear belief in a natural *law* or an all-encompassing moral order. Mention of natural law or higher moral norms does not generally appear in the new liberal sources. A clear-cut positivism seems to rule. Though, in practice, they do at times end up appealing to norms of justice not embodied in the positive law.

On freedom, conservatism is clearly closest to the Church; a serious weak spot is its espousal of an excessive notion of economic freedom. It agrees with the Church in holding the following: freedom is limited by moral norms beyond man; for true freedom to flourish order is required; personal actions usually affect the community; freedom can and must be limited for virtue's sake; and that economic freedom (and property rights) are essential for political freedom. The old liberalism does stress the need for order, limits, and duties, but is basically weak on the latter. It stresses rights *too* much, although not as irresponsiblly as the new liberalism does (in some areas). While denying that it seeks to make freedom its end, the theory of the old liberalism nevertheless treats freedom essentially as such. It laments that freedom or democracy, in effect, does not have the hold of a religion on men; and it does not realize that religion is needed to curb freedom's excesses.

The new liberalism carries individual freedom to an extreme, as seen in the fact that it believes various moral positions, such as those taken by the Church in such areas as sex and reproduction, infringe upon individual autonomy. The neoliberal wing of the new liberalism may even be a shade worse because, in addition to accepting individualism in areas such as these, it stresses it in economics. Even though conservatism may be the most extreme of the three in the area of *economic* freedom, all three political ideologies accept and encourage, in different degrees, the pursuit of economic self-interest, and see this pursuit, rightfully, as a central feature of the economy.

On the subject of equality, the old liberalism and conservatism have similar views. Both favor racial equality (that was the old liberals' major concern in the area of equality, since it was still the Jim Crow era), equality under the law, equal opportunity, and political equality. (Conservatism, however, does not call for absolute political equality even as far as the vote is concerned.) Both are against egalitarianism (although, it will be recalled, that old liberals such as Lerner were quite favorable to some degree of democratic socialism). Neither the old liberalism nor conservatism allow the desire for equality to decimate standards of excellence in such areas as education. They both favor equal opportunity; they did not push for equal results or outcomes. Conservatism is particularly emphatic in its opposition to equality of condition, which it sees as being against nature. It holds that this natural inequality is reflected in differences in wealth and property. In its zeal to oppose egalitarianism, however, conservatism seems oftentimes reluctant to redress even *excessive* accumulations of wealth. Its greater spiritual orientation enables conservatism to emphasize, with the Church, a type of equality that is not mentioned by either version of liberalism: equality of human dignity.

We must conclude that on equality, the old liberalism is closer to the Church than conservatism, but only by a shade. This conclusion is arrived at because of conservatism's unwillingness to redress excessive accumulations of and considerable gaps in wealth and its hesitation about and greater restrictions on political equality. While, as we have said, the popes are not egalitarian and do speak of natural differences which lead to legitimate inequalities, they nevertheless call for a *greater* equality of wealth and other basic goods of society and in political decisionmaking. They are concerned about everyone being allowed to partake of God's abundance and collaborate in public decisionmaking.

The new liberals are farthest from the Church because of their clear espousal of egalitarianism—in many different spheres—and advocacy of the equal results idea, which, as noted, offends Christian notions of prudence and justice.

Conservatism clearly best understands communism, in light of Church teaching. Of the three ideologies, only conservatism opposes communism for as many reasons—political, economic, social, philosophical, and religious—as the popes do, and only conservatism opposes it for the most *fundamental* reason the popes oppose it: its hostility to man's spiritual nature. Also, only conservatism seems ready to join the popes in seeing communism as intrinsically evil. The old liberalism is generally sound in its views on communism, but has weak spots in not realizing fully enough the character of Communist ideology's assault on human nature and in sometimes seeing benevolent aspects which are not there. As mentioned, it opposed communism mostly because of the latter's opposition to political freedom and democracy. The new liberalism does not even betray a sense of communism as a fundamentally evil ideology and suggests that it might be theoretically accommodated to Western humane principles (even while realizing that all is not right with communism and in Communist regimes). Conservatism is deficient in not seeing communism's suppression of religion as the most central problem posed by it, and in its tendency to take an uncompromising military stance toward the Communist nations (bordering on confrontation). The popes, of course, are uncompromising themselves when it comes to the theory and ideology of communism, but on the level of international relations, they call for nations to strive for peace in spite of East-West ideological differences.

To summarize, on the role of *politics and government,* the old liberalism is closest to the Church, conservatism is next closest, and the new liberalism is last, but the latter two are not far from the old liberalism. On the subject of *God, religion, and the natural law* as the basis of politics, conservatism is clearly closest, the old liberalism next, and the new liberalism last (the latter two are not close to conservatism). On *freedom,* conservatism is first and behind it (in this order), and not very close, are the old liberalism and the new liberalism. On *equality,* the old liberalism is first with conservatism close behind it, and the new liberalism far behind both. Finally on *communism,* conservatism is clearly first, the old liberalism a respectable but not really close second, and the new liberalism last.

When we bring these five areas together, it is clear that neither conservatism nor liberalism in either of its post-World War II periods conforms fully to Church teaching. It is apparent from the above that conservatism comes closest, the old liberalism is next (though not far behind), and the new liberalism is least in accord with her teaching. Although we have examined the various groupings within conservatism only to come to a "consensus" position that could be said to represent the thinking of "conservatism per se" (and not to draw a comparison among the groupings) in the five areas, we could probably conclude that cultural conservatism is the closest of the groupings to Church teaching. It could also be judged to be closer to it than the overall conservative position (i.e., the consensus conservative position). (On the next page is presented a table and point values assigned to each ideology on the basis of being closest (lst), second closest (2nd), and farthest (3rd) from the Church to illustrate how these conclusions were reached.)

Now, we turn to our conclusions on the six specific public policy issue areas. At the end of Chapter Four, we concluded that on economic and social welfare policy, the old liberalism was just slightly ahead of the new liberalism—in spite of the fact that the economic views of the latter are more like the popes'. This is so because the old liberals stress cooperation, and their social welfare ideas are slightly better as well (on the basis of their superior policy ideas concerning the family and subsidiarity). Except for health care and housing, the new liberalism seems too eager (judged from the 1984 Democratic platform) to let the federal government move aggressively into these areas. Conservatism, on many points of social policy, agrees with papal teaching, and is superior to either version of liberalism in its respect for subsidiarity and in the self-help emphasis it puts into its welfare programs. Its distance from the Church on unemployment and the matter of cooperation in the economy, and possibly also on fairness in taxation and women in the economy, however, results in its ending up as third behind the old and the new liberalism as far as conformity to her teachings overall in this first public policy area.

TABLE 1

RANKING OF THE THREE IDEOLOGIES ON THE BASIS OF THEIR CLOSENESS TO CHURCH TEACHING IN THE CATEGORY OF "THE GENERAL PHILOSOPHY OF POLITICS AND GOVERNMENT."

	Ideology		
Ranking	OL	NL	C
1st (closest to Church)	2	0	3
2nd (next closest to Church)	3	0	2 (both close)
3rd (farthest from Church)	0	5	0
Total points —	12	5	14 points

(Numbers in the above columns indicate the number of areas of the five for which each ideology had the respective ranking. The five areas are: General Purposes of Government; God, Religion, and the Natural Law as the Basis for the Political Order; Thinking about Freedom; Thinking About Equality; View of Communism.)

3 points are assigned for each ranking of 1st; 2 points for each ranking of 2nd (2.5 for each ranking of 2nd if close to 1st); 1 point for each ranking of 3rd (1.5 for each ranking of 3rd if close to 1st).

Key: OL - old liberalism
     NL - new liberalism
     C - conservatism

On agriculture and the environment, we can say the following. On agriculture, all three perspectives are about equally close to the Church. All favor appropriate assistance to the rural sector and furtherance of its economic well-being, support the family farm concept, and call for protections for non-owner farm workers. The point that moves conservatism ahead of either version of liberalism is subsidiarity. On the environment, as stated, the new liberalism is ahead of the old because it really was not much of a concern of the latter during a much earlier period. The new liberal and conservative plaforms are about equal in their endorsement of good environmental policy, but both appear to be somewhat deficient as far as the Church is concerned. Perhaps on the basis of its enunciation of a sound philosophy behind environmental protection—i.e., stewardship of our God-given resources, which conforms to the Church's thinking—and because of subsidiarity (with the new liberals having a stronger emphasis on federal government activity), we can say that conservatism is closest to the Church.

So, on the basis of the platforms, conservatism is narrowly first on the environment, the new liberalism close behind, and the old liberalism last.

What was noted about the American Convervative Union's positions, however, suggests that conservatism's environmental support may not be as strong as the platforms indicate. In light of this, it is difficult to determine how to rank the three. Perhaps the way to resolve the problem is to eliminate the advantage the platforms give to conservatism and put it in second place behind the new liberalism, (in spite of the latter's subsidiarity problem) on the basis of conservatism's thus possibly having a somewhat questionable commitment to environmental concerns (though the strong platform statements are difficult to simply ignore).

When considering a ranking for this whole category of "Agriculture and the Environment," conservatism would seem to have to be considered *at least equal* to the new liberalism because of the latter's neglect of subsidiarity in agriculture. It would be *ahead* of the new liberalism if we were considering the 1984 Republican platform alone. The old liberalism (if one faults it for not thinking about the environment in a period when it was not yet popular to do so) would be third. If, on the other hand, we nullify this as a consideration, the old liberalism would be tied with the other two ideologies, hampered by its neglect of subsidiarity in agriculture. (We shall not so nullify, however, because, as noted, conservatism even in 1952 was saying somewhat more about protecting the environment than the old liberalism did; also one cannot give credit for something not even dealt with.)

On civil rights and civil liberties, we have already pointed to the sharp contrast between the old and new liberalism and the reason why the former is clearly closer to the Church: the new liberalism conflicts with Church teaching on matters concerning sexual morality and the family. By means of the new putative rights it advocates, the new liberalism obliterates legitimate differences

in favor of egalitarianism (especially on gender questions), spurns the importance of religion with an extreme notion of church-state separation, and perhaps
undercuts prudence and sows group conflict with its "equal results" idea of
civil rights. As we noted, the old liberalism was much closer to the Church with
its strong opposition to unjust discrimination and unequal treatment of persons
because of race, religion, ethnic origin, and wealth. Even though the new
liberals treat areas of unjust discrimation which the old liberals ignored (e.g.,
against the disabled and, in many areas, women), the latter still come out ahead
because they stressed traditional, not ersatz, rights.

Conservatism has addressed those areas of rights that the popes address (but which the old liberals did not)—e.g., rights of the disabled, right to
life of unborn children, rights of parents (the latter, inadequately). It should be
recalled, again, that these matters were not at issue in 1948. At the same time,
by and large, it rejects the new liberalism's "equal results"-oriented positions
that conflict with Church teaching. Conservatism is thus at least equally close
to the Church as the old liberalism, and we might be able to judge it a notch
ahead because has gone into these additional areas. (It is difficult to fault the
new liberalism for omitting these, however.)

On education, there are two main issues— subsidiarity and parental
rights—which determine how the three perspectives are ranked with regard to
their closeness to Church teaching. All three perspectives are concerned about
helping education and increasing educational opportunities. The new liberalism,
is, however, farthest from the Church in this area. This is both because of its
seeming eagerness for a greater federal role in this area (it was noted that the
claims of the 1984 Democratic platform to, in effect, be upholding subsidiarity
were not convincing) and its opposition, for all practical purposes, to aid for
non-public schools and to enable parents to send their children to such schools.
(The non-public school aid issue, it can be argued, is really a parental rights
issue because it involves the restricting of parental choice in the education of
their children. The new liberalism thus puts itself in opposition to an important
aspect of parental rights). Both conservatism and the old liberalism are in
conformity with Church teaching about education, although conservatism has
the edge because of its pronounced emphasis on parental rights. (It must again
be remembered, however, that these kinds of questions were not public issues
in the old liberal era and so would not have been addressed by political
ideologies or party platforms.)

On foreign policy, the old liberalism stands out as closest to papal
teaching. On every point it treats—the understanding and attitude about communism, emphasis on negotiation, need for international cooperation and organizations, promoting economic development in poor nations and providing
them with economic aid, respecting the rights of other nations, and human

rights—the old liberalism conforms to the Church. The new liberalism is probably next in line, but is not very far ahead of conservatism. The former's agreement with the old liberalism and the Church on the foregoing points must be balanced off against its misapprehension of communism and its support for international population policies which violate the natural law. Conservatism stands most distant from the Church because of its many ambiguities and contradictions of morally sound policy positions which are recapitulated in the "Conclusion" to Chapter Six. On these specific matters, conservatism has several more debits than the new liberalism does when compared to Church teaching, although none may be as serious as those of the new liberalism.

Lastly, how do the three ideologies fulfill the Church's expectations concerning defense and disarmament? It was explained, in the "Conclusion" to Chapter Four, why the old liberalism was just slightly closer to the Church in this area than the new liberalism. It was stated in Chapter Six that on a full range of questions, about which we get an especially thoughtful discussion in the 1984 Republican platform (e.g., arms for the sake of deterrence and promoting peace, the concept of SDI to render nuclear war unlikely, the opposition to the MAD policy, military assistance to forces rebelling against oppressive governments, mutual and verifiable arms agreements, nuclear non-proliferation, opposition to terrorism), conservatism is definitely in agreement with the Church. On the point about arms control, it seems that conservatism over time has moved closer and closer to the Church. It is difficult to decide whether conservatism over time or the old liberalism is the *closest* of the three. We are inclined to say that they are *equally* close to the Church and, since we said the new liberalism is slightly behind the old liberalism (due to its seeming downplaying of the legitimate defense role of government and its confusion about what peace demands), it is also slightly behind conservatism.

We now summarize and bring together these six specific issue areas to determine which ideology is closest to the Church. We said that, on *economic and social welfare policy*, the old liberalism was just slightly closer to the Church than the new liberalism. Conservatism is farthest from the Church, although not an extreme distance behind the two versions of liberalism. On *agriculture and the environment*, conservatism and the new liberalism are equally close and the old liberalism lags behind. On *civil rights and civil liberties*, conservatism is narrowly ahead of the old liberalism in closeness to the Church and the new liberalism is, by far, the farthest. On *education*, conservatism is, again, closest by a shade, the old liberalism is second, and the new liberalism a distant third. On *foreign policy*, the old liberalism is closest, the new liberalism is next—but clearly in second—and conservatism is last, although not too far behind the latter. On *defense* and *disarmament*, the old liberalism and conservatism are equally close to the Church and the new liberalism is slightly behind them.

Taken together, this means that in these public policy issue areas overall, the old liberalism—which is closest to the Church in three of the areas and a close second in the other three—must be judged to be most in conformity with the Church. Conservatism—which is first in four of the areas ("tied" with the old liberalism in one of these and with the new liberalism in another), a close third in one, and a distant third in another—is next closest to the Church (not too far behind the old liberalism). The new liberalism is third, fairly far back. (In Table 2 point values have been assigned to each perspective on the basis of being closest [1st], second closest [2nd], and farthest [3rd] from the Church to illustrate how these conclusions are reached, as was done with the three political ideologies on their general philosophy of politics and government).

Frankly, if we were considering conservatism before, say, the 1980s, the old liberalism would possibly be even farther ahead of it in the "policy proposals" category—and would possibly edge past it overall (see below). The development of its thinking (even though there was no extremely sharp or fundamental change in its outlook such as would have created two distinct versions of conservatism, as with liberalism) in such areas as disarmament has moved it closer to the Church than it previously was. **Again, it must be pointed out that none of the ideologies conforms fully to the Church; each is wanting in some key areas.**

When we put the two categories of our analysis together—1) the general philosophy of politics and government and 2) the issue areas—we find conservatism to be first, barely ahead of the old liberalism. The new liberalism is a distant third, by far the farthest from the Church. (Conservatism can rightfully be judged to have the edge by considering that in the first category it was first in three of the five areas and a close second in the other two, and in the second category it was first in a full four areas [two were "ties"]. The old liberalism's better overall performance in the second category—three "first places" (one a "tie"), two close "seconds" and one third—does not seem quite enough to overtake it. This impression that one arrives at by simply looking over the findings is confirmed by our comparison of point totals: conservatism had 14 for the first category and 14 for the second for an overall total of 28; the old liberalism had 12 for the first and 15 for the second for an overall total of 27).

It must be understood that this result—that conservatism is slightly closer to Church teaching than the old liberalism and that, is fact, they are almost equally close—is based only, of course, on performance in the various areas of these two categories, *taken equally*. The Church certainly wants all of her teachings about social morality—all of the natural law as respects the social aspects of men's lives—to be accepted and followed. Nevertheless, certain points are clearly more central and, in any serious analysis, would be weighted more heavily.

TABLE 2

RANKING OF THE THREE IDEOLOGIES ON THE BASIS OF THEIR CLOSENESS TO CHURCH TEACHING IN THE CATEGORY OF "SPECIFIC PUBLIC POLICY PROPOSALS."

| | **Ideology** | | |
Ranking	OL	NL	C
1st (closest to Church)	3 (1 tie)	1 (1 tie)	4 (2 ties)
2nd (next closest to church)	2 (both close)	2 (1 close)	0
3rd (farthest from Church)	1	3 (1 close to first)	2
Total points —	15	11	14 points

(Numbers in the above columns indicate the number of areas of the six for which each ideology had the respective ranking. The six areas are: Economic and Social Welfare Policy; Agriculture and the Environment; Civil Rights and Civil Liberties; Education; Foreign Policy; and Defense and Disarmament.)

3 points are assigned for each ranking of 1st; 2 points for each ranking of 2nd (2.5 for each ranking of 2nd if close to 1st); 1 point for each ranking of 3rd (1.5 for each ranking of 3rd if close to 1st).

Key: OL - old liberalism

NL - new liberalism

C - conservatism

For instance, the truth that Catholics must believe in the Creed and the fact that God is the central reality and source of human purpose indicate that that which pertains to belief in God and the importance of religion is paramount. It seems likely that if such facts as these are not taken into account, we skew our results to some extent. This being the case, conservatism would seem likely to come out even further ahead of the other ideologies as far as closeness to the Church is concerned. Further, it can be argued that the Church in different eras gives particular emphasis in its social teaching to certain issues which are especially crucial for the time—those involving particularly dangerous implications for mankind—and so would perhaps judge ideologies more stringently on the basis of what they hold about these.

In our current era, probably the social questions which the Church has most stressed have been: the sanctity of human life, disarmament and mass destruction from warfare, and, possibly, the plight of the world's poor and development. It may be dangerous to factor these into the equation, however, because it could lead to the charge of subjectivity in the analysis and conclusions. This would not be so convincing of a counter to the argument above that an ideology's emphasis on religion should be weighted more heavily; it *would* be, however, in speaking about particular issues.

Actually, if we were to give the greater emphasis to issues such as these, this would probably not change the results we have gotten by weighing the different areas equally: conservatism would remain far ahead of the new liberalism on human life issues, but the old liberalism could not really be judged to be worse than conservatism because it did not call for legalized abortion, etc. On disarmament, the different ideologies would be about equally close to the Church. On development and aid to the world's needy, the two versions of liberalism would be ahead of conservatism and equally close to the Church, but conservatism would not be an overwhelming distance behind. The old liberalism, then, comes out slightly closer to the Church on these three putatively more important questions taken together and this might be enough to make up its slight disadvantage *vis-a-vis* conservatism in an equally weighted comparison of the various areas of the two categories. Its greater strength on the subject of religion, however, would still keep conservatism ahead.

Perhaps the vital point that gives conservatism its advantage when equally weighing the categories is subsidiarity. This gives it its slight advantage over the old liberalism and it accentuates its advantage over the new liberalism (which is already substantial on the basis of the fundamental content of different positions).

The poor performance of the new liberalism in comparison with Church teaching, and its proving to be considerably farther away from the Church than the old liberalism, definitely confirms the thesis of Professor

Hitchcock. Liberalism in America is now something that presents itself as much more problematical for the devoted Catholic to attach himself to.

It must be emphasized and remphasized, however, that even the closest perspective to the Church, conservatism, is *by no means* fully in agreement with her teaching. The specific points on which it diverges have been discussed. It is true that if all of conservatism—diverse as it has been shown to be—followed the thinking of the school that we have called the "cultural conservatives," and to have carried out this thinking into the public policy realm, it would be even closer to the Church. It would be *very* close if, especially, the John Courtney Murrays and the Russell Kirks were followed. (A major complicating factor with Murray, however, was his advocacy of a rather strict separation of church and state with government basically removed from any concern with religious matters and treating all sects absolutely equally. This position is at odds with that stated by Pope Leo XIII in Chapter One).

Explanation

There are three important questions that must be asked in light of the above results. First, why does conservatism have a perspective and policy positions which, overall, come closest to the Church? The second is, why did the old liberalism develop a perspective that compares so favorably with Church social teaching, especially in light of the condemnations of "liberalism" in Pope Leo XIII's time? And finally, most basically, why do both liberalism and conservatism deviate from Church teaching at all?—Why do the old liberalism and conservatism, in spite of their comforming to the Church on many points, still depart from her in significant ways? The answer to these questions is found, in substantial part, in the historical background to these two ideologies.

In the final analysis, the crucial reasons why conservatism is closest to the Church is because it best upholds the natural law and is most supportive of religion (even though, as we have seen, it is not fully adequate in either of these). This is the case because, as the popes have said, God, religion, and the natural law are the basis for the political order. The reason why the new liberalism, conversely, is so distant from the Church is because it has become so secularized and has gone far in the direction of rejecting the natural law, especially in the area of sexual morality.

The old liberalism scores well, probably for the very reasons Hitchcock and our own comments touched on in Chapter One. It is clear from our comparative analysis that the new liberalism is much more secular and, in some ways, more hostile to religion than the old. Hitchcock said, it will be recalled, that many of the old liberals were really quite secularly-oriented as well, but sublimated their true feelings because they had to work to keep their alliance with Catholic and other religious elements (which were all part of what was called the old liberalism). The old liberalism, then, was a coming together of groups which had disparate motivations, backgrounds, and ever basic world views in order to promote common ends. These ends were largely focused on economics, social welfare issues, and foreign policy; the people who coalesced in this liberal front ranged from devout Catholics and urban ethnics to secularist and agnostic intellectuals.

Thus, as Hitchcock noted, the very pragmatism of American politics—the concern about achieving public policy objectives even if it meant that ideology was not maintained pristinely or even necessarily spelled out substantially—made possible a seemingly odd political coalition. It is also perhaps because of this same pragmatism and blurring of more basic beliefs (along with the very fact that so much of American Catholicism was part of this old liberal coalition and that the old liberalism was responding with its policy ideas to the everyday, practical demands of a democratic electorate not very interested in ideology) that it could be as close to the Church as it was. So, even if the truly devoted, ideologically committed old liberals had the kinds of philosophical, religious, and political beliefs that Pope Leo XIII had placed under the rubric of a condemned liberalism, it is not so clear that the old liberalism *overall* did. Thus, it may well be that the old liberalism was not basically liberalism at all, or at least not substantially. It was rather an amalgamation of fundamentally different philosophies which were, paradoxically, compatible in their conclusions (so long, at least, as the conclusions which were emphasized, or which were brought into the public forum, concerned only certain types of things).

Still a certain rationalist philosophical outlook came forth in the old liberalism, especially in the writings of its secularized major spokesmen. This was seen in the examination of its general philosophy of politics and government in Chapter Three. It was primarily because of this that the old liberalism fell behind conservatism in its comparison with the Church. It is this worldly outlook on certain basic principles which is the reason for its deviation from the Church. It is because conservatism shares these basic principles with both versions of liberalism (although in a less thoroughgoing manner) that conservatism also deviates from the fullness of Catholic social doctrine.

It is important to briefly discuss the common background of liberalism and conservatism. (This is a subject which, by itself, would probably require a full book, so we can treat it only briefly here.)

The first point we must consider is that, as Professor Leo Strauss puts it, "[t]he conservativism *[sic]* of our age is identical with what originally was liberalism, more or less modified by changes in the direction of present-day liberalism."[1] As was stated in Chapter One, in the twentieth century, liberalism generally underwent a transformation from what it had been in the nineteenth century (the liberalism of the latter is often termed, it will be recalled, "classical liberalism"). For example, it reversed its previous *laissez-faire* position, especially in economics, and it embraced the idea of big government and substantial government regulation of the economy as well as many other areas of human activity. The result has been a complete reversal of positions and terms. As Professor Crane Brinton states:

> Radical Tom Paine in 1790 wanted a government that would govern very little, cost very little, and that would let nature take its beneficent course; if you want that in the United States in the 1960's, you are an old-guard Republican, not a radical.[2]

(We should add that the same is true in the 1990s as in the 1960s). Actually, this ideological switch should not be seen as altogether surprising. As Professor Rossiter tells us, "[T]he Conservative...wishes his critics would stop confusing liberty with Liberalism [for] Conservatism, too, is a philosophy of liberty." Like liberalism, conservatism's "taproot goes deep into the tradition of freedom under law." All told, "[m]any institutions and values that shallow men credit to Liberalism have been part of Conservative thinking from the beginning."[3] Indeed, Edmund Burke, the British statesman and political thinker who is usually credited with establishing the modern ideology we call "conservatism," was actually a member of the Whig faction, which is regarded as the embodiment of early British liberalism.[4] The principles of Whig liberalism later became important elements of what the Conservative party in Britain came to stand for, and, as Kirk tells us, were principles—i.e., liberty under law, economic freedom—which were received into the thinking of virtually all colonial Americans regardless of their political persuasions.[5]

Moreover, conservatism has also shared with liberalism a belief in the value and possibility of progress. Professor Rossiter suggests that this belief has always been a part of conservatism and is a fundamental part of its system of philosophy[6] (a position which seems to be confirmed by what is stated below; others say that conservatism has taken on this belief because of the influence of liberalism.[7]) It is further contended that conservatism has even been influenced by the egalitarian thrust of liberalism,[8] although precisely how and to what extent in America is in question in light of the findings of this study. Perhaps it is true that liberalism has pushed conservative thinking more towards political equality, although this effect has been felt much more profoundly in Europe than here.

The implication of all of this, for our purposes, is that conservatism and liberalism both deviate from Church teaching to the degree they do, because the former has become like the latter and, since the latter deviates from the Church, we can expect the former will, too. The difference will just be a question of the degree of deviation because of different positions taken on individual key questions. Conservatism will simply not go as far on something as liberalism does.

Probably, however, the main reason why each ideology deviates from the Church is their common origin in early modern political philosophy, and more generally in the thought which has characterized Western culture since the dawn of modernity. As Strauss says, "what now goes by the name of conservativism *[sic]* has...a common root with present-day liberalism and even with Communism....[T]his...would appear most clearly if one were to go back to the origin of modernity, to the break with the premodern tradition that took place in the seventeenth century."[9] We must remember that this new wave of thinking, beginning in the Renaissance (i.e., the fourteenth to sixteenth centuries), was a secular one—in ways, *rampantly* secular—and one which changed radically the notion of natural law. The latter was no longer viewed as having the nature of a moral law, imposing obligations, made known to man through his reason, stressing both commonality of men and their individual dignity by means of the common good—to something promoting extreme individualism, downplaying or ignoring duties in the name of rights, being more like a physical or mathematical law than a moral one, and supposedly emphasizing human reason (but really disparaging it because it elevated and liberated the passions and assumed reason could not help men distinguish right from wrong or tell them how to conduct their lives).

Professor Joseph Cropsey affirms what Rossiter said above about the common roots of freedom of liberalism and conservatism, and also notes the philosophical dimension of this commonality. He tells us that both see man, basically, in a condition of natural liberty. This implies the notion that men should be free to pursue their own interests in their own ways. (To the extent that the two ideologies differ, it is in the areas they permit freedom to be pursued in an unrestrained fashion, or in the extent to which it should be unregulated.) Men's supreme end for both seems to be "the desire and need to preserve themselves." Freedom, in effect, is necessary to achieve this end.[10] If conservatism's endorsement of equality was stimulated by liberalism, the roots and basic commitment to it are implicit in its own doctrines, in the same way as they are in liberalism's. Equality, as stated, is simply being equal in one's freedom, or in the possiblity of being free. This is an objective of both the freedom-loving ideologies of liberalism and conservatism, and is grounded in their common roots.

We noted the change in the notion of natural law which occurred in early modern times, around the time of the Enlightenment of the eighteenth century. While it is clear from our analysis that conservatism has a sounder conception of natural law than liberalism and is closer to the Church in asserting its role in political life, it nonetheless bears the marks of this earlier modern change. That is why there is any deviation from the Church at all in its perspective. Cropsey tells us that conservatism, like liberalism, was affected in its origins by that godfather of modern political philosophy, Thomas Hobbes (although we could trace it back, in some ways, even further to Niccolo Machiavelli). It was the metaphysics, psychology, and political philosophy of Hobbes that helped to render reason "impotent...to ascend to the principles or nature of its objects."[11] That is, his relativism, positivism, and nominalism made true philosophical speculation, searching for first principles and, from them, moral truths, impossible.

In different ways (Cropsey tells us), liberalism and conservatism reflect their Hobbesian heritage: liberalism does not reach for first principles "because their existence is denied"; conservatism does not do so because of its preference for traditions and conventions which are "the ingrained habits and beliefs...[that make up] the fiber of political community."[12] *Both* liberalism and conservatism, then, are "conventional." The deference of conservatism to conventions is, by definition, "conventional" because conventions are standards of conduct developed from human consensus; they are "artificial." The liberal, with his orientation to change and reform, is also conventional: he seeks to right wrongs by means of "human contrivance or upon what is artificial rather than natural." In each case, then, there is positivism. Of course, the conventionality or positivism of each ideology is expressed differently and is not thoroughgoing (e.g., Cropsey tells us that liberalism opposes human traditions by, in essence, appealing to nature, to something above human contrivance, and conservatism appeals to "an unchanging human nature" to resist what it sees as reckless liberal reform), but positivism is still expressed one way or another.[13]

We can see, already, the problem that both ideologies pose, as far as the Church is concerned, in their common basic, original view in support of extreme freedom without a sense of an ultimate, transcendent end for man. Both ideologies, Cropsey goes on, come to their thinking about freedom on the basis of "a morally normless nature," which in turn is based upon a nonteleological view of society[14] which is the outcome of the triumph of modern science, or rather, we should say, of the scientistic perspective it made possible (i.e., the view that physical nature aims for no purpose, so it follows that man does not either). This emerged from the rising secularism of the Enlightenment. Christianity, of course, teaches that even physical nature—to say nothing of man—is teleogical because it exists for the purpose of glorifying God.

In fairness to conservatism, it must be said that its positivism is especially exacerbated by the *laissez-faire* economics orientation of some of its elements. This results particularly, according to Cropsey, in a self-interest ethos that "leads to the collapse of morality into Utilitarianism."[15] Thus, one sees the same outcome as with liberalism with its more fundamental relativism which conflicts profoundly with Catholic morality. The appeal to tradition and thus to convention, as we have said, also contributes to these tendencies, but in a much less obvious or pronounced degree. Cropsey contends that each ideology still tries to adhere to moral positions reflective, in effect, of the old, true natural law—conservatism in the areas we today call "traditional" or "personal moral-ity," and, as we have seen, social morality in some respects, and liberalism tries to do so in social morality—but their efforts, as Cropsey says, are "unsatisfactory."[16] This is because such particular positions go against the basic underlying political philosophy and metaphysical perspective of each ideology, which essentially involves the preoccupation with freedom that we have spoken of. Even if we were to judge Cropsey's assessment of, specifically, conservatism as too harsh—e.g., its putative utilitarianism—it is clear that, as stated, the reason for its deviations from the Church is its non-acceptance of certain points of the natural law (and it also seems clear that this indeed is because of the freedom problem we have discussed).

This leads us to say, again, that if the cultural conservative school of thought or perspective within conservatism were predominant—in effect, were synonymous with conservatism—conservatism would deviate much less from the Church, especially in the matter of its neglect of social morality (which is conservatism's major problem). This is because cultural conservatism enunciates a philosophical framework consonant with Christian teaching and is more correct in its understanding of the natural law. Or, if we were to conclude that a few of the other conservative groupings accept the natural law to the full extent as cultural conservatism does, we must say that the latter has the deepest and most profound understanding of the natural law.

The Alternative For American Catholics

We have seen how neither major American political ideology of today fully corresponds with the teaching of the Church. The question thus follows: Can Catholics espouse either liberalism or conservatism and still be faithful Catholics?

As far as advocating its policy perspectives, they could still consider themselves proponents of the old liberalism—advocating some of its basic principles of political philosophy is more problematical—but they would do so as loners. They will also not find themselves able to attach themselves to organized political efforts that promote the whole agenda of the old liberalism without also having to accept the morally objectionable aspects of the agenda of the new liberalism. This is because there is no longer a viable American political movement identifiable with the old liberalism.

It seems out of the question for Catholics to identify themselves with the new liberalism, either in terms of its general philosophy or its public policy positions, since that ideology is so much out of line with the Church on so many points. It has been scandalous for the Church in the U.S. that, for example, some prominent Catholic politicians have seemed to be new liberals first and Catholics only second. They have allowed the outlook and positions of the new liberalism, and not Catholic teaching, to shape their thinking about important public moral issues, such as abortion. Names such as Mario Cuomo (Governor of New York), Geraldine Ferraro (1984 Democratic Vice Presidential nominee), Lucy Killea (California State Senator), and U.S. Senators Daniel Patrick Moynihan (New York) and Edward M. Kennedy (Massachusetts) come to mind in this regard. What, then, about conservatism? On first impression, it would seem possible for Catholics to do with conservatism what so many of them did with the old liberalism. They could line up with conservatism (i.e., with the organized political movement of conservatism as it finds expression in the Republican party and in certain other organizations) rather than with the ideology itself (its positions on economics, especially, are in conflict with the Church). The problem with this, however, is that while the old liberals were willing to subvert their secularism to maintain their common issue front with Catholics on matters such as economics, social welfare, and communism, it is very unlikely conservatives would do this on economics because the classical liberal perspective on this is so basically a part of their structure of beliefs.

As far as espousing the *ideology* of conservatism is concerned, Catholics could probably be more at ease in espousing cultural conservatism than the other schools or perspectives. But even here, we have seen that there is an excessively individualistic emphasis in economics, at least with some of the authors, and, moreover, the different schools in conservatism do not exist in the actual world in isolation form each other. They are involved with each other and, in spite of their disagreements, often make a common front. Conservatives typically see their points of agreement as stronger than their points of difference. The upshot of all this is that we believe it is problematical for a Catholic to simply embrace the ideology that we have been speaking of called "conservatism." Of course, Catholics, like anyone else, will loosely use the terms "liberal" or "conservative" in describing their positions and outlook on different matters. This is different from attaching themselves to the actual ideologies that go under those names.

Probably the best thing for Catholics to do is simply to do what they ought in any event to be doing: to *be* Catholic in the sense of accepting *in full* the teachings of their Church on social matters, and being faithful to what the popes have meant when interpreting and applying them to different situations. There is perhaps room for Catholics to carry these teachings into the political marketplace, even specifically calling them "Catholic." This could serve as a tool for evangelization as well as an attempt to influence general political thinking and the direction of public policy in America (*if* Catholics explain them well and show why they are so reasonable).

Actually, however, the problems of religious pluralism in America and traditional anti-Catholicism—never very far beneath the surface—may be enough to motivate some people to oppose such an explicitly Catholic attempt irrespective of its merits. (Moreover, we should not underestimate the force with which people will defend such a deeply-seated perspective in America as economic liberalism.) Perhaps emphasizing the demands of the natural law is a better approach, at least when going to the center of public debate and dialoging with political decisionmakers. Our nation's ideals emerged from the natural law tradition and many of the principles and positions that Catholics would be putting forth can be found in our own heritage.[17]

We also should not be sanguine about the possibility of a Catholic bloc in the American electorate asserting its influence to get public policy on social questions to conform more closely with Catholic teaching. This approach did not succeed very well in the past when American Catholics generally were more obedient to the teachings of the Church and to the hierarchy. It was more successful in influencing public morals, however, but it is much less likely to succeed now when so many dissent in belief and praxis and Catholics are more divided politically. This analysis suggests that to promote a social order based on the teachings of the Church—and on the natural law—Catholics will have to re-evangelize their own people as well as reach out to other Christians.

On this first point, it is obviously necessary to bring Catholics back to, simply, Catholicism; to restore their faith on the most basic level so they will not pick and choose which doctrines of the Church they will uphold (so-called "cafeteria Catholicism"). Faith, of course, is a gift from God. We cannot give it to our fellow humans, but we can help them to open up to receiving it through evangelization. It is from this renewed faith that commitment to social justice and social charity will occur. As Russell Kirk points out about Christianity, it had its social impact because it first recast the human heart and soul.[18]

On the second point, we perhaps can try to seek out non-Catholic Christians who would be receptive to Catholic social principles to try to form a more broad-based front to influence public discourse and public policy. This makes one think of the formation of the Christian Democratic party (CDU/CSU) in West Germany.[19] We are not specifically suggesting a political party here, but perhaps there is room for organizations of Christians which would try to influence public debate on social questions. We are not oblivious to the difficulties here: Protestants who would be close to Catholics in their commitment to the basics of Christian belief and on, say, human life issues would not be close on economics (e.g., evangelicals); and those who would be close to

Catholics on economic and social welfare matters tend to be the ones who would have succumbed the most to secularization and be at odds with Catholics on sexual morality and human life issues (e.g., mainline Protestants). Actually, if some kind of common front could be established, at least among a small number of Catholic and Protestant Christians, the idea of even a Christian Democratic political party would not be without merit. The latter would not at all be likely to become a major party in this country—both because of the American attachment to the two-party system and our suspicion of religion becoming intertwined with politics—but it would perhaps help further the kind of public debate desired and draw attention to the attempt to assert Christian social principles as an alternative in shaping public policy. In this way, it could perhaps influence the major parties (which is the major contribution that third parties have made in American history[20]). The Republican party seems to be the one which is now the more open one to religious perspectives, and could be influenced. A Christian third party could also provide an alternative in the active political arena for Catholics and other Christian voters who do not wish to formally line up with either liberalism or conservatism because of the conflict with the teachings of their churches.

Another, and perhaps more viable, option for Catholics is simply to work within the major parties, especially the Republican. Working within the Republican party is an option that has been pursued by many politically active orthodox Catholics and perhaps accounts for the shape of its 1984 platform, which is quite satisfactory from the Catholic perspective in many areas. If those same Catholics had not been so ready to simply attach themselves to conservatism, the 1984 platform could have been even better. The increasing division in the Republican party over abortion and its growing reluctance to stand foursquare against abortion now make it problematic for Catholics to place their confidence in it. The awareness of the obstacle posed by a stubborn commitment in the party to some version of a *laissez-faire* economic idea also should not be underestimated.

Catholics, of course, will have to work and deal with "liberals" and "conservatives" in an American political order we all share. As we have seen, there *can* be some common ground. If Catholics are to be successful in bringing about a more Catholic, more moral, natural law-oriented public policy—if they are to positively influence liberals and conservatives who *are* open to listening—they will have to know the social teachings of the Church (i.e., the teachings of the *popes*) and will have to put them forth clearly. Obviously, there will be compromises in the making of public policy; compromise is the essence and inevitable reality of political life. So, Catholics cannot expect that their principles will be fully realized in public policy. Nevertheless, they should understand what compromise means and how it is desirably brought about. They should learn how to practice the great political virtue of prudence. Prudence indicates that there should be a willingness to compromise on specifics or in nonessentials, or even in essential matters (if necessary) on the level of solutions or practical policies, while at the same time always enunciating and aiming for the realization of the true principles. Any policy solution that has the effect of surrendering the basic principles of social morality—of weakening them or compromising their integrity—is to be resisted. Thus, Catholics should work with liberals and conservatives, but should not rush to espouse either's ideology. If they do so, it is unlikely that they will be able to continue to vigorously enunciate the full corpus of the social teachings of the Church, or even to enunciate them at all. They will cease, if you will, to be a *witness* for these teachings to liberals and conservatives. Then, they will have followed so many of today's Catholic politicians to become liberals or conservatives first and Catholics second, and then they effectively will no longer be working for a *Catholic* social order.

Finally, it should be said that the attempt to promote Catholic social teaching in the American public arena today is best organized and spearheaded by *laymen*. The Church has emphasized that political activity is an area of endeavor more suitable for lay than clerical activity.[21] Further, the American Catholic hierarchy has perhaps been too influenced in its own thinking about public issues—i.e., about how to apply Church social teaching to various particular questions in American life[22]—by liberalism, especially by way of advisors who embody this perspective.[23] We are thus in the interesting situation that the laity are actually in a far better position than the clergy or hierarchy to transcend the limitations and constraints of a liberal or a conservative outlook.

ADDENDUM

CENTESIMUS ANNUS

Pope John Paul II issued his third social encyclical, *Centesimus Annus* (*The Hundredth Year*) in May 1991, as the original version of this book was about to go to press. This lengthy encyclical, written to commemorate the hundredth anniversary of *Rerum Novarum*, is in many ways a compendium of the Church's social teachings since Pope Leo XIII's great encyclical. In *Centesimus Annus*, John Paul announces that he will try to show the "fruitfulness" of *Rerum Novarum's* principles as a basis for analyzing and solving our present social situation, the "new things" of today. (*Rerum Novarum* means "new things.") These principles are perennial; they are part of the Church's "doctrinal patrimony and as such involve the exercise of her teaching authority."[1]

This Addendum summarizes the major points of *Centesimus Annus,* explains how its teachings compare to the previous social encyclicals, and determines whether its contents alter the conclusions we have come to about American liberalism and conservatism in reference to Church social teaching.

Chapter 1 of the encyclical is the main chapter which recounts and reaffirms the various teachings and principles of *Rerum Novarum*: the dignity of labor; the right of private property; the right to form employer-worker associations and labor unions; the rights to the "'limitation of working hours,'" rest, and the different treatment of women and children in work; the condemnation of socialism and liberalism; and the fact that the weaker, laboring classes must be protected by government.[2] The chapter notes that *Rerum Novarum* made clear that "teach[ing] and...spread[ing]...[the Church's] social doctrine...is an essential part of the Christian message."[3]

Building upon the foundation of *Rerum Novarum* and the other social encyclicals, *Centesimus Annus* addresses an assortment of both domestic and international social questions.

The Family and Respect for Human Life

All of the Church's teaching on these subjects is taken as a given by *Centesimus Annus*, of course. To underscore the importance placed on them, *Centesimus Annus* includes "*[a]mong the most important* of...[human] rights" the right to life "an integral part of which" is that of the unborn child; "the right to live in a united family"; the right to a good "moral environment" for children; and "the right freely to establish a family, to have and to rear children through the responsible exercise of one's sexuality."[4]

The encyclical also speaks about the family in two other specific contexts. One is a call for a rejuvenation of the family. Pope John Paul says that this requires that people accept marriage as a stable commitment characterized by mutual giving, not a vehicle for self-gratification.[5] The other is in conjunction with his insistence that the way "to overcome today's widespread individualistic mentality...is a concrete commitment to solidarity and charity, beginning in the family." It is because of this that the state must support the family. It must "promote not only family policies, but also those social policies which have the family as their principal object." Such policies would "assist the family by providing adequate resources and efficient means of support both for bringing up children and for looking after the elderly."[6]

Regarding human life, John Paul reiterates his condemnation in *Sollicitudo Rei Socialis* of systematic anti-childbearing campaigns.[7]

Obviously, all of the above is consistent with previous encyclicals.

The Role of the State

On this subject, *Centesimus Annus* might be said to build on, and be completely consistent with, *Pacem in Terris* and *Laborem Exercens*. Pope John Paul says that the role of the state includes the following: 1) establishing the "juridical framework" within which economic affairs take place in order to safeguard "human rights in the economic sector" and insure the needed equality in economic relationships (i.e., commutative justice); the "human rights" spoken of apparently range from the workers' rights spelled out in *Rerum Novarum* and other encyclicals to private property;[8] 2) protecting, *in conjunction with the private sector*, workers from unemployment[9] (this almost certainly follows from *Laborem Exercens'* contention that unemployment is always evil); 3) providing a stable currency and efficient public services in order to encourage efficient and honest work;[10] 4) guaranteeing, *in conjunction with the private sector*, a family wage;[11] 5) preserving "common goods" (e.g., the environment and basic human rights) which the market cannot sufficiently protect.[12] The principle of subsidiary clearly applies for each of these. Some of the points below elaborate on these.

There is no sharp change from previous encyclicals in the above. In many places, *Centesimus Annus* also stresses the state's role, mentioned repeatedly in the social encyclicals, of promoting and maintaining the common good.[13]

As far as forms of government are concerned, *Centesimus Annus* reiterates the Church's contemporary preference for democracy (i.e., representative government or a republican form) because of the available forms it best guarantees human rights, citizen participation, accountability of those in governing positions, and peaceful changes of power. Like Leo XIII, however, John Paul II notes the danger that in democracies truth will be suppressed because the majority will not accept it. Echoing Leo, he says that "if there is not ultimate truth to guide and direct political activity, then ideas and convictions can easily be manipulated for reasons of power." Even in democracies, rights can be suppressed. He singles out for special mention in this regard the right to life (especially of the unborn child), various family rights, the right to pursue the truth, and the right to a just wage. He insists that "[a]uthentic democracy" requires the rule of law and "a correct conception of the human person."[14]

Economics and Various Aspects of the "Social Question"

Centesimus Annus elaborates considerably on, and gives unprecedented emphasis to, the teaching of previous encyclicals about the need for private economic initiative, the right of free commerce, and the legitimacy of profit. It reaffirms that there is a natural right to private property, which is required for freedom but is not absolute (due to the social dimension of property [i.e., "common use"]).[15] In continuing to develop his theology of work begun in *Laborem Exercens*, John Paul notes that there is now another form of property "no less important than land: the possession of know-how, technology and skill." He says, in fact, that today "the decisive factor of production is increasingly man['s]...knowledge."[16] Human work and knowledge have replaced land and capital as the chief factors in production.[17]

The encyclical goes on to strongly commend the "free market" or "business economy"[18] or "capitalism" in a certain sense of the word.[19] Capitalism as "an economic system which recognizes the fundamental and positive role of business, the market, and private property and the resulting personal responsibility for the means of production as well as free human creativity in the economic sector" is desirable. If, however, capitalism is to be understood as a "system in which freedom in the economic sector is not circumscribed within a strong juridical framework which places it at the service of human freedom in its totality and which sees it as a particular aspect of that freedom, the core of which is ethical and religious," then it is to be rejected.[20] As Pope Paul VI said (see Chapter Two of this book), the market must be limited, so as to keep it just and moral and human.

As part of its expression of support for the free market, the encyclical speaks about the legitimacy, within limits, of the pursuit of self-interest and the profit motive. In effect, it calls for a balanced understanding of the role of self-interest. Man's self-interested actions are not necessarily to be condemned. Instead, the paradoxical role of self-interest must be understood: man "can transcend his immediate interest and still remain bound to it." A stable social order is one which "takes this fact into account" and "seeks ways to bring...into fruitful harmony" "personal interest and the interests of society as a whole." When self-interest is "violently suppressed," as in Communist regimes, "it is replaced by a burdensome system of bureaucratic control which dries up the wellsprings of initiative and creativity."[21] Earning profit shows that "productive factors have been properly employed" and "human needs...satisfied."[22]

Entrepreneurship is singled out for a special accolade. Again, while the stress and attention given to it are unprecedented, the importance of private economic initiative and entrepreneurial-type activity had been noted in previous encyclicals.[23] John Paul states that entrepreneurship demands such "virtues" as diligence, industriousness, courage and prudence in taking risks, etc. *Centesimus Annus* also underscores the importance of wealth-creation for society.[24]

By contrast, *Centesimus Annus* repeats the teaching of previous encyclicals about the dangers of an unrestrained market, self-interest, and the profit motive. If unrestrained, they can create injustice, suppress human dignity, neglect fundamental needs which the market cannot meet, make production and consumption the center of life (i.e., "consumerism"), and thwart the effort to establish dignified work as the main feature of the economic order (needed for men to "express their creativity and develop their potential").[25] Economics cannot be made the central concern for man. If it is, economic freedom becomes disconnected from man's distinctly human character and ends up "alienating and oppressing him."[26]

Pope John Paul, then, promotes a vision of economic society in which market mechanisms operate, but in which work is truly dignified and in which "the quest for truth, beauty, goodness and...common growth determine consumer choices, savings and investments." Further, work is understood as a naturally cooperative endeavor, undertaken in association with others and for the benefit, at least in part, of others. The latter is why the encyclical restates previous papal admonitions about worker participation in industrial enterprises.[27]

The implication of the above is that the Church has not simply embraced American "liberal economics" and abandoned her search for a "third way" in economics as the result of *Centesimus Annus*, as some have claimed.[28] We have noted above the two conceptions of capitalism that the encyclical mentions. John Paul also speaks critically about "alienation" and "consumerism" in the West—the home of liberal capitalism. Indeed, he says that "[i]n spite of the great changes which have taken place in the more advanced societies, the human inadequacies of capitalism and the resulting domination of things over people are far from disappearing" and that "it is unacceptable to say that the defeat of so called 'real socialism' leaves capitalism as the only model of economic organization."[29]

What is the "third way" that Pope John Paul holds out for economic life? What is the "alternative" to both "capitalism"—which "uphold[s]...the absolute predominance of capital" (he here apparently means capitalism in the pejorative sense discussed above)—and socialism—"which in fact turns out to be state capitalism." It is "a society of free work, of enterprise and of participation." This kind of society "demands that the market be controlled by the forces of society and by the state so as to guarantee that the basic needs of the whole society are satisfied."[30]

While upholding the proper economic and social welfare functions of the state delineated in previous encyclicals,[31] John Paul rejects the Western-style "welfare state" or "social assistance state." The latter results in a loss of human initiative, massive increases in public spending, and less concern with those being served than with "bureaucratic ways." As John Paul says, "it would appear that needs are best met by people closest to...those in need" (he speaks specifically of greater reliance on the family, neighbors, and the Church).[32] This, of course, echoes *Rerum Novarum*. The principle of subsidiary is specifically reemphasized, and the role and value of "other intermediate communities" besides the family underscored.[33]

The "preferential option for the poor" is reaffirmed, with the insistence that it pertains to the culturally and spiritually impoverished as well as the economic.[34] The roots of this were seen in *Rerum Novarum's* teaching that the poor need the state to protect them. *Centesimus Annus* makes clear that poverty, including economic poverty, of different sorts is found in developed countries as well as underdeveloped ones.[35]

The discussion in *Centesimus Annus* about the state's shared role in protecting against unemployment (noted above) develops further the teaching of *Laborem Exercens*. The former encyclical says that this protection has historically been provided by either "unemployment policies aimed at enduring balanced growth and full employment or through unemployment insurance and retraining programs" which enable workers to shift to healthier parts of the economy.[36] Which approach is to be chosen by the state is not for the Church to decide. This does not change the requirement of *Laborem Exercens* that the state either make grants for the subsistence of the unemployed and their families or insure that this is done in some way, as discussed in Chapter Two.

While the above indicates that *Centesimus Annus* in some sense expands the economic role of the state, the encyclical holds that actual, direct state interventions in the economy must be as limited as possible. Examples of when such interventions would be justified would be to help stimulate business activities (which are needed to create jobs) when lacking, to check monopolies which impede development, or even to "exercise a substitute function" when the private sector is weak. John Paul calls such interventions "supplementary," and says they must be undertaken only for "urgent reasons touching the common good" and be "as brief as possible."[37]

In both the discussion of the state's role in dealing with unemployment and of other aspects of its economic role, the principle of subsidiarity is clearly seen as controlling. The state has both an "indirect" economic role of "creating favorable conditions for the free exercise of economic activity"—which "will lead to...employment and sources of wealth"—and a "direct" role of placing the necessary limits on economic autonomy so as to defend the weak and provide "necessary minimum support" for the unemployed.[38]

As in previous encyclicals, the dangers of consumerism (i.e., wasteful or damaging consumption and consumption which elevates material concerns over spiritual ones) are stressed. Echoing his 1989 ecology statement, Pope John Paul speaks about the need of wealthy nations not just "to draw on...surplus goods" to help those in poor countries, but "above all" to "change...life-styles... [and] models of production and consumption."[39] It should be noted that this admonition goes beyond those of previous encyclicals. This provides the jumping off point to discussing *Centesimus Annus'* international points.

"The International Question"

Centesimus Annus upholds and elaborates on the principles of previous encyclicals on international matters. It reiterates points mentioned in Chapter Two of this book on such subjects as communism, the Cold War arms race and emergence of East and West power blocs, terrorism, the rights of nations, the plight of poor nations and the imperative and collective responsibility for development, and the need for international cooperation.[40] The following new specific points and admonitions are set forth: a nation's economic development requires international, as opposed to isolated, economic activity; a concerted effort by the most powerful countries, as well as the endeavors of international agencies, is needed to direct international economics toward the common good; when making aid decisions, international agencies must "always give sufficient consideration" to nations which are in the situation of having the greatest need but "little weight in the international market"; and if "hunger and despair" and "unbearable sacrifices" will result from requiring underdeveloped nations to repay international debts, the debts should "be lighten[ed], defer[red], or even cancel[led]."[41] John Paul gives a particularly strong emphasis to the need to reject war in the contemporary world. He says in the encyclical, as he has in various talks, "never again war."[42] Of course, the Church's teaching about just war does not change, but John Paul no doubt wishes to underscore the urgency of turning men away from war at a time of its unprecedented destructiveness.

He says that steps must be undertaken to insure that the rule of law, instead of warfare, is allowed to regulate international affairs as it does domestic.[43]

Communism

Some of the most profound papal reflection ever on communism and totalitarianism appears in *Centesimus Annus*. An entire chapter is devoted to the collapse of the Communist regimes in Europe in 1989. The Pope says that it resulted from the suppression of workers' rights, economic inefficiency (caused by the violation of human economic rights), and, most fundamentally, the spiritual void brought about by atheism.[44] The latter is the reason why communism could not be opposed merely by economic means—i.e., stressing the satisfaction of material needs while "excluding spiritual values."[45]

John Paul discusses the characteristics of all totalitarian regimes: rejection of transcendent truth, rejection of the Church, tendency to absorb all lesser associations, and the claim that the state or party is the repositor of all truth.[46]

In light of all this, the Pope reiterates how "impossible compromise between Marxism and Christianity" is.[47] He brings the discussion of communism back to the economic realm by saying that its extreme suppression of self-interest (mentioned above) reflected the ill-conceived utopian ambition to "make...evil impossible" by means of a purported "perfect social organization."[48]

Other Aspects of Freedom Threatened

Centesimus Annus' stress on the need for economic freedom is seen above. The encyclical reiterates the Church's general teaching about human freedom that John Paul mentions was spelled out so well by Leo XIII in the encyclical *Libertas Praestantissimum*: there is "an essential bond between human freedom and truth, so that freedom which refused to be bound to the truth would fall into arbitrariness and...self-destruction."[49] This, of course, is the basis for John Paul's distinguishing between the two types of capitalism above. It is also the basis for his concerns about the threats to freedom from the contemporary media and some religious fundamentalists. He says that true freedom and human development can be hindered by "manipulation by...mass communication...impos[ing] fashions and trends of opinion."[50] The intolerance of "new forms of religious fundamentalism" poses a current threat to religious liberty.[51] (The Church, of course, has held the latter to be one of the most central of human rights.[52])

Finally, it is important to note that Pope John Paul makes clear that social questions and problems cannot be approached as natural phenomena alone. Man needs to turn to God. He insists, as Leo XIII did, that "there can be no genuine solution" of these questions "apart from the Gospel."[53] It is "[t]he kingdom of God...[which] throws light on the order of human society, while the

power of grace penetrates that order and gives it life. *In this way,* the requirements of a society worthy of man are better perceived, deviations are corrected,
the courage to work for what is good is reinforced."[54] John Paul leaves no doubt
that the Church's attempt to rectify social wrongs and to elevate the earthly
situation of man is part of her sacramental and evangelistic mission: "When the
Church proclaims God's salvation to man, when she offers and communicates
the life of God through the sacraments, when she gives direction to human life
through the commandments of love of God and neighbor, she contributes to the
enrichment of human dignity."[55]

In sum, we see that *Centesimus Annus* continues and builds on the teaching
of previous social encyclicals.

ASSESSMENT OF THIS STUDY'S CONCLUSION IN LIGHT OF *CENTESIMUS ANNUS*

Centesimus Annus alters neither our analysis nor conclusions about the
three American political ideologies. The only areas in the category of "The
General Philosophy of Politics and Government" that might call for reconsid-
eration are the purposes of government and the view of freedom. On the former,
while conservatism's respect of subsidiarity and agreement about government
providing the "juridical framework" for a free economy commend it, it still is
handicapped by conceding too insufficient of an economic (both domestic and
international) and social welfare function to the state. This justifies its continued
placement behind the old liberalism in this area. Conservatism was already
judged closest to the Church in its thinking about freedom. The enhanced
emphasis of the new encyclical on the necessity of economic freedom, however,
does not remove conservatism's major liability in this area which is an *excessive*
notion of economic freedom. *Centesimus Annus,* as noted above, stresses the
evils encouraged by the latter. Nothing is addressed in the encyclical which
would change our comparisons in the areas of God, religion, and the natural law
as the basis of the political order, equality, or communism. In fact, the new
encyclical's strong repudiation of communism reinforces conservatism's status
as clearly closest to the Church on this subject.

Questions could possibly be raised about our conclusions in only two of the
six specific public policy issue areas surveyed, in light of *Centesimus Annus.* On
economic and social welfare policy, the above observations apply. While the
new encyclical's assertions about the private sector economic role, the welfare
state, and government economic intervention are plusses for conservatism and
minuses for both versions of liberalism, they do not sufficiently overcome
conservatism's stated drawbacks in this area (e.g., an excessive stress on competition, too little stress on cooperation, insufficient concern about unemployment). If any change in the ordering (first-old liberalism, second-new liberal-

ism, and third-conservatism) in this issue area were justified, it would probably be the dropping of the new liberalism into third place. This would be due to the strong papal criticism of the welfare state and the enhanced stress on subsidiarity. These problems of the new liberalism are not newly created, just highlighted, in light of *Centesimus Annus*, however. Thus, overall, we believe the ordering should stand.

The above indicates that Pope John Paul holds that environmental problems are rightfully in the state's arena of responsibility—although he does not say exclusively, nor does he say that the level of government has to be the national or central. This papal position might be construed as favoring the new liberalism, but this does not change our assessment of the three ideologies on the environment. The new liberalism was viewed as closest to the Church and remains so. *Centesimus Annus* just strongly reinforces this. Conservatism remains second and the old liberalism third. There is no reason to reevaluate our ranking on agriculture. Thus, it would seem that the ranking in the overall category of "Agriculture and the Environment" should not change: conservatism and the new liberalism tied for first, and the old liberalism third.

There is nothing new about the areas of civil rights and civil liberties and education in the new encyclical, so there is no need to change our analysis. The encyclical's statements about international matters are not substantially different from previous papal teaching, so our conclusions in the issue areas of foreign policy and defense and disarmament are still valid.

Centesimus Annus **thus reaffirms previous Church teaching and sustains our conclusion that, overall, conservatism is closest to the teaching, the old liberalism is next closest, and the new liberalism is farthest away.**

NOTES

CHAPTER ONE NOTES

1. On the tendency of the legalization of abortion to have these effects, see Sacred Congregation for the Doctrine of the Faith, *Declaration on Procured Abortion*, para. 20 and Krason, Stephen M., Abortion: *Politics, Morality and the Constitution* (Lanham, Md.: University Press of America, 1984), pp. 305-306.

2. For an examination of how liberals have been more sharply and consistently "liberal" and conservatives more sharply and consistently "conservative" in recent years than in the twenty years right after World War II, see Nie, Norman H.; Verba, Sidney; and Petrocik, John R., *The Changing American Voter* (Cambridge, Mass.: Harvard Univ. Press, 1976, Chap. 8.) They also discuss how rank and-file and activists Democrats have become more liberal and Republicans more conservative in recent years (pp. 194-204).

3. As social teachings scholar Anne Fremantle writes, "the cumulative teaching of the so-called 'social encyclicals'...can be taken to be...a complete documentation of Catholic social doctrine." (Fremantle, Anne, ed., The Social Teachings of the Church [N.Y.: New American Library, 1963], her Introduction, p. 17.) On the point about the encyclicals as the immediate source of Catholic social teaching, we are aware of Pope John Paul II's saying in his encyclical *Laborem Exercens* (1981) that "the Church's social teaching finds its source in Sacred Scripture, beginning with the book of Genesis and especially in the Gospel and the writings of the Apostles." (Pope John Paul II, *Laborem Exercens* [Boston: St. Paul Edns.], Part I, Sec. 3, p. 10 [hereinafter referred to as "*LE*"].) Christian Revelation, which includes all of its moral teachings, is complete, of course, with the close of the Apostolic Age. (Sacred Congregation for the Clergy, *General Catechetical Directory*. [Wash., D.C.: USCC, 1971], Sec. 13, pp. 15-16.) The *ultimate* source of the social teaching, then, is Divine Revelation, but it is also the natural moral law; both, of course, come from God himself (Fremantle above makes it clear why we can appropriately say the encyclicals are its *immediate* source which we can consult to know its content). Since the natural law is involved, of course, even the human mind which is ignorant of Revelation can come to a knowledge of the moral precepts involved. (Fremantle, her Introduction, pp. 12-13.) The Church, which authoritatively defines faith and morals, is, of course, the authoritative

interpreter of Revelation and of both the moral and natural law. (See Second Vatican Council, *Dogmatic Constitution on the Church* [*Lumen Gentium*], 1964, Chap. III, Sec. 25, in Flannery, Austin, O.P., gen. ed., *Vatican Council II: The Conciliar and Post Conciliar Documents*. [Boston: St. Paul Edns., 1975]; General Catechetical Directory, Sec. 59, p. 46.) Encyclicals can be defined as papal pastoral letters addressed generally to all Christians or all men and whose primary purpose is "to diffuse...[the] infallible teaching of the Church, to defend it if necessary, and to apply it to some particularly important problems of the day...[often] aris[ing] in social and political life." (Gilson, Etienne, ed., *The Church Speaks to the Modern World: The Social Teachings of Leo XIII* [Garden City, N.Y.: Doubleday [Image Bks.], 1954], his Introduction, p. 4.) As far as the obligation of Catholics to obey the teachings of encyclicals is concerned we might cite this quote from Gilson:

> [T]he "extraordinary magisterial teaching of the Church"...enjoys, in each and every one of its parts, without any reservation, the grace of infallibility. This grace belongs to the so-called "ecumenical councils"...[and] also belongs to the pronouncements of the Pope when, speaking in his capacity as pastor and teacher of all Christians, and by virtue of his supreme apostolic authority, he declares that a certain doctrine concerning faith or moral conduct should be held as true by the whole Church.

> [T]he "ordinary" teaching of the Church...The encyclical letters are the usual means by which the Popes exercise this definite teaching function. These letters are the highest expression of the ordinary teaching of the Church. To the extent that they restate the infallible teachings of the Church, the pronouncements of the encyclical letters are themselves infallible. Moreover, while explaining and developing such infallible teachings, or while using them as a sure criterion in the condemnation of errors, or even while striving to solve the social, economic, and political problems of the day in the light of these infallible teachings, the Popes enjoy the special assistance of the Holy Spirit, a higher guidance in which the supernatural gift of prudence plays a decisive part.

> That is to say, the teachings of the Popes, as found in their encyclical letters, can by no means be considered as expressing mere opinions which anyone is free to hold or to reject at will. Even though they may not be binding as to faith in all their parts, the teachings of an encyclical are all directly related to faith by the supreme teaching authority of the Church with the special assistance of the Holy Spirit. There always is grave temerity in not accepting the teaching of an encyclical on any one of the points it touches. (Gilson, his Introduction, pp. 4-5).

Our source about the authority of other types of papal statements and documents of the Congregation for the Doctrine of the Faith is Dr. Allan Schreck, Chairman of the Department of Theology at Franciscan University of Steubenville, who has authored several books on Catholic theology.

By the way, it is worth pointing out, in light of the confusion about this in the minds of some people in the Church in the U.S., that episcopal conferences—e.g., the National Conference of Catholic Bishops (NCCB) in the U.S.—have no teaching authority, as a body, for the Church (as do individual bishops in union with the popes).

4. A good brief survey of the changes in American liberalism from the late eighteenth and nineteenth centuries to the twentieth century—presented in the context of discussing the changes in the philosophy of the Democratic party over this time—is found in Bailey, Thomas A., *Democrats vs. Republicans* (N.Y.: Meredith, 1968), pp. 136-150.

5. Schrems, John J., *Principles of Politics: An Introduction* (Englewood Cliffs, N.J.: Prentice-Hall, 1986), p. 144.

6. Baradat, Leon, *Political Ideologies: Their Origins and Impact* (2nd. ed.; Englewood Cliffs, N.J.: Prentice-Hall, 1984), p. 304, cited in Schrems, *ibid.*

7. *Ibid.*, p. 145.

8. Skidmore, Max J., *Ideologies: Politics in Action* (N.Y.: Harcourt, Brace, Jovanovich, 1989), p. 7.

9. *Random House Dictionary of the English Language* (N.Y.: Random House, 1967), p. 707.

10. See, for example, his *Enemies of the Permanent Things: Observations of Abnormity in Literature and Politics* (New Rochelle, N.Y.: Arlington House), 1969.

11. This was stated in comments by Kirk at an Intercollegiate Studies Institute seminar on the topic of the twentieth century at his home at Piety Hill, Mecosta, Michigan, Memorial Day weekend, 1986.

12. *Random House Dictionary*, p. 707.

13. We shall refer to post-1932 liberalism as "contemporary liberalism"; this might be less confusing than calling it "twentieth century liberalism" since there was, of course, some of the twentieth century before this time. The "old liberalism" is the version of contemporary liberalism which ran from 1933 to roughly, 1960. The "new liberalism" is that version of it which began around 1960 and continues to the present. We apologize for the obvious confusion present here, but some terms have to be given to these different notions to distinguish them.

14. Grivetz, Harry K., *The Evolution of Liberalism* (N.Y.: Collier, 1963), pp. 153-154.

15. *Ibid.*, p. 154.

16. Canavan, Francis, S.J., "The Dilemma of Liberal Pluralism," *The Human Life Review*, Vol. V, No. 3 (Summer 1979), pp. 6-7.

17. Berns, Walter, *Freedom, Virtue, and the First Amendment* (Baton Rouge, La.: LSU Press, 1957), p. 72.

18. Spitz, David, "A Liberal Perspective on Liberalism and Conservatism," Goldwin, Robert A., ed., *Left, Right, and Center* (Chicago: Rand McNally, 1965, 1967), pp. 34-35.

19. Cropsey, Joseph, "Conservatism and Liberalism," in *ibid.*, p. 53.

20. *Ibid.*

21. Spitz, *ibid.*, p. 30.

22. Beer, Samuel H., "Liberalism and the National Idea," *ibid.*, p. 161.

23. *Ibid.*, p. 158.

24. *Ibid.*, p. 162 quoting Croly, Herbert D., *The Promise of American Life* (Hamdem, Conn.: Shoestring Press, 1909), Chap. III, Sec.2.

25. Rossiter, Clinton, *Conservatism in America: The Thankless Persuasion* (2nd. ed., rev.; N.Y.: Random House [Vintage], 1955, 1962), pp. 12-13. Emphasis is in the book. (Hereinafter referred to as "Rossiter 1962.")

26. *Ibid.*, p. 13.

27. *Ibid.*, p. 18. Emphasis is added.

28. *Ibid.*

29. *Ibid.*, p. 17.

30. Kirk, Russell,*The Conservative Mind: From Burke to Eliot* (7th rev. ed.; Chicago: Regnery, 1953, 1986), pp. 7-8. (Hereinafter referred to as "Kirk I.")

31. *Ibid.*, pp. 8-9.

32. Pope Leo XIII, *Libertas Praestantissimum* (*On Human Liberty*) (1888), para. 15, in Gilson, p. 66 (Hereinafter referred to as "*LP.*")

33. *Ibid.*, 17, p. 68.

34. *Ibid.*, 16, p. 67.

35. *Ibid.*, 23, p. 72.

36. *Ibid.*, 24, p. 73.

37. *Ibid.*, 30, p. 75.

38. *Ibid.*, 39-40, p. 79.

39. Sarda y Salvany, Felix, *What Is Liberalism?* (Tr. Conde B. Pallen; Rockford, Ill.: Tan, 1979; originally published in the U.S. in 1899 by B. Herder, St. Louis), p. 22. (When published in the U.S., the book was adapted to the American situation.)

40. *Ibid.*, pp. 26-27.

41. Letter from Fr. Jerome Secheri, O.P. (Secretary of the Sacred Congregation of the Index) to a Spanish Bishop who had sought to have the Church ban Sarda's book, Jan. 10, 1887, *ibid.*, p. iv.

42. Bailey, pp. 144-146.

43. Gleason, Philip, *The Conservative Reformers*. (Notre Dame, Ind.: Univ. of Notre Dame Press, 1968), p. 5.

44. *Ibid.*, pp. 29-45.

45. *Ibid.*, p. 5.

46. *Ibid.*, pp. 3, 104-105.

47. *Ibid.*, pp. 104, 205.

48. *Ibid.*, p. 4.

49. *Ibid.*, pp. 194-195. It might be noted that the Bishops' Program received mixed reactions from the Central-Verein (see pp. 194-197).

50. O'Brien, David J., *American Catholics and Social Reform* (N.Y.: Oxford Univ. Press, 1968), pp. 121-122, 130. Ryan, it should be noted, resigned from the ACLU over disagreement with some of its positions.

51. *Ibid.*, pp. 135-136.

52. *Ibid.*, p. 139.

53. *Ibid.*, p. 128.

54. Nie, Norman; Verba, Sidney; & Petrocik, John R., *The Changing American Voter* (Enlarged ed.; Cambridge, Mass.: Harvard, 1976, 1979), pp. 229-231.

55. Campbell, Angus; Converse, Philip E.; Miller, Warren E.; & Stokes, Donald E., *The American Voter* (Abidged paperback ed.; N.Y.: Wiley, 1964), p. 92.

56. Nie, Verba, & Petrocik, 1976, p. 267.

57. *Ibid.*, p.259.

58. *Ibid.*, pp. 258-260. This study found specifically that in the 1950s 35 percent of all Catholics were found to be in the three most liberal deciles of a political attitude spectrum set up by researchers on the basis of responses to questions about certain political issues. 21 percent were in the three most conservative deciles. In the 1970s, the percentage in the three most liberal deciles remained the same, while that in the three most conservative increased to 30 percent.

59. Flanigan, William H. & Zingale, Nancy H., *Political Behavior of the American Electorate* (Boston: Allyn & Bacon, 1987), pp. 99-101, 104, 116.

60. My sources for these assertions and data about Catholic presidential voting behavior are the following: Campbell, et al., pp. 159-301; Lowi, Theodore J., "An Aligning Election, A Presidential Plebecite, "Nelson, Michael J., ed., *The Elections of 1984* (Wash., D.C.: CQ Press, 1985),p. 290; Nie, et al., p. 383; Scammon, Richard and Wattenberg, Ben J., *The Real Majority* (N.Y.: Cloward, McCann & Geoghegan, 1971), pp. 64-65, 174; *The New York Times* (Nov. 9, 1984), p. 1, col. 6; *Time* (Nov. 21, 1988), p. 34; and *The Wanderer* (Nov. 19, 1992), p. 10. The three elections in the period 1932 to 1976 in which a plurality of Catholics voted for the Republican candidate were 1952 and 1956 (an unusual circumstance since the popular wartime figure Eisenhower was running) and 1972, which perhaps further illustrates the growing Catholic dislike of liberalism because the Democratic candidate, George McGovern, was perceived to be farther left than the mainstream of his party was at the time.

61. Kirk I, p. 245.

62. DeTocqueville, Alexis, *Democracy in America* (ed. J.P. Mayer; Garden City, N.Y.: Doubleday [Anchor], 1966, 1969), Vol. Two, Pt. I, Chap. 6, p. 450.

63. *Ibid.*, Chap. 15, pp. 542-546.

64. *Ibid.*, Chap. 6, p. 450.

65. Kirk I, p. 245.

66. *Ibid.*, pp. 246-249.

67. O'Brien, David, *Public Catholicism* (N.Y.: MacMillan, 1989), p. 64.

68 *Ibid.*

69. *Ibid.*, p. 83.

70. *Ibid.*

71. *Ibid.*, pp. 71, 75, 77.

72. *Ibid.*, Chaps. 4,6.

73. Quoted in *ibid.*, p. 91.

74. *Public Catholicism*, pp. 139-142.

75. *Ibid.*, p. 137.

76. *Ibid.*, p. 133.

77. *Ibid.*, p. 87.

78. Hennesey, James, S.J., *American Catholics: A History of the Roman Catholic Community in the United States.* (N.Y.: Oxford U. Press, 1981), pp. 184-185.

79. *Public Catholicism*, pp. 88, 123.

80. *Ibid.*, pp. 133-134.

81. Ireland, quoted in Ellis, John Tracy, *The Life of James Cardinal Gibbons*, Vol. 1 (Milwaukee, 1952), p. 532. The quote, from the Gibbons source, appears in O'Brien, p. 88. The rest of the information being footnoted here is also from O'Brien, p. 88.

82. *Public Catholicism*, pp. 88, 133.

83. *Ibid.*, pp. 178, 180.

84. Hennesey,. p. 261.

85. *Public Catholicism*, p. 180.

86. Hennesey, p. 293.

87. *Public Catholicism*, p. 178.

88. *Ibid.*, pp. 177, 178.

89. *Ibid.*, p. 176.

90. Hennesey, p. 261; *Public Catholicism*, p. 175.

91. Hennesey, p. 274.

92. *Public Catholicism*, pp. 174-175.

93. The article, as it appears in America, runs from pp. 186-190. The article was reprinted, with editing, as "Catholics and Liberals," in *The Human Life Review*, Vol. II, No. 4 (Fall 1976).

94. Pope Leo XIII, *Longinque Oceani* (*Catholicity in the United States*), para. 6, *The Great Encyclical Letters of Pope Leo XIII* (N.Y.: Benziger Bros., 1903), pp. 323-

324. Pope Leo also attacked the theological position of "Americanism" which was heretical, in his apostolic letter to Cardinal Gibbons *Testem Benevolentiae* (*True and False Americanism in Religion*) in 1899. This position, which was attributed to some in the Church in the U.S., included the following errors: that the Church should adapt itself doctrinally to modernity, that she should relax her doctrine and dicipline, that religious vows should be deemphasized, and that she should "give greater scope for the action of the Holy Spirit on the individual soul" (which conjured up thoughts of Protestantism). (Ellis, John Tracy, *American Catholicism* Chicago History of American Civilization Series. [Chicago: Univ. of Chicago Press, 1956], pp. 118-119).

95. Hitchcock, James,"Catholics and Liberals: Decline of Detente," *America* (March 16, 1974), p. 186.

96. *Ibid.*, pp. 186-188.

97. *Ibid.*, p. 188.

98. *Ibid.*, p. 189. Indeed, in such other countries as India and Communist China, the ugly monster of coercive family planning has already reared its head in recent decades.

99. *Ibid.*, pp. 186, 189.

100. *Ibid.*, p. 189.

101. Kennedy made his statement during a question-and-answer period after a speech to the Greater Houston Ministerial Association on September 12, 1960. According to Theodore H. White in *The Making of the President 1960* ([N.Y.: Atheneum, 1961], p. 261), Kennedy was asked if he would "accept Church direction in public life." He responded as follows: "'If my church attempted to influence me in a way which was improper or which affected adversely my responsibilities as a public servant, sworn to uphold the Constitution, then I would reply to them that this was an improper action on their part, that it was one to which I could not subscribe, that I was opposed to it, and that it would be an unfortunate breech—an interference with the American political system. I am confident there would be no such interference.'" He went on to say that "'if he found any conflict between his conscience and the responsibility of the Presidency, he would resign that office.'"

102. The decisions were, respectively, *Torcaso v. Watkins*, 367 U.S. 488 (1961), *Engel v. Vitale*, 370 U.S. 421 (1962), and *Abington School District v. Schempp*, 374 U.S. 203 (1963). These decisions were readily supported by liberals, including President Kennedy. (See *Public Papers of the Presidents of the United States: John F. Kennedy*, 1962, p. 511).

103. Podhoretz, Norman, "Making the World Safe for Communism," *Commentary* (April 1976), pp. 32-34.

104. See Schaefer, David L., "Introduction, "in Schaefer, David Lewis, ed., *The New Egalitarianism* Port Washington, N.Y.: Kennikat, 1979, pp. 3-4.1

CHAPTER TWO NOTES

1. Pope John XXIII, *Mater et Magistra*, Gibbons, William J., S.J. ed., *Seven Great Encyclicals* (Glen Rock, N.J.: Paulist Press, 1963), Part I, Paras. 9, 28, pp. 223-225. (Herinafter cited as *"MM"*.)

2. *Ibid.*, I,50, p. 229.

3. Fremantle, *op.cit* (Chap. One), her Introduction, p. 17.

4. Second Vatican Council, *Apostolicam Actuositatem (Decree on the Apostolate of Lay People)*, Sec. 11, quoted in Pope John Paul II, *Familiaris Consortio* (Apostolic Exhortation on the Family), Part III, Sec. 3. (Hereinafter referred to as *"FC."*)

5. *FC*, III, 3.

6. Pope Leo XIII, *Rerum Novarum*, Sec. 14, in Gilson, *op. cit.* (Chap. One), p. 212. (Hereinafter referred to as *"RN."*)

7. *FC*, III, 2.

8. *Ibid.*, III, 3.

9. *RN*, 14, p. 212.

10. Pope Paul VI, *Populorum Progressio* (Boston: St. Paul Edns.), Part I, Sec. 3, Parag. 36, pp. 22-23. (Hereinafter referred to as *"PP."*)

11. See *FC*, III, 1. In Pope Paul VI's apostolic letter, *Octogesima Adveniens (The Coming Eightieth* [1971], he opposes a "false equality which would deny the distinctions [between men and women] laid down by the Creator Himself and which would be in contradiction with woman's proper role..at the heart of the family," but says at the same time that legislation should be directed not only to protecting this role but also to "recognizing her independence as a person, and her equal rights to participate in cultural, economic, social and political life" (Sec. 13).

12. *Ibid.* This basically reiterates what Paul VI said (note 11 above).

13. *Ibid.*

14. Pope John Paul II, *Laborem Exercens* (Boston: St. Paul Edns.), Part IV, Sec. 19, pp. 46-47. (Hereinafter referred to as *"LE"*.)

15. *FC*, III, 1.

16. *MM*, IV, 193, p. 259.

17. Sacred Congregation for the Doctrine of the Faith, *Declaration on Procured Abortion* (1974). (Boston: St. Paul Edns.), Part IV, Sec. 15, p. 15.

18. Sacred Congregation for the Doctrine of the Faith, *Declaration on Certain Questions Concerning Sexual Ethics* (1975) (Boston: St. Paul Edns.), Sec. 8, p. 13.

19. The list appears in *FC*, III, 3. The rights are as follows:

—The right to exist and progress as a family, that is to say, the right of every human being, even if he or she is poor, to found a family and to have adequate means to support it;

—The right to exercise its responsibility regarding the transmission of life and to educate children;

—The right to the intimacy of conjugal and family life;

—The right to believe in and profess one's faith and to propagate it;

—The right to bring up children in accordance with the family's own traditions and religious and cultural values, with the necessary instruments, means, and institutions;

—The right, especially of the poor and the sick, to obtain physical, social, political, and economic security;

—The right to housing suitable for living family life in a proper way;

—The right to expression and to representation, either directly or through association, before the economic, social, and cultural public authorities and lower authorities;

—The right to form associations with other families and institutions in order to fulfill the family's role suitably and expeditiously;

—The right to protect minors by adequate institutions and legislation from harmful drugs, pornography, alcoholism, etc.;

—The right to wholesome recreation of a kind that also fosters family values;

—The right of the elderly to a worthy life and a worthy death;

—The right to emigrate as a family in search of a better life.

20. Hardon, John A., S.J., *The Catholic Catechism* (Garden City, N.Y.: Doubleday, 1975), p. 334, quoting *Didache*, II, 2.

21. *Declaration on Procured Abortion* V, 20, pp. 18-19.

22. *Ibid.*,V, 22, pp. 19-20.

23. This topic has been increasingly discussed and addressed by American prelates. The issue of their excommunication was raised by John Cardinal O'Connor of New York City (see *The Wanderer*, June 28, 1990, pp. 1, 7). In this same article, Fr. Joseph Penna, a canon lawyer and professor at St. Joseph's Seminary, Yonkers, N.Y., was quoted as saying that Canon 1399 of the new Code of Canon Law would justify the excommunication of a Catholic politician who supported abortion legislation if (upon the determination of his ordinary) scandal was being caused perhaps by his action giving someone else occasion to sin (*ibid.*, p. 7).

24. *LP, op. cit.* (Chap. One), 21, p. 71.

25. *RN*, 32, p. 222. In his encyclical *Immortale Dei* (*On the Christian Constitution of States* [1885]), Pope Leo XIII says that government must "be of a nature to insure the general welfare" (Sec. 4, in Gilson, p. 163). In *Mater et Magistra*, Pope

John XIII says "The State['s]. . .purpose is the realization of the common good in the temporal order. . ." (*MM*, I, 20, p. 224). These are all different ways of making the same point.

26. *RN*, 35, p. 224.

27. Pope John XXIII, *Pacem in Terris*, in Gibbons, Part II, Para. 62, p. 303. (Hereinafter referred to as "*PT*.")

28. *RN*, 34, p. 223.

29. *PT*, II, 57, p. 302.

30. *Ibid.*, II, 56, p. 301.

31. See *RN*, 34, p. 223 and *PT*, I, 43-44, p. 298.

32. *PP*, I, 3, 23, p. 16, quoting a letter he had written to the 52nd Session of the French Social Weeks in 1965.

33. *PT*, I, 9, p. 291.

34. For a philosophical discussion of how rights and duties are inextricably intertwined, see Father Thomas J. Higgins, S.J.'s solid Catholic ethics textbook, *Man As Man: The Science and Art of Ethics* (Rev. ed.; Milwaukee: Bruce, 1958), Chap. XV. The book bears the imprimatur of the late Archbishop Albert G. Meyer of Milwaukee.

35. *PT*, I, 11-27, pp. 291-294.

36. Second Vatican Council, *Inter Mirifica* (*Decree on the Means of Social Communication* [1963]), Chap. I, Para. 12, in Flannery, *op. cit.* (Chap. One), p. 288. (Hereinafter referred to as "*IM*.")

37. *PT.*, I, 29-31, p. 295. In connection with the matter of social communication, *Inter Mirifica* holds that while the media has rights, as mentioned, it also has a duty to respect the moral law. Civil authorities also have a duty "to ensure. . .that public morality and social progress are not greatly endangered through misuse of these media" (I, 11-12, pp. 287-288).

38. See Pope John Paul II, *Sollicitudo Rei Socialis*, Part IV, Sec. 33, in *L'Osservatore Romano* (Eng. ed.; Feb. 29, 1988), p. 8. (Hereinafter referred to as "*SRS*.")

39. *SRS*, VI, 44, p. 12. Emphasis is in the encyclical.

40. Higgins, pp. 434-436, 457-458. The quote is from pp. 457-458. By "juridic cause" of the state, Higgins means the free agreement of families—whose joining together is the source of every state—to come together into a bond of civic justice whereby they assume the rights and duties necessary to constitute a sovereign state.

41. *PT.*, II, 68, p. 304.

42. *Ibid.*, II, 51-52, p. 300.

43. *RN*, 13, p. 211; Pope Pius XI, *Quadragesimo Anno*, in Gibbons, Part II, Sec. 1, Parag. 49, p. 138. (Hereinafter referred to as "*QA*.")

44. See *MM*, II, 109, p. 241.

45. *Ibid.*, II, 57, p. 231.

46. *QA*, II, 1, 45, p. 137.

47. *PP*, I, 3, 22, p. 15. He is quoting from the Vatican II document *Gaudium et Spes* (*Pastoral Constitution on the Church in the Modern World* [1965]), Chap. III, Part (Sec.) 2, Sec. 69. (Hereinafter referred to as "*GS*.")

48. *RN*, 46, p. 230. Emphasis is added.

49. *MM*, II, 82-83, pp. 236-237.

50. *LE*, 7, p. 18.

51. *Ibid.*, 13, p. 32.

52. *QA*, II, 4, 71, pp. 144-145.

53. *RN*, 46, p. 230.

54. *QA*, II, 4, 71, p. 145.

55. *MM*, II, 71, p. 234.

56. *Ibid.*

57. *LE*, 19, pp. 46-48. Emphasis is in the encyclical.

58. *QA*, II, 4, 74, p. 146.

59. *LE*, 18, p. 43.

60. *Ibid.*, 19, p. 47.

61. *RN*, 20, p. 215.

62. *Ibid.*, 49-51, pp. 231-233.

63. *LE*, 20, p. 50. Emphasis is in the encyclical.

64. *Ibid.*, 22, pp. 52-53. Emphasis is in the encyclical.

65. *Ibid.*, 23, pp. 54-55. Emphasis is in the encyclical.

66. *Ibid.*, 19, p. 47.

67. *RN*, 20, p. 215.

68. *QA*, II, 2, 57, pp. 141-142. On profit, see also 4, 65 and 72, pp. 144,145.

69. *Ibid.*

70. *LE*, 20, pp. 49-50. Emphasis is in the encyclical.

71. *MM*, III, 128, p. 246.

72. *Ibid.*, 131, p. 247.

73. *Ibid.*, 142, p. 249.

74. *Ibid.*, 143, p. 249.

75. *Ibid.*, III, 144, p. 249.

76. *Ibid.*, III, 146, p. 250.

77. *LE*, 21, pp. 51-52.

78. *MM*, III, 127, p. 248.

79. *Divini Redemptoris*, Parags. 9-11, in Gibbons, pp. 180-181.

80. *Ibid.*, 11, p. 181.

81. Issued under the signature of Joseph Cardinal Ratzinger, Prefect of the Congregation, on August 6, 1984.

82. Issued under Ratzinger's signature on March 22, 1986.

83. See Congregation for the Doctrine of the Faith, *Instruction on Christian Freedom and Liberation*, Introduction. (Boston: St. Paul Editions), p. 1.

84. *Ibid.*, Chap. II, Part V, Sec. 42, p. 25.

85. *Ibid.*, Secs. 37-42, pp. 21-25.

86. *SRS*, V, 36, p. 9. Emphasis is in the encyclical.

87. See *RN*, 14-15, pp. 212-213; *QA*, III,2,155-160, pp. 155-160; *MM*, I, 34, p. 226.

88. *QA*, III, 2.120, p. 158.

89. *Quod Apostolici Muneris*, Secs. 5-6, in Gilson, pp. 192-193.

90. *Ibid.*, 9, pp. 195-196.

91. *GS*, III, 2, 69, p. 975.

92. *Ibid*, pp. 975-976, n.11.

93. Aquinas says (at II-II, q. 66, a. 7) that "according to the natural order. . .[of] Divine Providence, inferior things are ordained for the purpose of succoring man's needs. . .Hence whatever certain people have in superabundance is due, by natural law, to the purpose of succoring the poor...each one is entrusted with the stewardship of his own things, so that out of them he may come to the aid of those who are in need. Nevertheless, if the need be so manifest and urgent, that it is evident that the present need must be remedied by whatever means be at hand (for instance when a person is in some imminent danger, and there is no other possible remedy), then it is lawful for a man to succor his own by means of another's property, by taking it either openly or secretly: nor is this properly speaking theft or robbery." (Benziger Bros. ed.; N.Y.: 1947, Vol. II, pp. 1480-1481.)

94. *QA.*, II, 5, 88, pp. 149-150.

95. *Ibid.*, III, 1, 108, p. 153.

96. *SRS*, VI, 41, p. 11. Emphasis is in the encyclical.

97. *QA*, II, 5, 88, p. 150. In order to make sure that the crucial terms "social justice" and "social charity" are clearly understood, it is best to define them. "Social justice" is defined by Higgins as follows: "the virtue which moves the individual to contribute his due share to society by promoting the common good. Since there is a quasi identification between the social part and the community, justice demands that the part support the whole in due measure. Hence social justice looks toward an equilibrium of duty toward the social whole which each part must maintain." This definition is elaborated on by Johannes Messner in his massive *Social Ethics: Natural Law in the Western World* (Rev. ed.; tr. J.J. Doherty; St.

Louis: B. Herder, 1949, 1965, carrying the imprimatur of the late Joseph Cardinal Ritter of St. Louis): "'social justice' refers especially to the economic and social welfare of 'society,' in the sense of the economically cooperating community of the state. Owing to the division of labor, the national economy constitutes a cooperative economic unit, whose members in their various groups and classes are all interdependent in their work, making provision for their sustenance. The national economy, therefore, constitutes a socio-economic community whose common good demands for all groups and for their members a due share in the fruits of their cooperation which is commensurate with their contribution. These shares are distributed in the form of prices, wages, interest, dividends, rents, and social and private insurance benefits. Economic cooperation in society and the consequent distribution of its fruits give rise to obligations of natural justice. . .In the negotiations and agreements of the various groups, these must allow one another their due share in the output of their socio-economic cooperation. Social justice, therefore, imposes obligations on employer and on employee in the course of negotiations of collective labor agreements. It not only demands a just distribution of the social product, but also binds the groups cooperating in society to make the efforts in rendering their services, necessary for the firm establishment and development of the common good in all spheres and for economic and social progress. . . .The obligations of social justice also relate to the will and to the cooperation of the social groups in creating the social institutions necessary for the most perfect fulfillment of the demands mentioned. . ."(pp. 320-321). "Social charity," according to Messner, "demands 'community sense above all.'" He approvingly cites theologian J. Hoffner's definition, which does not see a basic difference between social charity and simply the theological virtue of charity. Among what he includes as an important part of social charity is a true attitude of love toward our country and our fellow citizens. Some "special expressions" of social charity are "readiness for self-sacrifice for the common good, especially in times of grave emergency, then care for the vital common good values of religion and morality." Another "sphere of duties" associated with social charity involves the relations of professions, groups, classes, and individuals to help others as members of society, and not just as individual men. Benevolence—the positive esteem for the state community and its citizens—is the basic feature of social charity (p. 338, citing J. Hoffner, *Soziale Gerechtigkeit and Soziale Liebe* [1935], pp. 93-102.)

98. *Ibid.*, II, 5, 79-80, p. 147.

99. *PP*, II, 3, 33, p. 21.

100. *LE*, 18, p. 43. Emphasis is in the encyclical.

101. *MM*, II, 117, p. 243.

102. *QA*, II, 1, 49, p. 138.

103. *LE*, 14, p. 35. Emphasis is in the encyclical. See also *SRS*, VI, 42, pp. 11-12.

104. *Ibid.*, Emphasis is in the encyclical.

105. *Ibid.*, pp. 36-37.

106. *RN*, 47, p. 231.

107. *MM*, III, 132, p. 247.

108. *RN*, 37, pp. 225-226.

109. *Ibid.*, 38, p. 226.

110. *Ibid.*, 52, p. 233.

111. *Ibid.*, 30-43, pp. 221-222.

112. *LE*, 18, pp. 42-43.

113. *MM*, III, 135-136, p. 248.

114. *SRS*, VI, 42, p. 11. See also *Instruction on Christian Freedom and Liberation*, IV, II, pp. 41-45.

115. *Instruction on Christian Freedom and Liberation*, IV, II, 66-68, pp. 41-44.

116. *RN*, 16, p. 213.

117. *QA*, III, 3, 127, p. 160.

118. *RN*, 19, p. 214.

119. *MM*, II, 91, p. 238.

120. See *QA*, II, 5, 81-87, pp. 148-149.

121. *RN*, 48-49, 50, pp. 231-233.

122. *RN*, 45, p. 230.

123. *MM*, III, 208, p. 262.

124. *PP*, II, 3, 66, p. 40.

125. *SRS*, II, 9. p. 2.

126. *Ibid.*, III, 17, p. 4. Emphasis is in the encyclical.

127. *Ibid.*, IV, 33, p. 9.

128. *Ibid.*, III, 26, p. 6.

129. *PP*, I, 1, 19-21, pp. 13-14.

130. *SRS*, IV, 33, p. 8. Emphasis is in the encyclical.

131. *Ibid.*, V, 39, p. 10. Emphasis is in the encyclical.

132. *Ibid.*, IV, 33, p. 8.

133. *PP*, II, 1, 48-49, p. 30. John Paul II calls for the same sort of thing in *SRS*, V, 39, p. 10.

134. *MM*, III, 165, p. 254.

135. See *MM*, III, 202, p. 261; PP, I,3,35, p. 22.

136. *PP*, II, 1, 50-51, p. 31.

137. *PP*, II, 1 ,54, p. 33.

138. *PT*, IV, 132-141, pp. 316-319.

139. *SRS.*, VI, 43, p. 12. Emphasis is in the encyclical.

140. See *PP*, II, 2, 64, pp. 38-39; *SRS*, VI,45, p. 12. The quote is from the latter. Emphasis is in the encyclical.

141. *PP*, II, 2, 58-61, pp. 35-37.

142. *SRS*, VI, 43, p. 12.

143. *PP*, I, 3, 24, p. 16. There would have to be a just amount of compensation given for any expropriation, however. (See *GS*, III, 2, 71, p. 978.)

144. *PP*, I, 3, 24, p. 16.

145. *SRS*, VI, 44, p. 12.

146. *PP.*, I, 1, 7, p. 7.

147. *Ibid.*, II, 2, 62-63, pp. 37-38.

148. *PT*, I, 44, p. 298.

149. *RN*, 34, p. 223.

150. *Ibid.*, I,3,31, pp. 19-20.

151. *Ibid.*, III, 94-97, pp. 309-310.

152. *Ibid.*, III, 103-108, pp. 311-312.

153. *MM*, III, 185-194, pp. 257-259. Pope John was prescient in doubting the validity of the claim about population outstripping food and resources. In spite of much propaganda to this effect in the 1960s and 1970s, there appears to be little evidence that such population "crisis" is upon us. See Clark, Colin, *Population Growth: The Advantages* (Santa Ana, Calif.: A Life Quality Paperback, 1975); Sassone, Robert L., *Handbook on Population* (4th ed.; self-published, 1978); and Simon, Julian, *The Ultimate Resource* (Princeton, N.J.: Princeton U. Press, 1981).

154. *SRS*, III, 25, p. 6. Emphasis is in the encyclical.

155. *SRS*, IV, 34, p. 9.

156. Pope John Paul II, "Peace With God the Creator, Peace With All of Creation", World Day of Peace Statement (Dec. 8, 1989), published in *L'Osservatore Romano* (English language edn.), Dec 18-26, 1989, reprinted in *The Wanderer*, Jan. 4, 1990, pp. 1,7.

157. *Ibid.*, Sec. II, p. 7.

158. *Ibid.*, I, p. 7.

159. *Ibid.*, II, IV, p. 7.

160. *Ibid.*

161. *Ibid.*, II, p. 7.

162. *Ibid.*, IV, p. 7.

163. *Ibid.*, III, p. 7.

164. *Ibid.*, IV, p. 7.

165. *Ibid.*, III, p. 7.

166. See Hardon, pp. 346-347.

167. *Ibid.*, p. 348.

168. *GS*, V, 1, 80, p. 990.

169. Higgins, p. 548.

170. *PT*, III, 120,124, pp. 314-315.

171. *PP*, II, 1, 54, p. 33.

172. *PT*, III, 93, p. 309.

173. Pope John Paul II, *Negotiation: The Only Realistic Solution to the Continuing Threat of War* Letter to the U.N. General Assembly (June 11, 1982). (Boston: St. Paul Edns.), p. 11. Emphasis is the Pope's. (Hereinafter cited as *Negotiation*.)

174. Pope Pius XII, *The Function of the State in the Modern World*, section entitled "Proud Illusions." (Boston: St. Paul Edns.), pp. 31-32. By "treaty" is meant any agreement between nations. Higgins notes that there are caveats to this general teaching of the Church (which is also, of course, a part of the natural moral law): "[A] nation's obligations cannot ask too much of it, for example, to observe terms which would lead to loss of independence, acute misery of its people, or spoliation of the fundamental means of development." (This does not, however, involve *rescinding* a treaty.) The grounds upon which a treaty ceases to bind a party are "mutual consent [to abrogate a treaty], impossibility of performance, extinction of one party, and the like." He cites favorably another authority who says there is only one circumstance in which "a nation may upon its own initiative declare itself freed of treaty obligation: . . .when an implied condition, necessary to impose obligations at the time of the treaty is made, no longer holds good." Two examples are: "when one party has substantially failed to live up to its part, the other party may declare itself free of all obligation. . .[and] when fulfillment would involve loss of independence for one party" (unless the treaty was meant specifically to apply even then) (pp. 541-542).

175. *PT*, III, 112, p. 312. Emphasis is added.

176. *GS*, V, 1, 81, p. 990.

177. *PT*, III, 112, p. 312.

178. *Negotiation*, p. 9.

179. *PT*, III, 113, p. 313.

180. *Negotiation*, p. 11.

181. *Ibid.*, pp. 10-11.

182. Hardon, p. 349.

183. *SRS*, III, 20, p. 5. It should be emphasized here that even though the encyclical is critical of the actions of both blocs and of the economic ideologies of each, there is no presumption of a *moral equivalence* between the two. This is clear from the encyclical *Divini Redemptoris*, the instruction on liberation theology, and many other papal pronouncements over the years. Papal social teaching builds on itself; new documents or pronouncements expand upon previous ones; they do not repudiate them. Nevertheless, John Paul here makes clear, as every social encycli-

cal since *Rerum Novarum* has, that liberal capitalism is not compatible with Church teaching. It is incompatible as Marxist collectivism is incompatible; whether it is not as bad on a number of points is irrelevant to the fact of its being incompatible in the final analysis. (Something is not partially in the condition of being incompatible; its basic principles or its essential aspects are either compatible or incompatible—in the case of liberal capitalism it is the latter.) The argument could be made that the West does not any longer follow the tenets of liberal capitalism as they were originally put forth in the eighteenth and nineteenth centuries, that changes have occurred in the twentieth century. Indeed, John Paul seems to acknowledge this by using the adverb "historically" before "inspired" when discussing liberal capitalism in the West. (He uses the present tense "is inspired" when speaking about Marxist collectivism in the East; he writes before the developments of 1989, although communism has certainly not disappeared form the face of the earth.) Nevertheless, a serious analysis of the economics of the West today would show it still to be basically built around these principles. This fact may become apparent in places in this book.

184. *SRS*, 22, p. 5. Emphasis is in the encyclical.

185. *Ibid.*, III, 24, p. 6.

186. *PP*, II, 3, 76, p. 45.

CHAPTER THREE NOTES

1. Schlesinger, Arthur M., Jr., *The Vital Center* (Boston: Houghton Mifflin, 1948).

2. Lerner, Max, *Actions and Passions* (Port Washington, N.Y.: Kennikat Press, 1949; reissued in 1969.) (Hereinafter cited as "Lerner I.")

3. Commager, Henry Steele, *Majority Rule and Minority Rights* (N.Y.: Oxford Univ. Press, 1943). (Hereinafter cited as "Commager I.")

4. Commager, Henry Steele, *Freedom, Loyalty, Dissent* (N.Y.: Oxford Univ. Press, 1954). (Hereinafter cited as "Commager II.")

5. Stevenson, Adlai E., *What I Think* (Westport, Conn.: Greenwood, 1953). (Hereinafter cited as "Stevenson I.")

6. Stevenson, Adlai E., *Putting First Things First* (N.Y.: Random House, 1960). (Hereinafter cited as "Stevenson II.")

7. Some would argue that a figure representative of the people who clustered around Henry Wallace's "Progressive movement" in 1948 should be discussed here. We do not believe they were in the mainstream of the old liberalism, however. Lerner concurs and discusses—as have others—how his movement was dominated by Communists. (Lerner, pp. 225-228, 234-236, 240-243; see also Manchester, William, *The Glory and the Dream: A Narrative History of America 1932-1972* [Boston: Little, Brown, 1973, 1974], pp. 208, 457-458.) Schlesinger castigates the Wallace people as "doughface progressives" (see Schlesinger, Chap. III).

8. *RN, op. cit.* (Chap. Two), 35, p. 224.

9. See Commager II, pp. 42, 91-92; Schlesinger, p. 29; Stevenson I, p. 112.

10. Lerner I, p. 99.

11. Schlesinger, p. 252.

12. *Ibid.*, pp. 28-29.

13. *Ibid.*, p. 176.

14. *PT, op. cit.* (Chap. Two), II, 62, p. 303.

15. Schlesinger, p. 176.

16. *Ibid.*, p. 250.

17. *Ibid.*, p. 170.

18. Lerner I, pp. 10-11. One does wonder if Lerner does not have some temptation to blame society and institutions for individuals going astray, however. This is seen in his discussion of how a fourteen-year-old murderer—an uncommon phenomenon at the time he writes—was perhaps led to his crime by conditions in our civilization and culture (pp. 64-66).

19. See *ibid.*, p. 246.

20. See Krason, *Abortion: Politics, Morality, and the Constitution, op. cit.* (Chap. One), pp. 397-398.

21. Stevenson I, p. 50.

22. Schlesinger, p. 176.

23. *Ibid.*, p. 173.

24. Lerner I, pp. 130, 136-137.

25. *Ibid.*, pp. 190-199.

26. *Ibid.*, pp. 97-99.

27. Stevenson I, pp. 52, 112.

28. *Ibid.*, p. 53.

29. Commager II, p. 71.

30. Stevenson I, p. 140.

31. Schlesinger, pp. 153, 182-183.

32. Lerner I, p. 292.

33. *Ibid.*, p. 299.

34. *Ibid.*, pp. 244-246.

35. Stevenson I, p. 50. See also Stevenson II, pp. 9-11, 54-55.

36. Lerner I, pp. 353, 358.

37. Schlesinger, p. 165.

38. Stevenson I, p. 53.

39. Stevenson I, p. 53. Emphasis is added.

40. Lerner I, pp. 146-147, 28.

41. *Ibid.*, p. 359.

42. *Ibid.*, p. 149.

43. *Ibid.*, p. 104.

44. Commager II, p. 155.

45. This is from the quote from Spitz, *op. cit.*, in Chapter One. See note 18 to Chapter One for the precise citation.

46. Commager II, p. 54. Emphasis is in the book.

47. *Ibid.*, p. 54,84.

48. *Ibid.*, p. 34.

49. *Ibid.*, p. 155.

50. *Ibid.*, p. 98.

51. Commager I, p. 79.

52. Lerner I, p. 12.

53. *Ibid.*, pp. 97-99.

54. *Ibid.*, p. 27.

55. *Ibid.*, p. 21.

56. *Ibid.*, p. 147.

57. Commager I, p. 80.

58. *Ibid.*, pp. 91-92.

59. *Ibid.*, p. 18.

60. *Dignitatis Humanae. (Declaration on Religious Liberty)*, in Flannery, *op. cit.* (Chap. Two), Sec. 1, pp. 799-800.

61. See Lerner I, pp. 115-123.

62. *Ibid.*, p. 93.

63. *Ibid.*, p. 207.

64. *Dignitatis Humanae*, Sec. 14, p. 811.

65. Lerner I, pp. 137-138. The Supreme Court decision referred to is *Pierce v. Society of Sisters*, 268 U.S. 510 (1925).

66. *Ibid.*, pp. 133-140. Catholic schools receive or did receive state funding for a long time in such countries as West Germany, Italy, Spain, and Canada. State aid has been sought for Catholic educational institutions in the U.S. for most of this century, but the efforts especially intensified in the 1960s until the Supreme Court decisions of the 1970s disallowed it. Today, the major proposals seem to center around vouchers or tuition tax credits for parents of parochial and other private school children.

67. *Ibid.*, pp. 157,246.

68. Schlesinger, p. 244.

69. *Ibid.*, p. 249.

70. *Ibid.*, p. 248.

71. Lerner I, p. 350.

72. Schlesinger, p. 253.

73. *Ibid.*, pp. 245-246. Emphasis is in the book.

74. *Ibid.*, pp. 189-191; Lerner I, pp. 97-102.

75. Lerner I, pp. 123-126.

76. Commager I, pp. 117-118.

77. Lerner I, p. 246.

78. Stevenson I, p. 49.

79. *Ibid.*, p. 148.

80. *Ibid.*, p. 106.

81. *Ibid.*, p. 227.

82. *Ibid.*, pp. 211-213. See also, generally, Commager I and II.

83. Schlesinger, pp. 213-215.

84. *Ibid.*, p. 96.

85. *Ibid.*, p. 223.

86. *Ibid.*, p. 174.

87. *Ibid.*

88. Lerner I, p. 207.

89. *Ibid.*, p. 248.

90. *Ibid.*, p. 58.

91. *Ibid.*, p. 59.

92. *Ibid.*, p. 311.

93. *Ibid.*, p. 96.

94. *Ibid.*, p. 207.

95. *Ibid.*, pp. 313,317. That Lenin, et al. never wanted a repressive, totalitarian state to develop is, at best, highly doubtful. The evidence clearly indicates otherwise. (See Carroll, Warren H., *1917: Red Banners, White Mantle* [Front Royal, Va.: Christendom College Press, 1981.]) In another of Lerner's books, he speaks about pre-Stalinist Soviet Russia having been a "humanist socialism and a planned democracy." (Lerner, Max, *Ideas for the Ice Age* N.Y.: Viking, 1941, p. 182.)

96. Lerner I, p. 317.

97. *Ibid.*, pp. 320-321. This interpretation of developments in the Soviet Union in those years is hotly disputed. (See d'Encausse, Helene Carrere, *Confiscated Power* [N.Y.: Harper & Row, 1980, 1982], especially Chap. I.)

98. *Ibid.*, pp. 201-202, 323.

99. *Ibid.*, p. 356. He also sees it as reflecting the normal realities of international politics that the nations with the greatest amount of power compete with each other.

100. Lerner, Max, *World of the Great Powers*, Headline Series No. 61 (Jan-Feb. 1947), pp. 23-24, 21.

101. *Ibid.*, p. 20.

102. Lerner I, p. 346.

103. *Ibid.*, p. 344-346. We do not believe he held the full-blown position that Truman, not the Soviets, was responsible for starting the Cold War that the later revisionist historians did, but this point was certainly one that the latter made.

104. Humphrey, Hubert H., *The Education of a Public Man* (Garden City, N.Y.: Doubleday, 1976). (Hereinafter cited as "Humphrey I.")

105. Humphrey, Hubert H., *Beyond Civil Rights: A New Day of Equality* (N.Y.: Random House, 1968). (Hereinafter cited as "Humphrey II.")

106. McGovern, George, *Grassroots* (N.Y.: Random House, 1977). (Hereinafter cited as "McGovern I.")

107. McGovern, George, *An American Journey* (N.Y.: Random House, 1974). (Hereinafter cited as "McGovern II.")

108. Douglas, William O., *The Bible and the Schools* (Boston: Little, Brown, 1966). (Hereinafter cited as "Douglas I.")

109. Douglas, William O., *International Dissent* (N.Y.: Random House, 1971). (Hereinafter cited as "Douglas II.")

110. See, for example, Price, David E., *Bringing Back the Parties* (Wash., D.C.: CQ Press, 1984), pp. 274-275, 292.

111. Peters, Charles and Keisling, Phillip, eds., *A New Road for America: The Neoliberal Movement* (Lanham, Md.: Madison Bks., 1985).

112. See, for example, McGovern II, pp. 21, 86, 89-90, 100, 104, 107.

113. *Ibid.*, p. 53.

114. See *ibid.*, pp. 52-58, 84-96, 97-102.

115. *Ibid.*, p. 6.

116. *Ibid.*, p. 28.

117. *Ibid.*, p. 53.

118. *Ibid.*

119. See *ibid.*, pp. 216-217, 224.

120. *Ibid.*, p. 10.

121. *LE, op.cit.*, (Chap. Two), 20, p. 49.

122. McGovern II, pp. 19, 22-23, 29.

123. *Ibid.*, p. 23.

124. Humphrey I, p. 47.

125. See especially his speech to the New York Society of Security Analysts, New York City, Aug. 29, 1972, printed in McGovern II, pp. 137-152.

126. McGovern II, p. 152.

127. *Ibid.*, p. 22.

128. *Ibid.*, p. 35.

129. This is inferrable from *QA, op.cit.*, (Chap. Two), II, 5, 78, p. 147 and *LE*, 17-18, pp. 40-45.

130. *Ibid.*, p. 9.

131. McGovern I, p. 262.

132. Peters, Charles, "Appendix: A Neoliberal's Manifesto," in Peters & Keisling, pp. 193-194. This piece was originally published in *The Washington Monthly* (May 1983), pp. 8-18.

133. *Ibid.*, p. 194.

134. *Ibid.*, pp. 195,206.

135. *Ibid.*, p. 200.

136. See the comments of former Arizona Governor Bruce Babbitt, Senator Thomas Eagleton, Bill Honig, and Peggy Holliday in *ibid.*, p. 31.

137. Peters, Charles, "Opening Address," in *ibid.*, p. 10.

138. 343 U.S. 306.

139. 343 U.S., at 313.

140. 367 U.S. 488, 495. Emphasis is added.

141. 370 U.S. 421 (1962).

142. 366 U.S. 420, 563 (1961).

143. Quoting *McGowan*, 366 U.S., at 564.

144. 370 U.S., at 443. Emphasis is added.

145. 374 U.S. 203, 229.

146. See *LP*,30, 31, 36, 37, in Gilson, *op. cit.* (Chap. Two), pp. 75, 76, 78-79.

147. For a discussion of the increasing hostility to religion in the aftermath of the Supreme Court's religion decisions of the 1960s and 1970s, see Ferrara, Peter J., *Religion and the Constitution* (Wash., D.C.: Free Congress Fdn., 1983), pp. 75-80, 136-137. About the sex education point, see Likoudis, James, "Classroom Sex Education: Undermining Parental Rights," in Krason, Stephen M. & D'Agostino, Robert J., eds., *Parental Rights: The Contemporary Assault on Traditional Liberties* (Front Royal, Va.: Christendom College Press, 1988), pp. 93-113.

148. Douglas I, pp. 47-48.

149. 370 U.S., at 443.

150. *Ibid.*

151. *Ibid.*, p. 59.

152. McGovern II, pp. 205-212.

153. *Ibid.*, pp. 30, 54, 124, 224.

154. *Ibid.*, p. 169.

155. *Ibid.*, p. 151.

156. Douglas opinion for the Court in *Griswold v. Connecticut*, 381 U.S. 479, 486 (1965).

157. McGovern II, p. 185.

158. *Ibid.*, p. 194.

159. Douglas opinion in *Griswold*, at 484.

160. Lemann, Nicholas, "Values" section in Peters & Keisling, pp. 76-80.

161. Townsend, Kathleen Kennedy, in *ibid.*, pp. 93,96.

162. Barber, James David, in *ibid.*, p. 81.

163. Etzioni, Amatai, in *ibid.*, p. 86.

164. 410 U.S. 179. It, of course, was decided with *Roe v. Wade*, 410 U.S. 113.

165. 410 U.S. 211.

166. *Byrne v. Karalexis*, 396 U.S. 976, 979 (1969).

167. 410 U.S., at 213. Actually, Douglas did not take too literally his claim that a person has "freedom of choice" in the education and upbringing of his children. He was the lone dissenter in the Supreme Court's *Wisconsin v. Yoder* decision, 406 U.S. 205 (1972), which held that Amish parents had the constitutionally-protected right to refuse to send their children to high school for religious reasons.

168. *Ibid.*, at 214-215.

169. 403 U.S. 713 (1971).

170. 403 U.S., at 724.

171. 401 U.S. 437 (1971).

172. 401. U.S., at 466.

173. Etzioni, in Peters & Keisling, p. 86.

174. *Ibid.*, pp. 86-87.

175. Stern, Philip, in "Law and the Courts" section of Peters & Keisling, p. 37.

176. See *FC, op. cit.* (Chap. Two), III.

177. See Canon 774, Sec. 2 in *Code of Canon Law* (Latin-English ed.; [Wash., D.C.: Canon Law Society of America, 1983]), p. 291.

178. See Higgins *op. cit.* (Chap. Two), pp. 496-497.

179. Humphrey II, p. 120.

180. *Ibid.*, p. 124.

181. *Ibid.*, p. 125.

182. *Ibid.*, p. 140.

183. *Ibid.*, p. 189.

184. *Ibid.*, p. 142.

185. *Ibid.*, pp. 140, 142, 188-189.

186. *Ibid.*, p. 147.

187. *LE, op. cit.* (Chap. Two), 20, p. 49; *PT*, III, 97, p. 310.

188. *MM, op. cit.* (Chap. Two), II, 70, p. 234.

189. *Ibid.*

190. Peters, Charles, "Opening Address," in Peters & Keisling, p. 10.

191. *Ibid.*, pp. 10-18.

192. *Ibid.*, pp. 189-208.

193. Humphrey I, pp. 424-425. The containment policy was instituted by the Truman Administration. It sought to limit or contain the expansion of Soviet influence and control to those nations which Stalin occupied after World War II.

194. McGovern I, pp. 95-97, 100, 105, 288.

195. *Ibid.*, p. 295.

196. *Ibid.*, p. 294.

197. *Ibid.*, p. 287. One might possibly argue that Humphrey and McGovern have different views than the old liberals because of changes that occurred in the 1960s and 1970s in the Communist world. It is highly doubtful that changes of great significance occurred in it during the time they wrote. The Soviet Union, for example, was at the peak of its international strength and aggressiveness and was still clearly totalitarian in 1980. True changes began to take place in her and other Communist countries only at the end of the 1980s.

198. *Ibid.*

199. *Ibid.*

200. *Ibid.*, p. 284.

201. Douglas II, pp. 150-151.

202. Douglas II, p. 151.

203. Perhaps the most thorough discussion of this background to the American political order is found in Kirk, Russell, *The Roots of American Order* (Malibu, Calif.: Pepperdine U. Press, 1974.) (Hereinafter referred to as "Kirk IV.")

204. Peters, Charles, "Introduction," in Peters & Keisling, p. 7.

205. *Ibid.*, p. 6.

CHAPTER FOUR NOTES

1. *The New York Times*, July 18, 1984, p. A17, col. 3.

2. *Congressional Quarterly Almanac (1984)* (Wash., D.C: Congressional Qtrly. Service, 1985), p. 64-B. (Hereinafter cited as "*CQA '85.*")

3. See *National Party Platforms*, Vol. I (1840-1956). Compiled by Donald Bruce Johnson. (Urbana, Ill.: Univ. of Illinois Press, 1978), pp. 430-436. (Hereinafter cited as "*NPP.*")

4. See *CQA* '84, pp. 73B-106B.

5. See *NPP*, pp. 450-454.

6. See *Congressional Quarterly Almanac (1980)* (Wash., D.C.: Congressional Qtrly. Service, 1981), pp. 91B-121B. Interestingly, the 1988 Democratic platform was the shortest in a long time, comprising only 7 1/2 larged-sized pages. Some commentators said that the reason was that the detail and specificity of previous platforms had gotten the Democrats into political trouble. Incidentally, the 1988 Democratic platform—like the 1988 Republican one—represents no change from the party's basic principles and public policy positions of 1984. The 1984 platform still works as an excellent statement of the current new liberal position, as the 1984 Republican platform serves as an excellent statement of the conservative one.

7. 1948 Democratic party platform in *NPP*, p. 430. (Hereinafter this platform will be cited as "1948 platform," with the page number in the *NPP* text.)

8. 1948 platform, pp. 432-433.

9. *Ibid.*, p. 433

10. *Ibid.*, p. 435.

11. *Ibid.*, p. 433.

12. *Ibid.*

13. 1948 platform, p. 430.

14. *Ibid.*, p. 433.

15. *Ibid.*, p. 435.

16. A good summary of the assessments of legal experts about the ERA and of the serious legal and constitutional problems with it appears in Hatch, Orrin G., *The Equal Rights Amendment: Myths and Realities* (Conservative Press, 1983).

17. *Ibid.*, p. 433.

18. *Ibid.*, pp. 433-434.

19. See *LE, op. cit.* (Chap. Two), 17-19, pp. 40-48.

20. *LE*, 17, p. 40.

21. 1948 platform, p. 432.

22. *Ibid.*, p. 434.

23. *Ibid.*

24. *Ibid.*

25. *RN, op. cit.*, (Chapter Two), 8, p. 209. Emphasis is added.

26. 1948 platform, p. 435.

27. *Ibid.*

28. *Ibid.*

29. *Ibid.*, p. 433.

30. *Ibid.*, p. 435.

31. *Ibid.*, p. 431.

32. *Ibid.*

33. *Ibid.*, p. 432.

34. *Ibid.*, p. 435.

35. *Ibid.*, p. 431.

36. *Ibid.*, p. 432.

37. *Ibid.*, p. 435.

38. This is seen in *Inter Mirifica*, which says that "[i]t is for the civil authority...to defend and safeguard—especially in relation to the press—a true and just freedom of information, for the progress of modern society demands it" (*IM*, I, 12, [Chap. I]), in Flannery, *op. cit.* (Chap. Two), p. 288. It is echoed in the post-Conciliar document called *Communio et Progressio* (the *Pastoral Instruction on the Means of Social Communication*)[1971]): "If public opinion is to be properly formed, it is necessary that, right from the start, the public be given free access to both the sources and channels of information and be allowed freely to express its own views. Freedom of opinion and the right to be informed go hand in hand." (*Communio et Progressio*, Chap. I, Part II, Sec. 33, in Flannery, p. 305.)

39. *Ibid.*, p. 430.

40. *Ibid.*, p. 431.

41. *Ibid.*, p. 436.

42. *Ibid.*

43. *Ibid.*, p. 432.

44. *Ibid.*, p. 431.

45. "1984 Democratic National Platform," (in booklet form). (Wash., D.C.: Democratic National Committee,) p. 9. (Hereinafter cited as "1984 platform.")

46. *Ibid.*, p. 11.

47. *Ibid.*, p. 15.

48. *Ibid.*, p. 14.

49. *Ibid.*, p. 15.

50. *LE*, 19, p. 47.

51. 1984 platform, pp. 9-10.

52. *Ibid.*, p. 10.

53. *Ibid.*

54. *Ibid.*

55. *Ibid.*, pp. 10-11. Elsewhere, they extol competition in the transportation industry (p. 18).

56. *Ibid.*, p. 17.

57. *Ibid.*, p. 18.

58. *Ibid.*, p. 19.

59. *Ibid.*

60. *Ibid.*

61. *Ibid.*, p. 16.

62. *Ibid.*, p. 11.

63. *Ibid.*, p. 19.

64. *Ibid.*, p. 12.

65. *Ibid.*, p. 35.

66. *Ibid.*, p. 12.

67. On these points, see: Pride, Mary, *The Child Abuse Industry* (Westchester, Ill.: Crossway, 1986), and Krason, Stephen M., "Child Abuse: Pseudo-Crisis, Dangerous Bureaucrats, Destroyed Families," in Krason, and D'Agostino, *op. cit.* (Chap. Three), pp. 153-196.

68. 1984 platform, p. 12.

69. *Ibid.*, p. 16.

70. *Ibid.*, p. 19.

71. *Ibid.*, p. 20.

72. *Ibid.*, p. 8.

73. *Ibid.*, pp. 22, 57.

74. *Ibid.*, p. 23-24.

75. *Ibid.*, p. 27.

76. *Ibid.*, p. 28.

77. *Ibid.*, pp. 27-29.

78. *Ibid.*, pp. 27-28.

79. *Ibid.*, p. 34.

80. See the *Declaration on Religious Liberty (Dignitatis Humanae)*, *op. cit.* (Chap. Three).

81. 1984 platform, pp. 34.

82. *Ibid.*, p. 37.

83. 1984 platform, pp. 34-35.

84. *Ibid.*, p. 35.

85. *Ibid.*, pp. 37-38.

86. *Ibid.*, p. 42.

87. *Ibid.*, p. 38.

88. *Ibid.*, p. 39. Emphasis is added.

89. *Ibid.*, pp. 39-40.

90. *Ibid.*, p. 34.

91. *Ibid.*, p. 37.

92. *Ibid.*

93. *Ibid.*, p. 36.

94. *Ibid.*, p. 12.

95. *Ibid.*, p. 13.

96. *Ibid.*, pp. 12-13.

97. *Ibid.*, p. 13.

98. *Ibid.* Emphasis is added.

99. *Ibid.*, p. 13.

100. *Ibid.*, pp. 13-14.

101. *Ibid.*, p. 13.

102. See, for example, *Lemon v. Kurtzman*, 403 U.S. 602 (1971), *Committee for Public Education v. Nyquist*, 413 U.S. 756 (1973), *Sloan v. Lemon*, 413 U.S. 825 (1973), *Meek v. Pittinger*, 421 U.S. 349 (1975), and *Wolman v. Walters*, 433 U.S. 229 (1977).

103. The rationale for this claim of a natural law mandate is found in Waters, Raphael T., "Values and Rights in Educaton," Krason, Stephen M., ed., *The Recovery of American Education: Reclaiming a Vision* (Lanham, Md.: University Press of America, 1991), especially pp. 34-37.

104. 1984 platform, p. 51.

105. *Ibid.*

106. *Ibid.*, pp. 50.

107. *Ibid.*, pp. 50, 52.

108. *Ibid.*, p. 57.

109. *Ibid.*, p. 56.

110. *Ibid.*, p. 57.

111. *Ibid.*

112. *Ibid.*, p. 55.

113. *Ibid.*, p. 57.

114. See *The Wanderer*, May 24, 1984, pp. 1, 6; *ALL About Issues*, Dec. 1984, p. 21.

115. See 1984 platform, pp. 50-58.

116. *Ibid.*, p. 55.

117. See *Ibid.*, p. 51, para. 6 and p. 55, para. 6.

118. The argument that the new liberals' insistence on treating totalitarian and authoritarian regimes equally really became a preference for the former— i.e., Communist or Marxist regimes—was made forcefully in Jeane Kirkpatrick's noted article, "Dictators and Double Standards," *Commentary* (Nov. 1979), pp. 34-45.

119. *Ibid.*, p. 48.

120. *Ibid.*, pp. 47-48.

121. *Ibid.*, p. 49.

122. See *ibid.*

123. *Ibid.*, pp. 50, 53.

124. *Ibid.*

125. *Ibid.*, p. 47.

126. Brock, Clifton, *Americans for Democratic Action* (Wash., D.C.: Public Affairs Press, 1962), pp. 2, 3.

127. ADA statement, quoted in Brock, p. 7.

128. Schlesinger, *op.cit.* (Chap. Three), p. 166.

129. Brock, citing *U.S. News and World Report* (specific issue unspecified), p. 57.

130. Brock, p. 113.

131. *Ibid.*, p. 47.

132. Phone conversation with the ADA national office, July 23, 1990.

133. *Ibid.*, pp. 26, 52, 113.

134. *Ibid.*, p. 20, from an ADA circular.

135. *Ibid.*, p. 164.

136. 1948 ADA ratings of Congress.

137. Brock, p. 112; 1948 ADA ratings.

138. *Ibid.*

139. See Brock, pp.95-99.

140. 1948 ADA ratings.

141. Brock, p. 52.

142. *Ibid.*, pp. 145-146; 156-157.

143. *Ibid.*, pp. 180-181.

144. Brock, p. 112; 1948 ADA ratings.

145. *Ibid.*, p. 97.

146. *Ibid.*, p. 180.

147. *Ibid.*, p. 52.

148. *Ibid.*

149. 1948 ADA Ratings.

150. Brock, p. 20 (from an ADA circular), 180.

151. *Ibid.*, p. 117.

152. *Ibid.*, pp. 64-65.

153. *Ibid.*, p. 117.

154. *Ibid.*, pp. 64-65, 91.

155. *Ibid.*, p. 52,56-58,63-67, (featuring a leaflet for a 1958 Roosevelt Day Dinner).

156. 1984 ADA ratings.

157. Brock, pp. 113, 180.

158. *Ibid.*, p. 113.

159. 1984 ADA ratings.

160. *Ibid.*

161. *Ibid.*

162. Brock, p. 113.

163. 1984 ADA ratings.

164. See also Brock, pp. 109, 202.

165. Brock, pp. 109, 180.

166. 1984 ADA ratings.

167. Brock, *passim.*

168. 1984 ADA ratings.

169. *Ibid.*

170. 1988 ADA ratings.

171. *Ibid.*

172. See Brock, p. 113.

173. July 23, 1990 phone conversation.

174. 1984 ADA ratings.

175. *Ibid.*

176. 1984 and 1988 ADA ratings.

CHAPTER FIVE NOTES

1. Nash, George H., *The Conservative Intellectual Movement in America: Since 1945* (N.Y.: Basic Bks., 1976, 1979), pp. xvi-xvii.

2. *Ibid.*, p. xvii.

3. *Ibid.*, p. 145.

4. Evans' article appeared in *Modern Age* (Spring 1971), pp. 130-137 and was reprinted in Brudnoy, David, *Viewpoints: The Conservative Alternative* (Minneapolis: Winston, 1973), pp. 25-31. We shall cite from this latter source.

5. Nash states that there were three general groupings of intellectual conservatives which emerged in the years after World War II: "classical liberals" or "libertarians," who were concerned about "resisting the threat of the ever-expanding State to liberty, private enterprise, and individualism"; "new conservatives" or "traditionalists," who "urged a return to traditional religious and ethical absolutes and a rejection of the 'relativism' which had allegedly corroded Western values and produced an intolerable vacuum that was filled by demonic ideologies" like Nazism and communism; and "militant, evangelistic anti-Communists," mostly "ex-radicals," who successfully promoted on the right "a profound conviction that the West" was facing "an implacable adversary" in communism which sought the "conquest of the world" (Nash, p. xvi).

6. Evans, pp. 26-27. He divides this "traditionalist" grouping into the categories of theological, Natural Law, and cultural conservatives individually, instead of running them together into one as we do here. He also breaks the "Natural Law conservative" category into a sub-category called "majority rule conservatives." Actually, the various major groupings we have adopted from him appear in this article only as what might be called specific groupings within three broad groupings: "traditionalists," "centrists" or "fusionists," and "libertarians." We do not use these broader groupings because Evans provides definitions, for the most part, only by referring to the specific groupings which are part of them and because by considering writers from each of the *specific* groupings one gets a more precise picture of each of the strains of conservative thought. It will be noted that we take the fusionists and at least some of the libertarians—which are *general* groupings—and discuss them as *specific* groupings within conservatism, partly because Evans does this also to some extent and also because they are important perspectives within conservatism which need to be examined to get a complete picture of it.

7. *Ibid.*

8. *Ibid.*, p. 27.

9. Nash, p. 69. As stated in the Notes to Chapter One, *The Conservative Mind* will be referred to as "Kirk I."

10. The revised edition of *The Conservative Mind* (Chicago: Regnery, 1953, 1960) is the edition of this work referred to this Chapter.

11. Kirk, Russell, *A Program for Conservatives* (Chicago: Regnery, 1954). (Hereinafter referred to as "Kirk II.")

12. Kirk, Russell, "Libertarians: The Chirping Sectaries," in *Modern Age*, Vol. 25, No. 4 (Fall 1981), pp. 345-351. (Hereinafter referred to as "Kirk III.")

13. Kendall, Willmoore, *The Conservative Affirmation* (Chicago: Regnery Gateway, 1963, 1985).

14. Murray, John Courtney, S.J., *We Hold These Truths: Catholic Reflections on the American Proposition* (Kansas City, Mo.: Sheed and Ward, 1960).

15. Eidsmoe, John, *God and Caesar: Biblical Faith and Political Action* (Westchester, Ill.: Crossway, 1984).

16. Evans, pp. 27-28.

17. Meyer, Frank S., *In Defense of Freedom* (Chicago: Regnery, 1962).

18. This is suggested by both Nash, pp. 313-316, and Robert Nisbet, another well-known intellectual conservative (see Nisbet, Robert, "Conservatives and Libertarians: Uneasy Cousins," *Modern Age*, Vol. 24, No. 1 [Winter 1980], pp. 2-8.) On the other hand, another noted intellectual conservative, the late Senator John P. East, indicated that libertarianism has been a part of this postwar mainstream. However, he seems to refer mostly to economic libertarianism and fusionism, which we have included, and to also exclude the Randian-Rothbardian perspective. (See, East, John P., "The American Conservative Movement of the 1980's: Are Traditional and Libertarian Dimensions Compatible?" *Modern Age*, Vol. 24, No 1 [Winter 1980], pp. 34-38.)

19. Evans states that the libertarian elements associated with Rothbard "attempted to link up with libertarian elements in the New Left" (p. 30). Rothbard published in the New Left journal *Ramparts* at times.

20. See Nash, pp. 283-289.

21. Evans, p. 29.

22. Friedman, Milton, *Capitalism and Freedom* (Chicago: University of Chicago Press, 1962).

23. Roepke, Wilhelm, *A Humane Economy* (Indianapolis: Liberty Fund, 1971).

24. Evans, p. 29.

25. Most of the thinkers we have chosen to examine in the groupings that were in existence at the time of Evans' article—whether we use his name or another for the groupings—have been selected because he mentions them. These are: Kirk, Kendall, Murray, Meyer, Friedman, and Roepke.

26. We should point out that the terms "neoconservatives" and "new right" are used only because those are the labels—first given no doubt by political commentators—which have been used to identify these groupings. Other perspectives have carried the same or similar names. For example, Meyer, who we shall discuss, called conservatives such as Kirk "New Conservatives" in the 1950s and 1960s. This is why we have tried to carefully explain the grouping or perspective we are referring

to at a particular time. The potential for ambiguity and confusion is great, as with the terms "liberalism," "old liberalism," and "new liberalism."

27. It should be noted that Nash, whose book was published five years later, does discuss the neoconservatives.

28. Kristol, Irving, *Reflections of a Neoconservative* (N.Y.: Basic Bks., 1983), p. xii. (Hereinafter referred to as "Kristol I.")

29. *Ibid.*

30. *Ibid.*, p. xiii.

31. Kristol, Irving, *On the Democratic Idea in America* (N.Y.: Harper & Row, 1972), p. viii, quoted in Nash, p. 332 (Hereinafter referred to as "Kristol II.")

32. Cited *supra*.

33. As is the case with political perspectives, one has to be careful about definitions of terms connoting religious groupings. "Evangelical Protestant" can have many different meanings, but we shall adopt that of Thomas Howard, a former professor of English at "evangelical" Gordon College in Wenham, Mass.: "In America, evangelicalism came eventually to refer to an *outlook* rather than to any specific doctrinal position. . . .[T]he word. . .ordinarily impl[ies] an especially ardent form of Christian profession. Evangelicals are to be found scattered throughout all Protestant denominations; but they also have had a lively history of starting literally hundreds of new, small denominations. . . .[T]he evangelicals believe the undiluted, miraculous account of. . .events [such as] the Virgin Birth, Christ's miracles, the Resurrection, the Ascension, and so forth. [In other words, they accept literally the traditional faith teachings of Christianity, but would join other Protestants in rejecting the Catholic doctrines on such matters as the papacy and the Virgin Mary.]. . . Evangelical worship. . .[is] informal. . .by liturgical standards. . . .[And b]y far the most important task of the church. . .is to instruct the people in the Bible." The Bible is the center and source of all Christian truth for evangelicals and the general rule for them is that the teachings and events in it are to be taken literally; all evangelicals, though, would not necessarily be fundamentalist in the sense of believing that *every* event in the Bible, particularly as regards the Old Testament, is to be taken as an actual historical happening with no room for imagery. A final, crucial aspect of evangelicalism that Howard points to is the oft-discussed belief that one's soul is "saved" the moment he "accepts the Lord Jesus Christ as. . .[his] personal Saviour" (Howard, Thomas, "From Evangelicalism to Rome," in Baram, Robert, ed., *Spiritual Journeys* (Boston: St. Paul Editions, 1987), pp. 153-155.

34. Wolfe, Gregory, "The New Right and the Politics of Reaction," *Hillsdale Review*, Vol. II, No. 4 (Winter 1980), pp. 8-11. The quotation about the community is from p. 9.

35. In his book, *The New Right: We're Ready to Lead*, Richard A. Viguerie says of Weyrich that of the people who built the early new right movement, he had "perhaps. . .the broadest vision." He continues: "I can think of no one who better symbolizes or is more important to the conservative movement than Paul Weyrich" (Viguerie, Richard A., *The New Right: We're Ready to Lead* [Falls Church,

Va.: The Viguerie Co., 1981], p. 53). In his anthology, *The New Right Papers*, Robert W. Whitaker singles out Viguerie and Weyrich as the ones who are "building. . .a New Right alternative in Washington." (Whitaker, Robert W., "Foreword," in Whitaker, *The New Right Papers* [N.Y.: St. Martin's, 1982], p. xix.)

36. Weyrich, Paul & Marshner, Connaught, eds., *Future 21: Directions for America in the 21st Century* (Greenwich, Conn.: Devin-Adair, 1984).

37. *Cultural Conservatism: Toward a New National Agenda* (Washington, D.C.: Institute for Cultural Conservatism, 1987). (Hereinafter referred to as "Institute.")

38. *Ibid.*, p. 10. Kirk's support was mentioned to us in a phone conservation with Mrs. Russell Kirk in late winter 1988.

39. *Ibid.*, p. 11. We believe this book is also a good one to select because its 1987 publication makes it a good statement of a "mature" new right thought.

40. Goldwater, Barry M., *The Conscience of a Conservative* (N.Y.: Macfadden-Bartell, 1960). All further cites to "Goldwater" refer to this book.

41. Crane, Philip, ed., *Liberal Cliches and Conservative Solutions* (Ottawa, Ill.: Green Hill, 1984).

42. Goldwater, Barry M., *The Conscience of a Majority* (Simon & Schuster [Pocket Book], 1971). Originally published by Simon & Schuster in 1970.

43. Kirk III, p. 350, 349.

44. Eidsmoe, p. 4. This is also the specific role of human law, which issues forth from government. (Eidsmoe, p. 6.) Murray agrees that "self-preservation and self-protection" is a central purpose of government, although he does not say it is the *most* central one (Murray, p. 159).

45. See Kirk I, p. 536; Eidsmoe, pp. 106-109.

46. Kirk II, pp. 160-161.

47. Kirk I, p. 539.

48. See Eidsmoe I, pp. 16-18.

49. Kirk, Russell, "Promises and Perils of Christian Politics," *Intercollegiate Review*, Vol. 18, No. 1 (Fall/Winter 1982), p. 20.

50. For example, Kirk states that "it is from the Church that we receive our fundamental postulates of order and justice and freedom, applying them to civil society." (*Ibid.*, p. 21.)

51. Kendall, p. 17. Eidsmoe makes this same argument very strongly (see Eidsmoe, pp. 84-90).

52. Murray, pp. 333, 33, 35.

53. *Ibid.*, p. 334.

54. *Ibid.*, pp. 155-174.

55. Kirk III, p. 350.

56. *Ibid.*

57. *Ibid.*

58. Higgins, *op cit.* (Chapter Two), pp. 415, 452.

59. *Ibid.*, p. 438.

60. Murray, p. 333.

61. Kirk II, p. 160.

62. *Ibid.*

63. Murray, pp. 92-95. The contrary view is seen in Kendall, p. 23.

64. Meyer, pp. 95-96, 97.

65. *Ibid.*, p. 97.

66. *Ibid.*, p. 95.

67. *Ibid.*, pp. 140,147.

68. *Ibid.*, p. 136.

69. *Ibid.*, p. 137.

70. *Ibid.*, p. 135.

71. *Ibid.*, p. 82.

72. On this entire point, see generally Meyer, Chap. V ("Leviathan").

73. Friedman, p. 15. It should be noted that throughout his book, Friedman does not actually refer to himself as a "conservative," but as a "liberal." He means a nineteenth century or "classical" or "*laissez-faire*" liberal. This is a position which, rightly or wrongly, is frequently identified with present-day conservatism.

74. Friedman, p. 23.

75. *Ibid.*, p. 34.

76. *Ibid.*, see Chap. VI.

77. *Ibid.*, p. 23.

78. See Roepke, Chaps. III and IV.

79. Kristol I, pp. xii-xiii.

80. Kristol II, pp. vii-viii, quoted in Nash, p. 332.

81. Nash, p. 332. Strauss and many of his followers have supported the notion—influenced by the thinking of the ancient Greeks—of the state playing an important role in the shaping of individual character along the lines of classical virtues.

82. Kristol I, pp. xiii, 235.

83. Institute, pp. 96, 23. The principle of subsidiarity was discussed in Chapter Two in examining the Church teachings and has been mentioned in this Chapter. "Mediating institutions" relate to it. They include, first and foremost, the family; also: churches, political parties, voluntary organizations, business enterprises, unions, trade and professional groups, the press and media, etc.

84. *Ibid.*, pp. 24-25.

85. *Ibid.*, p. 25.

86. *Ibid.*, pp. 25-26 (which is where the quotes appear), 101-107.

87. *Ibid.*, pp. 134-135.

88. *Ibid.*,pp. 52, 87, 88, 107.

89. Marshner, Connaught, "Family Protection: The Imperative of the Future," in Weyrich & Marshner, pp. 160-161.

90. See Institute, pp. 84-89.

91. See Goldwater, Chap. Three.

92. *Ibid.*, pp. 33-35.

93. *Ibid.*, Chap. Nine.

94. Livingston, Bob, MC, "Which Is the Fat Cat Party?" in Crane, p. 21.

95. See Lungren, Dan, MC, "Should Bureaucrats Run Businesses?" in Crane, pp. 130-138.

96. Livingston, *Ibid.*, p. 21.

97. See Bliley, Tom, MC, "What Really Helps Families?" in Crane, pp. 1-9.

98. Courter, Jim, MC, "What Kind of Defense is Best?" in Crane, p. 44.

99. Goldwater, Chap. Ten. The quote is from pp. 97-98.

100. Higgins, p. 355. In *Pacem in Terris*, Pope John defined the common good as that which *"embraces the sum total of those conditions of social living whereby men are enabled to achieve their own integral perfection more fully and more easily."* (*PT*, II, 58, p. 302 [emphasis in the encyclical]). He refers here to the common good of the whole human community.

101. Kirk says the following: "Now the enlightened conservative always has stood for true community, the union of men, through love and common interest, for the common welfare. It was the liberals and radicals of the eighteenth and nineteenth centuries, not the conservatives, who did everything in their power to abolish the traditional concept of community and substitute a doctrinaire individualism, which led inevitably to collectivism, as a natural reaction." (Kirk II, p. 140). This perhaps suggests, as was already stated by Friedman, that at least some present-day conservatism is really liberalism of a previous era. This is addressed more fully in the final chapter of this book.

102. In fairness to conservatism, some of its adherents, such as Kirk, seem to be unenthusiastic about such efforts directed at the rest of the world for the reason that they tend, in some sense, to promote avarice, to motivate poor peoples in the rest of the world simply to want what we in the West and in America possess, and generally to overemphasize material needs and wants to the exclusion of more impor-tant spiritual ones. (See Kirk II, Chap. VIII.) Kirk's concern is understandable—after all, the popes have condemned "economism," which is what this is, and have said that the poor countries are not free to repeat the environmental, etc.

excesses of the industrialized countries as they develop—but it ignores some very important truths: the goods of the world are put here by God and belong to *all* men; all men are brothers regardless of where they live, according to Christian teaching, and we must help our brothers who have needs—whether they are spiritual or material; we are in an increasingly interdependent world, as recent popes have emphasized, and all nations have no choice but to develop economically because of the demands made on them by this interdependent world; the people of the poor nations find out readily enough today that they are lacking and other nations have an abundance and, like it or not, this creates expectations, sometimes quite legitimate, that require redressing if international instability is to be avoided; influential elements in these poor nations—again, like it or not—are going to lead their nations toward pernicious doctrines such as communism if a serious attempt is not made by advanced free nations to aid them in their plight, and this is going to be done in spite of any claims, no matter how valid, that these other nations should have to assume the burden of economic development themselves in the way Western countries did; and the governments of advanced nations are, inevitably, going to have to be involved in this giving of aid. Direct overseas aid on a substantial scale—as will be needed—seldom comes from other than government sources. Even if much of it would be so derived—the popes do not specifically say it has to be governmental aid and, in any event, the subsidiarity principle holds here as it does in domestic matters—governments would still determine how private organizations within their borders would be able to channel that aid, to which countries, under what circumstances, etc. This is because foreign policy is one of the sovereign functions of the state, and *only* the state. So government is inevitably involved. Finally, giving material assistance does not, by any means, have to imply a diminution of spiritual values. Man is body and soul and needs "development" in *both* areas. The aid, of course, would have to be handled prudently so that it does not breed avarice and envy.

103. Kirk I, p. 7. This is, of course, very similar to the statement, mentioned in Chapter One, attributed to such figures as Cardinal Manning and Irving Babbitt.

104. Kirk I, p. 536.

105. Kirk I, p. 8.

106. Kirk II, p. 194.

107. Murray, p. 336.

108. *Ibid.*, p. 30, quoting the Supreme Court opinion in *Zorach v. Clausen* (1952).

109. See Kendall, Chap. 5. The quoted material is on p. 93. Kendall rejects the common idea that the Founding Fathers were primarily Lockeans.

110. Kirk I, p. 6. Emphasis is added.

111. Kirk II, p. 168. Emphasis is added.

112. Kirk III, p. 350. Emphasis is added.

113. Kirk I, p. 539; Kirk III, p. 350. Emphasis is added.

114. Kendall, p. 94. Emphasis is added.

115. *Ibid.*, p. 179.

116. Eidsmoe, p. 76.

117. *Ibid.*, p. 35.

118. See Murray, pp. 30-43, 310-327.

119. Evans, p. 27.

120. Meyer, pp. 47, 165.

121. *Ibid.*, pp. 44, 45, 47-48, 53, 68, 72, 73.

122. *Ibid.*, p. 69.

123. *Ibid.*, p. 71.

124. *Ibid.*, pp. 165-166.

125. Friedman, pp. 26-27. Emphasis is added.

126. *Ibid.*, p. 12.

127. *Ibid.*, pp. 18-21.

128. *Ibid.*, p. 33.

129. *Ibid.*, p. 133.

130. Roepke, pp. 148-149. His speaking about "counterbalancing" individualism, utilitarianism, and legal positivism actually does not indicate an endorsement of these. Elsewhere in the book he specifically criticizes utilitarianism (pp. 108-109) and the context of his other, scattered comments makes clear that he does not promote individualism or legal positivism (he favors a substantial measure of individual freedom, obviously, but that is different from *individualism*). In this quote, he apparently is just taking note of the reality that exists in many countries in this capitalistic era and telling us what is needed to limit the damaging effects of it.

131. *Ibid.*, p. 125.

132. *Ibid.*, p. 5.

133. *Ibid.*, p. 107.

134. See, for example, Hayek, Friedrich, A., *The Constitution of Liberty* (Chicago: Univ. of Chicago Press, 1967 [especially Part I]) and Von Mises, Ludwig, *The Historical Setting of the Austrian School of Economics* (Auburn, Ala.: Mises Institute, 1969, 1984), pp. 34-39. (Von Mises indicates here that there are natural laws which are perennial and universal, but [despite criticizing the Enlightenment] it is clear that he means Enlightenment-type rigid economic "laws," instead of the natural law.) His massive *Human Action* (New Haven, Conn.: Yale Univ. Press, 1949) makes clear that there is really, in his mind, no set natural law and that he does not believe religious principles should shape social organization (see especially, pp. 155-157, 716, 719).

135. Kristol, p. xi.

136. The Church has followed the formulation of St. Thomas Aquinas that the natural law is a reflection of the eternal law, which is a reflection of the nature of God Himself. The Church's *General Catechetical Directory*, issued in 1971 by the Sacred Congregation for the Clergy, makes clear, following Galatians 2:20, that man needs God to persist in following the natural law (Sec. 61).

137. Kristol, p. 77.

138. *Ibid.*

139. *Ibid.*, p. 48.

140. Marshner, Connaught, "Right and Wrong and America's Survival: An Ethical System for the Future," in Weyrich & Marshner, pp. 129-130.

141. Institute, p. 8.

142. *Ibid.*, p. 14.

143. *Ibid.*

144. Marshner, in Marshner & Weyrich, p. 130.

145. For a strictly philosophical analysis of natural law which affirms also that man cannot be independent of God in ethics or other matters, see Higgins, *op. cit.* (Chap. Two), especially Chaps. IV-V.

146. Institute, p. 103.

147. *Ibid.*, pp. 14-15.

148. Goldwater, p. 34. Emphasis is in the book. When we say he supports "some version of a theory of it," we mean that it may not so much be the real natural law that he is thinking of here when he says this, but rather the natural rights thinking of, for example, a Locke or Jefferson (which definitely influenced our Founding) or some other modern political-jurisprudential theory that involves rights and other precepts not of human making that are put into the general category of "natural law."

149. *Ibid.*, p. 76. Emphasis is added.

150. Kemp, Jack, MC, "Introduction: Completing the Revolution," in Crane, no page number.

151. Bliley, in Crane, pp. 4, 6. Emphasis is in the book.

152. Kirk III, p. 349.

153. Kirk II, p. 249.

154. Kirk III, p. 350. By rights being "sanctioned by prescription," he means the long-standing recognition and exercise of some right so as to give it broad acceptance and to incorporate it into law.

155. Kendall, pp. 105-120, 152-155 (the quote is from p. 105).

156. *Ibid.*, p. 154.

157. Kirk I, pp. 7-8.

158. Kendall, p. 153.

159. Kirk III, p. 350.

160. Murray, p. 206.

161. Eidsmoe, pp. 17-18.

162. Murray, pp. 69-71; Eidsmoe, p. 18.

163. Eidsmoe I, p. 84.

164. Murray, p. 160; Eidsmoe, pp. 87-90.

165. Eidsmoe, p. 88.

166. Murray, pp. 160-174.

167. Murray, p. 334; Eidsmoe, pp. 89-90.

168. Eidsmoe, p. 108.

169. Eidsmoe, pp. 108-109.

170. Murray, p. 318.

171. Eidsmoe, pp. 76, 88.

172. Meyer, p. 50.

173. *Ibid.*, p. 53.

174. *Ibid.*

175. *Ibid.*, p. 67.

176. *Ibid.*, p. 69.

177. *Ibid.*, pp. 165-166.

178. We say this even while realizing that Frank S. Meyer ridicules—rightly—the notion of modern-day education that by dispensing with the actual teaching of the wisdom of civilization and stressing experiential, undisciplined learning the student will "somehow, magically" be educated (Meyer, pp. 158-159). We suggest that his thought may be inconsistent in not applying this same understanding to his thinking on freedom.

179. Meyer, pp. 36-37, 154-155.

180. Friedman, p. 8.

181. *Ibid.*, pp. 8-9.

182. *Ibid.*, p. 9.

183. *Ibid.*, p. 10.

184. *Ibid.*, p. 11.

185. *Ibid.*, pp. 18-19.

186. *Ibid.*, p. 20. In fairness to Friedman, he does say that advocacy of unpopular causes such as communism should not be "costless" for the advocate. He says the advocate must be prepared to "sacrifice," though he does not specify how or what type of costs there should be, except to say that the advocacy should not be subsidized by society.

187. *Ibid.*, p. 21.

188. Nash, p. 181.

189. Roepke, pp. 4-5.

190. Kristol, p. 50.

191. *Ibid.*, pp. 50-51.

192. *Ibid.*, p. 52.

193. *Ibid.*, p. 53.

194. *Ibid.*, p. 48.

195. *Ibid.*, p. 54.

196. *Ibid.*, pp. 76-77.

197. *Ibid.*, p. 193. The notion of the middle class being a source of stability and moderation in a political order and making it less likely to give way to tyranny dates at least from Aristotle. See *The Politics of Aristotle* (tr. Ernest Barker; N.Y.: Oxford U. Press, 1948, 1972), Bk. IV, Chap. XI, 1295a-1296b, pp. 179-184.

198. Weyrich, Paul M., "Bureaucracy: An Inherent Evil?" in Weyrich & Marshner, p. 195.

199. Institute, p. 8.

200. *Ibid.*, p. 13.

201. *Ibid.*, pp. 23-24.

202. *Ibid.*, p. 25.

203. *Ibid.*, pp. 71-72.

204. See Friedman, pp. 133-136.

205. Institute, pp. 69-70.

206. *Ibid.*, p. 71. This is easily inferred from the discussion of the principle of "independence"—that an individual is able to support himself and his family through work—which is said to necessitate "[c]reating economic conditions that offer personally rewarding work to as many people as possible" (p. 71).

207. This preference of the new right is apparent from the list of goals in Institute, p. 73.

208. Livingston, in Crane, p. 21.

209. *Ibid.*

210. Lungren, in Crane, p. 138.

211. Goldwater, pp. 44, 57.

212. *Ibid.*, p. 57.

213. *Ibid.*, pp. 43-44.

214. *Ibid.*, pp. 57-58.

215. Regarding the latter, see, for example, the works of the Heinrich Pesch, S.J.

216. Goldwater, p. 75; Hiler, John, "Can Housing the Poor be Done Better?" in Crane, pp. 118-129.

217. Bliley, in Crane, pp. 2-3.

218. Goldwater, p. 61.

219. *Ibid.*, pp. 62-63.

220. *Ibid.*, pp. 45-59.

221. Kemp, in Crane, no page number.

222. *Ibid.*

223. Hyde, Henry J., MC, "What Kind of Foreign Aid Helps?" in Crane, p. 117.

224. We must take special account of the fact that the conservatives must use language like this because they are operating within the context of American religious pluralism. Their appeal is typically to a group which is both Catholic and non-Catholic and so, even if their positions are based primarily on Catholic principles or the Catholic moral tradition, they will not solely attribute them to such.

225. *PT op. cit.* (Chap. Two), I, 28-31, p. 295.

226. *Ibid.*, II, 73, p. 305.

227. *Ibid.*, 73-74, pp. 305-306.

228. *SRS op. cit.* (Chap. Two), VI, 44, p. 12. Emphasis is in the encyclical.

229. *PT*, I, 30, p. 295.

230. Higgins, p. 355.

231. *RN op. cit.* (Chap. Two), 34, p. 223.

232. See Higgins, Chaps. XXI and XXIV.

233. See *RN*, 34, pp. 223-224.

234. See Blotzer, Joseph, "Inquisition," *The Catholic Encyclopedia*, Vol. VIII, p. 36; Murray, p. 86.

235. Kirk I, p. 7.

236. *Ibid.*, pp. 9, 7. Emphasis is added.

237. Kirk II, p. 172.

238. Kendall, pp. 17-18.

239. Kirk I, p. 7.

240. Kendall, p. 18.

241. *Ibid.*, pp. 17-18.

242. *Ibid.*, pp. 17-19.

243. Murray, p. 181.

244. *Ibid.*, p. 81.

245. Kirk I, p. 7.

246. Eidsmoe, p. 77.

247. Murray, pp. 81-82.

248. *Ibid.*, pp. 145-146. Interestingly, even though he says it was always immoral, he claims it could still have been defended, for a time, on "sociological" grounds "in view of the unenlightened state of public conscience, the temporarily inferior cultural status of the Negro, etc." (Murray, p. 145). This position is not unlike that taken by most of those who wanted to abolish slavery at the time of the Civil War. They did not think American society was prepared for even full political equality between blacks and whites and were not prepared to accord it.

249. Kirk II, p. 170-172.

250. Eidsmoe, p. 77.

251. Meyer, p. 9.

252. *Ibid.*, p. 161.

253. Friedman, p. 34.

254. Roepke, p. 55.

255. See Friedman, pp. 92-93.

256. *Ibid.*, p. 5.

257. Roepke, pp. 142-144.

258. Friedman, p. 5.

259. Friedman is not alone among well-known authors in this grouping in not giving much attention to this. Hayek and Von Mises also have little to say about it.

260. Roepke, p. 5.

261. Friedman, pp. 117-118.

262. Kristol, p. xiv.

263. *Ibid.*, p. 200.

264. *Ibid.*, p. 245. Emphasis is in the book.

265. *Ibid.*, p. 244.

266. *Ibid.*, p. 52, note.

267. *Ibid.*

268. As an obvious example of this, we can point to the clamoring for government to pay for abortions for poor women on welfare.

269. *Ibid.*, p. 53.

270. *Ibid.*, p. xiv.

271. Institute, pp. 101, 12, 68-70, respectively.

272. *Ibid.*, p. 114. Emphasis is in the book.

273. *Ibid.*, p. 133.

274. *Ibid.*, p. 6.

275. *Ibid.*, p. 3.

276. *Ibid.*, p. 133.

277. *Ibid.*, p. 134.

278. *Ibid.*, p. 68.

279. Kemp, in Crane, no page number.

280. Goldwater, p. 64.

281. *Ibid.* Emphasis is in the book.

282. *Ibid.*, p. 85.

283. Livingston, in Crane, p. 21.

284. Murray, p. 223.

285. *Ibid.*, p. 224.

286. *Ibid.*, p. 226.

287. *Ibid.*, p. 236.

288. Kirk II, pp. 168, 170.

289. Eidsmoe, pp. 77-78.

290. *Ibid.*, p. 107.

291. *Ibid.*, pp. 107-108.

292. Kendall, p. 220. The review is of C.J. Friedrich's 1957 book, *Constitutional Reason of State* (Providence, R.I.: Brown Univ. Press, 1957).

293. Murray, p. 236.

294. Kendall, p. xxviii.

295. Meyer, p. 10.

296. *Ibid.*, p. 27.

297. *Ibid.*, p. 10.

298. *Ibid.*, pp. 9-10.

299. *Ibid.*, p. 171.

300. Roepke, pp. 103-112, 187-188.

301. *Ibid.*, p. 111.

302. *Ibid.*, p. 13.

303. *Ibid.*, p. 10.

304. *Ibid.*, p. 15.

305. *Ibid.*, p. 14.

306. Kristol, p. 119, 120.

307. *Ibid.*, pp. 325-326.

308. *Ibid.*, p. 120. It was perhaps this disinterest— discussed so well by d'Encausse (*op. cit.*, Chap. Three)—which presaged the recent decline of communism in the U.S.S.R. (See d'Encausse, especially Chapter 6.)

309. *Ibid.*, p. 324. On the point about communism being a version of gnosticism, see also Voegelin, Eric, *The New Science of Politics* (Chicago: U of Chicago Press, 1952, 1987.)

310. *Ibid.*, p. 21.

311. Moser, Charles A. "Foreign Policy and the Conservative Blueprint," in Weyrich & Marshner, p. 107.

312. *Ibid.*, p. 108.

313. Institute, p. 70.

314. *Ibid.*, p. 137.

315. Moser, in Weyrich & Marshner, p. 104.

316. *Ibid.*, p. 107.

317. *Ibid.*

318. Spence, Floyd, MC, "Does Appeasement Ever Work?" in Crane, p. 83.

319. Goldwater, p. 89.

320. *Ibid.*, pp. 90, 91.

321. *Ibid.*, p. 91.

322. Spence, in Crane, pp. 82-83.

323. Goldwater, p. 92. Emphasis is in the book.

324. *Ibid.*

325. *Ibid.*, p. 92-93. On this latter point, see also Reilly, Robert R., "The Nature of Today's Conflict," in Lawler, Philip F., ed., *Justice and War in the Nuclear Age* (Lanham, Md.: University Press of America, 1983), pp. 17-18.

326. Goldwater, pp. 97-98; Hyde, in Crane, p. 112.

CHAPTER SIX NOTES

1. Rossiter, Clinton. *Conservatism in America* (NY: Alfred A. Knopf, 1955), p. 186. This is the edition which is referred to in this Chapter (to avoid confusion it will be referred to as "Rossiter 1955"). The citation given in Chapter One was to the second edition, revised, of this book, published in 1962, to which Rossiter appended the subtitle *The Thankless Persuasion*. In that edition, he refers to Taft as "the very model of the American conservative" (Rossiter, *op. cit.*, [Chap. One], 1962, p. 173).

2. Manchester, *op. cit.* (Chap. Three), p. 616.

3. David, Paul T.; Moos, Malcolm; and Goldman, Ralph M., *Presidential Nominating Politics in 1952* (Vol. One: *The National Story* [Baltimore: Johns Hopkins, 1954]), p. 90.

4. Rossiter, for example, considers him to be definitely of that persuasion (see Rossiter 1955, Chap. V), but other well known conservative writers believed his administration to be essentially pursuing the policy directions of the liberal FDR and Truman administrations before him. (George H. Nash cites their comments. See Nash, *op. cit.* [Chap. Five], pp. 253-254.)

5. See Manchester, *op. cit.* (Chap. Three), p. 614.

6. See White, Theodore H. *The Making of the President 1964* (NY: Atheneum, 1965), pp. 202-213.

7. Some might argue, particularly with an eye to the question of whether there has been a fundamental shift in conservative principles comparable to that which occurred from the old to the new liberalism, that the span of time covered is not great enough. It might be argued that such a shift may actually have occurred from conservatism early in this century to the variety existing after World War II, so Republican platforms from that time should also be examined. My response to this is, first, that a cursory examination of the Republican platforms from the first third of the twentieth century did not demonstrate such a difference in basic conservative principles. Secondly, this is not a historical study of conservatism or of the Republican party throughout the twentieth century. It is a study of conservatism and liberalism in their contemporary cast, of the past generation or at least since the New Deal, which decisively altered American politics into what exists in the present day, and how they measure up to Catholic teaching. It is thus proper to confine the scope of my investigation of conservatism to the period covered by the platforms and, in fact, is only fair to do so since this is the period that is also essentially covered by the Democratic platforms considered.

8. It appears, upon surveying a number of other Democratic platforms, that general statements of political philosophy seldom appear. The Republicans seem more likely to include brief statements of this at the beginning of their platforms.

9. 1952 Republican party platform, in *National Party Platforms* (Vol. I [1840-1956]), *op. cit.* (Chap. Four), p. 496.

10. *Ibid.*

11. *Ibid.*, p. 497.

12. See Aristotle, *Nicomachean Ethics* (tr. Martin Ostwald; Indianapolis: Bobbs-Merril, 1962), Bk. Five, 15-20, p. 113; Aristotle, *Politics* (tr. and ed. by Ernest Barker; London: Oxford U. Press, 1946, 1972), Bk. III, Chap. xiii, 3, p. 132.

13. We use the words "liberty" and "freedom" here interchangeably, as might be done in common discourse and as is done in the platform. We are aware that for the philosopher, these terms have a different meaning. The philosopher emphasizes that there are different kinds of "freedom," which involves the power of choosing among various goods. "Liberty" is one of these kinds of freedom, involving the willing of our true end, the goal which fulfills our nature, which the Christian recognizes is the way of God. (See Sullivan, Daniel J., *Introduction to Philosophy* [Rev. ed.; Milwaukee: Bruce, 1964], Chap. 15). It should be noted that the platform seems to speak of "freedom" and "liberty" in the very limited way of freedom from government coercion.

14. 1964 Republican party platform, in *National Party Platforms*, (Vol. II [1960-1976]), *op. cit.* (Chap. Four), p. 677.

15. *Ibid.*

16. *Ibid.*, p. 678.

17. 1984 Republican party platform, printed in *Congressional Record*, Wed., Sept. 5, 1984, p. 2. (Reprinted in handout form by the Republican National Committee.)

18. *Ibid.*, p. 9.

19. *Ibid.*, p. 17.

20. *Ibid.*, p. 2.

21. 1952 platform, p. 505.

22. 1964 platform, p. 677.

23. *Ibid.*

24. *Ibid.*, p. 690.

25. 1984 platform, p. 1.

26. *Ibid.*, p. 9.

27. *Ibid.*

28. 1952 platform, p. 499.

29. 1964 platform, p. 677.

30. See pp. 678, 684, 685, and 687.

31. 1984 platform, p. 1.

32. *Ibid.*, p. 17.

33. *Ibid.*, p. 21.

34. See 1952 platform, p. 502; 1964 platform, p. 684; 1984 platform, p. 2.

35. 1984 platform, p. 2.

36. 1964 platform, pp. 684-685. See also 1952 platform, p. 500.

37. See, for example, 1952 platform, pp. 500-501; 1964 platform, pp. 684-685; 1984 platform, pp. 3, 4-5, 6, 9-10.

38. See all three platforms, *passim.*

39. *MM, op. cit.* (Chap. Two), Sec. 57, p. 231.

40. *QA, op. cit.* (Chap. Two), III, 1, 105-108, p. 153.

41. 1952 platform, p. 500; 1964 platform, p. 685. However, it should be noted that Republican administrations have not always been so vigorous in enforcing anti-trust laws. The Reagan Administration was especially known for shortcomings in this area. So, conservative principles do not always seem to be upheld in practice on this subject.

42. 1952 platform, p. 502.

43. 1964 platform, p. 683.

44. 1984 platform, pp. 2, 4.

45 See 1952 platform, pp. 500-501; 1964 platform, p. 685; 1984 platform, pp. 3, 4.

46. 1964 platform, pp. 680, 683, 684; 1984 platform, p. 18.

47. 1952 platform, p. 502; 1964 platform, p. 685; 1984 platform, p. 19.

48. 1964 platform, p. 685; 1984 platform, p. 19.

49. 1952 platform, p. 502; 1984 platform, p. 19.

50. *Ibid.*, pp. 504 and 17, respectively.

51. 1952 platform, p. 502.

52. 1964 platform, p. 686.

53. 1984 platform, p. 6.

54. See, for example, *ibid.*, pp. 13-15.

55. 1952 platform, p. 17; 1964 platform, p. 683; 1984 platform, p. 16.

56. 1964 platform, p. 683; 1984 platform, p. 10.

57. 1952 platform, p. 504.

58. 1984 platform, p. 11. The 1964 platform also supports federal assistance for medical research and its application (see p. 683).

59. *Ibid.*, pp. 10-11.

60. The 1952 platform supports the operation of Veterans Administration hospitals (p. 503).

61. The point about inflation is indicated in the 1984 platform, p. 10.

62. 1964 platform, p. 680. Emphasis is added.

63. *Ibid.,* p. 683.

64. 1984 platform, p. 10.

65. *Ibid.,* p. 17.

66. *Ibid.,* p. 10.

67. *QA*, II, 2, 5, 7, p. 142.

68. See the comments on health care above and civil rights/ civil liberties and education forthcoming.

69. 1984 platform, p. 10.

70. The 1984 platform does not even oppose and seek legal sanctions against pornography, except child pornography (see p. 16). The 1964 platform *does,* however (p. 683). 1984's *does* express "deep concern about gratuitous sex and violence in the entertainment media" (p. 16).

71. 1984 platform, p. 10.

72. 1952 platform, p. 501.

73. 1964 platform, p. 681.

74. 1964 platform, pp. 684, 686.

75. 1984 platform, p. 3.

76. *Ibid.,* p. 18.

77. *Ibid.,* p. 8.

78. 1952 platform, p. 499.

79. 1984 platform, p. 8.

80. *Ibid.*

81. 1952 platform, p. 501.

82. 1984 platform, p. 5.

83. *Ibid.,* p. 8.

84. See *ibid.,* pp. 5-9.

85. 1964 platform, p. 683.

86. 1984 platform, p. 7.

87. *Ibid.,* p. 8. Emphasis is in the platform.

88. 1964 platform, p. 684.

89. 1984 platform, p. 6.

90. *Ibid.,* p. 7.

91. *Ibid.,* p. 6.

92. 1952 platform, pp. 501, 502; 1964 platform, p. 683; 1984 platform, pp. 6-8.

93. See 1952 platform, pp. 501-502; 1984 platform, p. 8.

94. 1952 platform, pp. 501, 502.

95. 1964 platform, pp. 681, 686.

96. 1984 platform, p. 21.

97. *Ibid.*, pp. 11-12.

98. 1964 platform, p. 16; 1984 platform, p. 17.

99. 1952 platform, p. 504; 1964 platform, p. 683; 1984 platform, p. 18.

100. 1952 platform, p. 504; 1964 platform, p. 683.

101. 1952 platform, p. 504.

102. 1984 platform, p. 18.

103. *Ibid.*, p. 4.

104. *Ibid.*, p. 5.

105. *Ibid.*, p. 18.

106. *Ibid.*

107. *Ibid.*, p. 29.

108. *Ibid.*, p. 14.

109. *Ibid.*, p. 19.

110. *Ibid.*, p. 16.

111. *Ibid.*, p. 15.

112. 1952 platform, p. 504.

113. 1964 platform, p. 683; 1984 platform, p. 14.

114. Pfeffer, Leo, *God, Caesar, and the Constitution: The Court as Referee of Church-State Confrontation* (Boston: Beacon Press, 1975), p. 219. Pfeffer notes, however, that the support of the U.S. bishops and the U.S. Catholic Conference for such an amendment has been uneven.

115. 1964 platform, p. 685.

116. 1952 platform, p. 504; 1964 platform, p. 683; 1984 platform, p. 19.

117. 1984 platform, p. 20.

118. *Ibid.*, p. 9.

119. *Ibid.*

120. 1964 platform, p. 683.

121. 1984 platform, p. 16.

122. *Ibid.*, p. 11.

123. *Ibid.*

124. *Ibid.*, p. 22.

125. *Ibid.*, pp. 20, 22.

126. 1952 platform, p. 504.

127. 1964 platform, pp. 682, 683, 684.

128. *Ibid.*, p. 682.

129. *Ibid.*, p. 684.

130. *Ibid.*, pp. 13-15.

131. 1984 platform, p. 14.

132. *Ibid.*, pp. 13-15.

133. *Ibid.*, p. 14.

134. See, for example, Waters, Raphael T., "The Basis for the Traditional Rights and Resposibilities of Parents," in Krason and D'Agostino, *op. cit.* (Chap. Three), pp. 13-38 and Waters, "Values and Rights in Education," in Krason, *The Recovery of American Education: Reclaiming a Vision, op. cit.* (Chap. Four), pp. 17-53.

135. 1984 platform, p. 14.

136. *Ibid.*, pp. 14, 15.

137. See 1952 platform, p. 498; 1984 platform, p. 26; 1964 platform, p. 687 (the source of the quotation). For a learned discussion of the point about self-interest, see Morgenthau, Hans J. and Thompson, Kenneth W., *Politics Among Nations: The Struggle for Power and Peace* (Sixth ed.; [NY: Alfred A. Knopf, 1948, 1985]).

138. See 1952 platform, pp. 497, 500; 1964 platform, pp. 680, 689; 1984 platform, pp. 23, 29.

139. 1952 platform, p. 500.

140. 1964 platform, pp. 689, 687.

141. 1984 platform, pp. 23, 29, 22. Even as changes were sweeping through the Soviet Union in 1990 which carried with them the promise of better relations with the West, the U.S. was resisting giving economic aid to her because, our government said, she was continung to give aid to Cuba and other hostile countries. For a discussion of Cuba's role in insurgent and revolutionary activities in Central America, see Turner, Robert F., *Nicaragua Versus United States: A Look at the Facts* (Wash., D.C.: Corporate Press, 1987), Chap. 2. Cuba's activities in Nicaragua, specifically, are chronicled in Belli, Humberto, *Breaking Faith: The Sandinista Revolution and Its Impact on Freedom and Christian Faith in Nicaragua* (Westchester, Ill.: Crossway/Puebla Institute, 1985), *passim*.

142. *Ibid.*, p. 22.

143. 1952 platform, p. 498; 1964 platform, pp. 688-689; 1984 platform, pp. 22, 24, 26-27.

144. 1952 platform, pp. 497, 500; 1964 platform, pp. 678-679; 1984 platform, p. 23.

145. See, for example Goldman, Eric F., *The Crucial Decade—and After, America 1945-1960.* (N.Y.: Vintage, 1956, 1960), pp. 113, 126, 248, 284; Manchester, pp. 658-659; Nixon, Richard M., *Memoirs* (Vol. 1; N.Y.: Warner Books, 1978), p. 136.

146. 1952 platform, p. 498.

147. *Ibid.*, p. 500.

148. 1964 platform, p. 689.

149. 1984 platform, pp. 22, 23.

150. 1964 platform, p. 687.

151. See footnote 174 for Chap. Two.

152. See, e.g., former President Harry S. Truman's comments in Miller, Merle, *Plain Speaking: An Oral Biography of Harry S. Truman* (N.Y.: Berkley, 1973, 1974), pp. 217-218; Roosevelt, Eleanor, *Autobiography* (Boston: Hall, 1984; originally published by Harper, 1961), pp. 382-383.

153. 1952 platform, p. 498.

154. 1964 platform, p. 688.

155. 1952 platform, p. 499. In a way, this is a curious statement for this platform to make. It speaks also, as noted, about the utter hostility communism has for the principles identified with the West. The U. N. has included Communist nations from the beginning, and the platform gives every indication of believing that they accept what their official ideology stands for. How, then, could it hold, without contradiction, that the U. N. was based on "agreed concepts of justice"?

156. 1984 platform, p. 26.

157. 1964 platform, p. 688.

158. 1984 platform, p. 26.

159. *Ibid.*, p. 23. It mentions this in connection with El Salvador.

160. See, e.g., Second Vatican Council, *Nostra Aetate* (*Declaration on the Relation of the Church to Non-Christian Religions*) (1965), Sec. 4, in Flannery, *op. cit.*(Chap. One), p. 741.

161. See Fenno, Richard F., Jr., *Congressmen in Committees* (Boston: Little Brown, 1973), pp. 69-70, 215-216.

162. 1964 platform, pp. 685, 689.

163. 1984 platform, p. 6.

164. *Ibid.*, p. 25.

165. *Ibid.*

166. *Ibid.*, p. 26.

167. *Ibid.*, pp. 23, 25, 26, 27.

168. *Ibid.*, p. 25.

169. *Ibid.*, pp. 26, 27.

170. 1952 platform, p. 499.

171. 1964 platform, pp. 689, 690.

172. 1984 platform, p. 27.

173. See Morgenthau and Thompson, pp. 227-228.

174. 1984 platform, p. 29.

175. *Ibid.,* p. 27.

176. *Ibid.,* pp. 28, 31.

177. *Ibid.,* p. 28.

178. *Ibid.,* p. 31.

179. Codevilla, Angelo, "Justice, War, and Active Defense", in Lawler, Philip F., ed., *Justice and War in the Nuclear Age* (Lanham, Md.: University Press of America, 1983), p. 95.

180. Reagan said this during his second debate with Walter Mondale during the campaign.

181. 1984 platform, p. 28.

182. 1964 platform, p. 680.

183. On this point, see, for example, Codevilla, pp. 83-97.

184. Higgins, *op. cit.* (Chap. Two), p. 549.

185. 1984 platform, p. 23.

186. *Ibid.,* pp. 22, 25.

187. Messner, *op. cit.* (Chap. Two), p. 499.

188. *Ibid.*

189. *Ibid.*

190. 1984 platform, p. 22.

191. Messner, p. 499.

192. 1984 platform, p. 23.

193. Messner, p. 500.

194. 1984 platform, p. 30.

195. *Ibid.,* pp. 22, 26, 30.

196. Compiled from "The American Conservative Union Annual Report" (for 1987), pp. 2, 3. The assessment about how influential it is was made by *Newsweek* magazine and is quoted in the Report, p. 3.

197. When information could not be gotten from the 1984 ratings, the ones of years right after that—1985, 1986, 1987, and 1988—were consulted. On a few points, additional information was gotten from a phone conversation with the ACU national office on July 23, 1990.

198. 1984 ACU ratings.

199. 1986 ACU ratings.

200. 1988 ACU ratings.

201. July 23, 1990 phone conversation.

202. 1984, 1986, 1987, and 1988 ACU ratings, respectively.

203. 1984 ACU ratings.

204. 1984 and 1987 ACU ratings, respectively.

205. July 23, 1990 phone conversation.

206. 1987 ACU ratings.

207. 1984 ACU ratings.

208. *Ibid.*

209. July 23, 1990 phone conversation.

210. 1986 ACU ratings.

211. 1984 ACU ratings.

212. 1985 ACU ratings.

213. 1984 and 1985 ACU ratings.

214. 1984 and 1988 ACU ratings.

215. 1984 ACU ratings.

216. See 1984, 1985, 1986, 1987, and 1988 ACU ratings.

217. 1985 ACU ratings.

218. 1986 ACU ratings.

219. 1988 ACU ratings.

220. Contra Aid votes appear in the 1984, 1985, 1986, 1987, and 1988 ACU ratings; aid to EL Salvador appears in the 1984 and 1986 ratings.

221. 1984 ACU ratings.

222. 1985 ACU ratings.

223. 1984 ACU ratings.

CHAPTER SEVEN NOTES

1. Strauss, Leo, *Liberalism Ancient and Modern* (N.Y.: Basic Books, 1968), p. vii.

2. Brinton, Crane, The *Shaping of Modern Thought* (Englewood Cliffs, N.J.: Prentice-Hall, 1950, 1963), p. 183.

3. Rossiter 1962, *op. cit.* (Chap. One), p. 55.

4. See *ibid.* and Sabine, George N., *A History of Political Theory* (N.Y.: Henry Holt, 1937), p. 535.

5. Kirk IV, *op. cit.* (Chap. Three), p. 292.

6. Rossiter, 1962, p. 55.

7. Vierhaus, Rudolf, "Conservatism," *Dictionary of the History of Ideas* (Vol. I.) (N.Y.: Chas. Scribner's Sons, 1968, 1973), p. 481.

8. *Ibid.*

9. Strauss, p. vii.

10. Cropsey, Joseph, "Conservatism and Liberalism," Goldwin, ed., *op. cit.* (Chap. One), p. 47.

11. *Ibid.*, p. 58.

12. *Ibid.*

13. *Ibid.*, pp. 43-44.

14. *Ibid.*, p. 49. Obviously, some of the conservative groupings we have examined could be said to have a teleological outlook, at least to some extent. Also, it is clear that certain conservative groupings are more inclined to concur with liberalism in stressing excessive freedom and individualism than others, but most conservatives (as discussed) exhibit such in economics.

15. *Ibid.*

16. *Ibid.*

17. About our natural law background and how it was reflected in many of our particular beliefs and practices, see Kirk IV; Murray, *op. cit.* (Chap. Five); and Corwin, Edward S., *The Higher Law Background of American Constitutional Law* (Ithaca, N.Y.: Cornell U. Press, 1955).

18. Kirk IV, pp. 146-147.

19. "CDU" stands for Christian Democratic Union and "CSU" stands for Christian Social Union, the Bavarian affiliate of the CDU. They were together in a union, a united party, since the earliest years of the West German republic, and now continue in such association in a united Germany.

20. Rossiter, Clinton, *Parties and Politics in America.* (N.Y.: New American Library [Signet], 1960, 1964), p. 16.

21. See Second Vatican Council, *Lumen Gentium* (*Dogmatic Constitution on the Church*) (1964), Chap. IV, Sec. 31, in Flannery, *op. cit.* (Chap. One), pp. 388-389; Sacred Congregation for Religious and Secular Institutes, *Le scelte evangeliche* (*Religious and Human Advancement*) (1981), Part I, Sec. 10, in Flannery, Austin, O.P., gen. ed., *Vatican Council II: More Postconciliar Documents* (Northport, N.Y.: Costello, 1982), p. 269; Synod of Bishops, *Ultimis temporibus* (*The Ministerial Priesthood*), Part II, Sec. I, Sub-Sec. 2, in *ibid.*, p. 685.

22. We are thinking here of the U.S. bishops' positions and statements on economic, social welfare, and defense and arms control matters, not on human life issues like abortion.

23. On this point, see Benestad, J. Brian, *In Defense of a Just Social Order* (Wash., D.C.: Ethics and Public Policy Center, 1982).

ADDENDUM NOTES

1. Pope John Paul II, *Centesimus Annus* (*The Hundredth Year*), Introduction, Sec. 3, published in *Origins*, Vol. 21, No. 1 (May 16, 1991), p.3. (Hereinafter, referred to as "*CA*.")

2. *Ibid.*, Chap. 1, 6-10, pp. 4-6.

3. *Ibid.*, 1, 5, p. 4.

4. *Ibid.*, 5, 47, p. 18. Emphasis is added.

5. *Ibid.*, 4, 39, p. 15.

6. *Ibid.*, 5, 49, p. 19.

7. *Ibid.*, 4, 39, p. 16.

8. *Ibid.*, 2, 15, pp. 7-8; 5, 48, p. 18.

9. *Ibid.*, 2, 15, p. 7.

10. *Ibid.*, 5, 48, p. 18.

11. *Ibid.*, 2, 15, p. 7.

12. *Ibid.*, 4, 40, p. 16.

13. See, e.g., *ibid.*, 1, 11, p. 6; 5, 47, p. 18.

14. *Ibid.*, 5, 46-47, p. 18.

15. *Ibid.*, 1, 6, p. 5; 2, 13, p. 7; 4, 30, p. 12.

16. *Ibid.*, 4, 32, p. 13.

17. *Ibid.*, 4, 31-32, pp. 12-13.

18. See *ibid.*, 2, 19, p. 9; 4, 34, p. 14; 4, 42, p. 17.

19. *Ibid.*, 4, 42, pp. 16-17.

20. *Ibid.*, p. 17.

21. *Ibid.*, 3, 25, p. 10.

22. *Ibid.*, 4, 35, p. 14.

23. See, e.g., *QA, op. cit.* (Chap. Two), II, 5, p. 150; *MM, op. cit.* (Chap. Two), II, 57, p. 231; *PP, op. cit.* (Chap. Two), I, 3, 25, pp. 16-17.

24. *CA*, 2, 15, p. 8; 4, 32, p. 13; 4, 43, p. 17.

25. *Ibid.*, 2, 17, p. 8; 4, 35, p. 14; 4, 34, p. 14; 4, 36, pp. 14-15; 4, 33, p. 13.

26. *Ibid.*, 4, 39, p. 16.

27. *Ibid.*, 4, 31-32, p. 13; 4, 43, p. 17.

28. See, e.g., Simon, William E. & Novak, Michael, "Pope's Encyclical Advances Liberty, Prosperity," in *National Catholic Reporter* (May 24, 1991), p. 32; Novak, Michael, "Magnificentesimus," in *Crisis* (July-Aug. 1991), p. 2.

29. *CA*, 4, 41, p. 16; 4, 33, p. 13; 4, 35, p. 14.

30. *Ibid.*, 4, 35, p. 14.

31. See *ibid.*, 1, 10, p. 6; 2, 15-16, pp. 7-8; 5, 48, p. 19.

32. *Ibid.*, 5, 48-49, p. 19.

33. *Ibid.*, 5, 49, p. 19.

34. *Ibid.*, 6, 57, p. 21.

35. *Ibid.*

36. *Ibid.*, 2, 15, p. 7.

37. *Ibid.*, 5, 48, p. 19.

38. *Ibid.*, 2, 15, pp. 7-8.

39. *Ibid.*, 6, 58, p. 21.

40. *Ibid.*, 2 *passim*, pp. 6-9; 5, 52, p. 20; 6, 56-58, p. 21.

41. *Ibid.*, 4, 33-34, p. 14; 5, 52, p. 20; 6, 58, p. 21.

42. *Ibid.*, 5, 52, p. 20.

43. *Ibid.*

44. *Ibid.*, 3, pp. 9-12.

45. *Ibid.*, 2, 19, p. 9.

46. *Ibid.*

47. *Ibid.*, 3, 26, p. 11.

48. *Ibid.*, 3, 25, p. 10.

49. *Ibid.*, 1, 4, p. 4.

50. *Ibid.*, 4, 41, p. 16.

51. *Ibid.*, 3, 29, p. 12.

52. See, e.g., *SRS*, IV, 33.

53. *CA*, 1, 5, p. 4.

54. *Ibid.*, 3, 25, p. 11. Emphasis is added.

55. *Ibid.*, 6, 55, p. 21.

INDEX